A MOST
DESPERATE
SITUATION

A TwoDot Book

© 2000 Larry Len Peterson

Published by Falcon® Publishing, Inc., Helena, Montana

Printed in Canada

 2 3 4 5 6 7 8 9 0 TP 05 04 03 02 01 00

Cover images: Background portrait of Walter Cooper courtesy of Larry Len Peterson.
Inset painting, *Carson's Men* by Charles M. Russell (1913) courtesy of Gilcrease Museum.

All interior photographs and C.M.R. pen & inks (unless noted below) are property of
Larry Len Peterson.

C.M.R. pen & ink on page 135 property of Cooper Barnette.

Visit our website at www.Falcon.com.

Library of Congress Cataloging-in-Publication Data:

Cooper, Walter, 1843–1924.
    A Most Desperate Situation: Frontier Adventures of a Young Scout, 1858–1864 /
    Water Cooper ; edited by Rick Newby ; introduction and afterword by Larry Len Peterson.
        p. cm.
    Includes bibliographical references (p.).
    ISBN 1-56044-891-
        1. Cooper, Walter, 1843–1924. 2. Frontier and pioneer life—Montana. 3. Frontier and
    pioneer life—West (U.S.) 4. Pioneers—Montana—Biography. 5. Pioneers—West
    (U.S.)—Biography. 6. Montana—Biography. 7. West (U.S.)—Biography. 8. Bozeman
    (Mont.)—Biography. I. Newby, Rick. II. Title.

F731 .C67 2000
978'.02'092—dc21
[B]
                                                                              99-058750

Falcon® Publishing, Inc.
P.O. Box 1718, Helena, MT 59624

A MOST
DESPERATE
SITUATION

Frontier Adventures of a Young Scout 1858–1864

TWODOT

Walter Cooper (n.d.). Photo by Ernsberger & Ray, Auburn, New York.

INTRODUCTION

On April 30, 1803, Thomas Jefferson doubled the size of the infant United States by purchasing for $15 million more than 800,000 square miles of French-owned land from Emperor Napoleon. The first Americans to explore the wonders of the land gained in the Louisana Purchase were Meriwether Lewis and William Clark and their Corps of Discovery, 1804–1806. Tales of their explorations were widely circulated back East and sparked generations of future trailblazers. Lewis and Clark's influence on these "voyageurs" or mountain men cannot be overstated. First came fur trappers, then gold seekers and miners, and finally the homesteaders. Some of the early explorers led adventurous and dangerous lives on the edges of American civilization, and they became legendary. To the "old west" names of Daniel Boone and Davy Crockett, the "new west" added Kit Carson, Jim Bridger, and John Colter—but not Walter Cooper. If the tale that follows is true, or even partly true, then the story of Walter Cooper is the stuff of legend, but until now, it's been a tale known to none.

Like so many others, Walter Cooper was an easterner who came West at a young age to seek fame and fortune. Cooper's story of adventure and discovery in the West begins on an October day in 1858 when he was living in Michigan, still in his mid-teens. This is an epic tale, written by Cooper himself in the early 1900s and never before published; it concludes in 1864 after his arrival in the area we now call Montana. On his way to Montana he trapped beaver with Jim Bridger, panned for gold in Colorado, visited with Kit Carson in New Mexico, and found himself in most desperate situations with Navajos, Comanches, Apaches, and later, Mexican vaqueros.

Walter Cooper's subsequent life in Bozeman, Montana, was distinguished in many ways. He was a successful entrepreneur and businessman. He owned gold mines, coal fields, a flour mill, a railroad wood-tie company, and a fur business, and he had numerous real estate holdings. He was patent holder on several innovations he made on the Montana Sharps rifle.

On the civic side, Walter Cooper was one of the incorporators of Bozeman and one of the founders of the local college, now known as Montana State University. He was a delegate to the first Montana Constitutional Convention in 1884 and to the second in 1889; he was president of the Society of Montana Pioneers and chairman of the state Democratic party. Along with such great Montanans as William A. Clark, Granville Stuart, Paris Gibson, Frank Linderman, and Charlie Russell, Walter Cooper shaped the history of the state he so loved. Unfortunately, his accomplishments have fallen into relative obscurity.

As close as can be determined, Cooper began writing this story sometime after the turn of the century, when he was close to sixty years old. This impressive labor comprises almost fifteen hundred pages of handwritten manuscript. Whether this is autobiography or novel is uncertain—many adventures are so grand it makes one wonder if fact wasn't stretched a little. Perhaps author Charles Guernsey said it best in 1936 when he described his book, *Wyoming Cowboy Days*: "True to life, but not autobiographical, romantic, but not fiction, facts, but not history."[1]

Walter Cooper's life is highlighted in *Progressive Men of the State of Montana* (1902). He was born on July 4, 1843, in Sterling, Cayuga County, New York, the third son of Andrew and Sarah Cooper. Andrew Cooper married Sarah McGilvra in Sterling on October 30, 1832. By 1845 they had moved with their four sons to Shiawassee County, Michigan, where two more sons were born. Tragedy struck the family in 1851 when a boat carrying Andrew and a load of his horses capsized on Lake Michigan. While he survived the accident, Andrew soon developed pneumonia and died. Walter, age eight, was sent to live with a maternal aunt in Lansing, Michigan, while Sarah and her younger children headed back to New York. Around age twelve, Walter ran away to work the lumber camps and farms of northern Michigan. That is where *A Most Desperate Situation* begins.

In the first book, Cooper places himself in the spring of 1859 in Kansas, where he wins a great foot race among whites and Indians. It is there that he meets the legendary Jim Bridger. Stanley Vestal, in his biography of Bridger, does mention Bridger heading west from St. Louis in the spring of 1859, so it is likely that Cooper did, indeed, cross paths with Bridger in Kansas.[2]

Progressive Men next places Cooper in the San Juan Mountains prospecting for gold in the spring of 1860 and eventually traveling to Mexico. In Walter's account, en route to Mexico he visits Kit Carson in Taos, New Mexico. By the time Cooper crossed his path, Carson was an Indian agent spending most of his time helping the army bring the Indians under government control. After his perilous adventures in Mexico, Walter returned to Colorado in the winter of 1861 and spent the summer and fall of 1862 near Colorado Springs, at times acting as a scout for the First Colorado Regiment. In November 1863, he started for the Montana Territory and arrived in Virginia City in February 1864. *A Most Desperate Situation* ends just before Walter began prospecting for gold in Alder Gulch.

In 1913, Cooper commissioned Montana's "cowboy artist" Charles Marion Russell to illustrate this chronicle. The pen-and-ink drawings Russell executed for Cooper's manuscript have never before been reproduced. By chance, Walter's younger brother Ransom Cooper, an attorney in Great Falls, was a personal acquaintance of Charlie and Nancy Russell. It was through Ransom that the Russells agreed to accept the commission. As Charlie's business manager, Nancy Russell handled all deals, and the surviving correspondence between Nancy and Walter Cooper reconfirms this. Nancy once stated, "Charlie was not a businessman. He knew absolutely nothing about the methods used in the business world so when I came into his life, it filled a place that was needed so that he might go on with his work undisturbed by things that would have caused him to worry."[3]

By the turn of the century much of America viewed the West with nostalgia and regret for the destruction of its pristine wilderness and the American Indians' way of life. Charlie Russell had become a popular choice as artist to illustrate remembrance-type biographies, autobiographies, and novels. After Frederic Remington died in 1909, Russell was hailed as the king of Western artists.

Charles Wallace was the first author to use Russell illustrations in his 1894 biography on Mrs. Natalie Collins, *The Cattle Queen of Montana: A Story of Personal Experiences During Residence of Forty Years in the Far West*. This was followed by numerous other Russell-illustrated books, including *Then and Now, or Thirty-six Years in the Rockies* (1900) by Russell's close friend Robert Vaughn; *Adventures with Indians and Game, or Twenty Years in the Rocky Mountains* (1903) by Dr. William A. Allen; *Bucking the Sagebrush, or The*

C.M. Russell's sketch for pen & ink "Into the West." Final pen & ink on page 118.

Oregon Trail in the Seventies (1904) by Charles J. Steedman; *My Sixty Years on the Plains Trapping, Trading, and Indian Fighting* (1905) by W. T. Hamilton; *Chaperoning Adrienne: A Tale of the Yellowstone National Park* (1907) by Alice Harriman-Brown; and *Fifteen Thousand Miles by Stage: A Women's Unique Experience during Thirty Years of Path Finding and Pioneering from the Missouri to the Pacific and from Alaska to Mexico* (1911) by Carrie Adell Strahorn.[4]

By 1913, at Nancy's insistence, Russell was spending less time working on magazine and book illustrations that paid poorly and more time painting major watercolors and oils for wealthy clients. A year earlier, Russell had completed his masterpiece, *Lewis And Clark Meeting Indians At Ross' Hole*, a 12' x 25' oil for the House of Representatives at Montana's capitol in Helena, for which he was paid $5,000. Throughout 1913 and into 1914 he struggled with another commission worth $3,000, *When The Land Belonged To God*, a 42$^{1}/_{2}$" x 72" oil for the Montana Club in Helena. After 1911, Nancy generally only accepted book commissions from some of Charlie's closest friends such as authors Frank B. Linderman (*Indian Why Stories*, 1915; *Indian Old Man Stories*, 1920) and B. M. Bower (*Chip of the Flying U*, 1906), whose series of western novels had made her the most popular female writer of her day. Her 1913 novel, *The Uphill Climb*, and Cooper's commission were the only book projects accepted by the Russells for almost five years.

The illustrations Russell completed for Cooper's book are a testament to Charlie's admiration for Walter Cooper and the story he had to tell. Unusually large in size, 14" x 18", and fine in detail, the pen and inks are aptly named with such titles as *Bridger at the Stake, The Great Foot Race, Kit Carson's Farewell, The Chase, The Survivors, The Duel, The Bronc,* and *The Fight.* Their titles summarize many of the adventures described by Cooper in his story. For the first time, it is apparent that Russell's impressionistic oil, *Carson's Men*, also completed in 1913, was inspired by Cooper's story. In the painting, Walter Cooper is leading the men across the haunting southwestern desert landscape into unknown adventure.

Indeed, the correspondence between Nancy Russell and Walter Cooper gives us further insight into how at least some book commissions were handled. It is apparent that Russell was given general themes to work with, and he decided what media he would use. Only a short time before Charlie finished the drawings, Cooper wrote him asking if the works would be line

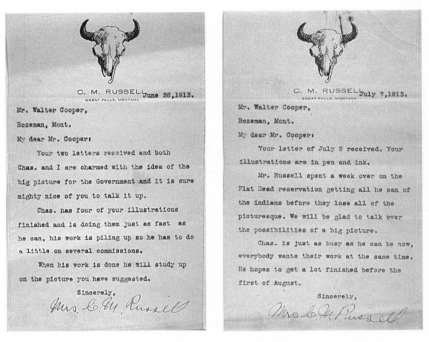

(above and facing page) Summer 1913 correspondence between Nancy Russell, Charlie's business manager, and Walter Cooper regarding the progress of Charlie's illustration work for Cooper's manuscript.

or wash drawings. Nancy, handling all business correspondence, notified Cooper that the drawings would be in pen-and-ink. One month later, around August 1, 1913, Cooper received the drawings on time, as promised. Most likely, Russell was paid only a few hundred dollars for the project.

Probably because of financial problems from a downturn in the economy, Cooper was unable to afford the publication costs, and the manuscript and pen and inks were set aside. After his death in 1924, his daughter Mariam inherited them, and upon her death, they were passed on to her daughter, Virginia.

I first became aware of these materials several years ago when Virginia, then in her late seventies, was actively editing the manuscript from her home

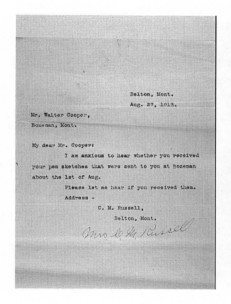

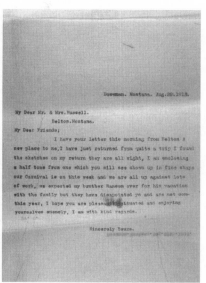

in northern California. I met with her several times to assist her with the editing process and publication of the manuscript. Her son Edmund coordinated our discussions and finally, in the fall of 1998, the project came together, in large part due to his efforts. I had just written *Charles M. Russell, Legacy: Printed and Published Works of Montana's Cowboy Artist*[5] for the C. M. Russell Museum in Great Falls and TwoDot Books in Helena. I was certainly excited the first time I viewed the pen and ink drawings and read the manuscript. It is a unique situation to have both a manuscript written by one of Montana's greatest pioneers combined with art from America's greatest twentieth century Western illustrator.

When it became apparent that we needed a professional editor, Rick

Newby immediately came to mind. Rick is not only a great editor, but also one of Montana's most gifted writers. He has done a superb job of transforming Walter Cooper's manuscript into a very enjoyable reading experience.

I would like to thank Elizabeth Dear, curator at the C.M. Russell museum in Great Falls, for introducing me to Virginia Barnett and the Russell pen-and-inks that were on loan at the museum.

The only sad note is Virginia's passing in early 1999. Virginia (Mrs. Edmund Barnett) I know would have been thrilled with the results. Her spirit lives on through her two sons, Edmund and Cooper Barnett, and so does the spirit of Walter Cooper and Charlie Russell through this publication. In 1917, Charlie wrote:

> *The west is dead my Friend*
> *But writers hold the seed*
> *And what they sow*
> *Will live and grow*
> *Again to those who read*

As you read, I hope the West, Montana, Walter Cooper, and Charlie Russell will come alive for you and take you back to an earlier time. If it does, then my mission is accomplished.

Your cowboy friend from Plentywood, Montana
LARRY "KID" PETERSON

---

[1] Charles A. Guernsey, *Wyoming Cowboy Days* (New York: G. P. Putnam's Sons, 1936): title page.

[2] Stanley Vestal, *Jim Bridger: Mountain Man* (Lincoln: University of Nebraska Press, 1970): 204.

[3] Nancy Cooper Russell, unfinished manuscript on C. M. Russell from 1928, now in the Helen E. and Homer E. Britzman Collection, Taylor Museum for Southwestern Studies of the Colorado Springs Fine Arts Center.

[4] Larry Len Peterson, *Charles M. Russell, Legacy: Printed and Published Works of Montana's Cowboy Artist* (Helena: TwoDot Books, An Imprint of Falcon Publishing in cooperation with C. M. Russell Museum, Great Falls, Montana, 1999): 39 (*Cattle Queen of Montana*), 143 (*Then and Now*), 156 (*Adventures with Indians and Game*), 179 (*Bucking the Sagebrush*), 181 (*My Sixty Years on the Plains*), 219 (*Chaperoning Adrienne*), and 262 (*Fifteen Thousand Miles by Stage*).

[5] Ibid.

EDITOR'S NOTE

As Larry Len Peterson notes in his introduction to *A Most Desperate Situation: Frontier Adventures of a Young Scout, 1858–1864*, the manuscript of Walter Cooper's memoir/novel stretches to nearly fifteen hundred barely legible handwritten pages. Some brave soul—perhaps after Cooper's death—typed up this document, religiously following the original text word for word. The resulting typescript, comprised of 531 double-spaced, legal-sized sheets, is the text upon which I made my editorial changes.

When I received the typescript, it had already been edited by several hands, each seeking—often in radically different ways—to trim, streamline, and otherwise make publishable Walter Cooper's marvelous episodic romance of the West. I took the liberty of ignoring almost all previous edits, acting upon the assumption that none of them were the author's. And even if some of them were in Walter Cooper's hand, I had no way of knowing which were authentically his and which were not. To my ear, very few had the ring of a true Cooper locution.

That I reverted to the original text, however, does not mean that I left well enough alone. First, much of the book had never been paragraphed, and those paragraphs that did appear came at apparent random. Second, Walter Cooper had clearly never finished his magnum opus, and he left many details unresolved, from the name of his protagonist—who is variously called Walter MacGilvra and Walter Cooper, with other variants penned in by later editors—to the fates of numerous minor (and sometimes major) characters. Sadly, I was unable to conjure up, out of whole cloth, the future adventures of stalwart Cooper characters like Old Tex, nor could I trace the post-manuscript biography of young Walter's beloved, the lovely señorita Maria Castillo. I did my best to make the disappearance of such key figures as painless to the reader as possible. On the positive side, I could ensure consistency in characters' names and correct Cooper's occasional lapses in continuity.

Walter Cooper wrote a vast, spirited, engaging, and sometimes wandering saga. My initial editorial charge—from editor Megan Hiller of TwoDot Books—was to take the manuscript of more than 230,000 words and trim it radically, preserving only the young scout's most riveting adventures. But as I worked through *A Most Desperate Situation*, I found that to follow our original editorial plan was to do violence to what was proving a much more ambitious work of literature than the dime Westerns it superficially resembled. There was something so involving, so thrilling, touching, and sometimes disturbing about this scarcely credible tale of a remarkable young man's coming West and coming to manhood. Megan and I concluded that we needed to let Walter Cooper tell his story fully.

I did cut certain passages that I deemed of little interest to modern readers and others where the author—or one of his secondary characters—waxed effusively and for several pages about the splendid qualities of the young scout. These cuts are either indicated by an editorial note in italics, recapitulating key events in the deleted text, or simply by an asterisk. Occasionally, an asterisk indicates that Cooper has made an abrupt leap in time and has provided no transition. Besides rendering the prose more active, I trimmed excessively elaborate clauses, which tended to sap energy from the story's otherwise compelling narrative momentum. In all cases, I strove to maintain Walter Cooper's distinctive idiom, poised halfway between Victorian formality and the crude energies of a Western vernacular.

A Most Desperate Situation ended up nearly twice its originally intended length, but it is my hope that readers will find here a Western that can hold its own beside other masterpieces of the genre, books like *Tough Trip through Paradise*, *Roughing It*, *The Virginian*, and *The Big Sky*. Somewhere between a memoir and a fiction, a potboiler and a folktale, *A Most Desperate Situation* offers the reader adrenaline-pumping action, a richly imagined Western landscape, complexly drawn characters both sympathetic and repellent, spell-binding speeches, scarifying tortures and breathtaking bravery, a tender love story, and the compulsive pleasures of an undeniable page-turner. It has been my pleasure to edit this extraordinary book.

RICK NEWBY
November 1, 1999

Walter Cooper, 1859. Photo by George Wakely, Denver City, Colorado Territory.

BOOK ONE

At the close of a bright October day in the year 1858, a one-horse buggy with a male occupant moved slowly along the Grand River Road in Shiawassee County, Michigan. A man on foot approached from the opposite direction. He carried on his back a bundle slung on a stout stick. The man on foot called out in a cheery voice, "Hello, Albert."

The man in the buggy answered, "Hello, Oscar," then added slowly, "You are back again, I see. Got your fortune, of course."

"Not quite," replied the man addressed as Oscar.

"When did you get back?" asked the man in the buggy.

"Today," replied the pedestrian.

"Got any gold?" asked the other.

"Some," was the answer.

"Let's see it."

Oscar slowly deposited his bundle on the ground and took out an old fashioned pocketbook of the long pattern. From one of the pockets he took a goose quill and handed it to the man in the buggy.

"Is that gold?" asked Albert. "And that is gold, is it? Well, well, gold, gold. Oscar, it this all you got?"

"Yes," replied Oscar. "It came from Pikes Peak, too. I got it there myself."

"How much is it worth?"

"Two dollars and fifty cents, down weight," Oscar answered proudly.

"Well," said the other, "was there any more left there?"

"Of course. There was plenty of it."

"Did I understand you to say that this was all you got?"

"Yes, that is all I've got."

"How much money have you got left besides this gold, Oscar?" asked Albert.

"One dollar and sixty-five cents in silver."

"One dollar and sixty-five cents. Let's see, you took away fifteen hundred dollars, I believe. Am I right?"

"Yes, that's what I had when I left."

"Well, Oscar, you have made a fine job of it. What are you doing back here now? Winter coming on, too. Come back to live on your wife and friends, of course. You ought to be ashamed of yourself. Sold a nice farm that belonged to your wife. Got the money; took it all away with you. Left your wife without a cent to earn her own living. I would have stayed there and got some gold, as much as I took away with me at least. Stayed there, yes, you bet I would."

The man in the wagon said, "Go along, Doll," and gave his old mare a lick with the whip. The mare broke into a trot and passed down the road a dozen rods or more. Then Albert pulled up and looked back. "Mary is down at my house. You can put your bundle in here and come along." The man in the buggy slid over to the near side of the seat. "Get in and don't keep the mare waiting all night. She wants her oats. She hauled this buggy five miles today and must be tired out. Go along, Doll. Sorry to keep you out so late."

The man in the buggy was Deacon Grubb, the most prosperous farmer in that part of the country. The returned gold seeker was his improvident brother Oscar. A few feet from where the men met, and just inside an old, crooked oak-rail fence, stood a fifteen-year-old boy, listening to every word they said. He wore coarse homespun trousers tucked into a pair of rough heavy boots and a hickory shirt. His hair was very black. Dark gray eyes peered out from under an old straw hat.

As the lad turned away from the fence to his work of husking corn, he might have been heard to remark, "Pikes Peak. Gold. I guess I would have stayed there. I never would have come back until I had gold enough to buy a farm at least." This may have been the best lesson of the lad's life. He had heard a lecture delivered, the point of which was that Oscar Grubb, having left his home for the gold fields of Pikes Peak, had abandoned the gold regions without having accomplished the object for which he went. The lesson went straight home to the boy. He would have stayed and honestly endeavored to make a success. He would have tried at least to have gotten enough gold to buy a farm. These thoughts haunted the lad, and when the sun was down and it began to grow dark, he started for the farmhouse where much work remained to be done.

When his chores were finished and he had washed up, he came into the supper table where sat his employer Mr. Payne, Mrs. Payne, their three daughters, and a son, a young boy of five years. During dinner, one of the girls engaged our young friend in conversation, asking him what he proposed doing that winter.

"I am heading for Pikes Peak," he answered. This remark created general merriment at the table. The lad sat quietly gazing at the fire.

"To Pikes Peak," said Mrs. Payne. "Whatever put such a thing as that into your head?"

"When are you going, Walter?" asked Mr. Payne.

"When my time is out with you, Mr. Payne," answered the lad without moving his eyes from the fire.

"Your time is out in December. You won't start until spring, will you?"

"Yes, I will go then at once. I expect to pass the winter some place west and cross the plains in the spring." The lad had been at the Payne home six months. He was a cheerful, handsome lad, and so a great favorite with all the family.

Mrs. Payne gave a sigh, "Walter, what can I do without you?" And sure enough, the boy had become a fixture in the Payne household. Whatever he had been asked to do, he did promptly and cheerfully. When Mr. Payne was sick, the work on the farm went forward just the same.

Mr. Payne had told his wife that very day, "Walter's not quite so strong, but he's quicker and more willing than most men. I will take him for another year."

"I'm so glad," the lady had answered. "We all like him so much. His manners are so nice, and he is so kind to the girls and Willie."

The tired boy went up the stairs to bed. "Why, Jabe," said Mrs. Payne to her husband, "persuade Walter to stay. Give him another dollar or two a month, and tell him you will keep him for a year or more."

"What are you talking about, Jane? That boy is going to do what he says he will do. Depend on that. No, I will stir myself and sell my wood so I can pay him his wages when his time is out. And Jane, you had better fix him up woolens and such things to take with him, for surely if ever a boy earned his way, Walter has."

Matters went on as usual at the Payne farm until Mr. Payne was kicked by one of his colts and was hurt so badly that all the work on the farm was left to Walter. But nothing was neglected. One day the boy said to Mr. Payne, "The pasture fence is down again, and those old rails are so broken that it does not seem possible to repair it again. I had better go down in the timber and split some rails and put in a new fence."

It was some time before Mr. Payne answered. When he did, he asked, "How about the corn in the field?"

"It is all husked and in the crib. The fodder is all in, and I don't see much else to do until you get out again," answered Walter.

"Well, son, you can do as you like. If you think you can split those rails, I would like it done. There is some nice white and black oak timber there that I have been saving for that fence. It ought to have been built last spring, but somehow I could not get around to it."

For the next two weeks, little was seen of Walter except at mealtimes. And then Mr. Payne was around again. He had not yet visited the timber. One evening, he asked casually of Walter, "How many rails have you made today, son?"

"One hundred and one, and yesterday, one hundred and two," was the answer, "and Monday, one hundred and five."

Mrs. Payne said to her husband, "I heard you say one day that one hundred was a day's work for a man."

After Walter had gone to bed, Mr. Payne said to his wife, "I must go down tomorrow and see what Walter has been doing. To tell the truth, I feel guilty. I can see that Walter is somewhat worn."

"Yes, Father," said his daughter Dott. "He went to sleep today at noon and seemed so ashamed when he thought I saw it."

"One hundred white oak rails is too much for that boy. I will put a stop to it," said Mr. Payne. "Really, I think he has enough for the pasture fence anyway. I calculated that it would take fourteen hundred, and if he has enough, I shall put a stop to it."

"And if he has not enough, Father, I suppose you will let him finish the rails and himself, too," the kindhearted Dott said with some warmth.

Toward evening on the following day, when Mr. Payne came in from the timber, he said, "Well, Jane, that boy is a captain. He has split fifteen hundred as fine eleven-foot white oak rails as I ever saw. He has averaged more than one hundred a day. I don't know, but I might rebuild the orchard fence, too, but his time is up Saturday."

"Did you put a stop to it, Father?" asked Dott. "Don't you think it would be nice to tell him he need not go to the timber anymore and just have a day or two rest?"

"Why, Dott, he just felled a big white oak and it will make a good many rails. I told him he could work up that tree if he liked. I think it will be done by Saturday noon."

Just then, Walter came in for the milk pails. Mrs. Payne said, "Jabe, that boy is tired. I'll just go out and help milk those cows." And out she went but soon came in, saying Walter would not hear of it, "and he said it in such an earnest way that I just came in and will finish getting supper."

Saturday afternoon, Mrs. Payne came in from back of the house and said, "Jabe, I wish you would look down the back lane. Someone is coming up very slow. It can't be Walter, can it?"

"No, not him, he always comes on the trot. He never lags."

Dott went to the back door and had no more than glanced out when she cried, "Father, quick! It is Walter, and he is hurt." She flew over the fence and down the lane. It was Walter, sure enough, but he was in a terrible condition. He limped along supported by a strong stick, his face as white as a sheet and his foot bleeding profusely even though he had bound his jacket around it. Dott supported him all she could while he protested that he was not hurt much and could go alone and for her to never mind. All helped the injured lad to the house.

They removed his boot and exposed a fearful gash in the top of his foot. The doctor was summoned and the foot was dressed. The doctor found that the bone was injured, and he had to probe before he could sew up the gash. The lad never flinched or complained.

For some weeks, the boy was compelled to remain indoors. He had lost so much blood that it took considerable time before he had the strength to move about the house. All helped him cheerfully. Dott took entire charge of the injured foot, notwithstanding his earnest protest. The foot healed very slowly.

Walter's Aunt Betsy was heartbroken to see his pale face. She was, however, most worried at the new prospect of losing him altogether, because of his intended departure for Pikes Peak. "It's no use, Jane," she said to Mrs. Payne, when the latter suggested that perhaps he might now forego the trip.

"It's no use," repeated Aunt Betsy. "If he said he was going, he will go. I have never known him to change his mind when once he has decided, and he's never at a loss to know how to meet a difficulty. Now you know those maples in front of our house. I said one day that I feared they might blow down and strike the house. What did he do but climb those great trees and saw off the tops. Why, there was not one of the men that dared try it.

"He is a brave boy, a brave boy. Did I ever tell you about the turkeys he killed for me? It was a year ago last Thanksgiving. Well, Archibald and Samuel were home, and it had been years since we had all had an opportunity to get together. I planned to have roast pig and a good dinner. Well, I said to Mattie one day when we were planning dinner that I wished Mr. McCay was well. I might get him to kill me a wild turkey. I did not know Walter was near. Well, you know he has a new double-barreled rifle. I made a good deal of fuss when he bought it, but it done no good. He got the gun but—up to this time—had not been out hunting.

"Well, that night he had that gun down, molded bullets, and oiled and cleaned it and was up and out before daylight, long before anyone else. He didn't get anything, and he was up the next morning even earlier, and about seven o'clock he came to the back door with two great big turkeys. One was a gobbler, the largest I ever saw. It dressed thirty-nine pounds, fat as it could be. Turkeys fatted on beech nuts are the finest flavor in the world. The other was a nice young turkey. I never was so proud of anything in my life as I was over those turkeys.

"Well, that night I got Walter to tell me how he got them. He said the first morning he was too late. The turkeys went into Deacon Grubb's back cornfield and left it by sunrise. So the next morning he was up at 3 o'clock. He went across the Maple River bottom and stood near the field. Presently he heard the turkeys calling, so he concealed himself. They went straight into the corn. He went around into a piece of woods on the other side of the field and waited. As the turkeys came out, he shot one with each barrel. He was quite proud of himself. We shall never again have another such family gathering. We are so scattered now, and then Walter is going so far away, we may never see him again."

That same afternoon, Frank McGregor and Dan McCarty came to see Walter. He was out at the barn, the girls said. When Aunt Betsy got through with the turkey story, she said to Frank, "I have never forgiven you for taking Walter out that night after coons. You might tell us about it now.

It is so long ago it won't do any hurt now."

"Oh, tell us, tell us!" the girls cried, clapping their hands.

"Well," replied Frank, "that boy could climb any tree in the woods, and he was not afraid of anything. So when McCay and the other boys agreed to go cooning in the maple bottoms, McCay said that if we can take Walt along we can get their old coon dog to go with him and save chopping down so many trees. The coons always go up the biggest tree they can find, and sometimes it takes two hours to cut down the tree and then sometimes if the coon strikes it just right he gets up another tree out of reach of the dogs and then you have got your work to do all over again. Cooning is hard work, but I never seen a fellow who did not like the fun."

"Why didn't some of you go up the tree yourselves?" asked Aunt Betsy.

"Well, you see it's rather ticklish climbing in the night and every fellow can't climb, and some that can climb are afraid to climb in the night, and most of the boys are mighty afraid of cats."

"Well," answered Aunt Betsy, "I should think you would be ashamed of yourselves to encourage a young lad like Walter to do what you were all afraid to do."

"Well," continued Frank, "I said, 'It's no use. Aunt Betsy won't let him go.'"

"'Oh, we'll fix that,' said one of the others. 'Just take a pole and put it up to that back window, and he'll come down quick enough.' And sure enough, he saw Walt and fixed it all up, and about 9 o'clock, we came along to your house, got your dog quiet, put up a rail against the house, and down came Walt and away we went. We crossed the bridge and went up the river on the other side, back of the Grubbs' place. The dogs went out and seemed to tree a coon near the river. The brush was pretty thick. The animal went up a big elm. It was dark so we built a fire, and we could see it pretty well up and away out on a big limb. Under the tree, there was a dense thicket of prickly ash, terrible to get into. Well, Walt went up the tree and went out on the limb but couldn't shake the beast off. So he went back and cut a stick to knock him off with. Walt edged his way back out there and then got down astraddle the limb and hitched along until he was pretty close. As he raised his club to strike, the creature struck at him with its feet and made a screech. Then we knew it was not a coon.

"I called to Walt to go back, that it was a wild cat or a lynx, but he paid no attention and kept pounding it. Finally it sprang toward him and must have struck him for he lost his balance and rolled off. The cat jumped at the same time, and the dogs went for it. Walt went down through those prickly ash bushes, and when we got to him, he was a sight. His clothes were nearly torn off his back and his face was covered with blood. He had two deep cuts under his left eye and one on the back of his head. He was in bad shape but never whimpered.

"Aunt, you didn't know that we took him over to Mrs. Crane's and had his head sewed up. The gash was about two inches long. Mrs. Crane, dear old woman, said we ought to be thrashed. She cried all the time she was sewing him up. We washed him good and took him home, and he went up the rail to bed. Must have been about 4 o'clock in the morning.

"McCay said the animal must have been a lynx, for a cat could never have used up the dogs as it did. Why, it killed our old dog Sport right there on the ground. It tore his entrails out, and he died in no time. McCay's young hound lost one eye and was literally torn to pieces, and the old half bull of Jenney's was so badly cut up it died in less than two weeks."

The tears ran down Aunt Betsy's cheeks while Frank told of this adventure. "Dan McCarty," she said, "you are another man I haven't forgiven for your treatment of Walter. You see, Walter was up in the lumber woods last winter, and Mr. McCarty was up there, too. They hunted together considerable. When they started home, McCarty made up his mind to come down in two days—and it's a hundred miles!—and do you know, that boy walked that hundred miles in two days. McCarty told me afterwards that he thought he would tire the boy out. He said he was afterward ashamed of himself. He said the last few miles the boy sat down every chance he had, but never even said he was tired. It did not seem to hurt him any. He was all right in a few days."

"Say, McCarty," Frank said, "I hear you hunted with Walter some, something about a bear hunt you had with Walter up in the north woods. But I never heard the particulars."

McCarty laughed, "It was way up at the forks of the Cass, a very wild country. You see, Walter's cousin Jack's lumber camps were on the Cass, and Walter went up there with me when I went hunting. I was glad to have Walter for company. We went about twenty miles back in the wilderness. There was not a settler within seventy miles, and the woods were full of animals. One day we saw two little bear cubs. The cubs went up a basswood tree and into a big hollow. We waited for the old one to come, but she did not appear, nor did the little ones even stick out their heads. Finally Walter said he would go up the tree and look in. Maybe he could get the cubs.

"I had no business letting him go up, but he did. We peeled some basswood bark and made a stout cord, which Walter took to the den about forty feet up. There was a convenient limb to stand on near the hole. Walter peeked in, and sure enough there was a big den and there were the cubs. He reached in, and after a lot of snarls and growls he got hold of one and tied the string to his leg. The cub made a great howl as Walter let him down to the ground and I tied him to a tree. The cub kept crying at a great rate.

"Walter was just pulling up his basswood rope when he heard a noise back in the woods and saw this great black bear coming at a breakneck pace. I called, 'Look out there! She is coming.' I caught up my gun and waited for the bear to stop so I could shoot her, but she did not stop. When she got near the tree, I fired and missed her. She made for me, and she surely would have got me only for the cub crying. She turned back to the cub and smelt around for some time. Then she cuffed the cub with her paw, which broke the string. The little one went straight up the tree to the nest. The old bear, after running around a good deal, also started up to the den.

"I called out to Walter, 'Look out. She will get you.'

"Walter asked me calmly why I did not shoot the bear. 'You know I have no gun,' he said.

"That brought me to my senses, and I realized the great responsibility that rested upon me. The bear was now twenty feet from the ground and on the opposite side of the tree. Walter had not moved but was looking around, evidently for some avenue of escape. Finally, he seemed to decide upon a plan of action. He glanced down at the bear and then started farther up the tree. For the first time, the brute realized that a new enemy was near her cubs. She gave a tremendous roar and redoubled her energy and climbed faster. Meanwhile, Walter had gotten well up the tree and was standing on a big limb, looking toward a tall, slender ash tree near at hand. The limb of the basswood came quite close to the ash tree, but not near enough for him to reach it in safety. He stood there looking around. I saw him raise his hand over his head. He seemed to be reaching for a slender limb of the ash tree that extended above and past his limb quite a distance over his head. He glanced back. The bear had just reached the limb upon which he stood.

There was a fork in the limb. I could see that Walt could go no farther out. My heart was in my mouth. The old bear had stayed on the opposite side of the tree from me, cunningly working around as I tried to get a shot at her. She cautiously walked out toward the boy. Her body was fairly sheltered from me by limbs and leaves. The boy looked back over his shoulder. Then he bent his knees and I felt sure he was going to jump for the ash tree, but he did not jump. He began to spring the limb up and down, and now I thought he would try to shake the bear off. She stopped and moved more cautiously forward. What would the boy do? Still he teetered the limb, and each time it bounded more and more. The weight of the bear seemed to aid him. All at once, when the beast was no more than four feet from the lad, he swung his right hand up over his head and caught the limb of the ash tree. He kept springing the limb, and nearer came the bear. Now my heart stood still. She put out her paw as if to measure the distance between herself and her intended victim. He glanced back, then swung forward with a springing movement into space. If he did not reach the ash, he would certainly meet death in the great plunge downward.

"Thank God! He had made a correct calculation of the distance, and he clasped the body of the ash with his legs and was for the moment safe. He rested and watched the bear. She could not reach the lad. He quietly went farther up the ash tree. I kept prospecting around for a shot at the bear. She went back to the trunk of the basswood tree and climbed up to the level of the boy. He called to me that he thought he would come down. Accordingly, as he descended, the bear did the same, keeping even with him, growling hideously all the time.

"Finally the boy got to the bottom limb, and as it looked as if the bear would reach the ground at the same time as he did, he called to me. I told him that he had better go back up the tree. This he did. At the same time, the bear went back up the basswood tree. I still could not get a good shot at her. I knew I had better try for a sure shot, as she might get very troublesome wounded. Finally, she went into the den, and Walter again started down the tree. Again, the bear came out and maneuvered as before. After a rest, Walter climbed the ash again. Again, the bear went into her den. The boy waited quite a long time and then quietly slid down the ash. The bear did not come out this time.

"On reaching the ground, Walter at once got hold of his gun and tried in every way to induce the bear to come out. He pounded on the tree with his small hatchet, but the bear would not appear. I persuaded him to give up the effort and go to camp, promising to come back early next morning with an ax. I assured him that we would get the bear. The boy, though very much aroused, was tired with the exertion of climbing the large tree and the excitement attending the adventure. It was about five miles to camp, and we arrived just at dark. We turned in early and were up early in the morning and started for the bears' den, better equipped than we had been the previous day.

"To tell the truth, I was not so very anxious to get there, for the ferocious beast had made quite an impression on me. The animal was a large black bear, not very fat. She could go up a tree like a squirrel. As she had come at us through the brush and over the logs, she made a barking noise not unlike a wild boar. I have often wondered how that boy kept his wits about him in the trying moments and yet had the foresight to plan a safe retreat. I feel sure that I never could have made my escape, nor is there one man in a thousand who could have done so under the same circumstances.

"When we arrived at the tree, Walter looked over the ground and said at once, 'The bears have gone.' And sure enough, so it proved. I could hardly keep him from going up to the den. We finally felled a small tree, which lodged against the old basswood. We went up the leaning tree until we could look into the den, but the bears had gone. We tried to track them, but the leaves were dry and we soon lost the trail. We separated and agreed to meet at camp in the evening. I had no luck and got to camp early. Walter came in shortly after dark. He had been more successful, having killed a fat young deer. We stayed at this camp several days. We killed quite a number of deer, but we saw nothing more of the old bear or her cubs.

"We went back to the lumber camp and hunted in the vicinity for some time. One day an Indian family came along and stopped for dinner at the lumber camp. When evening came, we learned that Walter had gone away with the Indians. This Indian family lived at the head of the Cass most of the time, occasionally coming down to sell their furs and skins and to secure such supplies as they wanted. One of the men said that the old Indian took a fancy to the boy and invited him to go home with him for a hunt. I was worried about him, but there was no help for it now.

"Walter was gone about a month and came down the river in a birch bark canoe he had built himself, with quite a number of deerskins. He said that he had had a very nice time. We all teased him a good deal about the young daughter of the old Indian. I saw the old Indian the next spring, and he was anxious to know about the lad who, he said, was a fine hunter and 'very much good.' Walter had evidently made himself agreeable, for he was certainly very popular with them all. The old Indian said, 'Boy heap climb tree, catch coon. Learn Indian talk.' The Indian laughed and told about hunting one day when they wounded a young buck, and the boy went up to it to cut its throat. As soon as he pricked the animal with his knife, it sprang to its feet. The boy had hold of its hair, and a lively scene followed. The Indian said, 'Me heap laugh, boy hang on hair of buck and the deer fight viciously and heap tear boy's shirt.' The deer did not seem anxious to escape but was bent on a fight, and by the time the fight was over and the deer had gotten away, the boy had very few clothes left on his back." McCarty laughed as he finished his tale and stood to go.

※

It was the twenty-ninth day of January, and the Payne family were all sitting around the fire. It was a cold night. Walter turned to Mr. Payne and said, "I think if it will not discommode you too much, I will go away on Tuesday."

"This is Friday," said Mr. Payne. "I will go to town Monday and sell my wood and give you your pay."

"I leave your house with regret, and I shall never forget you and your good kind family," said Walter. On Tuesday morning, as he packed his bag to depart, Walter found a pair of nice woolen stockings and a pair of woolen mittens. When he came downstairs, there was evidence of tears on his cheeks. Mr. and Mrs. Payne shook his hand, and each said, "Make our house your home at any and all times and as long as you like." When the boy hurried out after a farewell with the girls, there were tears in all eyes. Walter was the most affected of all.

He left behind a letter to Mr. Payne, which read: "I shall remember my service with you and shall always be thankful that I worked for you. I never before worked for a man who seemed to think that a boy had any thoughts or feelings. I shall pray that you may prosper, sir, on your splendid farm. If you see Deacon Grubb, I wish that you give him my kind regards. I like him very much. If you will, be kind enough to say to Dott that in my room I left a box containing a few old books for her if she would take them."

Sitting around their big fireplace, the Payne family talked of the absent boy. "He left a box full of books," said Mr. Payne.

"A box of books?" said Dott. She rose, saying to her sister, "Come and go up to the garret with me."

"No, girls," said Mr. Payne. "I will go up and bring them down for you." When Mr. Payne returned, he set down quite a heavy box, which all now remembered that the boy had had when he first came there to live. All crowded around to see it opened.

"Why," said Mrs. Payne, "I never saw him reading." On the top of the first volume was a neatly folded note addressed to Miss Dott Payne. Mr. Payne handed it to his daughter.

Dott read aloud: "Miss Payne, I feel so indebted to you for your great kindness and tender care of me when my foot was injured that I cannot go away without leaving you something as acknowledgment of my appreciation. While these books have been treasures to me, I can't think that a girl could care for them, yet you can give them to some friend and perhaps add happiness somewhere. This I know would please you, for it seems to be your only study, to do good to others." As the girl finished reading, there were tears in her eyes.

The volumes were taken out one by one. Among them were a standard school reader, a spelling book, an old arithmetic, a geography, an history of England, an history of the French Revolution, Demosthenes's *Orations*, an old, musty volume of Shakespeare, a volume of *Michigan Revised Statute*s, a volume of Josephus's *Works*, a Franklin's *Poor Richard's Almanack*, together with several other old books. In one corner of the box was a package of tallow candles.

"Well, land sakes," said Mrs. Payne, "don't that beat all. That boy must have read those books nights. Now that puts me in mind of what old Mrs. Russell told me some time ago, and I thought it strange then. She was visiting here and asked me what our hired boy did with so many tallow candles. 'Why,' says she, 'he buys them from me right along, sometimes five pounds at a time and pays the cash, too. I thought it strange, for I know you make your own tallow candles.'"

"Well," said Mr. Payne, "now I remember that the Abbotts have asked me several times what we kept a light in our south garret window at night for. Abbott says it has been there all summer and fall. He said that the night his wife was sick and he had to go for the doctor and got home at 2 o'clock in the morning, the light shone from the garret window."

Dott, who had been looking over the books, remarked, "I understand now why Walter used such good language. Don't you remember, Mother, what the minister said about that?"

"Why, yes," said Mrs. Payne, "he said that the boy talked like an educated person. Where on earth did he get his education? He's lived in this neighborhood all his life. He never went to school more than a few years. To be sure, he don't talk much, but what he does say, he says well."

"This explains all to me," said Mr. Payne. "The boy is a student, and he has read these books nights and Sundays. That explains why he stayed in his room so much."

"Dott, are you going to keep the books?" asked Addie, her sister.

"Keep them? I guess I will. I will never part with one of them." Then with a blush, Dott said, "You call all read them, if you wish. They are just what I like. Father, do you not remember the night you took Walter and me to the spelling and debating school up at the corners in October?"

"Yes, daughter, I do remember," replied Mr. Payne, "and you chose him on your side both times. He was so bashful that we could hardly persuade him to take part, and he was a pretty good speller."

"Yes," added Dott, "he saved the day in the debate for our side. The schoolmaster said afterwards that the boy knew more about the War of 1812 than he did."

＊

Meanwhile Walter passed down the road at a brisk pace, though his injured foot caused him to limp somewhat. He had his all in his pocket and in a satchel which he hung on the barrel of his gun. The distance to Aunt Betsy's was about six miles, and he arrived there in good time for dinner. She would not hear of him going farther that day, so he spent the night. Aunt Betsy also filled his satchel with more woolen socks and other little articles of comfort.

Early the next morning, Walter bade his kind Aunt Betsy good-bye. "My son," said Aunt Betsy, "you are going far away from me. I shall likely see you no more. I give you this little testament. It is small and will take but little room in your pocket. Read it often for my sake. Do not swear or drink liquor or play cards. Say your prayers always when you go to bed and when you are in trouble. If you are earnest and truthful, always trying to do right, your prayers will be answered. Remember that you are to do unto others as you would have them do unto you. I shall pray for you each night and ask the good Lord to watch over and protect you."

After leaving his aunt, Walter took the train to Grand Haven, arriving there early in the evening, and he at once took the boat for Milwaukee, where he purchased a ticket for St. Louis. He reached St. Louis in due time. He was now among strangers, and his money was soon at a low ebb. Upon inquiring, he found that it would be some time before he could get passage on a boat to the upriver points. Therefore, he thought it wise to get work and thus save the small amount of money he had left.

This, however, seemed a hard task. Had he been larger and more robust, he might have been more successful. After many days of fruitless effort, he was one evening on the outskirts of the city and went into the yard of a big house and asked for employment. The man who came to the door was coarse and abusive, telling the boy to get out, and when Walter did not move as fast as he was told to go, the man caught him by the shoulder and thrust him rudely out of the gate, giving him a smart kick as he went out.

As quick as a flash, the boy caught up a piece of brick and threw it after the ruffian, striking him on the hip. The man called out in a loud voice for a policeman. Shortly, one came around the corner. The man told the officer to take that scamp into custody, which the officer promptly did. After they had passed out of sight, the policeman said, "What are you doing in this part of town?"

"I was looking for work, sir," said the boy.

"I guess it is well for you that you didn't get it from that old divvle. He's the meanest man in the city. What's your name, my boy?"

"Walter Cooper."

"Where are you from?"

"Shiawassee County, Michigan."

"How long have you been here?"

"Two weeks."

"Where are you going?"

"To Pikes Peak."

"What! A lad like you going to Pikes Peak?"

"Yes, sir," said the boy.

"Now, tell me all about this trouble." The lad recounted to the officer all that occurred. "Did you give the fellow any sass or back talk?"

"No, sir, I did not. I have told you the truth and all that happened."

"You did throw the brick, did you?"

"Yes, sir," said the boy.

"Did you throw it hard?"

"Yes, sir, as hard as I could."

"Do you think it hurt him?"

"I think it did. I meant to hurt him, but I suppose it was wrong."

"I guess it was," said the officer, "but bedad, I believe I would have done the same thing."

"Are you going to take me to jail?" asked the boy in alarm.

"I think I will have to, my boy, but let's hurry along to the station, and if the old man is there, he may be easy with you."

At that moment, a polished old southern carriage came rattling along and turned up to the walk opposite the officer and the boy. Waiting to board the vehicle was a fine-looking southern gentleman and a young girl. The gentleman wore a broad-brimmed, soft, white hat and a neat-fitting suit of homespun. He had a heavy, gray mustache and goatee. The girl was young and pretty. She had dark-brown hair and eyes. She wore a heavy winter suit with handsome furs and a brown hat with feathers. The team was a fine pair of bright bay thoroughbreds. The driver, an old black man with gray hair, answered to the name of Sampson. He talked constantly to the restless horses as he waited for his passengers to board.

"Mr. Morley," called the gentleman, addressing the police officer. "What are you going to do with that lad?"

"Sir, I am taking him to the police station for throwing a stone at Professor Zillflig."

"Father," said the young girl, "do ask him to let the boy go."

"Now, see here, Morley," the gentleman said, "I saw the whole thing from my piazza across the way and so did Alice here. We were just about to start out when the lad went to the door. We saw Zillflig push the boy rudely out and kick him. We saw the boy throw the stone. I hope the magistrate will not lock him up. My boy, what were you doing at that house?"

"I went in to inquire for work," Walter replied, and he repeated all that had passed.

"That's about so," said the old gentleman, "about so. I did not hear what was said, but I saw all that was done. I wish I had time to go down to the police station. I would see to it myself, but I can't. I must go to the wharf and catch Todd's boat before she pushes out. Where are you from, my boy?"

"I come from Shiawassee County, Michigan, sir."

"From the north, way north," said the gentleman in an undertone. "Got some grit though. Where are you going, my boy?"

"I am going to Pikes Peak, sir. I wanted to go up the river, and there is no boat going up for some days, and I wanted to work while I was waiting, sir."

"Yes, yes, I see," said the gentleman. "Morley," he continued, "I feel some interest in this boy. I suppose Zillflig will be on hand in the morning with his tribe to make the lad trouble. I wish you would make a statement to the magistrate. Say, if you wish, that I saw the whole thing and will appear in the morning at his police court to tell what I saw." Then turning to the boy, he said kindly, "If you will call this evening at 8 o'clock at my house and inform me at what hour your case will be called, I will be on hand to help you."

"I will, sir," replied the boy. "Yet I do not like to trouble you so much. I am very sorry this happened, sir."

"Never mind, lad, never mind," said the old gentleman. "I saw it all, and I will stand by you until you are out of it. I don't believe in standing abuse, especially from such upstarts as that Yankee professor. Let me see, what is your name?"

"Walter Cooper, sir."

As the carriage moved away, the boy raised his hat and bowed respectfully. Morley called to the gentleman, "I will tell the old man what your honor says, and I will just put in a word meself for I like the lad, I do."

When Walter and Morley arrived at the police station, they went before the police magistrate. The officer told all he knew about the case. Turning to the lad, the magistrate asked him to tell his story, which he did in a straightforward way. "Were you in the street when he kicked you?"

"No, sir, just inside his gate."

"I wish it had been just outside," said the magistrate. After a few words with the police officer, he turned to the boy and said kindly, "You may go, if you will report here at ten o'clock tomorrow morning."

"I will be here in the morning," replied the boy, bowing politely as he turned to go.

Promptly at 8 o'clock that evening, Walter knocked at the door of the mansion opposite the scene of his misfortune earlier in the day. Presently, the same old retainer, Sampson, opened the door. Bowing, he said, "Walk right in, sir, walk right in. Take a seat right there. Master Hudson will be in directly, sir."

Left alone, Walter had time to survey the large drawing room warmed by an open fireplace in which burned a bright fire of hickory wood. On the left was a picture of a gentleman dressed in an officer's uniform. Near it hung a large portrait of a beautiful woman much younger than the man. The lad thought he could trace in the portrait of the lady a resemblance to the young girl he had seen that afternoon. High up between the two portraits hung an elegant sword with jeweled hilt.

Walter's meditations were interrupted by the rustling of silk coming from an alcove to the left of the entrance hall. The girl came forward smiling and offered her hand to the caller. "I am so glad you came. I have been so worried about your misfortune, and Papa is also worked up about it. My name is Alice Hudson. I have a brother. His name is Gerald. He is away off in the West, and I always think of him when I see young men and pray that if he should get into trouble that he would find some kind friend to aid him."

The gentle, frank manner of the young lady soon put the young stranger at his ease. He forgot his almost painful bashfulness and felt as natural as if among old friends. "Is your brother in the Pikes Peak country?" asked the boy.

"Yes, he went there this spring. He left here with friends of our family. The last we heard of him, he was at Santa Fe, New Mexico. He was about to leave that place for a town called Denver where he was to look for mines. Oh! I am so lonesome without him. He should not have gone away, but he was twenty-one and Papa said he was his own man and had a right to do as he pleased. He does not say in his letters anything about coming back. Boys seem restless to go to new places. I do not think it is so bad to go where people live, but in that wild, far-off mountain country where the Indians and wicked, rough people seem to predominate, it is awful. This is my brother's picture."

The boy took the picture in his hand and at once glanced at the portrait on the wall.

"Oh!" said the girl, "you see it. Do you think he strongly resembles Grandpa?"

"I certainly do think he strongly resembles that portrait," Walter replied, pointing out the lines of resemblance.

"Exactly what Captain Gilbert says: the eyes, chin, and forehead. Yes, those are the very points Captain Gilbert mentioned. How old are you?" inquired the girl.

"Past sixteen, almost seventeen," Walter answered.

"Are your parents living?"

"My father is dead. My mother and brothers live in New York."

"Then you take care of yourself."

"Oh, yes, I have done that for a long time."

"Is it not hard to earn one's living?" she asked.

"Oh, no, I do not find it so. I feel more independent when I do that."

At this moment, the gentleman Walter had seen that afternoon—and whom he had heard Morley call Colonel Hudson—came into the room. The colonel came forward with hand extended. "I judge," said the colonel, "that they let you go until tomorrow."

"Yes," the lad replied. "The magistrate told me to appear tomorrow at ten in the morning. I so dislike to bother you, but I came to tell you as I promised I would." Walter rose and moved toward the door. "I thank you very much for offering to aid me, but you must be a busy man."

"I'm not too busy to help a stranger when he is pursued by such a scoundrel as that cowardly Yankee professor."

"I shall never have an opportunity to return the favor," said the boy.

"Never mind that," replied the colonel. "I have a boy myself, and I hope he will meet friends should there be a time offered."

"Father," said the young lady, "I showed Gerald's portrait to Mr. Cooper. He at once pointed out the same points of resemblance to Grandpa as Captain Gilbert pointed out to us."

"Why, that is a little strange. Captain Gilbert is a celebrated art critic," explained the colonel. "You are not going, lad. No, sir, not tonight, at least not until after dinner, which will be called at once." While the young man protested that it was necessary for him to go, dinner was announced. Walter followed his host into the dining room, where a splendid southern dinner was served. Walter declined the wine.

"Well, Alice doesn't take wine either. You are on the right track, and I am glad you do not use liquor. I am sorry to say that some of our southern boys use too much."

Dinner over, the men sat until late, talking of Pikes Peak and the West. Finally, the young man rose to take his leave. The colonel then insisted upon sending the servant Sampson with him, saying that he was in a strange city where things did not look the same at night and that it was a long distance to his lodgings.

"I cannot permit your man to go so far with me," Walter protested.

"Well, then," said the good colonel, "be our guest for the night. We shall be pleased to have you with us."

So it was arranged for the morning. The colonel would take his young guest to the police department. At ten sharp, the accused was on hand. Sitting near him was Colonel Hudson. On the other side of the room sat Professor Zillflig, his wife, and his hired man. The police magistrate entered promptly and took his seat. There were other prisoners, both male and female, charged with all sorts of offenses: picking pockets, fighting, drunkenness, stealing, and other misdemeanors. After reading the docket, Walter hung his head.

"Never mind, my boy," said the colonel, "your case is not like the others. You have done no more than any person of honor and spirit would be forced to do under the same circumstances."

After reading the list, the magistrate glanced around the room. Noting Colonel Hudson, he nodded his recognition to that gentleman. "Mr. Morley," asked the magistrate, "is the youth Walter Cooper present?"

"He is, your honor," replied the policeman.

"Let the lad stand at the bar. My lad," said the magistrate, "you are charged with assaulting Professor Zillflig with a stone upon his own premises. You may sit down for the present. Have you any counsel?"

"No, sir," replied the lad. "I do not want any. I have no money to pay for such service."

"Let Professor Zillflig be sworn," the magistrate said. "You may state when and where and the nature of the offense committed by this lad."

"Well, sir, he came to my house yesterday afternoon and asked for work, and when I told him I had none, he swore at me and called me names. I took hold of him and pushed him out of my yard. He then picked up a stone and threw it at me with great force, and he continued to call me vile names and to throw stones, hitting me many times. I told him to go away, but he would not go, and I called for a policeman and had him arrested."

"Professor," asked the magistrate, "are you sure that this lad used abusive language?"

"Yes, sir," was the answer.

"Where was he when he used this language?"

"In my house and on the street?"

"Did he go into your house?"

"Yes, sir," Zillflig replied.

"How many stones did he throw at you?"

"A great number."

"Did he throw more than one stone at you?"

"He did, sir, throw many."

"You say you pushed him out of your place. Did you strike or kick the lad while you were doing this?"

"No, sir."

"What language did you use toward the boy? Was it loud and threatening and abusive or mild and gentle, such as a man of your age should use toward a lad?"

"I was very mild and gentle, sir, just as I would be with my own son."

"That will do, professor. Have you any eyewitnesses?"

"Yes, your honor, my wife and my man Johnson here." Both Mrs. Zillflig and Johnson were sworn, and they told similar stories corroborative of the professor's statement.

"Have you any further testimony, Professor?" asked the magistrate.

"No, your honor," answered that worthy.

"You may stand aside then." The professor and his wife then exchanged meaning glances and nods while Johnson, the hired man, hung his head and looked sheepish under the steady gaze of Morley.

The magistrate then turned to the boy and said, "Walter, you may state when and why you went to Professor Zillflig's house and what transpired."

"I went to his house," replied the lad, "as I had gone to other houses and asked for work. He opened the door and said, 'Go away. I have no work. Go now, go quick, or I will throw you over the fence.' He then took me by the shoulder and pushed me toward the gate, and as we came to the gate, he kicked me, saying, 'Begone, you young thief.' I stooped to the walk and picked up a piece of brick, and as he ran toward the house, I threw it after him. He called, 'Police! Police!,' and Mr. Morley came along and brought me here."

"My boy," asked the magistrate, "how many stones or bricks did you throw at the professor?"

"I only threw one, sir," came the reply.

"Are you sure you did not throw any more?" again asked the magistrate.

"Yes, sir, I am sure."

"Is it true," continued the magistrate, "that you used abusive language and swore at the professor?"

"Sir," answered the lad with dignity, "I do not swear. I did not call him names. I did not go in his house. I simply asked him for work, and when he said he had none, I turned to go away and he pushed me roughly through the gate and kicked me."

"How hard did you throw the brick bat?" asked the magistrate.

"I threw as hard as I could," was the answer. "I now know it was wrong, but I tried my best to hurt him."

"That will do," said the magistrate. Patrick Morley whispered to a fellow officer and nodded approvingly at the boy. "Is there any other evidence, Mr. Morley?"

"I think, your honor, that Colonel Hudson saw the fracas."

Colonel Hudson rose and said, "Your honor, in behalf of this boy who was raised in the country and I believe is honest and truthful, I want to say that I saw him—as did my daughter Alice—go to the door of the professor. He did not go in. I saw him when the professor seized him and pushed him from his door. I saw the professor kick the boy viciously as he passed him out of the gate. I heard the professor call the boy vile names, such as thief and rascal. I saw the boy pick up a missile of some kind and throw it at the professor. I saw the professor run like a coward from this brave boy who had the courage to defend his person and his honor as all true Americans should do. I heard all the lad said, and I am sure he did not use any improper language. I've heard the testimony of Professor Zillflig and, of my own knowledge, know that it was in the main false. In conclusion, I ask that this brave boy be discharged and that the professor, who is here as prosecutor, using the weapons of the coward, malice and falsehood, be fined in such sum as your honor may elect, for wasting your time with a frivolous charge supported by perjured witnesses and for disgracing our city by mistreating a stranger." The colonel took his seat.

The magistrate turned slowly around and surveyed the scene before him. It was plain to see that there was but one sentiment in the room. "My son," said the magistrate, "you are discharged. While you really committed an assault, which is unlawful, yet the court feels the provocation was very great. Nothing that has been alleged in the complaint beyond the mere assault has been proven or sustained against you. The court believes and asserts that the worst part of the crime charged in the complaint, that of swearing and the use of vile language, has utterly failed of proof. The court therefore admonishes you in future to abstain from throwing missiles at persons older than yourself, no matter what the provocation may be. The court wishes you well and a prosperous future."

"Professor Zillflig," continued the magistrate, "you have brought a frivolous charge against this boy before this court and attempted to sustain it by evidence which in the main has been proven to be false. While a portion of your complaint has been admitted by the defendant, the provocation which the defendant alleges was ample to warrant the assault on your person. The assault made by you upon the person of this defendant has been clearly proven. You deny this assault, the court believes falsely. You are therefore fined one hundred dollars and the costs of this case, and you will be taken into custody to there remain until the fine and costs are paid."

✳

Upon Walter's release from custody, his new friend Colonel Hudson found him a job working on a plantation not far from St. Louis. Within two weeks, however, after being turned down for a place with the American Fur Company (because of his youth and small size), Walter met a man named Purdy on the St. Louis docks. Purdy needed help bringing a band of horses home to Leavenworth, Kansas, by steamboat, and in exchange for Walter's assistance, he offered to pay for the young adventurer's fare and food.

Before departing, Walter paid his respects to Colonel and Alice Hudson. The colonel gave Walter a letter to his son Gerald, as well as letters of introduction to the "houses of Jones & Cartwright and of Walingford & Murphy," both of Denver. Alice took Walter aside and confided that her "brother is somewhat wayward." "If you should be so fortunate as to meet him," she begged her young friend, "will you promise me to help him if you can?" Walter promised to do so, and Alice too gave him a letter addressed to Gerald Hudson.

Walter's trip by steamboat to Leavenworth was relatively uneventful, though Walter "saw something new and interesting in each bend of the river." The passenger list included U.S. Army officers bound for Fort Leavenworth and trappers and scouts headed for "Salt Lake, Pikes Peak, and the different trading posts at or near the Rocky Mountains." Among the latter was Jim Beckwith (also known as Beckwourth), the renowned mulatto mountain man and subject of the popular biography, The Life and Adventures of James P. Beckwourth, Mountaineer, Scout, Pioneer and Chief of the Crow Nation, *published in 1856. Walter was clearly impressed by Beckwourth's knowledge of the ways of the West, though he noted that "he was quite loudmouthed and talked a great deal about his exploits. . . ." The historical record notes that Beckwourth was in St. Louis in 1858 and that he did travel to the Pikes Peak region the next year to work as a storekeeper and supplier. Beckwourth died in 1866 while visiting the Crow, the tribe into which he was adopted during the 1820s.*

Walter contracted dysentery from drinking the "muddy water of the Missouri," and upon his arrival in Leavenworth, he was nursed back to health by Mrs. Purdy, "a most excellent woman, kind and motherly." He soon found work as a government teamster, and when that ended, he "hired out to husk corn." Finally a merchant heading for the gold fields of Colorado hired Walter as a teamster at the rate of $20 per month. The merchant, a Mr. Bohn, had purchased a team of horses that "proved balky," and throughout the trip west, they provided "much annoyance and trouble." Walter proved to be up to the challenge, and Mr. Bohn was "much astonished at the patience of the boy."

As they passed through Kansas, Walter learned more about the deep divisions between the "Free and Slave State Partizans," and he witnessed the "constant fear" of raiding parties with which all Kansans lived. Every "home had its tale of woe, few homes having escaped the heavy hand of one party or the other." Walter

*was also impressed by the "rich and fertile" soils of Kansas and by the territory's
"vast plains . . . her heavily wooded streams . . . a picture both sublime and grand
beyond description."*

*Merchant Bohn moved slowly through Kansas, trading with the settlers and, as
the opportunity arose, with the Indian tribes that made their homes in the territory. Walter was particularly taken with a group of Pottawattamies, originally
from Michigan, who had settled along the Kaw River. He "met young people who
had the advantage of schools and found them bright and intelligent." And apparently, while he was there, Walter ran in a footrace. The race ran over a course of
two miles and, to his own surprise, Walter beat all comers.*

*As Bohn's party turned south, they encountered a "great assemblage of all the
Indians from the surrounding country in a general council." The gathering brought
together the Indians—who were unhappy about the government's failure to pay
their cash annuities for two years—government representatives, settlers, and traders. Besides the question of annuities, the council would address the Indians' con-
cerns about the government's failure to carry out treaty stipulations and to make
"certain amendments to old treaty rights and to make new treaties." Walter witnessed many speeches by tribal leaders, but one in particular, by an old chief,
struck him with its eloquence and wisdom. The old chief began:*

> I have lived long in these parts and have heard much about the
> Great Father. I have always been told that he was wise, just, and
> great, and that he had but one tongue, two eyes, and that his ears
> were large, that the voices of his children, the Red Men, he always
> heard; that he had promised to care for them and that in exchange
> for their lands . . . each year so much money should be paid to
> each member of his tribe. We surrendered our lands because the
> Great Father wanted it and we wanted the money because it would
> buy food and clothing. What does the Great Father think his chil-
> dren have lived on these two years? Can his children eat the grass
> like the horse and sleep on the prairie like the wolves, without
> blankets? No, they cannot. His children have been hungry. Their
> women and children have cried out for food and clothing. . . .

*Given the unrest among the Indians, the government authorities proposed to
complete the council with "as much expedition and as little friction as possible." To*

accomplish that end, they arranged a "series of feasts and attractions such as races. . . . an almost continual round of pleasure which sometimes interfered with business discussions." Walter described two of the horse races, including one in which the white men had cheated, using "fine race horses" when they had agreed not to. Trouble was averted when the panel of judges—made up of two Indians and a white man—ruled that the Indian horse had won, thereby punishing those "who had the unblushing effrontery to resort to trickery and unsportsman-like acts. . . ."

"The great event," however, "to which all looked forward with eager expecta-tion was a footrace open to all comers." Though the footrace had been announced well before the council began, no date had been set, and tension built as the date was kept a mystery day after day. Finally, the council organizers announced—in English and in all languages "spoken by any of the assembled tribes"—that the great race would be held the following day at 2 o'clock in the afternoon. The manager of the races, a Mr. Godfrey, set out the rules and the grand prize:

"The race is open to all comers. No entrance fee will be charged. Those wishing to enter must apply to Major Greene at the Settlers' tent. All entries will close at 10 o'clock tomorrow. The competitors for the prize must be on the ground, ready to start at 2 o'clock sharp. They will pass down the course two and one-half miles, pass around the red flag, and return to this point. The first one touching the rope here will receive the prize, which is the handsome thoroughbred race horse, saddle, bridle, and spurs, standing yonder. The same rules will govern this race that governed all previous races. The race will be judged at each end of the course. Each racer as he passes around the flag must give the record judge his name. All persons are warned to keep the course clear. There must be no interference with the runners. Each runner is free to wear whatever he chooses. The animal which will be the property of the winner will be on exhibition at this place for one hour."

The horse was then led in front of the stand and its saddle removed. He was five years old, fifteen-hands high, and of about ten hundred and fifty pounds weight. He was a dark iron-gray with a broad chest and fine quarters, clean-limbed with perfect feet, and hoofs as black as jet. He had never been shod. His head was small, large eyes standing well out. The forehead was broad. The ears were small, well tapered. His mane and tail were black, the tail almost touching the ground. The neck arched and the withers were high, the back short, the loins heavily muscled, every part indicating speed and high character. Mr. Godfrey announced that one thousand dollars would be paid the winner for the naked horse—should he wish to part with him. The animal submitted to the examination quietly, which showed a good disposition. He was nervous and restless, however, when closely approached by the Indians and would paw the ground impatiently when one attempted to put a hand on him. He was certainly a most magnificent creature and was much admired by all.

Mr. Bohn watched while his young driver handled the horse with perfect confidence, the animal seeming to enjoy it as much as the boy who took up every foot, looked into his mouth, and patted him affectionately. Walter looked back at the horse many times as he departed in company with Bohn, who said, "That's a fine horse, don't you think?"

"Yes," said the boy, "I never saw one that I liked so well."

"Why don't you go into the race and win him?" said his employer.

"Oh, I don't think I could do that," said the boy. "There will be too many swift runners for me to win such a race."

"Why, you won that race up on the Kaw River easy, and they say those Indians were big runners," said Bohn. On reaching their quarters, Bohn talked of nothing else. Finally he said, "Now you just try, and I know you can win."

But the boy insisted that he would not have a winning chance against such odds as he thought would most likely be in the race.

Bohn said, "Well, I am going over and find out all I can about who will be in the race." He accordingly repaired to the Settler's tent, where several men were congregated discussing the coming event. Mr. Bohn made so many inquiries that he attracted the attention of both Mr. Godfrey and a stranger named Bridger, who inquired why he was so much interested.

"It was just like this, gentlemen. I've got a boy with me what can run just like a deer."

"How do you know he can run?" asked Godfrey.

"Well, he beat the best runners over on the Kaw a few days ago."

"How far was it?" asked Bridger.

"It was two miles."

"This is five miles," replied the trapper.

"Well, I don't care. My boy can run ten miles."

"What do you call him 'your boy' for?"

"Oh," Bohn said, "he works for me."

Bridger inquired, "Where is the boy?"

"He was over at my tent. Just you come over and see him."

"What are you so anxious to have him run for?" asked Godfrey. "If he wins, the horse will be his, not yours."

"Well, I know that. I don't want the horse. I want to win some money."

"Do you mean if the boy enters you will bet your money on him?"

"Yes," replied Bohn, "I will bet my money on him if he will go in the race."

"How much will you bet?"

"I will bet one thousand dollars," replied Bohn.

"James," said Godfrey, addressing Bridger, "suppose you go over with this man and look the boy, as he calls him, over?"

"Now, gentlemen, when you see that boy, don't talk about betting, for if you do, he won't run for money. I think he is a little religious. Talk about the horse. He likes the horse, and if he had friends here, I think he would enter."

"Well," replied Bridger, "I will go over with you."

Bohn returned to his tent in company with a stranger, a large, fine-looking man whom he introduced to the boy as Mr. Bridger. After a time, the conversation turned on the race.

Bridger said, "My lad, your friend here, Mr. Bohn, says you can run."

"I cannot run much and have had no experience as a runner or racer," the lad modestly replied.

"But you won the race up on the Kaw, he tells me," continued the trapper.

"Yes, I did win that race, but it was only two miles and this is five. And they will, I think, have faster runners than See-ma-tah was."

"Now, my boy," said Bridger, "let me look you over." He then examined the boy very carefully, felt of his limbs and body most critically. Finally he said, "I think you had better enter this race. You are well built, and there is only one thing I question and that is your endurance."

"I can hold out," said the boy.

Bridger got up and said, "I would like to go over the course with you. It will do you no harm to have a good sweat, if you don't mind. I will get my horse and go with you."

The boy finally consented. After they came back, Bridger said to Bohn, "I think we can win the race, and I wish your young friend would go over and enter for it."

"Do you think, Mr. Bohn," the boy asked, "that there would be any harm in my entering?"

"No, of course not," and so it was decided that Walter would compete in the great race. Mr. Bridger told the boy that it was a friendly competition for a prize and no harm in it from a moral standpoint.

The race was called promptly at the appointed time. A list of the entries was read as follows:

Ca-so-to, was the first entry,
Sac-tok, the second,
See-ma-tah,
Ah-son-to,
Me-ma-on-to,
Antoine Andrew,
Charles Galick,
Andrew Gordon,
Walter Cooper,
De-ah,
Ten in number.

The runners were now given their places, beginning on the left of the judges or stand starters, the positions having been assigned by lot. They were as follows:

Ca-so-to, No. 1
Walter Cooper, No. 2
Sac-tok, No. 3
Andrew Gordon, No. 4
Charles Galick, No. 5
See-ma-tah, No. 6
Antoine Andrew, No. 7
De-ah, No. 8

Me-ma-on-to, No. 9
Ah-son-to, No. 10

Among the tribes of Indians represented at the council were Delawares, Iroquois, Wyandots, Miamis, Ottawas, Pottawattamies, Creeks, Sac and Fox, Choctaw, Osage, Shawnees, Kiowas, and Cherokees. Of the Kansas Indians, there were the Kaws and Pawnees and still others.

Thousands of the Indians lined the racecourse on either side except for a space about one hundred feet square in front of the judges' stand. This had been fenced off with ropes to prevent interference with the race. Wagons and carts had been placed together on both sides of the course for a long distance above the judges' stand. This left ample room for the racers, and no person was allowed inside this enclosure except those in charge of the race. The wagon and carts were filled to capacity with spectators. Under the wagons, every inch of space as taken with more men, women, and children, while outside the enclosure were congregated Indians on horseback, half-breeds, and white men. Other anxious onlookers had taken a stand on a large tract of elevated ground just back of the horsemen, but near enough to hear the words of the judges and recognize the runners. Flagged poles had been placed along the track, and outriders were stationed here and there to warn away excited onlookers.

When the first name was called, a gigantic Sac and Fox Indian came forward and took his place amidst great applause from the Indians as-sembled. As Ca-so-to took his place, covered with an ermine robe, it was easy to understand that he was not only a very popular man among his friends, but was well known beyond the limits of his own tribe.

When the second name was called, there did not at first seem to be much movement, and the name was called a second time before the runner made his way to the enclosure through the dense throng. As he took his place, there was no applause such as had greeted the giant at his side—who now looked down upon the newcomer with a seeming look of contempt. A ripple of merriment started among the Indians, one of whom called out in a loud voice, "Heap papoose." A roar of laughter followed, and it was long before quiet was restored. In response to each new sally of witticism at the expense of No. 2, the Indians would break into uncontrollable fits of mer-riment. The object of the mirth stood in calm indifference while the jokers laughed and shouted themselves hoarse at his expense.

Finally, the runners had all taken their places unnoticed, with one exception. When the last man, Ah-son-to, stepped forward, he was greeted
with some applause and calls of approval. It was evident that he was no
novice and was well known to both whites and Indians.

The roll was then called. Three men came down from the stand and
directed the runners to disrobe and prepare for the start. No. 1, the Sac and
Fox giant, threw his robe behind him, and a friend took it. No. 2 took off a
large overcoat, which had completely covered his body, and not until then
was the difference in size between the first two runners fully realized. The
cry of "papoose!" was again raised but was soon hushed as all were now
eager for the start.

Godfrey and Bridger came down into the enclosure, followed by Bohn.
They examined closely all the contestants. As they walked along, Godfrey
said, "Why, Jim, that boy don't stand any more show to win this race than
I would, and I am fifty-five years old, all crippled up with rheumatism.
There is just two in the race, the Sac and Fox and the Delaware, Ah-son-to.
The others are dunghills."

"Look here, Sam, don't you call my new, young friend a dunghill. If you
don't like him, bet on your favorite, but don't abuse him in my presence.
Didn't I go over the course with him, and didn't he go over that track without a puff? I know a thoroughbred when I see him, and he's the only one of
the lot. The only thing I fear is that he may not overcome the lead that this
big, red cuss here will get on him the first three miles. If he can keep in
sight, he'll win—just as sure as my name is Jim Bridger."

"Don't get mad, Jim," said the other. "I meant no harm by my remark,
but remember he's only a novice. Both of these Indians are great runners.
Why, that Delaware was with Harney and made a hundred miles in a day
carrying dispatches, and that Fox has beat every Indian on the frontier. But
I'll stay with the boy if you say so, and because he's got no friends here and
because they made so much fun of him."

"That's right," said Jim. "Now you talk like an American and a free trapper. Let's look him over. Feel of those legs, Sam." So saying, the friends went
over to Walter. "Son," said Bridger, "this is Major Sam Godfrey, Colonel St.
Vrain's secretary. He feels an interest in you 'cause you don't seem to have
many friends here. I told him you would win if you could."

"Yes," said the major, "and another thing. I don't want that horse to fall into the hands of those Injuns. They don't know how to appreciate a good thing. They would kill him in six months. Why, that horse came from Kentucky, and he is a full thoroughbred. He's worth fifteen hundred dollars to any man who can afford him."

At this point Bohn came up and said, "Walter, do you see that big fellow over there? That is the Indian you beat over on the Kaw, See-ma-tah they call him."

"Yes," said the boy, "I don't think he will stay long in this race. That man over there on the end, the last man, Ah-son-to, is I think the best among the Indians."

"You are right," said Major Godfrey. "He is a great runner. I don't know how fast he is, but he is long-winded."

Godfrey and Bridger stopped in front of the giant Ca-so-to and walked around him. As he stood there perfectly naked except for a breechclout, his dark limbs shone like polished rosewood. His hair hung down his back in two heavy braids, and in his ears were heavy, brass rings. Around his neck he wore a necklace of bear claws. The Indian stood there, indifferent to all surroundings. He was about twenty years of age and possessed a proud, manly, independent bearing.

"Well, Jim, it looks as though we have a Tartar here. Look at him. Why, he is six foot three in his moccasins. Look at that muscular development. You can't help admiring such a specimen of manhood. Those arms! How the muscles stand out, and those hips. What power! Look at that thigh and those legs."

"Well, yes, fur an Injun, I must say he is hard to beat, but, Sam, them legs have got to pack a pretty big load. That body weighs something like two hundred or better. That could count pretty well in a rough-and-tumble fight or a wrestle, but in a five-mile race, there is too much load. Mark what I tell you. Now, look here, Sam. Just look at this lad. Of course, he ain't naked like that monstrous critter there. Look at that broad forehead, close-cut black hair, that handsome face, that eye. I never saw an eye like that that wasn't unconquerable. He'll never quit, no, never. Look at them limbs. That Injun ain't built like that. Look at that round body. Go and feel of that Injun's leg, and then feel of this lad's limbs."

The major did so. "Say, Jim," he exclaimed, "you are right. That Injun's leg feels like beef. This boy's leg is like iron."

"That's so, Sam. How they taper! No surplus there. No heavy carcass to carry. I wish he were six inches taller, though. But I guess he'll do. Sam, that boy's built like a racehorse, like a deer, and if he can't win this race, no white man can." Seizing the major by the arm, Bridger said in a whisper, "He will run that five miles without a puff. Those iron limbs are tireless. He will win! He will win!"

At this moment, they stopped in front of the Delaware, Ah-son-to. He was a man about thirty years old, well built, weighing about 140 pounds, with no surplus flesh. "He's really a fine-built man," remarked Bridger as the friends turned away. "Yes, that man will surely win if the boy does not." They scarcely gave the other racers a passing notice.

Godfrey and Bridger now passed up into the elevated stand. Colonel St. Vrain was there, as was Major Greene. Godfrey asked Mr. Bohn up as a friend of the boy. Colonel St. Vrain asked Godfrey about the runners, and he described them, dwelling on the makeup of the boy runner. The colonel was much interested.

The runners had, in one way and another, decorated themselves in such a manner as would be recognized at a distance. One wore strips of red cloth tied to his arms. The others wore different colors, no two alike. "What are your boy's colors?" asked the colonel. None had been provided.

"I wish I had a flag," said Bridger.

"Here, take this sash," said the colonel. "It is red, white, and blue." He handed Bridger a long, light silk scarf. Such a scarf was often worn in place of a belt by Spanish and other gentlemen on the border. "Give it to him with my compliments."

Bridger hastened to comply. The lad bowed his thanks and knotted the sash around his body in the usual fashion.

The order was given to make ready. A mark in the earth had been made from one side of the track to the other. The runners now toed this mark, each competitor leaning forward with his eye on the farther end of the platform. They awaited the signal, which was to be a pistol shot. Rigid and still, they scarcely seemed to breathe.

The shot rang out, and a line of human forms leapt forward simultaneously. For the moment, it was not possible to distinguish which runner had the start. The Indians seemed to leap, rather than run. The white men, all save the boy, quickly fell behind. The boy stayed with the leader Ca-so-to for about a quarter mile, then seemed to slack his pace. The giant forged ahead, and Ah-son-to also passed the boy. Finally, See-ma-tah passed the lad, in which order the race continued for the first mile. The pace was a swift one which, if it continued to the end, would certainly bring the big Ca-so-to out ahead.

For the first half mile, the racetrack was no more or less than the main road. The remainder of the distance was a wagon road with a well-beaten track. From the point where it left the judges' stand, the road led in a bee line west for about a half mile up quite a grade. Then it bore north for a distance of one and a half miles, giving the spectators a very good side view. It then turned again to the west in an almost parallel line with the first half mile. It was difficult to tell what the relative positions of the runners were for the first and last half mile, but for the intermediate mile and a half, one could make a very close calculation of not only the speed of the runners, but their position and the distance separating them. The track followed the road in order to avoid the rough, bumpy places over which it was difficult to make rapid progress.

After the first mile, one white man and two Indians dropped out, being hopelessly outclassed. This left seven in the race. Colonel St. Vrain had been provided with a camp chair and sat on a small platform several feet above the others. He had a large field glass, and now he alone could see what was going on at the front.

Before the runners started, Major Godfrey gave orders to the marshal to send trusted outriders forward and to see that the racers were not interfered with. "Keep an eye on the boy," said he, "and see that he has a fair show."

"I don't think if I watch the leaders that I shall be able to look after him," growled the marshal. "He will be so far behind."

"Never mind, never mind," said the major. "Carry out my orders and see that you keep a sharp look-out."

Betting was lively. The Delaware was a strong favorite at first. The Indians, however, were betting heavily on the Fox. The excitement was rising. Godfrey, Bridger, and Bohn bet on the boy. They took every bet that was offered. Now came a halt as the lead of the Fox and the Delaware seemed too great.

"How are they now?" asked Bridger.

The Great Foot Race

"The Fox has turned the pole."

"And the boy?" asked another.

"He is a quarter behind the Delaware," said Colonel St. Vrain. "He has passed See-ma-tah."

"How is the Fox running?"

"Slowing up," said the colonel, "if I can correctly judge."

"And the Delaware?" asked another.

"Gaining on the Fox" was the answer.

"And the boy?" asked Bridger.

"Holding his own," replied the colonel. "The Delaware has turned the pole and is apparently keeping the same pace he set at starting. I am sure the Fox is easing down. The boy has turned the pole."

"How far behind the Delaware?" asked Major Godfrey.

"About two hundred yards," said the colonel.

"How far behind the boy is See-ma-tah?" asked Bridger.

"I should say one hundred and fifty yards."

"One hundred dollars on the Delaware," cried the settler Mr. Graham.

"I'll take that," said Bohn. "Make it two hundred," he continued, as he counted out the coin.

"Two hundred goes," answered Graham, covering the gold.

"My boy wins," whispered Bohn to Bridger. "Yes, he has not commenced to run yet."

At this moment, a government wagon master rode up and called out his horse saddle and bridle on the Fox, stroking the neck of a fine black stallion.

Bridger raised his hand and answered, "My brown mare and rig goes on the boy."

"It's a go," answered the wagon master, making a note in his book.

"Where are they now?" called Godfrey.

"The Fox has turned the bend, and the Delaware is closing the gap" was the answer.

Graham turned to Godfrey and said, "I go you one hundred on the Delaware."

"I take it," said Godfrey.

"Where is the boy?" asked Bridger.

"Coming down that stretch next to the pole," replied the colonel. "See-ma-tah has rounded the pole. The other three have dropped out. The Delaware has turned the bend one hundred yards behind the Fox. He is gaining on him. The boy rounds the bend, one hundred yards behind the Delaware. The Fox and the Delaware stick to that long lope, and my opinion is it will cost them the race."

"How is our boy?" asked Godfrey.

"Steadily gaining, I think" was the answer. By this time, large numbers of Indians mounted on horses had gone up the track and were crowding close to the course.

"Godfrey," said the colonel, "send a fast rider up the track to keep it clear." The necessary order was given, and a man flew up the track.

"How are the runners?" asked Bridger.

"The Fox seems to be about one hundred feet ahead of the Delaware," answered the colonel. "The boy is just holding his own. They are coming at a fast pace. The strain must be terrible."

"One thousand dollars on the boy," called out Bohn.

"I'll take five hundred," said Mr. Graham.

"All right," answered Bohn.

The excitement now became great and betting increased, mostly in small amounts. Horses, mules, robes, and every kind of property was freely and liberally staked on the issue of the race. The prairie was covered with Indians, and difficulty was apparently being experienced by the outriders in keeping the course clear.

"How are the runners, Colonel?" asked Godfrey excitedly.

"Coming down the track at a fast pace," replied the colonel. "They are passing the one-mile pole, the Fox and the Delaware neck and neck. I can't see the boy."

"He must have dropped out" was the answer.

"Five hundred dollars on the boy," cried Bohn, showing more excitement.

"I see the boy now," cried the colonel. "He has gained a little."

"Who will take my five hundred?" called out Bohn.

"You had better keep your money," said the colonel.

"I'll take it," said Graham, closing the stake.

"Godfrey," said the colonel, showing some feeling, "those Indians will break up the race. They are crowding in up there."

"Collins," directed Godfrey, "keep the track clear. Take help with you." Collins started to obey.

"Where are the runners?" asked Graham.

"The Delaware has passed the Fox," answered the colonel. "I can't see the boy."

"Here," called out Graham, "one hundred more on my Delaware."

"I'll take it and make it another hundred," said Bohn.

Bridger and Godfrey were surrounded by bettors and were taking every bet offered. At this point, a noted Cherokee chief appeared on the stand. He was named Ap-sat-ka, and was accompanied by a Cherokee interpreter, who said, "This man wants to bet ten horses on the Delaware."

"I'll take that bet," called out Godfrey. "I see the boy now. He is between the Delaware and the Fox. See-ma-tah is now close to the Fox. He may win. The boy and the Delaware are neck and neck. The boy has passed the Delaware! The Indians are crowding in. See-ma-ta has passed the Fox and is gaining on the Delaware. The giant is beaten. He falls back. The Delaware is forging ahead."

"Outrageous! Outrageous!" called out the colonel. "Those Indians constantly crowd in. They are trying to discourage the boy." For the first time since the race began, the colonel took down his glass and angrily addressed the Cherokee chief in his Indian language. The latter instantly jumped to the track and ran shouting up the course. Others beyond him followed his example. There was wild excitement. It was now seen that the course was rapidly being cleared. A crowd gathered at the beginning of the half-mile stretch. The runners could not be seen. Presently the Delaware came out in view. There was an excited mix-up.

"They have stopped the boy," shouted the colonel. "Outrageous!"

"No, he is coming."

"He is ahead."

"He has been delayed."

"He leaps over the backs of the ponies in his path and has cleared the group. How he runs. He can win. He will win. Bless him. Bless him. He's a hero. He's a hero."

Now in plain view, the runners were coming down the home stretch, the Delaware leading See-ma-tah by five yards. The boy was far to the right, and his exact position with reference to the others could not be judged. But on he flies. He is certainly abreast of them. He is ahead. The Delaware falls back. See-ma-tah grows weaker. The boy is one hundred feet ahead. He comes. He comes at what a pace after five, long, miles. He's here. He's here.

"The race is his," shouted the colonel, dropping his glass and swinging his hat in a perfect ecstasy of joy. The lad had crossed the line fully one hundred and fifty feet ahead of See-ma-tah, who was second. The latter was the first to greet the lad with a kind, hearty shake of the hand, saying, "Legs heap fast. Heap good. Too quick for Injun."

The boy's friends now crowded around him. The thoughtful Bridger gave him a large coat which covered him completely. Bridger gave his careful attention to the boy, rubbing the perspiration from him and keeping him out of the chill air. A tremendous rush was made by the Indians to get a close view of the lucky papoose who had vanquished the swiftest native runners to be found among twenty tribes.

After an hour spent under Bridger's watchful care and having recovered his composure and cooled down, Walter was anxious to go and take possession of his prize, the magnificent thoroughbred. When Bridger and the boy appeared to claim the horse, Godfrey came out and addressed the boy, who had taken hold of the halter to lead the horse away. "My young friend," said Godfrey, "you have won a great victory and with it a great prize. I am authorized to say to you that, pursuant to the announcement from the judges' stand at the beginning of the race, you will be paid one thousand dollars in gold if you prefer the money to the horse—or take the horse if you like. He is a very valuable animal, and it may be better for you to take the money as you might lose the horse. Use your own judgment about it. I think you had better leave the horse in our charge until you are ready to go away, as he will be guarded then with the other horses. Colonel St. Vrain wishes to see you."

The boy stood admiring the noble animal with all the pride and pleasure of one in possession of his first great prize. He finally said, "I think, sir, I would like to ride my horse now."

Godfrey turned to the groom, saying, "Saddle the horse and adjust the stirrups," and he let the young man take his first ride on the prize he had so bravely won. "When you come back," he told Walter, "come to the big tent there. The colonel wishes to see you."

Shortly after, a great shout was heard, and Bridger, looking across the racecourse where a great body of Indians were congregated, saw the boy riding down the course and receiving a great ovation from the Indians whose chosen champions he had just defeated in the greatest footrace ever run in the territory embracing the great plains of Kansas.

Fearing some accident, the trapper crossed over to the spot where horse and rider still stood. There he found Walter surrounded by his late rivals in the great contest, who were endeavoring to converse with him. The Sac and Fox giant was at his side and was feeling of his limbs when the trapper elbowed his way inside the circle. The chief turned to Bridger. "This little chief does not understand. Tell him that I will give him twenty horses for this one."

Bridger told the boy what the Fox had said. The boy shook his head. "No, I would not part with him for a hundred horses."

When Bridger communicated the answer, a great shout went up. All his late competitors praised the boy, saying that he had good medicine. He was certainly the lion of the hour.

Bohn—having reaped quite a rich harvest besides having sold some of his wares—reminded Walter that he wanted to reach Fort Scott in good time. So the boy took leave of Godfrey and Bridger, and they began a drive of about thirty-five miles across an unbroken prairie without a single habitation. Having started early and found a most excellent well-beaten road, they were nearing a heavy belt of timber with a stream running through it. When the timber looked to be some five miles distant, Bohn noticed a great black smoke rising to the west from nearly the direction they had come. Walter stopped the team, got up on the high wagon seat, and looked back over the prairie long and intently.

"Mr. Bohn," he said, "the whole prairie is on fire. We are in a dangerous situation. I fear the fire may overtake us before we can reach the timber." There was a cold wind blowing, and Bohn had insisted that the wagon sheet be put on to protect him from the wind; otherwise they would have discovered the danger sooner. The boy whipped up the horses to a fast trot and gradually pushed them to the top of their speed. While the distance to the timber was growing shorter, the fire was approaching at a much more rapid pace. Bohn crawled over the bundles to the back end of the wagon and watched the approach of the fire. Faster and faster it came, at times leaping hundreds of feet it seemed. Bohn became wild with alarm and urged

the boy constantly to whip the team, which the boy had already urged forward at the top of their speed. Now the smoke enveloped the wagon. He
knew the fire would soon be there, and he applied the whip without mercy.
On they rushed. On came the fire. The atmosphere was hot. Looking behind, the boy saw the flames and knew they would soon reach the wagon.

"Mr. Bohn," he cried, "cut off the loops of the sheet and let it go, quick!
No, no, cut the other side first; the wind will take it off then. Quick, I say, or
it will be on fire and burn you up. Hurry, sir! There it has caught. Cut the
loops." The excited Bohn could not, it seemed, do anything as he was told.
Jumping to the back of the seat, the boy soon accomplished what should
have been done much sooner. The wind caught the burning sheet and
whirled it far to the left.

The grass was now afire on all sides, but the path was yet open in front.
The roar and heat of the flames was terrible. Bohn's clothes caught on fire,
and he was on the point of jumping out of the wagon when the boy encouraged him, saying, "I do not know how near we are, but I think we will
escape. Don't look toward the flames, or you will lose your eyes."

On they flew. The horses were foaming. Their hair was scorching. The
bundles in the wagon caught fire. Several times, Bohn's whiskers caught
fire, but he managed to put them out. Bohn pulled his hat over his eyes and
now seemed to give himself up to his fate. Just at the moment when the boy
thought all was lost, they reached the timber and dashed on toward the
stream.

The grass on the edge of the timber was much higher than on the prairie,
and for a moment, it seemed that they had been hunting a worse danger
than had been passed. But gradually the bushes became thicker and the
grass less abundant, and now the danger was past. Approaching the river,
the horses dashed in, nor could they be restrained.

At Fort Scott, Bohn had to have his whiskers and hair cut off, as they
were so badly burned. They rested the team and themselves for a few days,
as both animals had injured themselves to some extent in their long race
for life. Walter's fine saddle horse had led the way for the team and was not
injured a hair. At the fort, Bohn succeeded in closing out all his remaining
goods, and they turned their faces toward home, traveling as fast as possible, as both Bohn and his young teamster were tired of traveling and wanted
a good rest.

＊

After two weeks in Leavenworth, where he again stayed with the kindly Purdy family, Walter was eager to head west to the gold fields. He soon found a position with a "pompous" gentleman named Whetmore. For his passage and twenty dollars, Walter was engaged to transport passengers by wagon to Denver. Whetmore charged the young man—"old for his years and tho small, very strong"—with the "responsibility of keeping the outfit together and providing for the needs of the passengers on the road." Once he arrived in the Pikes Peak country, Walter was, in Whetmore's words, to "take care of the team . . . until I or my son shall arrive . . . to claim and take possession of it." Though Walter did not like the "man very well," he took the position because he was short of money.

Walter fixed up the wagon, provisioned it, and took charge of a "fine large team of horses." On a Monday, his party—made up of "ten men from Georgia, three from Illinois, and a cook who had his own pony"—set out, and by the following Saturday, they had reached the Big Blue River, "estimated to be about one hundred and eighty-five miles from Leavenworth." The Big Blue, which was "much swollen," gave Walter and his party "some trouble in crossing," but the young driver's "good judgment, experience, and courage saved the outfit from utter destruction." Once on the west bank, Walter was greeted by a large group of travelers.

＊

Some of those persons had been many days encamped there in hopes the stream would go down sufficiently to enable them to cross in safety. Among the lot was a large government train. Some of the travelers were en route to Oregon or California and others to Salt Lake. On Sunday afternoon, a big crowd had congregated near the ford, and Walter went down to see what the excitement was. He was told that two teams of emigrants were about to make an effort to cross the river.

One of the men remarked that he was doing his best to discourage them, saying that there were women and children in the party, and if they started, there would surely be an accident and perhaps a very serious one. "After seeing you cross last night," he told Walter, "I have concluded that this stream in its present swollen state is a very dangerous proposition, especially to persons inexperienced."

The boy remarked that only the largest horses could keep their feet and only heavily loaded wagons could ford without floating around and turning the horses upstream.

"It does look as though they are going to try to cross to the west bank," remarked the man. Walter went over to his camp, saddled his horse, and came back to the riverbank, reaching the ford just as the front team started into the river. The team got along very well until they were about two hundred feet from the bank, when they came into deeper water. Presently, the horses lost their footing and began to drift downstream. A man, a woman, and two children clung to the wagon bows. The wagon began to rack and soon went over. The woman and children plunged into the stream. The man vanished from sight.

Below the ford there was a high bank which took a drop of some ten feet to the water. When the wagon toppled over, Walter spurred his horse to this high bank. The horse hesitated one instant and then plunged far out into the foaming water. Horse and rider disappeared but surfaced almost immediately. Walter stroked the neck of the horse, and the noble animal responded to the caress and breasted the torrent.

The woman and children had floated down the stream, now on the surface, now out of sight. She held in her arms her two-year-old infant, but the boy four years old had become separated from her. The man was nowhere to be seen. The four-year-old came to the surface and was caught by Walter and thrown across his saddle. The woman sank again. Walter turned his horse downstream, and when the woman came to the surface, he seized her by the hair and turned his horse toward the shore.

The noble animal struggled with all his might, but burdened as he was, he could not make headway against the awful current. They all drifted down the stream. The boy, realizing that his horse would drown, threw himself into the water on the lower side, with one arm over the saddle, where the older child was clinging. With his other arm supporting the woman and infant as best he could, Walter struggled to keep above the surface and urged his horse by every means toward the western shore.

The high-spirited creature—relieved of a good portion of its burden— struggled nobly. In the meantime, the people on the west bank ran down, keeping close to the bank in hopes of aiding in the rescue. As soon as the gallant horse struck the bank, willing hands seized the mother and children (who were at first thought to be past all help) and gave them every

The Rescue

attention. Walter and the horse were both entirely exhausted. The boy lay down on the grass while the horse stood panting over him. The man was still missing.

Some time later, when Walter got back to the ford, he saw that the horses and wagon had landed some distance below on the head of a small island. The man was perched on top of the wagon, awaiting rescue. No one seemed able to render the necessary assistance. Walter told the men on the bank that, if they would provide sufficient rope to reach the stranded wagon, he would go out and fasten it to the man and they could pull him in. The boy stripped down to his underwear and swam out to the man, fastened the rope around under his arms, and gave the signal to pull away. When he saw the man pulled to safety, Walter swam to the west shore. Thus the family was saved, but the horses were drowned and the wagon and its contents lost.

＊

As stated, a large camp of emigrants had congregated up the river some distance. To this camp, two of Walter's passengers—a Mr. Langly and a man by the name of Mason—went Saturday night and did not return. They remained away Sunday, and not until late Monday, too late to think of moving, was it possible to get them back. This delay caused some bad feeling among the passengers. The three men from Illinois were especially out of patience with the delay. This brought some hard words which came very near resulting in trouble between Langly and a young man by the name of Grover, but Langly was taken in charge by his Georgia friends.

Nothing came of this trouble until a few days later when Langly and two or three others of the Georgia party went at noontime to an Indian camp two miles off the road and did not return until five o'clock. In the meantime, the team had been unharnessed and was about to be fed. Supper was underway. Upon returning, the men—who had evidently been drinking— ordered in a boisterous manner that the team be harnessed and a start made. Having given this order, they went into the tent and commenced loading up their personal effects. Noticing that no attention had been paid to their order, they commenced to abuse the driver.

Walter walked over to where they stood and, addressing himself to one of the company who had not gone to the Indian camp, said, "It is now too late to move this evening. I was told by those emigrants who passed a short time since that it was twenty-two miles to the next convenient water and that it was a hard day's work to get there because the road is very sandy. I therefore think it best to stay here tonight and get a good start in the morning. It will be much better for the animals."

This angered Langly, and he was with much difficulty restrained from striking the boy. Every man had sid earms, and nearly all a Bowie knife. The boy turned and walked to his horse. He stood there, awaiting results. In the meantime, one of the men from Illinois, Mr. Richards, a mild, easygoing gentleman, spoke up, "I am very anxious indeed to get along, but I am of the opinion the boy is right and that we would be in danger of being forced to make a dry camp."

There was much bad blood and many bitter remarks made, but finally Langly and his friends had to acquiesce. Presently, supper was ready and the men who had been away to the Indian camp did not partake, saying that they had had their supper. However, Langly, who remained in the tent, called to the cook to bring him some coffee. The cook was at the moment engaged in waiting on one of the others but, as soon as relieved, obeyed Langly's order. But that gentleman was ugly and took the cook to task because he did not instantly obey. When the latter tried to explain, Langly struck him with his pistol, knocking him down, and began to beat him. Langly was soon stopped, several interfering.

After supper, Langly and the others who had been to the Indian camp started to go back again. Mr. Grover in the meantime took three or four of the Georgia men aside and asked them if they proposed to put up with such work, which was causing delay and trouble, and they said, "No," that they were anxious to get along as their provisions were getting short and there seemed to be no chance of getting a fresh supply.

It was decided to let Langly and party know that it was proposed to start at 7 o'clock sharp and to ask them to be on hand. They went away sullenly and did not return that night. Camp was astir early, and breakfast was over at seven and the party ready to move. Grover, Oliver, Richards, and two others were in favor of an immediate start, saying—when told by the others that there would be trouble—that they would take the consequences, whatever they might be, and that they had rights and did not propose to surrender them any longer. The other four of the Georgia party advised waiting until 8 o'clock, saying that they would then be ready to go if the party failed to arrive.

About dark the previous evening, two wagons had come in from the Big Blue. In the morning, one of the newcomers, an old man, walked up and spoke to Walter, saying, "My name is Collins. I saw you at the crossing. You did a very courageous thing when you saved that outfit. We all thought you were lost, and how you escaped from drowning, none of us watchers on the bank could understand."

"Oh, Mr. Collins," asked the boy, "did the mother and children come out all right? I did not hear how they got along."

"Why," replied Collins, "they came to after a long time and were doing well when I left. The mother wept when told of your brave deed and asked to see you, but no one knew where you had gone."

"I am glad to hear that they are all right," said Walter. "I cannot see how a man could jeopardize the lives of such a family."

"That is a noble horse you have there," said Collins.

"Yes," said the boy, "I guess he's the one who deserves praise. I do not think that I could ever have gotten out without him."

"Well," said the old man, "we are going on. I suppose you will come on later today."

Eight o'clock came, and yet there was no sign of the stragglers. Grover and Richards demanded that a start be made, but Walter said, "I think, gentlemen, we had better wait another hour. Then we will start. That is as long as we dare wait with a hope of reaching water before night." At 9 o'clock, all hands clamored for a start and the wagon rolled out. Sure enough, the road was very heavy and the team suffered much from the deep sand and constant drag. About 7 o'clock in the evening, the party reached the first water, a small creek, and the tent was pitched with some difficulty, owing to the severe rainstorm that set in just before their arrival. The cold storm was hard on the stock, and the animals now began to show signs of weakening under the strain of a heavy load. The supply of corn, owing to the delays, was also growing short.

Just as darkness set in, a voice was heard in the distance and was at once answered, and in came the stragglers, wet, hungry, and very hostile. A shooting scrape was just avoided by a great deal of talk and persuasion by cooler heads, but none believed that serious trouble could much longer be delayed under the conditions that existed in the unhappy company.

The storm cleared up during the night, and an early start was made, all being anxious to get out of the last camp which furnished no wood, shelter, or any of the comforts usually found in good camping places. Saturday night, about 5 o'clock, the party reached the Platte River and camped in a sheltered spot along the bank some distance above where travelers usually camped. Here they found good grass for the horses.

They had scarcely unloaded their traps to prepare for the night before it began to look as though trouble was brewing. Langly kicked the cook, and that person caught his pony and put on the saddle and was about to mount, leaving his trust, when Langly again attacked him. Seeing that the loss of the cook would complicate matters, the Georgia crowd themselves interfered and the cook was finally persuaded to stay.

Just as all hands were ready to sit down to the evening meal, Langly struck Mr. Oliver without any provocation. Grover sprang to his feet and dealt Langly a blow to the face with his open hand and called him a ruffian. The latter ran to the tent for his pistol, and Grover planted himself before the tent with a cocked revolver in his hand. When the Georgia crowd tried to interfere with him, he waved them away, saying, "You look after your crowd. I want neither your advice nor your help." Some had already gone to the tent, and after much talk, it was decided that seconds should be chosen and a duel fought. To this Grover readily assented and insisted that it should take place at once, but better counsel prevailed and supper was eaten in silence.

Before morning, this trouble was patched up and things looked better. Still Langly and Mason were ugly. They seemed to be angry at Walter for having left them the day before. On the other hand, Walter seemed to expect trouble and, as it turned out, was prepared for it. He had taken the big dragoon revolver out of his saddle holster and strapped it on his body under his coat.

Just as the lad had placed his wheel horses in position, Langly and Mason started for the wagon, intending—as Langly said—to punish the boy and teach him manners. The boy had just stepped in front of the horses when Langly approached him with a rapid stride, his cocked pistol in his hand. He had been talking loudly, and his intention was known to all. The boy stepped forward, saying, "Did you want to see me, sir?" looking Langly straight in the eye.

"Yes," said Langly, using an ugly epithet, "I'll show you how to leave me on the prairie," at the same time raising his weapon over his head as if to club the lad.

Like a flash, the boy whipped out his big dragoon pistol, cocked and ready, and had it less than two feet from the astonished desperado's nose. In a clear, calm voice, Walter said, "Drop that pistol, Mr. Langly." The order was instantly obeyed. "Kneel down there quick." Langly did so. "Now, you cowardly dog, apologize and take back your dirty, slanderous words, or I will scatter your brains on the grass here in two seconds." Langly took back his words. The lad then stepped forward, picked up Langly's pistol, and hurled it into the river. Taking a step forward, the boy kicked Langly in the side and said, "Go, you cowardly ruffian, and never come near me."

Turning to Mason, who was still standing some feet back from the tent and had all the time been under his eye, Walter said, "Sir, you have no right to delay this outfit, and you shall not do so any more. This team belongs to Mr. Whetmore. He agreed to take you and the other passengers here to Denver without unnecessary delay. He has carried out his agreement to the letter. You have not carried out yours. You have delayed this party to the damage of my employer, and I notify you that I shall do all I can to make time and will not wait for either of you men a moment, except for sickness, in the future. You called me a vile name a few moments ago, your language intending to reflect upon my mother. Take those words back, sir, instantly, or I will shoot you down like a dog." At the same time, Walter brought his pistol up in range of Mason's breast. Mason quickly apologized, and the boy said, "I court no trouble with anyone, but I know my rights and I will defend them. If you wish, sir, to carry this matter any further at this time, I am at your service here and now." Mason did not seem to care to have any more trouble, and the occurrence passed off and the outfit was soon on the road.

That evening, the friendly Mr. Collins came over to the boy's wagon from his outfit and seemed much alarmed. He said to Walter, "I would go on ahead, but I fear some accident will befall you. I was sure those desperate men would harm you."

"You need have no fear of Langly," said Walter. "He is a coward and will not again trouble me. Nor do I think anyone else will be bothered by him, but Mason I am not so sure about. I never let him get near me if I can help it. Of course he was at a disadvantage this morning. I did not think of or weigh the consequences. He could not do less than apologize to me. I am sure I am also anxious to see the end of this trip. Now, Mr. Collins, do not wait on my account. You can travel much faster than we can."

"No," said Collins, "I will stay. Of course, I could not aid you if it had to be done by fighting. But I could take care of you if you were wounded."

Nothing transpired for two or three days until one evening, on the twenty-second day out from Leavenworth, Mason was taken sick. Mr. Collins looked at him and said, "You have the measles. There were many cases in the big camp on the Big Blue." They made Mason a bed in the wagon and pushed on as fast as possible. While the measles were not considered dangerous, yet the state of the weather and constant exposure of the invalid to the rains which fell almost every day, together with the lack of proper medical attendance, gave the disease a tremendous hold on the strong young man.

Mr. Collins was all attention. He prepared a syrup from wild sage and other herbs, which gave the sick man some comfort. "For," said Mr. Collins to Walter, "one should give comfort to one's enemies when they are stricken."

"I wish you would do all you can for him," said the boy, "for I am very anxious that he should get well and that no harm or accident should happen to any in our party."

On the third day, Mason was blind and had not broken out. Some whiskey was found and administered under the direction of Mr. Collins, and on the fifth day, Mason was better. He thanked Mr. Collins most kindly.

"You need not thank me," said the old man. "Thank the warmhearted boy who drives this wagon. I came to you at his request." Mason made no answer, and Mr. Collins left him and did not again visit him.

That evening, a hailstorm came up suddenly and stampeded the work horses. Mr. Collins's stock and the mules of the two friends traveling with him also went. They were out of sight before their absence was discovered. Walter at once saddled his horse and gave chase. When the hail ceased, it turned to snow, and after a time, darkness came on. All night the storm raged, and the young man did not return. Morning dawned, the sun came out, bright and cheerful, but the driver and the horses were still missing. The day passed, and yet the lad did not put in an appearance. Several teams

passed each way, but none had seen, nor heard of, either the missing animals or the lad who had gone in pursuit of them. Another night passed and
another bright day dawned without any word.

Mr. Collins was very much disconsolate. He traveled from one camp to
another constantly. He kept saying, "I fear the boy was lost in that first
night's storm. I fear that he will never return." The old man was not heard
to express a single regret at the loss of the stock, but the absence of the boy
was a source of great distress. He would walk to the top of the bluff lying a
mile to the west of the encampment and gaze long and sorrowfully over the
vast expanse of prairie and then take his course back to camp where he
arrived each time more and more dejected.

As the sun was setting on the evening of the second day, Collins made
out a clump of animals far to the southwest of the road. They were traveling
fast, and in the distance, it could not be told whether they were buffalo,
Indians, or the missing animals. Shortly after dark, however, the boy came
in, driving the jaded animals. Walter said that the storm had driven them to
the west upwards of sixty miles. He advised that in future all animals be
hobbled each time they were turned out, for said he, "They travel fast and
far before such a storm." It was thought best to lay over the next day because of the worn condition of the animals.

It now seemed that the inaction had had a bad effect on the passengers.
They had constantly quarreled for the two idle days. More trouble had taken
place between Langly and the cook. The latter had, in some way, given offense and was again beaten by Langly. This led to an open rupture between
Joyce, another Georgian, and Richards and resulted in a rough-and-tumble
fight. Grover stood over the combatants with a cocked revolver, declaring
that he would shoot any man who touched them until one or the other
cried enough. Richards finally came out victorious, giving Joyce a good
mauling.

Long after the combatants were separated, Langly tried to pick a fuss
with Richards. This Grover took up, and the result was another challenge.
This time, it was to be a fight to the finish with pistols. The duel was set for
sunrise the following morning, that time being picked so that if a funeral
occurred it would not delay the party overmuch. All hands were on the
ground at the time appointed for the meeting, which took place behind
some willows just back of camp. Joyce was the second of Langly, and Richards

was Grover's second. The parties took their places. The distance was measured off twenty yards. The seconds threw up for choice of positions. Langly
won first choice and chose a position with his back against the sun. Grover
had to face it. He said afterwards that the sun dazzled his eyes so that he
could not see to shoot. However this may have been, it is fair to say that
both men did very bad shooting.

It was understood that the parties were to use navy revolvers and that
they were to fire at the word, and if neither party was hit, either or both
could demand a second shot. All being ready, the word was given and two
shots in quick succession rang out on the morning air. Langly hit the ground
to the left of Grover, and Grover fired far over Langly's head. The second
shot was also a miss on both sides, as was the third. Both men were excited,
especially Langly who could scarcely hold his pistol. With the fourth shot,
Grover's ball plowed through Langly's coat opposite the heart, and Langly's
went through the top of Grover's boot and plowed a furrow through the
calf of his leg. Both parties now declared that they were satisfied.

All hands took hold and prepared the breakfast, and by 8 o'clock, the
outfit was in motion. Mason now left the wagon and slept in the tent; during the day he rode Walter's saddle horse, by permission of his owner, with
whom he had now become friendly.

That evening, camp was pitched at the junction of the North and South
Platte rivers. There was universal good feeling in camp, the only trouble
being the task of cooking, which now had to be performed by the passengers. Some were disposed to saddle the burden of it on the man—Langly—
who had been instrumental in driving the cook from camp.

At this campsite, the travelers had their first opportunity to taste good
buffalo meat. A herd was crossing the river. The whole party rushed out
after the beasts, but it was not until the young driver tied up his team,
mounted his horse, and disappeared among the hills that it looked as though
fresh meat would grace the supper table. After an absence of a couple of
hours, Walter returned loaded with choice cuts from a fat buffalo cow. The
meat was on all sides pronounced delicious, and all hands enjoyed it abun-
dantly.

On the river bottom opposite the camp, a battle royal was witnessed
that evening. Some straggling buffalo were crossing the river. One family,
an old and a young cow with calves by their sides, was set upon by a band

The Duel

of a dozen big gray wolves. The cunning creatures seemed to lay deep plans to inveigle the young animals from their mothers' sides. The mothers acted very worried. They for a moment lost sight of their young ones, but a blat from one of the frightened calves brought the mothers to the rescue. They charged the wolves, who were almost in the act of pulling down their prey. So vicious and active were the assaults of the two mothers that they succeeded in saving their calves, but the younger mother was herself assaulted, and had it not been for the timely arrival of a couple of bulls, her bones would have been picked by the ravenous brutes.

✳

With no further trouble, Walter and his passengers pushed on, finally reaching Denver on April 1, 1859. Walter set up camp above the townsite. He found a ranch that would store the outfit—"horses, wagon, harness, tents, cooking equipment"—belonging to Whetmore, his employer, to whom he wrote a letter which detailed "everything that was of interest to him." He spent a few days in Denver in "hopes of meeting his friend, Mr. Collins." When Collins did not appear, "our restless young friend saddled his horse and started out to find something to do. . . ." Walter first worked for a rancher named William Sheppard, who also carried the mail from Denver to the mines at the head of Clear Creek. Walter was a herdsman, which he found "not irksome," but after a month, he "hired to a Texas firm by the name of Sowers & McKee, the owners of twenty thousand head of Texas cattle."

✳

This was an entirely new experience for Walter. Having joined the great camp, situated on the Cherry Creek divide, he was surprised to find an immense crowd of all sorts of men—Mexicans predominating but many Texans—all in all, a pretty rough class of citizens. Walter rode up to the lodge and called for Mr. Gant, the foreman. When that gentleman appeared, Walter told him, "I was hired by Mr. McKee to work for you."

"Have you ever done this work?" asked the foreman.

"No, sir."

"Want to learn, do you?" Gant said with a sneer and a curl of his lip.

"I want to do what you want done and earn my money."

"Got bedding?"

"Yes, sir, on my horse."

"Not much of a bed," said the Texan.

"It suits me, sir."

"Whose horse is that?" was the next question.

"Mine, sir" was the answer.

"Yours? Where did you get such a horse as that?"

"I brought him from Leavenworth with me, sir."

"Want to sell him?"

"No, sir."

"What do you want with a horse if you are going to work here? We got plenty of horses."

"He is my horse. If I can't keep him, I don't want to work for you."

"Where are you from?"

"Leavenworth."

"Where were you born?"

"State of New York."

"When did you leave?"

"When a child."

"Where was you raised?"

"In Michigan."

"Down among the nigger stealers, eh?"

"They don't steal niggers or anything else where I was raised in Michigan, sir."

"I don't think we've got a place for you here."

"Very well, sir," said the boy, and he vaulted into his saddle and started to ride off.

"Hello," called the foreman, and the boy turned in his saddle but did not ride back.

"Where are you going?" asked the foreman.

"To find work, sir."

"We want men here."

"You said you didn't want me, sir."

"Did you say McKee hired you?" asked the foreman.

"Yes, sir."

"What did he say?"

"He said his camp was on the head of Cherry Creek—that he wanted men—that I was to report to Mr. Gant, his foreman, and he would tell me what to do—that my wages would be forty dollars a month."

"Are you a man?"

"Mr. McKee saw me, sir." The boy looked back. "Is that all?" he asked.

"Well," drawled the foreman, "you can stay here."

The boy turned his horse and rode back.

"You can stop in there," Gant indicated a lodge nearby. Walter unsaddled his horse, took him out on the hill and picketed him, and came back to the lodge, which was full of men. He looked around for a place to lay his traps and saw none.

He finally spoke, "Gentlemen, Mr. Gant told me to sleep in here. Will you tell me where I can put my bed and not interfere with any of you?"

"No gentlemen in here, only buckaroos," said a coarse man sitting in the crowd.

"I might move out and let you have my bed," said a big man. This sally was greeted with a big laugh, in which all joined.

The boy turned around, looked the speaker square in the eye, and calmly answered, "I simply asked you where I could lay my things, so as not to interfere with any of you."

"The devil you say," answered the big bully, and another loud laugh followed.

At this moment, a big, quiet man spoke up in a kind voice, "Here, boy, put your traps here beside me. You and I won't quarrel. Bring in your saddle. You will need it as a pillow." The boy complied, while the man made room for him. "Make yourself comfortable as you can," said the big man. "What is your name?"

"Walter Cooper, sir."

"Why," said the man, "I have a brother named Walter—we call him Walt. I'll just call you Walt. I'm Stubbs."

Shortly a loud call was heard, "Grub pile here, grub pile!"

"Well," said Stubbs, "come along and have supper. You won't get much if you wait."

The cook camp was situated in the pines, some distance from the sleeping lodges, and Walter was surprised to see fully seventy men gathered around the mess. Truly these were a medley of all nationalities. Each carried a cup for coffee, a plate, and a belt knife. There was an ample supply of good roast beef, corn bread, and bacon. The lad was hungry and did justice to his repast.

The next morning, the herd was brought in, and all hands started for the corral with lassos. Stubbs gave Walter a rope and told him to rope anything he found in the corral to ride during the day. While he was not an absolute novice in the business of handling wild horses, Walter was by no means efficient. He watched several rope their horses, saddle and bridle them. He proceeded to do the same. After considerable trouble, he got his saddle on a wild fellow and got him out. All the men were lounging around, as he afterwards understood, to see the fun of a green hand taking a fall. When once outside, he adjusted the blind and vaulted into the saddle—and then raised the blind. His animal began to paw the air. "Give him the spur," called someone. Walter complied with this command, and the horse commenced to buck. After six or eight jumps, the saddle was empty. Amid raucous laughter, Walter again mounted and, as before, was hurled to the ground. Mounting a third time, he rode his horse for some distance, but was finally thrown. Now, however, Stubbs came up and said, "Come, Walt, that will do this time. I'll change horses with you. This one has had his morning exercise, and I guess you can stay with him. That one is a Tartar."

The day was spent scouting the hills, turning in stray bands of cattle that were getting out too far from the usual range. As they reached camp towards evening, the boy found himself pretty sore but he was all right in the morning. Stubbs pointed out a horse with which he had no trouble, and gradually he became expert. He was one of the most fearless as well as expert riders and ropers in the entire camp. He became a general favorite among the Texas cowmen.

One evening, Walter had an experience that doubtless placed him on a more solid footing with those reckless men than he would have enjoyed— had he been with them years—had it not happened. He had taken great pains to take fine care of his handsome horse until the horse was fat and sleek and universally admired. A certain big, burly Mexican greatly admired the horse. This man was recognized as a bully of the first water—and one who cared little for the rights of others.

On this particular evening, Walter had come in and at once noticed that

The Bronc

his horse was gone. He made inquiries, and one of the cooks told him that Jose had saddled him and ridden away that morning. Jose soon rode in with the foreman and quite a party of Mexicans. The horse's ribs were covered with blood, and he was a mass of foam. Walter met the man, who called out, "Purty good mustang." Walter walked to his side and, in a calm, dignified manner, said, "Yes, he is a good horse—too good for a cowardly brute like you to ride." Adding, "Get off my horse," Walter laid his hand on Jose's thigh. The Mexican raised in his stirrups and struck the boy in the head with the coil of his lasso. The boy sprang forward, seized the man by the shoulders, and hurled him to the ground. The Mexican was on his feet in a moment and, drawing his pistol, sprang toward the boy with his weapon clubbed. He struck Walter a glancing blow on the head, but throwing up his left arm, the boy partially warded off the violent blow. Quick as a flash, Walter whipped out his own revolver and dealt his assailant several stunning blows on the head and face. Following up his advantage, he seized the man by the hair with one hand and literally hammered him into unconsciousness, dropping his limp form only when he himself was exhausted. Whipping out his knife, he cut the latigo straps of Jose's saddle loose and threw the saddle on the now apparently lifeless form of the Mexican. Taking his horse to the brook, he proceeded to wash his bloody sides where they had been lacerated by the brute's wicked spurs.

For some days, Jose lay recovering in his tent, his face and eyes swollen out of all proportion. When the ruffian began to improve, the rumor circulated that Jose would kill the boy as soon as he was able. Several men warned the boy that Jose was a dangerous man and to look out. When Jose had so far recovered as to be able to go out on the herd, these rumors still kept coming. Thinking that it was high time to put a stop to such talk, the boy one evening walked up to Jose, in front of the lodges, and said, "I hear that you are going to kill me. I am tired of listening to such talk. You know very well that threats are not made by men who intend to carry them out. Now, I am here and at your service. I have waited until you got well and are able to defend yourself. What can I do for you?" Jose cowered before the calm, cool, and determined boy and said he did not care for any more trouble. From that hour, Jose was a different man. He no longer posed as a fighting bully.

*

After Walter had spent five months with Sowers & McKee, the outfit sold its cattle. Gant, the foreman, offered to take Walter to Texas, where the plan was to gather another large herd and head back to Colorado in the spring. Walter declined. Instead he bought a pair of pack horses and traveled south to the famous fur-trade post of Bent's Fort, twelve miles upriver from the confluence of the Purgatoire and Arkansas rivers, on the Arkansas's north shore.

*

There Walter found a large camp of trappers and traders getting ready to start out on fall and winter hunting and trapping expeditions. This was a strange congregation of men. There were Americans, Frenchmen, Spaniards, Mexicans, half-breeds, and a large number of Indians. There was continual excitement: drinking, gambling, horse trading, target shooting, and foot racing—in fact, every kind of sport known to the frontier. Among the crowd, Walter recognized Jim Bridger, but Bridger did not recognize him.

One day, there was a shooting match, and Walter entered as a contestant, bearing off the honors and prizes. Bridger was also in the match, and when it was over, he looked the boy over. He recognized the lad—notwithstanding the fact that he was now dressed in buckskin and moccasins—as the winner of the great footrace at Council Grove the previous fall. Nothing would satisfy him but that the boy must move to his camp. This Walter consented to do. Bridger was a rough but honest man who stood above the rank and file of the trappers. He very soon invited Walter to go with him for a winter expedition.

It was decided to go to the Green River country, as Bridger said they would surely reap a good harvest—if they had luck in steering clear of Indians. "A chance," said he, "we have to take, no matter which way we go. This is a great life," added Bridger. "I have followed it so long that I can't do anything else, and one winter won't hurt you."

Bridger was surprised to see that the boy still had his thoroughbred horse. "Too good a horse for such a trip and country as this, but as you won't sell him, and there is no safe place to leave him, you might as well take him along. You can't do more than lose him anyway. Now, about next week, I shall be all settled up, and we will pull for the buffalo range. I want you to have a good time while they are fat."

"I shall be glad to accommodate myself to your convenience, Mr. Bridger."

"Say, my son, don't 'Mister' me. My name is Jim Bridger. Don't you see they all call me Jim? If you keep calling me 'Mister,' I shall get stuck up and, like as not, get above my calling. I am just an old trapper."

As Walter walked away, Bridger joined a group standing nearby. One of the men spoke up, "Jim, got a son, I see."

"He ain't my boy, you know well enough."

"You seem to know him," said the fellow.

"Well, I do. Met him at Council Grove last year. You see that thorough-bred horse he is leading?"

"Yes, fine horse, Jim," said the other.

"Well, the boy won that horse in a five-mile footrace against the greatest runners 'tween here and St. Louis."

"Say, Jim, can't we get up a race and clean out the Arapaho and Comanche? Them two fellers are crack runners."

"Good idea, but no, he won't run for money," said Bridger. "Me and Godfrey tried him on that."

"You say he won't run for money. Kind of stuck up, ain't he?"

"No," said Bridger, "not stuck up at all, just a good, square, honest boy that's had a good mother and good raisin' and hasn't forgot it, as some boys do."

"Well, guess your stories don't hang together. Didn't he just shoot in that contest fur Andrews's outfit and was glad to get the money?"

"That's different. The * * * sutler over there," said Bridger, pointing back with his thumb toward the fort, "told him his old man, Andrews, had been wounded and had to go to the States and needed all the money he could get. They could get no one to take the chance, so the boy entered. He done it to help out."

"Well, I guess that's right," said the other.

"Yes," said Bridger, "if he had been stuck up, he wouldn'ta seen the real human side of it as he did. No, sir, he's all right. I wish I had such a boy."

"He's going with you, Jim, ain't he?"

"Yes," said Bridger, "I'm going to teach him all I know, and that ain't much."

*

A party was now being made up for the States, consisting of traders from Santa Fe and stray trappers who wanted to dispose of their furs. With this party, the poor fellow Andrews was to go. Andrews had been out on a long expedition. He'd made a good catch, but his camp was raided and he himself badly wounded in the leg. His leg had to be amputated, which was done in a most rude fashion. He had now recovered sufficiently to be able to travel. He had decided to leave the mountains for good. He had little left to take with him. His traps, Hawkins gun, and other property had been raffled off, raising $200. Walter won the raffle—and Andrews's outfit. A few of the trappers who knew the crippled man well put their heads together to try and raise some more money for him. In his day, he had been one of the most intrepid scouts and trappers on the prairie, and he ranked very high among the bravest and most valiant. He was, Bridger told Walter, "proud, independent, self-confident, always open handed, and ready to divide his last cent with a fellow."

A meeting was called to see what could be done for the man. Having failed to accomplish anything by way of subscription, as the burden fell on so few, a committee was appointed and came forward with this plan: A number of those best able raised a fund of $350 which was converted into Spanish dollars. This sum was to be offered as a prize for a four-mile footrace, to be open to all comers.

The plan was adopted for two reasons. First, because there were among the Indians two very noted racers, one belonging to the Comanches, the other to the Arapahos, and there was much rivalry between them. To see the race, all white men were to pay $10—and the Indians whatever they could. The race course was well situated for such a scheme, as the old road ran for three miles close to the riverbank, with a high bluff near the road, and on the opposite side, the trappers were to station themselves on the edge of the bluff and allow no one inside, except those who bore tickets furnished by the committee.

A council of Indians was called, and the trappers explained to the head men that if each Indian would give a robe, wolfskin, or its equivalent for admission, then the women and children could go in free. The committee, of which Bridger was one, now came to Walter and explained that the race was gotten up solely to raise money for the injured trapper. They asked him if he would enter and run, and he promptly said he would. He was told that a fee of $25 or its equivalent must be paid by each runner who entered. This money was to go to the injured man to further swell the donation. "Now," said Bridger, "we may as well tell you that men will be gambling and betting on this race, as all these people, Indians included, are more or less gamblers."

"I understood you to say," said the boy, fixing his eyes on Bridger, "that the entrance money paid by the runners, with all that is paid to see the race, goes to Mr. Andrews."

"Yes, sir, that is true."

"Very well," Walter replied. "I will enter, and here is my fee."

News of the race went up and down the river for a hundred miles, and a good many came in from outlying camps. By the day before the race, several entries had been made. It had been explained to the Indians that they must come prepared to pay, as a solid line of armed trappers would be placed between the river and the bluff, and that armed men would occupy the crest of the hill, so that it would be impossible to see the race without paying as they passed through the line. The Indians paid in robes, furs, and any kind of property that could later be converted into money at the trading post.

All the white men purchased tickets, paying in coin. Before noon, the Indians began to go in. This continued until the trappers were more than satisfied with the spoils they had taken in: more than five hundred robes, wolf and bear skins, and smaller furs. Then the gate was thrown open, and those who could not pay were allowed to go in.

About 2 o'clock, the race was called. The racers came forward and were assigned places by lot. Two could start in the roadway—a great advantage as the prairie was rough. And yet, when they got strung out, all would finally fall onto the smooth-beaten road, as the race was a long one and it could not be expected that any two would run abreast for any great distance.

Quite a number of the trappers, as well as a few Indians, were selected as outriders. Their duty was to keep the track clear and to see that no advantage was taken of a racer by any of the contestants or an outsider. Jim Bridger said, "There will be no trouble if everything is on the square, and it must be so, if I have anything to do with it." This point was made a rigid rule. If a dispute arose, two or three of the Indian chiefs were called in to assist in settling it.

Both the Arapahos and the Comanches, who were on the ground in large numbers, believed that their man was a sure winner and that they would reap a great harvest, and each was betting everything he could scrape together, one against the other. There was a small camp of Cheyennes at the post, and they had entered a man, so that there were three Indians, one half-breed, one Frenchman, and Walter.

As the men lined up for a start, the excitement became intense. Little attention was paid to the half-breed or the two white men. The Cheyenne was a light, thin warrior, exceedingly well built. He was a young chief, a very fine-looking, handsome fellow and good natured. He came up to the boy and shook hands with him, felt of his limbs, very carefully looked him over, and tried to talk with him. Bridger noticed him do this, stepped up to them, and acted as interpreter.

"This young chief is a Cheyenne," he explained to Walter. "He has run races and thinks he can beat the Arapaho and says he thinks he may beat the Comanche, but he says he don't know about you. He says the course is too long for the half-breed and Frenchman, says he has seen them run. He says they are fast for a mile. Says his friends are betting all their horses and property on him. He wants to know if you will bet with him a horse."

"Tell him, 'No,'" answered the boy, "that I do not bet."

"Well, then," said Bridger, "I will bet with him."

The Indians were all fine specimens of their race and seemed to be athletes of the highest order, if appearances went for anything. It developed afterwards that Bridger had told the trappers to bet everything they could on the boy. "For," said he, "if he lives to run the race, he will come in first."

The scene was certainly a lively one. You would see two Indians talking together; presently they would each take a robe and walk up to the general pile and throw the two robes into the pile. Again, two would meet on horseback, jump off their horses, tie them together, and give them either to a boy or a woman to hold, or let them stand. The winner would take both. So went the betting up to the time the start was made.

An old Indian chief was directed to fire the starting gun when all was ready. Lots were drawn, and two Indians, the Comanche and the Arapaho, won the road. All the rest started on the rough prairie ground. The Frenchman took the lead from the start, the half-breed ran second, the Arapaho third, the Comanche followed, the Cheyenne fifth, and the boy last. The pace at starting was a fast one, and the boy simply kept in touch with the other runners. The half-breed dropped out about the end of the first mile. At the end of the second mile, the Arapaho crowded the Frenchman, and Walter was close to the Cheyenne. As the pole was rounded, the Arapaho led the Comanche, third came the Cheyenne, fourth the boy, and last the Frenchman, who then dropped out. The home stretch was begun in this order.

The Cheyenne was closing the gap between himself and the Comanche, while the Arapaho increased his lead on the latter. The Arapaho seemed to be straining every nerve. The Cheyenne now passed the Comanche, as did the boy. For the next quarter, the contestants held their positions. At the end of the third mile, the Cheyenne passed the Arapaho, and for the next quarter, the boy remained just behind. Then the boy passed the Arapaho with apparent ease and began to crowd the Cheyenne, increasing his pace. At the three-and-a-half mile pole, the boy shot past the Cheyenne and now took the lead. The excitement became intense. The two Indians exerted themselves to the utmost to recover the lead, but without result.

It took all the energy of the outriders to keep the track clear. The boy was now 50 feet ahead. He steadily held his lead to the end, finishing in a fine spurt, crossing the line 105 feet ahead of the Cheyenne and 135 feet ahead of the Arapaho. The Indians seemed wild with joy—that is, the Cheyennes and Arapahos. The Comanches were quiet. They had lost heavily in horses and robes—mostly to the Arapahos. The Cheyennes were much excited that their young chief had defeated the Arapaho.

The runners now approached the trading post, and the trappers proposed to make the awards. The 350 Spanish dollars were brought to the boy in an iron kettle. He took up the kettle, walked up to the wounded trapper Andrews, and set the kettle by his side. "My friend," Walter said, "I hope you will accept these. I am most happy to have aided your friends in their kind efforts for your sake. May you reach your home in safety, and may you enjoy the bounty of your friends there." This action was so unexpected and such a surprise to the old man that he burst into tears and hugged the boy.

Bridger came up, with eyes moist, and grasped Walter's hand. "Boy, you have outdone us all."

The young Cheyenne chief pulled at Bridger's coat sleeve and asked, "What has Swift Foot done to the sick warrior?" Bridger told him that the boy had given the sick warrior all the silver. Taking off his big, fine robe, the Cheyenne approached the sick man and laid the robe at his feet. In his own language, which both Bridger and Andrews understood, he said, "Swift Foot has big heart. He is my friend. I am glad he won the race. I give One Leg my robe." Taking Walter by the hand, he pressed it warmly, saying, "Swift Foot my brother."

The traders and trappers were all dumbfounded at the boy's action, and one and all congratulated him on his generous course. When all the furs were sold, and the generous gifts figured up, the whole amounted to more than two thousand dollars in gold and silver. So delicately was all accomplished that the proud trapper felt that he was not the recipient of charity, but rather of Christmas blessings from warm and grateful friends. The warmhearted trappers surrounded the crippled man, bidding a last farewell to the intrepid hero of many deadly encounters. Many wrung his hand and called to his mind instances of his courageous and kindly assistance to them and other knights of the trail.

The young boy came into the circle—bearing a Hawkins rifle, powder horn and bullet pouch, belt and knife, and hatchet—and said, "Sir, your friends have told me of your past life among these great mountains, of your successes and disasters, in none of which have you been separated from this splendid rifle. I do not need it, sir. I shall be happy if you will take it with you on your long, homeward trail, and keep it always, for you must not be separated from a lifelong friend like this, which has never failed you."

Tears crept into the eyes of the trapper, and he said, "You must have read my thoughts, my son, for it broke my heart to part with my old gun that I have carried long. Thank you, my son. I shall never forget you. If you ever come to St. Louis, come to me. Take my address."

Colonel DeVost—who had taken charge of the trapper and promised to see him safe in St. Louis—now came forward and said the outfit was ready to move. Andrews was assisted to a comfortable seat in a wagon belonging to DeVost. As the team rolled away, more than a hundred men took off their hats and gave three hearty cheers for Andrews and then three more for the kindhearted DeVost. Thus went an active and successful trapper, who had enjoyed the freedom of the Rocky Mountains for more than twenty-five years, who endured untold hardships without the least complaint. He was going back to the home of his early childhood with ample means to care for his future wants.

"That last act of yours, boy," said Bridger to Walter, "touched both him and me deeply. I shall never forget it, never. I owed my life to him—to that man—and in all the years that have passed since that terrible day, I have never been in a position to pay the debt. Oh, he was a proud, independent, fearless man. It almost breaks my heart to see him so helpless now."

"Won't you tell me about him, Mr. Bridger?" asked Walter.

"Not now, son, not now. Some stormy night when we are roasting marrow bones far from here, I will tell you, son, but not now. Let us go to the lodge. I am hungry."

Within a few days, active preparations began for winter expedition. The trappers chose and corralled their packhorses, prepared and packed their supplies and grub, and gathered their bedrolls and personal gear. Bridger, Joe LeBassett, Walter, and Antoine, a Wyandot scout, sat around the fire in Bridger's lodge one night, discussing their plans. Bridger said, "I am of the opinion that the safest and best place for us to go is the Green River country. The Gila is too dangerous now; the Apaches are a restless lot, and they prowl all winter. I don't say the Green River is safe. We may run against Utes, Sioux, Arapahos, Cheyennes, or Snakes, but they don't roam the Green as constantly as the Apaches do the Gila."

"But," said LeBassett, "the Green has been overrun with trappers. We won't get much."

"Well," said Bridger, "I will answer for that part. I know of a hole that has never been touched, unless it has been trapped since spring, and that ain't likely. And another thing: Andrews is the only man that has ever been there to my knowledge besides myself. We, I believe, are safe for the winter. When spring comes on, I am not so sure about our safety near Green River."

In the morning, all was bustle and activity about the lodge, and by 9 o'clock, the camp was moving. Bridger decided to go by way of the Cache La Poudre and to push forward as fast as possible. The party had twelve packhorses, the horses the four men rode, and four extra saddle horses. It was October 20, and Bridger was anxious to push forward with as much expediency as possible, in order to get located before the November storms set in. On the tenth of November, they made camp at the mouth of Big Sandy, a small fork of Green River. The weather was fine. They found no buffalo in the region of Big Sandy, but there was much sign about ten days old, the buffalo apparently having moved up the main river.

The party now proceeded up Green River, constantly looking out for Indian signs, as they had discovered a few carcasses of buffalo which, Bridger said, were killed by a small party of Indians crossing the country from the south. On the third day, they found a few straggling bulls traveling up the stream. They made camp on a small island in a thicket of cottonwood, and Bridger took the boy and pushed up the river for a careful scout. About noon, they came to the mouth of a creek, which Bridger called Otter Creek and up which he proposed to pitch a winter camp. He said five miles up the creek, it entered an impassable canyon, about a mile in length, above which was a small lake and a fine valley, plenty of thick timber, and lots of beaver. "There," he said, "if anywhere, we are sure of a quiet winter. Now we must find buffalo."

Passing up the creek perhaps a mile, they suddenly came out upon a broad valley, about two miles wide by a mile or more long. This valley and the hillsides were covered with a vast herd of buffalo—largely cows and calves. Here Bridger stopped and made a careful survey of the scene before him. Turning his horse, he said, "Boy, we will go back to camp and move here tomorrow. Tomorrow night we will have plenty of marrow bones. We will try and pick up a fat calf on our way back for camp meat tonight. There is no danger, for these animals are quiet and not restless as they would be if they had been disturbed lately."

Instead of going back down the stream, Bridger led the way along the base of the hills for several miles. When about to cross a small creek, they came upon five buffalo. Picking out a small, dark-robed cow, Bridger killed it. At the report of the rifle, the animals stopped and listened. Presently they passed on without being frightened. When the herd had passed out of sight, Bridger and the boy butchered the fallen animal and took as much of the choice cuts to camp as could be conveniently carried.

Early the next morning, the trappers moved their camp to Otter Creek, and towards evening, they killed several fat cows and moved the meat to camp. The animals were quartered with the skin on and then hung up in camp for future use. The next day, Bridger, Joe LeBassett, and Antoine did extensive scouting. When they left camp, Bridger told the boy he might stay about camp and explore the creek through the canyon if he liked. "We," said Bridger, "want to make a wide circuit, to be sure there are no Reds near us. We must lay in a winter supply of meat before these buffalo get the grass cleaned up and leave this section, for we don't want to spend the time following them for meat."

That night about dark, all hands were in camp. Bridger and Joe reported having made a very wide circuit and not coming onto any sign whatever. They had found buffalo, and they were jubilant over the prospect of a quiet winter and a rich haul of beaver. "Now," asked Bridger, "what is your report, my son?"

"Did you not tell me, Mr. Bridger," answered the boy, "that the canyon above here in the creek was impassable?"

"Now, see here," replied Bridger, "I am not going to have you call me Mr. Bridger all the time. My name is Jim. Everybody calls me Jim. Nothing else seems natural. Just call me Jim. It will please me."

After a silence of some minutes, the boy answered, "I cannot do it, Mr. Bridger. You are much older than I, and it would not be showing proper respect to a man of your age and experience by calling him by his given name."

"What," said Bridger, somewhat sharply, for the first time showing a tinge of anger, "Won't call me Jim, by my own name?"

"No," replied the boy, "but Mr. Bridger, if you don't mind, I will call you Uncle Jim."

There was a long silence. Bridger sat gazing into the fire, his keen eye moist, and a kind, soft expression on his face. "Do it, boy," he finally said. "Do it. It will please me."

"Why not call me Uncle Joe?" broke in LeBassett, who had been a silent observer of all that had passed.

"It will please me much to do so," replied the boy, and from that time on, he never addressed either in any other way.

There was a long silence. Each seemed engaged with his own thoughts, when Joe finally joked, "How about your report, boy?"

Bridger laughed, "I remember, son, you asked me last if I had not told you the canyon was impassable. Why, yes, I said so."

"Well," said the boy, "I went through the canyon to the valley above.

There has been a great rock slide at the mouth of the canyon, which really bridges the stream, but when you have passed around that, which is easy, it is a good, smooth road through. You can go in the stream all the way and not make any trail over the hill. The valley above is a beauty. There are a good many deer in there, but no sign of buffalo or Indians."

"I am glad to hear that," answered Bridger. "The trail over the hill is steep and rocky. We can go into the valley and hide our trail completely. If the buffalo don't stampede out of here before we get what meat we want, they will cover all our signs anyway."

The basin that Bridger had proposed as a winter camp was one of remarkable beauty, but difficult of access, because of the high, rugged rocky ridge cutting the country from east to west. It could only be crossed by man or beast in two places. The small stream had broken through the ridge, leaving a high-walled canyon with walls almost perpendicular and several hundred feet high, absolutely impassable on either side. The canyon was about a mile long. At the lower end, a mighty cave had formed. The cliff had toppled over from the west side completely, covering and bridging the stream to a great depth. At first sight, the canyon seemed to be completely closed—the great wall of loose stone apparently blocked the way. In fact, so high was the barrier that one could see little of the canyon from a viewpoint in the valley below. One would certainly never suspect what a beautiful valley existed above that forbidding cliff.

The boy, with his quick eye, however, had noticed that from the bed of the stream on the west side a rugged path existed, although apparently it had never before been traveled. It led up the creek bank, turned sharply downstream, ascended gradually, and then turned to the south, ending against the rock flow, which Walter then crossed by a rough, zigzag path. The route then entered and followed the bed of the stream for a good mile to the upper end of the canyon, where the valley opened out broad and clear. There was no sign of a trail leading from or entering into the canyon from above.

Bridger stood on the edge of the rock flow, looking down the course of the stream that passed under the rocks. "I never suspected," he said, "that a passage existed here, and I had looked it over, having in view this spot for a winter camp. I was dreading crossing yon ridge." He pointed to the rugged height. "It has never been used, I am sure. By moving a few of these large stones," he continued, "this trail can be closed to the redskins."

Looking into the valley from this high point, a panorama of surpassing beauty unfolded itself before them. The valley was about three-fourths of a mile wide and some two and one-half miles long. The creek, which was some ten yards wide, was clear as crystal and passed through the center of the valley, the ground rising gradually from the stream toward the rocky bluff and the mountains that encircled the valley. On the left, two smaller streams entered the creek. About half a mile above, on the right, another joined the main stream. The valley was thickly wooded with willows, alders, and cottonwood, with an occasional clump of thick, tall fir trees and a few pine and spruce. The hills were fringed with pine, fir, and cedar, and patches here and there of aspen. The foliage had taken on its winter garb. The rosebushes and buckbrush were dark red, the aspen yellow. Along the streams, there was kinnikinnick with its white balls, water maple, and mountain ash, the latter cloaked in large clusters of bright red berries. All combined to make an autumn picture strikingly grand. Delighted by what they saw, the trappers returned to the valley of the buffalo for the night.

All hands were up early the next morning. Bridger suggested that they begin at once to slaughter what buffalo they could take care of each day. So the party divided, Bridger and the boy going up a small creek to the right, and Joe and Antoine riding up a dry, bushy run on the left. During the day, they killed ten fat young animals, quartered them, and took them to camp. Each was hung up and covered with brush to keep the magpies away— hung as high as possible to keep the bears from getting into the meat. At the end of three days, they had secured all the meat they could take care of, and as the weather looked threatening, they began to move camp. They experienced no trouble in going through the canyon, and after getting over the rock slide, they entered the stream and passed up its bed for about two miles to a grove of cottonwood and aspen, with many big fir trees scattered through the grove.

A suitable place was finally selected under the great fir trees, and they pitched their lodge. "The little smoke we will make," remarked Bridger, "will rise up among the fir limbs, spread and scatter, and not be noticed." When, after a second trip, they arrived at camp, they found four grizzly bears. The great bears had succeeded in getting down some of the meat. The bears were all killed, and Antoine stayed in camp to guard against future

raids, while Joe, Bridger, and the boy moved the balance of the camp equipment. It took three days to complete the move. Once they had set up the
lodge, they built a large pen of heavy logs, well notched down, in which to
keep the meat. When snow came, they would let the meat freeze. This, Bridger
said, would preserve it indefinitely. They now spent time drying and smoking a large quantity of the meat, especially the tongues, much of the hump,
and other choice tidbits.

When the men went out hunting, their camp was soon alive with bear,
wolves, birds of prey, and other offal destroyers, and in two or three days,
there was no trace of offal sufficient to attract even birds of prey—or that an
Indian might notice in passing through the country. The big timber wolves
were abundant, which is always the case where buffalo abound. Bridger
now suggested that all hands take hold of sharp knives and cut the tall
grass, which stood four and five feet high all over the bottom. "It may be,"
said he, "that the snow will get too deep for our animals to feed, especially
if a crust forms on top." They spent several days in this work, and a large
quantity of hay was stored up for a time of urgent need. This grass had a
head similar to rye, in which there was seed that has much nutriment, which
horses enjoy.

The hay gathering having been completed, the animals were turned loose
to roam wherever they chose. The trappers built a strong corral or pen in
which to place the horses at night. They took every care to provide large
quantities of dry willow, alder, and aspen wood for kindling, and while the
ground was bare, they used the saddle horses to haul heavy logs to a convenient place near the lodge. A saddle horse could pull almost as much from
the horn of the saddle, with a man on its back, as by collar and hames.

It was soon December. Fur was prime, and the men got out their traps
and cleaned and prepared them for use, and the work of gathering in fur
was begun by all parties. It taxed Antoine's skill and energy to the utmost to
stretch and dry the many skins. He then folded and stacked them in bales,
ready for transportation. The men spent the evenings in lounging around a
comfortable fire, talking, eating buffalo tongue, and often roasting marrow
bones. This process was very simple. They cleaned the large leg and thigh
bones of all meat, laying them on a flat stone in front of the fire out of the
ashes and dirt, and after a time, the intense heat would bake the bone until
it was brittle and would split easily—exposing the delicate morsel, which

was eaten on tongues, cornbread, and in almost any way. This was a great delicacy with trappers, travelers, and hunters who found themselves in buffalo country with little else for food, except the meat.

One evening, while they were thus engaged, Walter said to Bridger, "You told me at Bent's Fort that, when we got located in our winter's quarters—some cold night when we were roasting marrow bones—you would tell me the story of how Andrews saved your life."

"So I will, son, so I will," answered the trapper. After a silence of some moments, spent by the old scout staring into the fire, he began, "Bob Andrews came to Laramie in 1840 from the lower Missouri. He and I agreed to go together on a trapping expedition. In the fall, it was September, we had a good outfit, with a few goods in trade. We went over on the Snake River, hunted along the river, prospecting the creeks for beaver, and finally located on a creek which we called Swift Creek. There was plenty of beaver there, so we concluded to locate there for the winter. We made a good catch, packed up, and pulled out about the first of May. We had seven packs. We got back to Green River. Game was scarce and we had no meat, except dried meat, and we were tired of that. Andrews went out to hunt. Presently he came running back and said that there was a camp of Indians on the next fork. He said that we could not get out of the country without being discovered. As our horses were thin and would scarcely carry us, we talked it over. He said they had not seen us but would surely strike his trail in the morning. 'Now,' asked he, 'what do you think we had better do?' I proposed that we cache a couple of small packs of beaver and the rough skins we had, and pack up all the rest and go into the creek, and go up as far as we could—cache them and come back the same way—camp, and take our chances. Andrews said, 'All right.'

"We went up the creek as far as we could, made a cache in a thicket of alders—by making a platform high up on some good-sized trees. We had to think of the bears as well as the Indians. Well, we got back to our camp just at daylight, and we turned out our horses. Bob got breakfast while I watched the horses. Just after sunup, Bob motioned that they were coming. I brought the horses in and tied them to the small trees close to camp. The reds only had two horses. They wanted breakfast and coffee and tried to get into camp, but I told them they must stay together and keep away. I had both rifles, and each of us had dragoon revolvers. So they sat down about a hundred feet away from camp. There were fourteen Utes in the lot. After Bob got things ready, he poured the coffee into a bucket and told one of the reds to come and get it, which he did. I told them we were poor, that we had nothing but a very little dried meat, and we wanted that ourselves. They were not satisfied. Bob and I took each a cup of coffee, and each took a good chunk of dried meat and began eating. We stood our ground, and after they had drunk their coffee, they started to separate, but we took our rifles and made them keep in a body. Then we packed up, for we were in no place suitable for a fight.

"We pulled out north on the high ground. We could see them a long time. Finally we went over the ridge then Bob stopped and I pushed on. By and by, he came up and said that they had separated. One party had gone back to our camp, and other had crossed the valley to the creek. We were now skirting along the foothills. We pushed on until about 4 o'clock and then turned out. We grazed our horses until dark and then saddled up quick, crossed the creek, and pushed into the hills. We traveled until near midnight, then lay down and got some sleep. Just at daylight, Bob saw half the party on the high ground ahead of us. We at once saddled up and pushed out over the level country.

"We did not fear them as long as we could keep them in a level country, for they only had three or four guns and two horses. The rest had bows and arrows. Their horses were as poor as ours, and they could make no better time than we could. As soon as they passed over the ridge, Bob galloped ahead and I stopped behind a little butte. Bob motioned that they were pushing on fast, so I turned square to the right, intending to go on the right side of a high rocky butte. Bob joined me as soon as he could, and we pushed on all day, only stopping for an hour at noon. At night, we stopped for another hour, then packed up and backtracked for a couple of miles and went around the opposite side of the butte that we had already passed. Here we unpacked and had a good night's rest, besides a good feed for our stock. The next morning, we moved on more leisurely, because our stock was worn out. About noon, we had to go through a rocky canyon.

"I said to Bob, 'I don't think we'll get through.'

"He asked why.

"I said, 'I don't know, but I guess they are in there.'

"He said, 'No, we have shaken them. Don't you think so?'

"'Well,' I said, 'I will go through, and you take the hill. If I am taken, you stay out.'

"'I will do what you say,' he said.

"So I started on. I got through the canyon, and just as I got outside, in a little bend of the creek surrounded by bushes and rocks and overgrown with willows, they rushed on me. I saw at a glance that I was gone. I jumped off my horse and turned it loose. They had shot all their guns at me and missed. I downed one with my rifle and pulled my dragoon and killed two more and wounded another. It was a narrow place and in the open. Five or six were on me in a moment, and I was down and tied. We had made a mistake in separating, for we could have licked them had we remained together, but it was too late.

"Well, they went through our outfit. Two of them took the back track; the rest got dinner. They left the packs on our horses. I was too far away to hear what they were talking about, but they were ugly. They pushed on down the creek. Night came on. They camped in the brush, out of the wind, and I was thrown down on the ground. Finally, they began to talk, and I found out that they wanted to turn back, that they were on a scouting expedition and wanted to go and strike the Snakes, so I had to be disposed of.

"They said our horses were tired out and could not go much farther. They proposed to kill me, cache the horses and packs, and pick them up on the way back. The friends of the men I had shot were determined to have my scalp at once and proposed to burn me. At it they went. They cleared the brush from around a big, old cottonwood stump and tied me to it. They took big, wet strips of buffalo hide and tied them around my chest and around the tree and another around my hips and then another around my legs below the knees. They built an immense pile of brush and dry logs, and they were soon all dancing around me and howling. One big fellow had a brand of fire just ready to start the pile. I shut my eyes and said my prayers for the last time. I had given up. I thought of my old mother, whom I always loved, and knew I had neglected her in her old age. I was wondering if I would meet her after death.

"My mother was a Christian woman. She always prayed for me when I was little. She used to talk to me about Heaven and the immortal Lord. I did everything she asked me to do, but when I went away from home, somehow I forgot what she taught me. I did not pray very often, especially when

I was tired. I didn't drink whiskey for many years; somehow when I went to take a drink, I thought of Mammy. I didn't swear, either, and I didn't like to hear others swear. Oh, how my thoughts flew over these things. I found myself trying to make a mental promise never to do any of the things that Mammy prayed me not to do, but constantly came the awful warning, 'Jim, your time has come. Your race is run. What's the use now, after all these years of wickedness?'

"Something hot touched my cheek. I opened my eyes, and there that great, big painted varmint had that brand of fire close to my face, swinging it around my head. He made a thrust at my eyes, and I dodged to one side. I did this three or four times. He would give a terrible yell every time I fooled him. Then he danced over to the fire and got a fresh brand. I didn't look for him to fire my brush pile until he had put my eyes out and a brand had been crowded down my throat. While he picked out his new brand of fire with which to torture me, I said a long, silent prayer. This time I felt it was my last, sure enough. The big savage swung the firebrand over his head, slowly dancing towards me. He made a terrible thrust at me, which I again dodged. At this instant, I heard a deafening report close to me. I saw the savage who held the firebrand stagger and fall among his companions. Another had also fallen. I heard the most terrible yell that had ever reached my ears in all my life and saw a human form leap among the astonished Indians like a whirlwind. It was Bob.

"He had his hatchet in one hand and his big dragoon in the other. He split the head of one and shot another in a flash. The others jumped for the brush. Down went another, and another staggered and fell, as they passed out of the circle of the firelight. Bob flew after them. I found myself shuddering. I, who have passed through so many dreadful scenes. Pretty soon, Bob came back, with the bloody hatchet in one hand and a smoking pistol in the other. Without a word, he cut me loose, and down I fell. My limbs were stiff and numb. I could not stand.

"'Jim,' said he, 'I was in time, wasn't I?' Dear boy, he looked at me so gentle and kind like. 'Are you hurt?' he asked.

"'No,' I said, 'but Bob, you look out or you will be riddled with arrows.'

"'That's so,' he answered, and he dragged me behind the old stump into the brush, out of the firelight. Then he looked around. Pretty soon he laughed. 'Jim,' asked he, 'how many was there?'

Bridger at the Stake

"I said, 'Eight.'

"He laughed again and said, 'Jim, not one of them varmints had a thing to shoot with. Here is your gun and pistol and four more old flukes and eight bows with quivers of arrows. Guess we are safe now, partner.'

"Them Indians seemed to be perfectly paralyzed, so sudden was the attack, and so terrible was Bob's charge. He rushed them away from their arms that they had stacked up near the fire.

"He now left me and brought in the horses. I told him that I feared he had been killed by the two who were sent on the back track. 'Well,' said he, 'I was too far from you when they attacked to do any good, but I thought I might help you later. So I cached myself behind a big rock and waited for the two who took your back track. They walked right into my arms. I killed them both in their tracks. The first one by the first blow. I wounded the other and he ran, but I soon got him. I then left my horse and followed your trail on the outside and came up just in time, I think.'

"We concluded to watch the rest of the night by turns. Bob took the first watch, and by the time my turn came, my legs were all right again. In the morning, we looked over the ground carefully and found that the ones who had escaped took different routes, showing that they did not get together at once. Bob followed one trail for more than three miles. The fellow was bleeding, but he did not stop.

"In the morning, we took our back trail, raised our cache, and pulled out for Laramie. We got to the fort the middle of June. Our horses were in good condition. We gave them plenty of time when the grass got good. We met no other Indians. We found that the news of our trouble had already got there, through the Indians themselves. The story they told was that we killed twelve, so the wounded one must have died. We had only counted eleven. The report was that I was badly wounded, but that was a mistake. I did not get a scratch beyond bruises.

"Bob never cared to talk about that brush, but one day I said to him, 'Bob, how was it that you killed two of the Indians that night with the first shot?'

"He laughed and said, 'Jim, I crawled about that camp for an hour before I got close enough to get in on them to prevent them from killing you. I watched a long time to get two in range, and I finally got them right. That big fellow,' said he, 'who tried to punch out your eyes, I could have fixed him anytime, but I wanted to get two, and I believe that is what paralyzed them, for the second one fell dead right on top of the rest who were sitting down on the far side of the fire. He fell first, then the other fell, then I came in pretty swift, and they just stampeded. I always felt kind of mean, Jim, because I kept you waiting so long—knowing that that big fellow was dying to put out your eyes. But I was trying to get things my way, so I could make a sure thing of getting you out alive. I knowed I had to do my work mighty swift, for it was not hardly an even shake.'

"We made a good killing that winter, and both went down to Westport and finally to St. Louis and sold our beaver there. I have told you the story, son. Now I don't think another man in all these mountains would have got me out of that scrape against such odds. Bob Andrews was one of the bravest men I ever knew, and the most independent and kind-hearted. He never had much to say."

*

The winter wore away and seemed to pass quickly, as all were so busy with their work. One day in February, the boy went out into the hills and saw two peculiar foxes. He killed them both and brought them into camp. Bridger told him that he had killed two of the finest silver-gray foxes he had ever seen, as well as the largest, and that their skins were of great value. The party trapped many otter, marten, and fisher, with some mink, and a very large catch of beaver. One of the great delicacies relished by trappers, hunters, and travelers on the plains and in the mountains is the beaver tail, which—when properly prepared—is a delicious morsel.

Walter learned new lessons each day. He took his lessons very seriously. Besides setting traps, he learned to track like an Indian, he learned to endure long marches and to care for the large catch of beaver and other valuable furs, he learned how to speak bits of Indian tongues, and he perfected his use of the sign language.

Early one morning towards the end of March, Bridger and Walter started down the creek toward the canyon to look after their traps. They were walking on the crust of the snow, which had fallen to a depth of two feet. Following a thaw, a cold wave had come on and froze the heavy crust, sufficiently strong to hold a man easily. They had about reached the end of

their journey and were about to turn down to the creek, when Walter continued on some distance farther towards the canyon. Bridger stopped, waiting. Walter now turned and motioned Bridger to come to him. When the
older trapper reached the boy, Walter said, "I have noticed all the way from
camp that something has passed over this snow. Look at this." He pointed
to a slight disturbance of the crust.

"I guess," answered Bridger, "that a big gray wolf has passed this way."

"No," said Walter, "it is too heavy for that." And, following some distance
farther, he picked up some hair and showed it to Bridger.

"Boy," said the old man, "you are a born trailer. You are right. That is
buffalo hair."

They followed the dim trail some two hundred yards farther, at which
point the creature had crossed the creek and broken in with one foot. A few
yards farther on, they found more buffalo hair on a bush. Bridger stopped
short. "Walter," said he, "this is serious. This is the trail of an Indian. Our
retreat has been discovered, and our only safety lies in our overtaking this
chap. If we do not, he will be back with a war party, and we will likely be
taken in. You see, son, this fellow is, I think, a young Indian who wants to
become chief. He has started out alone to look up the rendezvous of some
trapper or hunter who has worked hard all winter and made a good haul.
Now he will go back to his winter camp, get a lot of his friends together,
come back, surprise and scalp us all, take all our horses and furs, and go
back in triumph to his camp. Now, son, your quick eye has perhaps saved
our necks. I see through his scheme. He has taken a piece of buffalo hide
and covered his moccasins so they are broad and wide. In this way, he can,
as you see, travel on the crust, making little or no impression. He travels
carefully, of course, and came very near deceiving us. Now, son, I wish you
would go back to the lodge and get Joe. Have him bring some dried meat,
his gun, and a couple of extra pairs of moccasins for each of us. Quick, we
must be on the trail, for a storm may come up suddenly and cover the little
sign he makes. But he will shed those shoe covers before he goes far, for he
is depending on having covered his trail so well that we will not see it."

Walter fairly flew up the creek on his errand and soon returned with Joe.
They overtook Bridger near the rockslide at the outer end of the canyon.
Bridger turned to the boy, saying, "We will follow this fellow and try and
overtake him. You take care of the camp and keep that fool Antoine from

shooting any more around camp. I suspect it is his foolhardy work that has got us into this trouble."

Walter stood a moment, looking down at the snow, then looking Bridger in the eye, said, "Uncle Jim, let Joe and I go on this mission. I am younger than you, and it, I foresee, will be a hard one. I am sure that Uncle Joe will not object."

"That I won't, boy, that I won't. Not I, not I," replied Joe.

Bridger stood for some time in deep thought. Turning to Walter, he asked, "Son, tell me, do you really want to go? Or do you just want to save me a hard trip?"

"Uncle Jim," said the boy, "first, I want to save you the fatigue of this journey—you know you have not been very well—and second, I want to go very bad. But I will do what you say cheerfully. I know it is important and that you hesitate to entrust the fate of our party to me, but Uncle Joe has great experience and I will stay by him and obey him implicitly."

"I know that, son, I know that, and I will stay. Have you extra shoes?"

"Yes," was the answer. "I have everything I need."

So the matter was settled.

"I will go along a piece with you," said Bridger, and the party moved rapidly forward. About a mile below the canyon, they found the shoe coverings of the enemy's moccasins, as Bridger had predicted. They had been thrown into the thick willows and were detected by the keen eye of Walter. These they carefully examined. They consisted of a heavy piece of buffalo hide, thick and stiff, cut out considerably wider than the outside of the moccasin. These were tied to the foot with strong leather thongs. Outside of this was a big broad shoe, made also of buffalo skin, with the hair outside. These broad shoes covered a wide space and made little impression on the snow, frozen as it was into a hard, firm crust. Near the shoes was an old piece of buffalo skin, made into a bag, which Joe recognized as one in which Antoine used to carry his lunch of dried meat on his daily trips to the traps.

"Is it possible," asked Bridger, "that this fellow has actually been to the door of our lodge and taken this bag which Antoine said contained some dried tongue? He told me this morning that a wolf had carried it away."

Before the party separated, Bridger advanced the theory that the savage was not far ahead, arguing that he could not safely have gotten to their camp while anyone was awake and that he had doubtless prowled around until well towards morning, especially as the night had been very dark, and he would surely stop for rest on the main creek. "Then," said Bridger, "when he starts from there, he will make a long trail and you will have to hustle." Bridger turned back toward camp, while Walter and Joe pushed rapidly forward.

The trail led due northeast and soon crossed the creek and left it, taking to the open country. LeBassett here stopped with the remark, "This won't do. We must go back, cross the creek, and keep out of sight. This trail will cross yonder divide." He argued that while they would have a longer trail, they could push along undisturbed and would likely make as good time as by following the trail.

Reaching the main stream, the pursuers turned up on the opposite side and pushed on until they came to a freshet that entered from the northeast. Following this stream to its head, they crossed the divide without encountering the trail of the fugitive. They took great care, keeping constantly under cover of timber or brush. It was the savage's evident intention to keep in the foothills, out of the flat country. LeBassett was now anxious to cross his trail and get to the higher ground, for two reasons: first, being above the short breaks, they could make better progress, and second, while the savage would closely watch the whole country, he would naturally expect pursuit only from the southwest, the direction of the trappers' camp.

The basin they were now traversing was thickly covered with willow and aspen thickets, and they had no fear of discovery. After crossing the basin, LeBassett shaped his course more to the north, saying that he wished to save all the distance possible. He thought that they would soon strike the trail of the fugitive if, indeed, they were not already ahead of the pursued, which he did not consider probable. They found the fugitive's trail about a mile farther on, much to LeBassett's satisfaction. "We have made a big cutoff," he said. "That fellow has had a sleep and rest, for this trail is fresh, and he is traveling fast. We must push on, with all the speed possible, and not let him get too much a start on us."

On they pushed until about 2 o'clock in the afternoon when on raising a ridge, they discovered that the trail led down into an open valley, with an open stretch of country of fully ten miles or more before them. After gazing long and thoughtfully in the direction that it now seemed sure the fugitive had taken, LeBassett turned on his back track. "He is surely two hours ahead of us," he said, "and just one of two things must be true." He added, "If he did not rest and eat back there, and now that I can better judge the distance he must have traveled, I think he may not have done so, he has stopped yonder and is now looking on his back track. We can't follow that trail."

Therefore they doubled back. After walking some distance, LeBassett turned and noticed that Walter was not following but was looking intently across the valley. After waiting a few moments, he asked impatiently, "What is it, boy?"

"Won't you come here a moment?" asked the boy. When the older man had joined him, Walter said, "Do you see that small clump of willows two thirds of the way across the plain and above somewhat where you thought the trail would run? Well, from that clump of willows, I think I can see an occasional puff of smoke. I may be mistaken, but I think not."

The older man leaned long and silently on his rifle, fixing his gaze intently on the spot indicated by the youth. "You are right, boy, you are right. I now see the smoke. It puffs, as you say. His wood is not very dry. The game will be ours. Let us push on."

Having located their quarry, they now needed to double back again for a mile or more, cross the mountain higher up in the timber, and skirt around the head of the valley under the cover of the timber and brush. Both entered upon their task with a determination to annihilate the distance with the utmost despatch that their tired limbs would carry them. One thing in their favor was the strength of the crust, which admitted of rapid progress, so that at times, on downhill stretches, they could half run without breaking through.

For two long hours, they pushed on. By this time, the afternoon was wearing away. At the end of the third hour, they were able to identify the place where they had discovered the smoke. It appeared to be about three miles below them. They now discovered that the point of brush where they had seen the smoke was the end of a small stream, thickly bordered with willow. "The creek," said LeBassett, "goes underground near where the brush ends. Let us go down and approach the fellow while he sleeps."

"Do you think it possible that he has moved on or may move before we reach the spot? Could not one of us keep on around and possibly head him off?" asked Walter.

"The very thing, boy," said LeBassett. "You go around and I will go down. Keep a close watch on the point of brush, for he may push out any time. I don't think he has left there. While we could not always see the point, he could not travel far without our seeing him."

The trappers separated, each pursuing his own way with rapid strides, for it was growing late. LeBassett pushed down the creek and was nearing the point where he felt sure the savage must lie. He was using every care in making the approach. The bushes were very thick. Once he thought he saw the outline of a human form, but he was not clearly certain. He still continued to approach the point, and when—within twenty yards of the end of the willows—he began to think the bird had flown, the Indian rose to an upright position in full view. The willows were so thick that LeBassett knew that he could not send a rifle ball through them with accuracy. He remained perfectly still. The savage too stood still as a statue, looking long and intently toward his back track. He then turned and examined the country ahead. Again he turned, facing the direction of the trapper, who had taken the precaution to cover his hat with snow, to as far as possible resemble the surroundings. Apparently the outlook was satisfactory, for the savage turned to the south and looked down the valley. At this instant, from under the very muzzle of the trapper's gun leaped a large jackrabbit, which rushed forward towards the spot where the savage stood. The frightened creature had been hiding in the deep snow, entirely unseen by the trapper, who crowded it from its winter bed. It leaped forward through the brush without regard to its own comfort, crushing the dry brush and making a tremendous racket. The Indian, knowing that some enemy, of which the timid animal was in deadly fear, had caused its alarm, was instantly on the alert. The trapper, on his part, believed he must strike. Grasping his rifle, he bounded forward. The warrior also seized his weapons. The trapper, being close to his enemy, raised his gun to fire. The warrior was first, launching a deadly arrow at his enemy. The shaft was turned aside by a bush, which was also the case with the trapper's rifle ball. The trapper drew his pistol and fired, missing the warrior, who also missed his second shot. The trapper, still rushing forward, fired a second shot from his pistol, which slightly wounded the Indian, who was now driven from the shelter of the bushes and ran towards the hills, across the open prairie.

When forty yards away, he turned for a parting shot at his enemy, which struck the trapper in the thigh, inflicting a dangerous wound. The trapper's shot, fired at the same time, also took effect, striking the savage in the leg. The Indian now pushed on towards the hills, soon passing over a small swell in the ground that concealed him from view. It was impossible for the Indian or the trapper to tell the condition of the other.

In the meantime, Walter had reached a point in the timber almost exactly in the path of the retreating Indian, who was now rapidly approaching. Walter looked in vain for his companion. He could not understand why LeBassett did not pursue the Indian. The savage was fully a mile away and seemed to be making progress with difficulty. In his effort to run, the Indian kept breaking through the crust. The boy, after surveying the surrounding country, concluded that he must try and meet the Indian. The day was far advanced, and if Walter did not stop him, the Indian was sure to escape. Having watched the Indian for some time, Walter noticed his form gradually disappearing, which he judged was because the Indian was passing into a gulch or depression. As soon as the savage disappeared, Walter pushed rapidly down the hill and, when near the foot, concluded that he would likely meet the Indian near the top of the ridge—and judging from the distance he had himself already traveled, that the meeting was near at hand. He therefore moved forward with great caution, as he knew that the sound of the breaking crust could be heard some distance.

He now neared the crest of the hill. He glanced up and down the ridge for a glimpse of the approaching enemy and listened intently. He bent low and crept forward. Directly he caught a bare glimpse of the feathers in the hair of the savage, some distance ahead. He glided rapidly forward for twenty-five or thirty yards, then again silently passed to the summit of the ridge. The savage was standing erect, bow in hand, looking back intently in the direction from which he had come. His back was partly to Walter, who could have shot him down from behind, but scorned to do so. He therefore raised his cocked rifle and awaited results. As the savage turned, he instantly saw his new enemy. Quick as thought, he sprang to one side and kept jumping first one way and then the other—all the time getting arrows from his quiver. Placing one in his bowstring, he stopped suddenly and sent the arrow with deadly aim at the boy. Walter felt the shaft grate on his ribs as it passed along his left side, and he felt the blood trickling down to his moccasins. Instantly the savage drew his tomahawk and bounded forward. His move was fatal. Walter fired. The shot took effect in the center of the neck of the savage and brought instant death. The boy now stepped quickly to the side of his fallen foe, pistol in hand, but further shots were useless. The warrior had passed to his happy hunting ground.

Walter was much alarmed. The sky was black with storm clouds, and night was closing in. Taking the weapons of his fallen foe, together with a long, buffalo-hide rope, he left the dead warrior and pushed forward rapidly to the scene of the encounter between LeBassett and the savage. The farther he went, the more alarmed he became. He could only travel so fast, on account of the crust on the snow. Just as dusk began to settle, he reached the scene of the struggle and found the trapper lying on his back.

"I am wounded, boy," said Joe, "and I am getting weak. The arrow must have cut a vein, judging by the way it bleeds." The trapper had taken off his belt and tried unsuccessfully to twist it around his leg above the wound. Cutting a piece from the buffalo hide rope he had taken from the dead warrior, the boy tied it loosely around the wounded limb. Then, taking a strong piece of willow, he twisted the rope tight enough to stop the flow of blood.

Walter then looked around to see what could be done to make the wounded man comfortable. He at once decided that the night could not be passed there. About three miles south, there was a large stream, and he made up his mind that they must reach that point in order to get wood sufficient to keep comfortable, as a storm was certainly brewing. The trapper thought he could walk, but the boy did not think he could. Joe insisted upon trying. After going about a quarter of a mile, LeBassett gave up and said he could go no farther. There was no time to be lost. The boy must get his friend to the timber on the big creek. He at once went to the willows and cut two of the largest he could find. These, with a lot of smaller ones, he dragged down to where the wounded trapper lay. He then made a narrow frame of stiff willows, stiff enough to carry the weight of the wounded man. He placed the two large willow butts underneath to act as runners. Having smoothed the bottoms of his makeshift runners, he raised the almost inanimate form of his friend and placed him upon the rude sled and started down the hill.

The ground fell quite rapidly towards the creek, and Walter was surprised at the ease with which he was able to haul his load. He got along nicely to

The Frontiersman

the foot of the hill, but when he struck level ground, he found the load very heavy. Finally, sometime in the night, he succeeded in reaching the stream and refreshed himself with a drink of cool water. To his great surprise, he found the trapper asleep. He pulled the sled into a dense thicket, made a good fire, and proceeded to build a shelter of brush and fir limbs where they passed the night. In the morning, Walter warmed some meat and gave the trapper water. LeBassett felt, he said, somewhat easier. The boy now concluded that the leg must be dressed. The tightly twisted cord had caused Joe great pain. Walter bound up the wound with a piece of his outside shirt, binding a tight band of buckskin around the outside. Then, with much care, he loosened the buffalo-hide rope a little and towards night took it off altogether. In the afternoon, he killed a deer and gave his patient a good meal of hot roasted venison. In the meantime, the storm had set in, and it continued for three days without intermission. Having provided good shelter, they passed the time fairly comfortably, having plenty of dry wood and a good bed of boughs. They were almost as comfortable as in their own lodge.

After the storm, they found that a foot of snow had fallen, and there was little prospect of moving. Walter wanted to go to camp for help, but the trapper insisted that horses could not travel and three men could not help him over the divide. Joe said he felt that in three or four days he would be able to walk over the divide. In the meantime, he said, they could fix up the sled to go down the hills easily and that in time they would be able to get home.

When Walter dressed Joe's leg, he found it badly swollen, and feeling that he could not leave his friend without his full consent, he set about making a new sled, well knowing that Joe could not travel for some time. Cutting down a young fir tree, he split two runners, which had a smooth, broad surface, dug two holes through each runner, and put them on a light frame of dry willows.

A strong wind had been blowing for two days, and Walter found that on the open ground the loose snow had blown away. He therefore determined to make an early start in the morning and try to get over the divide before night. While out scouting a route, he took the precaution to fix a camp and provide some wood on the first creek over the divide. This proved to be wise. They started early, before sunup. Walter covered the sick man with a couple of deer skins, and all day long he pushed on until they reached the summit an hour after dark. Having gotten this far, he zigzagged along steep side hills, pulling the sled with its heavy burden with great difficulty. After about two hours, they reached the new camp. Walter made a fire and got the wounded man comfortable for the night. Joe, however, complained for the first time of intense pain, and Walter became alarmed, fearing that the shaft had been poisoned and that death might follow before he could reach help. He wanted very much to push on, but the wounded man begged to lay over for the day. This course was finally adopted.

While the trapper slept, the boy picked out a path across the creek and over the lower ridge on the lower part of Otter Creek. On his return to camp, he was greatly alarmed to find a large pack of buffalo wolves within a few hundred yards of camp. Rushing over the stream, he found the sick man all right, but plenty of wolf tracks within thirty feet of the fire, which was still smoldering. This incident determined Walter to never again leave Joe beyond his sight. The wolves seemed famished and utterly without fear. During the night, they often came to the side of the lodge. When Walter got up to renew the fire, he threw live firebrands at the animals. As soon as it was light and the morning meal disposed of, the two trappers started out. The day was a most laborious one, but before sundown, they made a good camp and all arrangements to pass the night.

In the early morning, Walter was on the move with his burden, pushing on up the cliff. He thought it possible that Bridger, becoming anxious, might come down the stream in hopes of meeting his friends. About 4 o'clock in the afternoon, he saw a man on a high eminence, and he felt sure this must be Bridger. Going to the top of a little ridge, he swung his hat for a long time, but did not seem to have succeeded in attracting the man's attention. In desperation, he finally fired his pistol. This brought a response, and he was soon gratified to see the stranger making rapid progress in his direction. In about an hour, Bridger came up. He was almost overcome by the sight he beheld.

Putting his shoulder to the line, Bridger helped haul the sled, and by dark, they had reached their fall camp, about five miles from the lodge. While Walter built a fire, Bridger went to the lodge for Antoine and a robe to cover the sick man, who began to show signs of fever. After a good rest and some hot coffee, they made a start for the lodge. With three men, they made rapid progress, and midnight found them safely in the lodge. Bridger immediately prepared some herb tea for the patient and applied a balsam plaster. By the next day, Joe felt better. Bridger gave him some beaver-tail broth, and he now became more cheerful, not needing so much attention.

About this time, a warm southwest wind set in, and the snow began to settle. In four or five days, the hillsides were nearly bare, and the trappers once more turned their horses out to graze upon the abundance of fine grass that had been covered during the winter. All agreed that the chinook came in good time, as the woodpile was well-nigh exhausted, the hay provided in the fall was all gone, and the horses had begun to shrink in flesh. It was the tenth of April. LeBassett and Walter had been gone twelve days. The trappers now took up all their traps and made every preparation to leave their winter quarters as soon as the snow was entirely gone and the horses had picked up sufficiently to stand the hard travel.

LeBassett did not mend as fast as they had expected. His wound broke out on the inside, and they found that some fibers of dirty cloth had been driven into the wound with the arrow. Making a syringe from a piece of alder, Bridger drained the wound and it soon began to heal. The patient soon felt much better and rapidly recovered.

Walter—having appropriated the bow and quiver of arrows belonging to the savage he had killed—devoted much time to the practice of archery. Observing this, Bridger said, "That fellow was a warrior of the first class. I have never seen a finer bow nor more perfect arrows." The bow was made of red cedar, backed with a heavy coating of sinews, and covered with the skin of a snake. The arrows, seventy in number, were of the very finest quality and winged with robin feathers.

Day by day, Walter practiced archery. His worst trouble was to shoot with sufficient force. Bridger told him that that would come gradually, as his muscles grew stronger, and this was found to be the case. Walter no longer used a rifle for small game such as grouse, rabbits, and the like. Bridger allowed no rifle shooting, as war parties were on the move.

The warm hillsides were now covered with anemones and other hardy early flowers. The whole party was tired of inactivity and was anxious to move. The longer the matter was delayed, the more danger there was from war parties, who moved everywhere in the early spring. Bridger was beginning to fret, as he'd promised the government to be on hand for an expedition on the plains and he didn't want to disappoint them.

On the fifth of May, LeBassett was able to ride, and the trappers broke camp and started for Laramie. Their horses were in good fix and able to travel. They encountered no war parties on the trip, and they reached the fort on May 20, 1860. The party remained at Fort Laramie a few days. The prices offered for their cache of furs did not suit either Bridger or LeBassett, and so they decided to take them down to Westport. They joined up with a party that had wintered at Laramie and was just starting for Westport, having come in from Salt Lake late the fall before.

The evening before they started out, Walter told Bridger and LeBassett that he would part with them in the morning and would go on to Pikes Peak and into the gold mines. Both of the older men seemed much surprised and disappointed. They had become much attached to the boy.

"Why," urged Bridger, "we can't pay you for your share of the furs, and we can't get half price for them here. And I don't see what we can do. We may never meet again."

"Well," replied Walter, "I don't think that I have any interest in them anyway. I have done nothing, while you are two of the best trappers in the mountains. I have gained much knowledge and experience from you, and you have taught me much. I have enjoyed myself immensely while I have been with you."

There was a long silence. Then LeBassett spoke, "See here, boy, if you want to part friends with me, don't talk that way anymore." LeBassett turned to Walter with moist eyes. "Lad," said he, "Jim told me about your wound. To think I let you drag me over them hills, and you was hurt worse than I was." Then he broke down and could say no more.

After another long silence, Walter said, "Uncle Joe, you and Uncle Jim go on to Wesport or to St. Louis as you think best. Sell the furs for the best price you can get. When you come back, leave my share with the trader at Bent's Fort, or keep it until I see you and leave a letter telling me where I can find you. I don't need any money now; in fact, I have a little to spare, if you need it to pay Antoine. I can spare eighty dollars, if you need it—in fact, I want to pay my share." So they settled up in this way.

"Where are you going now, son?" asked Bridger.

"I am going to Pikes Peak and going to the mines. I will come down to Bent's Fort in the fall and will find you if you are there. I started out for the mines, and I want to go there. I do not want to go back to the States now."

"Do you know anybody in St. Louis, boy?" asked Bridger.

"Yes, I know Colonel Hudson."

"Colonel Hudson!" said Bridger in surprise. "I have met him many times. Well, if anything happens and we don't come back, we will leave your money with the colonel. If we do come back, we will leave your share at Bent's Fort." So all was arranged, and the party went to bed.

The boy was up at an early hour. He wrote letters to his friends, to Mrs. Purdy and Colonel Hudson and the colonel's daughter Alice. He explained to the Hudsons that he had not been fortunate enough to meet their son and brother but had left their letters at the place they had named. When he reached Denver, if their letters had not been claimed, he would take them and try hard to make a personal delivery. He told his friends that if the mines did not turn out as he hoped, he might go to New Mexico, in which case he might meet young Mr. Hudson.

All was bustle and confusion in the morning. Bridger and LeBassett loaded their furs into wagons and left the packs, and horses at the fort, taking only their saddle horses. Walter had packed his personal outfit and was ready to start for Denver. He extended his hand to Bridger. "I am sorry our trails divide here," he told the old trapper.

Bridger was barely able to stammer a good-bye. LeBassett, his eyes fixed on the ground, could not speak. As the boy mounted his horse and rode away toward the west, the old men saluted him with their hats—each stood silent, leaning on his long rifle until long after the retreating figure had passed from view. Then they mounted their horses and followed the wagons that carried their effects.

During the afternoon, as the two old men rode along, Bridger said, "He's mighty tenderhearted. He was modest as a girl."

"Yes," answered Joe, "but he's got the heart of a lion and a head as cool as yon snowbank on old Pikes Peak." The old mountaineers lapsed into silence, deeply absorbed in their own thoughts.

BOOK TWO

When Walter reached Denver on the first of June, he made inquiry at Jones & Cartwright concerning the letters he had left there the previous spring for Gerald Hudson. He was told that the letters had never been called for. The last word the firm had had from Hudson was that he was at Santa Fe, and they felt sure that he was still in that country. Walter told them that he would leave the letters there, and if he decided to go into the southern country, he would call and get them and try and locate young Hudson himself.

Remaining in Denver a few days to decide in what part of the mining country to locate, Walter finally decided to go to California Gulch, which had recently been reported as a new gold discovery. He therefore proceeded to Soda Springs, where he camped, and there he joined a party on its way to the mines. He reached the famed diggings in due time and temporarily located in California Gulch. It often happens that the pilgrim is disappointed on reaching the new Eldorado to find absolutely nothing to warrant the widespread reports that reach distant points. This was the case with California Gulch. Of the pioneers, there were but few.

There were perhaps a dozen claims staked off, no more than the actual miners on the ground, and no development work whatever had been done. Some gold had been panned out on the rimrock—and some small nuggets found in shallow prospect holes along the margin of the stream. The evening after Walter arrived, quite a party came in from Cherry Creek and Russel's Gulch farther north. These were mostly Georgians, among them many good miners, and from then on, people came in rapidly—each day adding to the population of the place.

Of course, one of the first steps to be taken on arrival was to stake off your claim, and it thus happened that all parties commenced to number their claims. They then built cabins and rude places of shelter. As they completed their abodes, the miners turned their attention to opening and prospecting their claims. About two weeks after Walter reached the gulch, a nearby miner struck the pay streak and rocked out five ounces of coarse gold in one day.

The excitement from this strike was great, and claims were in demand. It transpired that a good many of the early arrivals had staked claims for their friends, who were not on the ground, and had written them to come and take possession. The owners not being on the ground furnished an excuse for claim jumping. There were always adventurers about new mining camps ready to profit by others' misfortunes and mistakes. So it transpired that, if the owner of a claim was not actually on the ground, it was speedily jumped, the new claimant immediately moving onto the claim and beginning the work of development. This, of course, led to numerous disputes, and when the two claimants came together and could not settle their difficulties themselves, the disputes were usually settled at a miners' meeting. In such cases, notices were posted on the piece of ground in dispute and a day was set for the trial. Sundays were usually selected, as miners seldom worked on that day. They generally washed their clothes, fixed up about camp, or went for supplies.

The procedure in such cases was that—when the miners had assembled—they selected one of their number to act as chairman. The chairman then called the meeting to order, called for the selection of a secretary, and stated the object of the meeting. The principals were then called to come forward and state their cases in person or by attorney—the jumper took the place of plaintiff, and the burden of proof was on the plaintiff. Each party had the right to introduce evidence.

After the case had been heard, a line was drawn in front of the chairman and a vote was taken, the miners arranging themselves to the right and left of the line. The chairman counted the votes, and the majority ruled. Decisions of this kind were usually satisfactory. Sometimes, however, the parties were dissatisfied, quarrels occurred, and the misunderstandings resulted in bloodshed. It sometimes occurred that the parties settled their troubles on the ground with guns, pistols, and knives—in other words, duels were fought, and the victor took the claim.

When Walter had reached California Gulch, he—in common with other goldseekers—staked his claim, built his cabin, and began improvements.

One day, a big Georgian jumped his claim on the grounds that Walter was a minor and not entitled to the privileges of a citizen. When the man appeared and put up his notice, Walter was out hunting. It so happened that meat was very scarce in the gulch, and Walter was the only successful hunter thereabouts. The meat he killed was shared by all, and everyone helped themselves as long as it lasted. Many had tried to find game, but none had been successful. Walter, however, never failed to bring in an ample supply for his own use and the use of others who, in acknowledgment, frequently helped him for a few hours in the development of his claim.

When the lad came home that evening with his horse loaded with elk meat, he found his claim jumped. He was much worked up over the occurrence. He walked up to the tree where the notice was posted and read it carefully. Then he attended to his horses for the night. All the evening, the subject was not referred to among his immediate associates. The next day, the partner of the jumper came on the ground to arrange terms, stating that Mr. Malcolm, who had jumped the claim, would be down directly with his tools to go to work on the claim. Up to this time, the boy had said nothing, but now he walked up to the speaker and said, "You may go to Mr. Malcolm and say to him that he will not go to work on this claim while I am here. This claim I will defend until it has been decided that it is not lawfully mine."

The man said, "Young man, you had better not be too smart. Mr. Malcolm will take possession according to the custom of this camp."

"You had better tell your friend what I told you to tell him," replied the lad quietly. Turning on his heel, he walked into his tent.

Why Mr. Malcolm did not take possession has never been explained, but he did not appear that day. The next day, the same man came again and said he came to fix the date of the miners' meeting and proposed to try the case on Sunday.

"I will not try this case Sunday," said the boy.

"Not try it Sunday? When will you try it then?" he asked.

"Any week day you may name," answered the lad.

"Do you suppose that these miners are going to quit their work to settle your troubles?" asked the man.

"I have made no troubles," said Walter. "You and your partner have started this trouble, and if it is settled at a miners' meeting, I will have something to say about when and where it shall take place."

"Guess I won't fool any more time with you," answered Mr. Malcolm's agent.

"As you please, sir," said the boy, walking away.

It was not long before a half dozen men came down to the claim; among them was Malcolm's partner. A new spokesman came forward and in a very abrupt manner asked, "Are you the boy as claims this ground?"

"Yes, sir," said Walter, "I own this ground and have possession of it."

"Well, we came down to see about settling this dispute."

"You are all friends of Mr. Malcolm, I presume," said the boy.

"Yes, we are his friends," answered the spokesman.

"Well, sir, I decline to discuss this matter, except in the presence of an equal number of my friends."

"When will you have them here?"

"At 12 o'clock," replied the boy.

"We are here now. We are ready," answered Malcolm's spokesman.

"I will not ask my friends to leave their work before 12," said the boy in a quiet, firm manner.

Malcolm's friends consulted amongst themselves, and the spokesman said, "Being as you're a boy, we'll come back at 12. If you was a man, it'ud be settled now."

"As an American, sir, I stand upon my rights, and I ask no favors from anyone because of my youth," replied Walter.

The big, burly fellow stopped short, turned around, and looked the lad over carefully but finally followed his companions without further remarks.

At 12 o'clock, the same men returned. In the meantime, the boy had secured the attendance of six neighboring friends. The same man who had acted as Malcolm's spokesman earlier in the day opened the subject by stating what had happened at the meeting in the forenoon, adding that, as one of the disputants was a boy, they had come again, and now they proposed to have the matters in dispute settled.

At this point, Walter stepped forward and said, "My friends, this gentleman has correctly stated what happened here this forenoon. I will state my side of this controversy. When I was absent from my claim the other day, out hunting, a man signing his name as Malcolm put up yonder notice on my claim. I have not seen him. I declined to confer with them this morning, because I did not care to disturb you before the noon hour. Whatever you do or say in this matter, I wish it to be understood that I am here demanding the same rights as you who are men enjoy. I stand only upon my rights and want no extra consideration because I am looked upon as a boy."

"Well, let's get down to business," said the man who represented the jumpers. "When are we going to have this miners' meeting?"

"Gentlemen," replied Walter, addressing his friends, "I have told these men that I did not want the meeting to take place on Sunday. Select any other day you like, and it will be satisfactory to me."

"Well, we want it Sunday," said the jumpers' spokesman, in a most positive manner.

Turning to his friends, Walter said, "I have told you my wish in this matter. I have been taught to believe it wrong to do such things on the Sabbath. I do not want any dispute, by which I am to be benefited, settled on that day." Saying which, he sat down on the grass.

The spokesman for the jumpers and several others had a good deal to say—all of them advocating Sunday as the proper day, as it was a day of idleness.

At last, an elderly man by the name of Stoddard got up from among the friends of the boy and said, "Gentlemen, I have boys of my own, and I have taught them that Sunday is a day of rest. If our young friend here does not want this trouble settled on Sunday, suppose we have the meeting Saturday afternoon at 4 o'clock. You can appoint two, and we will appoint two men to get up and post the notices."

The spokesman of the jumpers then rose and commenced a long tirade, saying some pretty ugly things, when a big fellow sitting among the lad's friends raised his hand and said, "Say, mister, you're doing a good deal of talking. I'd like to know your name."

"My name is Bill Strong," answered the jumpers' representative.

"All right," said the big man.

Strong continued by saying he did not see why the custom should be changed. For his part, he did not propose to be bullied any more. The meeting would be on Sunday or not at all. "That boy has no business with this claim anyway, and I don't propose to take any more of his sass. He can just take his chances with the other fellows next Sunday."

The big man then got up and stepped over in front of Strong. Looking

him square in the eye, he said, "Mr. Strong, I asked you your name. My
name is Peter Stanford. I came over here at the request of this lad. I never
spoke to him before in my life. I did not care to mix up in this affair, but
since I came here, I have got interested because I believe in fair play. You
have come here to bully this lad, and yet you declare that you don't propose to be bullied. Who has offered to bully you? I have not seen any disposition on the part of this boy to either scare or bully you. On the contrary, he has acted a perfect little gentleman.

"Now, sir, I don't like your style," the big man continued. "As I said, I
came here disinterested. I am now interested. First, that this boy shall have
fair play; second, that he shall not be bullied or robbed out of his claim;
and third, that if he has honest scruples about trying his case on Sunday,
his wishes shall be observed.

"Mr. Stoddard here has made a sensible suggestion, that we meet on
Saturday at 4 o'clock to settle this question. If this suits you, Mr. Strong, just
appoint two men to arrange the preliminaries. If this plan don't suit you,
you can just pack yourself off this ground and say to your man that there
will be no miners' meeting to settle this difficulty and that this boy's friends
will defend his rights against all comers. Mr. Stoddard, kindly act as chairman and appoint two of us to arrange the preliminaries." Mr. Stanford sat
down beside Walter who, it was noticed, had seized the big man's hand
with both of his and seemed to be squeezing it very tight.

Stoddard then got up and said, "I appoint Mr. Stanford and Mr. Grey.
Come, boys," he added, "let's go to dinner."

All rose to their feet, and Mr. Stanford addressed himself to Strong, "Mr.
Strong, if you decide to appoint, come around to my claim after 6 o'clock,
or I'll come to yours. Which will it be, sir?" Stanford turned partly around
as if to depart. Waiting a moment, he said, "Decide, sir. I must go."

"Well," said Strong slowly, "if we decide to appoint, I'll come to your
camp."

"I guess you'll appoint," replied Stanford, as he walked rapidly away.

Before Stanford left, he said to Walter, "Say, boy, come down after 6."

"I will," replied the boy, and he did so after supper. When he arrived, he
asked Stanford, "Do you think those fellows will come?"

"Yes, I guess they'll come. I think they'd just as soon avoid a row, although
them Georgians are claimed to be on the fight and shoot, so they say."

"I was so glad," said Walter, "to hear you talk to that Mr. Strong as you did. He acts like a big bully. I am not afraid of any of them singly, but I don't want the whole pack on my hands at once. At the same time, I don't want to get you into trouble, Mr. Stanford."

"Oh, never mind me," said Stanford. "I really enjoy a good scrape. I am with you, boy. Now that I think of it, guess I'll sleep up there on your claim until this thing is settled. You see, if they get possession once, it would be hard to get them off the ground without a killing. They say possession is nine points of the law. Say, call me Peter, lad."

At 8 o'clock, Peter finally said, "Well, I guess they won't come after all." But just then, they detected the sound of footsteps. "Here they are," he said, and sure enough, up walked Strong with two others who had not before been seen.

Strong looked surly. He introduced his friends as Mr. Blaine and Mr. Logan. Both had the southern accent. Strong said at once, "Me and Blaine are the committee."

"All right," said Peter. "I'll just call Mr. Grey over."

Presently, Grey put in an appearance. He was a quiet man of small stature, with a slight stoop of the shoulders. He had thinning hair and a light blue eye, as did Stanford.

The men were now made acquainted. Stanford stood facing Blaine— apparently sizing him up. The three men representing the jumpers were all armed with revolvers and acted sullen and restless. Finally, Blaine broached the subject, saying, "We've concluded that 3 o'clock Sunday afternoon would be the most suitable."

Just before this, Peter had gone into his tent and now appeared with his coat on, and it was noticed that he had on his belt and most likely a pistol, although none was visible. "What's that, Mr. Blaine?" asked Peter. "I didn't catch what you were saying."

"I said that we had decided that Sunday afternoon would be the more suitable," Blaine answered.

"Well," said Peter, "you can just decide again, for as I told Mr. Strong, we will not hold the meeting on Sunday. That is the condition we made, and we won't change."

"Well," said Blaine, "it takes two to make a bargain."

"That's all right," answered Peter most decidedly. "Sunday is out of it, and we won't discuss it any further."

At this point, Logan got up and pulled his pistol around in front. Grey got up and faced Logan. All had been sitting on logs in front of the fire. Then Strong got up. As he rose, Walter—who had been sitting on the other side of Peter—rose and moved over in front of Strong, who eyed the boy closely. Walter had on a buckskin hunting coat, which hung loosely around his body, and no weapons were visible. Grey had on a belt, but his weapon was not visible either. The six men stood facing each other. So far, no one had made a hostile move beyond the action of Logan, which might have been made in the interests of comfort.

"I might as well tell you that we are not particular whether there is any meeting at all," Peter said. "We are perfectly satisfied with our position. Now, Mr. Blaine, we are done with this subject, except to set a time for the meeting, if you fellows want a meeting. We leave it to you, sir."

Blaine and Strong exchanged glances. Logan said nothing. Finally, Strong called Blaine to one side, and Logan soon followed. They conferred in a low tone for some time and finally came forward. Blaine said, "We have decided to accept your date—Saturday afternoon at 4 o'clock. Now, who will attend to your side of the case, and how many witnesses have you, and who are they?"

"So far as those matters are concerned, we will attend to our own side of the case, and you do the same," answered Peter. "We will have as many witnesses as we think proper; you have the same privilege. The meeting will have these things in charge. The only thing that remains to be done here is to frame a notice of the meeting and see that it is posted. We will post the notices down the gulch, if you will post them up the gulch. What do you say?"

"All right," replied Blaine. "It is agreed." They drew up a notice, and the parties separated.

After the Strong party had gone, Stanford turned to Grey and said, "I believe them fellows came here for a row and expected to have it."

"I think so, too," said Grey.

"Do you really?" asked Walter.

"Yes, boy," answered Peter, "but I guess they made up their minds we were ready for them. Do you think you could have managed Strong?" he asked Walter with a laugh. "He was the biggest of the lot, so we left him for you to look after, boy."

Grey smiled and left without a word.

"Walter," said Peter, "I am going up to your camp to sleep tonight. Don't know what these chaps may conclude to do. I don't much like them."

As they walked along, Walter asked Peter what kind of man Mr. Grey was. "He is so quiet, "said the boy. "Doesn't say a word."

"That's so," answered Peter, "but he's all right, especially in a row. He's a fighter. They don't want to try to bluff that chap. He'll sleep up here if you want him."

The next morning, the notices were sent down the gulch. Walter's supporters took good care to spread the word as far as possible so that all their personal friends would be sure to come to the meeting.

Down the gulch a short distance lived a man by the name of Jonathan Gore, who was something of a lawyer and a good talker. Walter was advised to get him to plead the case. He accordingly went down and saw Gore, who said he would take the case for one of Walter's horses—and if Gore won the case, Walter was to give him another horse.

There was good attendance at the meeting, and each party put in its evidence. The plaintiff had the opening and burden of proof. It was asserted that Walter, being a minor, was not entitled to hold a claim, and Blaine, having charge of the jumpers' side of the controversy, made a good showing. It was plain that he depended upon a preponderance of votes and on the fact that a good deal of prejudice had been worked up against the boy because he would not try the case on Sunday. This had some weight with a certain drinking element that had begun to congregate in the gulch.

In opening the jumpers' case, Blaine made the following statements, which he said were undisputed propositions of law: first, that the defendant was a minor and therefore under the law was not lawfully entitled to own or convey property of a real estate character; second, that Walter, being a minor, could not make a valid conveyance of real property; and third, that the only way Walter could acquire property was through a guardian, and he had no one whom he claimed as a guardian. This latter point was more clearly brought out on examination of the boy himself. After an excellent general speech lauding Malcolm as a man of family and one capable of taking care of one, Blaine ended his case.

Gore followed for the defense. He paid no attention whatever to the points raised by the plaintiff and instead simply ridiculed Blaine's position, stating that the boy was there first, had found the ground vacant, and took it—as he certainly had a right to do. Gore's remarks had a good effect.

Amos Stoddard, the chairman of the meeting, rose and put the question, stating that those in favor of the plaintiff—who had jumped the ground owned by the defendant—should stand to the right of the line marked out directly in front of him and that those in favor of the defendant retaining his ground should stand to the left of the line.

Peter Stanford gave a great hurrah, urging those in favor of giving first locators their rights to step to the left of the line—"this way, boys, over here." This rally came near raising a row among the friends of the jumper. When Stoddard announced the result, the boy had won his case by a majority of about twenty-five, out of two hundred miners and others present.

The friends of the winner cheered him lustily. However, the affair stirred up a good deal of bad blood. Many of the Georgians, who were friends of Malcolm, talked pretty loud. Finally, Walter and his immediate friends went home. The next day, they learned that, after they had gone, Malcolm's friends got together, elected a new chairman, and passed a resolution granting Malcolm a new trial, which was to take place on the next Sunday afternoon.

Walter knew nothing of this until a notice was served on him the next day. He went down at once to see Peter Stanford. Stoddard and Grey were called over to Peter's camp, and they held a consultation as to the best plan to proceed. They decided not to do anything until they had talked to Gore. Walter saw Gore the next day, and he told the boy that he had agreed to take the case for Malcolm. Gore's neighbors told Walter that Gore was to receive a pair of mules provided he won the case, and fifty dollars if he lost. The lad was much incensed at the course of Mr. Gore, who had violated his word, he having agreed to stay with the boy to the end of the controversy. Now Gore told the boy he could not hold his claim, that Malcolm had the best right.

On Friday night, about a dozen of Walter's friends came up to his claim to talk matters over. It was pretty well agreed that serious trouble would yet grow out of this affair. Stoddard said it was an outrage on the boy and an insult to him as chairman and to every man who had honestly participated in the proceedings. He said he would stand by whatever course the boy's friends decided to take. Peter said that no matter what others did, he would stand by the boy—and all the others assented. Finally, Walter rose gravely and said, "My friends, you are very kind, but it now looks to me as if trouble may come of this unfortunate business. As much as I would like to keep my claim, I will cheerfully give it up to save any of you from the danger of being injured or having serious bad feeling with residents in the gulch. I hope, therefore, you will not consider me in the matter."

As Walter seated himself on the grass, Grey arose. Every man looked at him with surprise, as he had never been known to have anything to say upon any subject. He usually just fell in with his companions. He said, "Gentlemen, this boy is right, and he shall not give up his ground. I will never desert him, no matter what happens." All those present agreed.

One other point was to be decided. Should Walter and his friends attend the meeting? Some were in favor of standing on the first decision, while others favored attending the meeting. All were somewhat disconcerted about the desertion of Jonathan Gore.

Stoddard turned to Walter and asked, "My son, you don't like to hold this meeting on Sunday. What do you think about it now?"

Walter replied, "This meeting was not appointed by us. We have our rights to protect and defend. We are in this community, and I am not certain but that it would be for the best interests of all to attend the meeting. Should we not do so, Malcolm would get the decision in his favor. In that case, I think his friends would insist upon taking the claim from me. If such a thing was attempted, it might result in trouble more serious than holding this meeting on the Sabbath. I think we had better attend. I do not know who to get to talk for me, but we will do the best we can." So it was decided to go to the meeting.

The meeting assembled quite promptly at 2 o'clock, and the jumpers succeeded in selecting Blaine as chairman. They first introduced their testimony, which merely consisted of the statements made by Malcolm in regard to staking the claim he had jumped.

When the defendant opened his case, he simply put the district recorder on the stand to show that his claim had been properly recorded. He then closed, to the disappointment of his friends. Jonathan Gore now opened his argument for the plaintiff, speaking quite a long time. He said that at the time he had been engaged to defend the boy in the first action, he did not fully understand the situation. He had thought the boy was older, and in fact he had not given the matter very serious thought. "Mr. Malcolm," he said, "is a man of family, and men of families should be encouraged rather than discouraged." He spoke feelingly on this point. He also said that, in his opinion, the boy should be sent back to the States and that this was no place for boys. He wound up with quite an eloquent appeal for his client, which warmed up the friends of the jumper, and he closed with the prediction that the verdict should be unanimous in favor of Malcolm.

As Gore sat down, a good deal of applause followed, and it looked somewhat gloomy for the boy and his friends. They had concluded that it would not be worthwhile to try to get any good speaker, as the jumpers had Gore, the only man in camp who had any pretensions as such. Stoddard, after much persuasion, said he would make a few remarks, but when he got up to speak, he had forgotten everything he had intended to say. Blaine followed with a good speech on the same lines as had been adopted by Gore.

Blaine said, "My friend, Mr. Malcolm, is an honest man. He has a family and a home in the state of Georgia. There is a large mortgage on his farm, and he came here in the hope of honestly accumulating sufficient money to pay off the mortgage and provide means to make his family comfortable for the remainder of their lives.

"He came to this gulch a poor man. He has four mules, a wagon and harness, provisions and equipment for one year, and a small sum of money. This constitutes his worldly wealth, which he has here with him. I have known Mr. Malcolm for many years. We live in the same county, go to the same church, and went to the same school when we were boys, and I reckon we will stay here together and be neighbors as long as either of us stays in these mountains."

A voice called out, "I guess you're partners."

Blaine paid no attention to the interruption but proceeded to say that, when Mr. Malcolm came to the gulch, he looked around for a location, but it seemed as though all the best ground was taken. He finally took a claim up the gulch, and lately some gold had been discovered above him. In looking over the claims that had been taken previously, he found that many claims had been staked for men who were nonresidents of the gulch, which he did not think right, as he believed that "first come, first served" was the right principle.

"Now," continued Blaine, "Mr. Malcolm found that this boy, a minor, had staked off a claim. Most likely he was holding it for some absent one or for some of the men who are taking so much interest in his personal affairs. Now, you know, gentlemen, that a minor has no right to hold real estate. He can't convey to you, if you wished to buy his claim, and should you buy his claim, he could make you restore it to him after you had struck pay, by hunting up a guardian and paying you back what money you had paid him.

"Now, gentlemen, this is a clear case, and there can be but one honest way to settle this matter, and that is to give Mr. Malcolm this claim, unlawfully held by this minor."

When Blaine ceased speaking, there was quite a good deal of talk, and it looked as if the case was as good as settled in favor of the jumpers, who were stimulated no doubt by the fact that a very good strike had been made Saturday evening on the next claim below the one in dispute. Walter's claim was therefore looked upon as one of the best in camp. A cry went up from all parts of the crowd, "Vote, vote! Let's vote!"

On the edge of the crowd stood Stoddard, Stanford, Grey, and a good many friends of the boy. Peter Stanford said, "It is plain that someone ought to say something." But no one seemed to think himself capable, and in the meantime, the cry was taken up again, "Vote, vote!"

At that moment, old Stoddard caught hold of Stanford, saying, "He's going to speak himself. I seen it in his face. When those two white spots come on his cheek, you can look out. He's going to talk."

The chairman, who was one of the Georgia party, had risen to put the vote, when Walter came forward with a quick, nervous step and signified a desire to address the crowd. The chairman seemed inclined to ignore him. Noting this, Stanford called out, "Hold on there. Give that boy a chance." This cry went up from every part of the crowd. Stanford, Grey, and many of the boy's friends rushed forward.

"All right," said the chairman. "The boy can speak, if he wants to."

Near where the chairman stood was a large pine stump with a flat top. When Walter came forward, being small in stature, the crowd could not see him. Someone called, "Get on the stump," and quick as a flash, Stanford seized the boy and lifted him to the top of the stump. Walter looked over the assembly, seeming much embarrassed. He stammered and blundered and seemed utterly speechless. The crowd began to jeer, "Speech! Vote, vote!" "Hello, there," shouted one fellow, "tell us why you don't like to hold meetings on Sunday." This brought a great laugh.

With burning cheeks, the lad faced the portion of the crowd from which the voice came. Reaching forth his hand, he said, "Sir, had you a mother that loved and cared for you and taught you your prayers? Does not the Lord Prayer's say, 'Remember the Sabbath day and keep it holy'? And is it not written in the constitution of our country that 'no man shall be deprived of life, liberty or property without due process of law'? Is it reasonable that the Christian people of all nations should recognize one part of the divine law, and discard the other? If you, sir, so soon forget that portion of divine law that teaches you it is wrong to work and hold business meetings upon the Sabbath day, will you not also forget that it is wrong to rob your neighbor or to take your neighbor's property without his permission?

"I have expected you to ask me, sir, why I am not at my cabin, and why I came to this meeting, which I have told you it is wrong to hold on Sunday and contrary to my teaching. Though, sir, you have not asked me this question, yet I will answer it.

"Turn your eyes which way you may, and you will find a snow-capped barrier surrounding this place, over which men cannot pass without much labor and exertion. In this valley, perhaps, there are three hundred human beings, cut off from legal interference and beyond the jurisdiction of courts of law. In such cases as this, it is the citizen's duty to obey the dictates of reason and justice. A correct solution can only be reached in such a case as ours by the wise exercise of the will of the majority. Judging from the number assembled here, I am of the opinion that it was the will of the majority of the residents of this gulch that this meeting should be held on this day and at this hour. I, sir, bowed to the will of the majority.

"Sirs, one week ago yesterday, a gathering took place of all or nearly all of the people of this beautiful valley—called together to settle a dispute between two persons who had been so unfortunate as to have a disagreement about a little piece of ground one hundred feet in length, in this wild, vast, and remote region. That gathering was upon this spot. The difference between these parties was discussed, a vote was taken, and a majority gave its sanction to the possession of this little piece of ground being made permanent by its original locator. The verdict so rendered seemed to suit all at the time.

"Later, it seems, some persons gathered together and assumed to annul the decision of the majority. In fact, the whole population of the place decided that there should be a new trial, and that it should take place on the Lord's day. Because American-born people are naturally tenacious of their rights, and good citizens, they will not, in violation of principle, tamely surrender them. I came to this meeting because I propose to act in unison and harmony with my neighbors. I am ready now to hear whether or not I am entitled to the same right as you yourselves hold, to enjoy the fruits of my labors.

"When I first came here among you, I think there were ten men in this community. My coming, I remember, seemed to please you then."

Voices called out from different parts of the crowd, "It did! It did!"

Walter continued, "I was then one of you. As others came, we rejoiced. The laws and rules we made were respected by my friends and associates. The claim I have my kind friend and neighbor over there, Mr. Stoddard, pointed out to me and helped me stake out. A father could not have been more thoughtful for my welfare than he. But I do not come before you to plead the baby act. I want no leniency shown me on account of my youth. I hold that a boy has no business away from his home until he can take care of himself." Great applause greeted this declaration.

"Therefore, gentlemen, I shall stand upon what I deem to be my rights under the laws and customs of American civilization. These rights I will defend and I will aid my neighbors in defense of them, should they appeal to me for such assistance. In the first trial of this case, Mr. Jonathan Gore was my paid spokesman. I shall not criticize his course, although he violated his contract with me. I shall leave his punishment to his neighbors and his own conscience. Mr. Malcolm is a stranger to me; I have not had the pleasure of his acquaintance. He placed a notice on my claim in my absence and has never been there since, to my knowledge.

"Gentlemen, let me call your attention to two matters that may have escaped your memory. First, when this district was organized, I was present. At that time, a general meeting was called of all the miners. I was then told it was necessary and customary in all new mining camps to so organize for mutual protection. Now, if my memory serves me, Mr. Stoddard was elected chairman of that meeting. Mr. Gates, you were elected secretary, and Mr. Graves was elected recorder of the district and he still holds that office.

"At that place and time, certain rules and bylaws were enacted for the proper government of the district. Among them I remember the following, which bear on this case:

First, the name of this gulch shall be California Gulch, and the name of the district shall be Summit District;

Second, every person who shall be a resident of this gulch shall be entitled to locate and hold one claim of one hundred feet in length up and down the gulch, which shall extend crossways of said gulch from rimrock to rimrock; after said claim has been staked with stakes at least five inches in diameter and three feet high, set firmly in the ground in such a manner as to be in plain view, with the name of the locator written thereon, said locator shall, within three days, record the same;

Third, every person who has so located and recorded a claim in California Gulch shall, within ten days after the same has been recorded, commence work thereon, in person or by agent, and shall show his good faith by the development of same;

Fourth, every person who shall engage in mining in California Gulch shall, in addition to one claim to which he shall be entitled by location, also hold one other claim acquired by purchase, but no more;

Fifth, any claim in this gulch that has been abandoned for a period of thirty days, upon which no work has been done for the period stated, shall be open for relocation;

Sixth, the recorder of this district shall hold his office for the period of one year, or until his successor has been elected and assumes the duty of the office; if the recorder shall resign said office, he must notify the chairman of this meeting in writing of such resignation;

Seventh, said recorder shall be entitled to charge a fee of one dollar for recording each and every claim and the issue of a certificate to said claimant; each certificate shall be numbered, stating upon its face the number of said claim, above or below discovery, as the case may be;

Eighth, said recorder shall keep a book and shall record each claim located in this gulch and describe same in such a manner that said claim can be identified in case of dispute; and

Ninth, these bylaws and rules shall not be altered or amended except at a general miners' meeting called for the purpose, in some central location, after ample notice has been given."

"Mr. Chairman, I object," shouted Strong.

"What is the objection?" asked Blaine.

"To these rules being considered."

"The objection is sustained," shouted the chairman.

"No, no, no!" came from every part of the assemblage.

"Mr. Chairman," continued Walter, "at the proper time, it might be in order to object to considering these rules and bylaws, should they be introduced, but up to this time, no rules have been offered to this meeting."

"You have been talking about them," called out Gore.

"That is true," said Walter, "and I shall continue to talk about them until I am through, and I do not think anyone will interfere with my arguments. I am simply exercising the same privilege that you exercised in making your speech and arguments, and if I am not permitted to have the same privilege that the plaintiff was given, Mr. Chairman, I shall appeal to this meeting, and I think they will at least vote to give me fair play."

"Yes, yes, yes, we will!" came from every part of the crowd.

"Gentlemen," Walter continued, "the bylaws of this district, which you will also find in the record book, can be found in the office or cabin of the recorder. While I have spoken of them from memory, having been present at their passage, I am sure you will find that I have given a correct version of them. There are at least seventy-five or one hundred men in this assembly who were present at the time I speak of, when this district was organized and these laws passed."

"That's so! That's so!" cried many.

"My friends, when were these bylaws repealed? Is there anything in them that disqualifies a minor, as I am styled, from holding and working a claim in this district? The bylaws distinctly say, 'Every person who shall be a resident of this gulch shall be entitled to locate and hold one claim. . . .' Has this rule changed? If so, when? Is not this the law duly enacted by the miners of this gulch?

"Now, gentlemen, the plaintiff in this action is the only man I know who has violated the existing bylaws of this gulch. He is only entitled to one claim by location and one by purchase. Instead, he has located one claim and has jumped another. Is that lawful and in conformity with your bylaws?

"Suppose a great lot of strangers should come to this gulch tonight, and tomorrow, jump your claims, and you found you had to prove that you owned and occupied and had located your claim. Where would you go, and how would you establish your rights? Why, by the books and records and in no other way, and yet you have taken claims away from men because they were not on the ground when they were located. Hence, you have permitted rightful owners to be robbed of their property, and you have permitted these men to override the law of your district without protest. Is it not time to halt? As I told you at the start, there is a principle involved here that must not be violated."

"Who," asked Blaine, "gave those men the right to make them laws for this district?"

"Sir," replied Walter, "that is a God-given right, recognized by all the people of this great republic, to whom we acknowledge allegiance whenever and wherever it is necessary. When it becomes important—in order to protect mutual interests—to bond together and enact rules, local laws for the government of small, isolated communities, it is done, and such acts are recognized. This, sir, is local self-government, to which a freeborn people are justly entitled and should never surrender as long as a spark of life or a honest drop of blood remains."

Great applause followed this announcement.

"And now," continued the boy, "I shall leave this case with you. I think I have shown you that you cannot find for the plaintiff without the most flagrant violation of every principle of law and justice and without placing in jeopardy every single claim owned, occupied, and worked by you. To so find is to annul every law, rule, and regulation that you have made for the preservation and protection of your own property interests in this district. Gentlemen, thank you for your attention. I regret having delayed you so long."

When the boy had ceased speaking, a strong man seized him from the stump and bore him on his shoulders back and forth through the throng, notwithstanding Walter's earnest protest. And finally, when the vote was taken, it was practically unanimous in the lad's favor. Not even Malcolm or his friends made any pretense at voting. Instead they hastily left the ground.

A good deal of bad blood had been stirred up by the controversy. The young man had made such a good showing that his friends were loud in their praise of him, while, of course, the friends of the jumpers were correspondingly surly. The effect of the trial, however, was to consolidate and determine a large majority of the substantial and foremost miners to stand by and uphold the bylaws which they had in the early days wisely enacted.

On the way home from the trial, Peter Stanford and Logan had some hot words, and they separated with the determination on the part of each that should they meet under favorable circumstances, they would have it out. Each seemed to understand that the other meant to stand his ground, and matters stood in this way for some time.

One evening, Strong, Malcolm, and Logan had been down to the saloon and had indulged to some extent in spirits and were returning home, when they met Peter Stanford. "Good evening," said Peter in a friendly manner.

"Good evening," replied Malcolm. Strong and Logan said nothing.

Peter was of a jovial and kindly disposition, and if he had to have trouble, he wanted it over and done with. So he said to Logan, "How are you? Are you well?"

"I want nothing to do with you," said Logan.

"Nor I," put in Strong.

"All right," said Peter. "If that is the way you feel, it suits me, and there will be no harm done."

"I think," answered Logan, "that you are a scrub."

"And," added Strong, "I can lick you any mark in the road."

"All right," replied Peter, seeing that it would be impossible to avoid trouble, "you will never have a better time to do it than right here. One at a time, gentlemen, is all that I ask."

"I think I am enough for you," growled Strong, attacking.

Just at this moment, Walter happened to be coming down through the timber with his gun on his shoulders, having been out hunting. He saw the beginning of the fight. The men had stepped down just below the trail to a smooth piece of ground and were hammering away at each other in good earnest. They were both strong, large men, and the encounter was a vicious one. Strong was the larger of the two and seemed to understand the game pretty well. He hit Peter twice on the forehead and once on the cheek. This seemed to stir up the good-natured Peter's blood, and he went at Strong in good shape.

Presently Peter struck Strong full in the nose. The blood flew, and the big fellow staggered and came near going to earth. Peter followed up his advantage and got in a stunner just under Strong's left eye. Before Strong could recover, Peter landed another terrible blow on the right eye. This also brought the blood. Strong staggered, and Peter followed with another on the chin, which brought Strong sprawling to earth.

By this time, Strong was furious and was using ugly language. Peter stepped back and remarked as he did so, "I make it a rule never to strike a man when he is down." Strong got up, rushed at Peter blindly, striking at him with all his strength. Peter stepped back and dealt Strong a blow at the butt of the ear, which knocked him completely off his feet.

Walter had reached a position but a few feet from the combatants and stood leaning against a tree, watching the progress of the battle. No one had noticed his presence. Strong rose to his feet, more furious than ever. He charged the good-natured Peter, who was now smiling at his furious foe. For some time, the men faced each other, sparring as if for an opening. Strong was on the uphill side. He had, by this time, learned to be a little more cautious and to act with greater deliberation. Watching his chance, he struck Peter a blow full in the face. This staggered Peter and, for a moment, threw him off his guard. Strong struck him another heavy blow, which brought him to the ground. Strong threw himself on the prostrate man and began to beat him in the face, saying as he did so, "I have you now."

With a great effort, Peter turned to his antagonist and said, "So, my man, that is the way you return my generosity, is it? I will just give you some of your own medicine." He proceeded to give Strong a terrible beating.

In the meantime, Logan had been acting as though he wanted to interfere, and now, seeing that his friend was powerless and must soon give up the fight, he drew his revolver and rushed to strike Peter in the head. But before Logan could carry out his purpose, he was knocked senseless by a heavy blow dealt by Walter, who had bounded to the scene of action like a panther. He struck Logan in the side of the head with the muzzle of his gun, and the latter fell as one dead. He had no sooner felled Logan than he had to take Malcolm, who had sprung to his feet with drawn pistol. The lad faced him with both barrels of his gun ready to fire, and he said in a low calm tone, "Drop that pistol, Mr. Malcolm." Malcolm hesitated but a moment, having met the flashing eyes of the boy. His pistol dropped from his hand, and he stood unarmed. "Step back, please," said the boy. The lad went forward and took up the pistol, also taking that of Logan.

Peter was so exasperated at his unfair antagonist that he would not let him up but continued to punish him in a most unmerciful manner. When Strong finally called out, "Enough," Peter let him up. Strong's face was a sight to behold. Both eyes were closed. But all hands now turned their attention to Logan, who had not yet moved. At first, they thought he was dead, but soon they detected signs of life. Malcolm and Peter removed him to the closest cabin, where he shortly came to his senses. Peter had his own face to wash, and he helped Strong wash and grease his bruised face. Both Strong and Malcolm were disposed to be ugly, but Peter stepped forward and said, "Look here, gentlemen, if you haven't got enough, say so, and I am ready for both of you. But if you don't want to finish this encounter here and now, just shut up and at another time I will try and entertain you. But, before you go, I want to say that you are the most cowardly lot I have ever met with."

By this time, Logan could walk and the three left. After they had gone, Peter took hold of the boy and hugged him. "My boy," said he, "you saved my life. I know those fellows intended to murder me. In fact, I thought so at the start, but I would not turn my back on them. They were all armed."

"That puts me in mind," said the boy. "I have their pistols. They have no right to carry pistols. Men who have no more honor than to assault a man when he is down are not entitled to proper consideration."

"Now," said Peter, "I look for more trouble. This will not end here. These fellows always go in twos and threes, but I'll take my chances anyway. You will not catch me away from home again unarmed. Depend on that." So saying, he walked on home.

Work in the gulch was being pursued vigorously. A good many had gone to bedrock without finding pay. Many others had encountered a thick body of cement gravel and could not go through it, consequently having to abandon their claims. There was some prospecting going on at St. Clair Flat, but very little had been found. News of rich strikes elsewhere reached the gulch, and many were leaving for new fields.

About this time, reports came from the San Juan country, and a great exodus took place from California Gulch. Among those to leave was Peter Stanford. He made a lucky sale of his claim and went away very suddenly with Grey and Stoddard. Not a day passed that some did not leave the gulch, bound for the heralded San Juan mines, the fame of which spread like wildfire through every gulch and valley in the mountains. Walter finally began to get the fever, also. Most of his friends had gone. Scarcely an acquaintance remained. He had all the time had faith in his claim and had worked very hard to get it open so he could commence mining, but after reaching bedrock without receiving the expected reward, he sank a new hole. In this, he struck the dreaded cement gravel and at last concluded to sell his claim.

Besides, he sadly missed the kindhearted friends who had left him alone, especially Peter Stanford. Walter felt many misgivings concerning Peter's departure, fearing that it was not all because of the sudden mining fever that had struck him. He knew that the wise Stoddard had quietly advised Peter to leave the gulch because of the Strong-Logan fight and more expected trouble, which all believed would ultimately result in Peter's death. Logan, Strong, and Malcolm had, on one or two occasions, hung around the store in hopes, it was believed, of catching Peter there alone. But after this trouble, his silent friend, the ever-watchful Grey, and the young lad always went with him, never leaving him for a moment when the enemy was near.

Now it seemed that few opportunities presented themselves to Walter to effect a satisfactory sale of his claim. At first, he left word at the store, not caring to disclose his intentions of leaving the gulch—for when it became known that men had the San Juan fever, he had noticed that buyers delayed, knowing well the effect would be to reduce prices. He found no takers, and finally, in a fit of desperation, he put up a sign, "Claim for sale." Many days passed before anyone made an inquiry. A stranger came down the gulch and asked the price of the claim. "Two thousand dollars," answered Walter.

After spending several hours prospecting the ground, the stranger said he liked the claim and would like to trade for it. He said he could not pay all cash, but he had some likely mules that he would part with. "I am camped down the gulch," the stranger said, "and I'll just move up tomorrow and camp here. If we can't trade, I will look above." In the morning, the man came up and pitched his tent near Walter's cabin. Said he, "Here is a good pair of mules. They are good travelers, weigh about fourteen hundred pounds, are five-years-old, and are true as steel. You can't find a better team anywhere." His leaders were a good pair of horses. "Those horses I can't spare. I want something to get out of the country with if I can't make the claim pay." He also had a fine saddle horse, about ten hundred weight, strong and stout, which he said would either ride or pack. "Now, young man," he said, "tell me the best you will do on a trade for that claim."

After some study, the boy said, "You can pay me one thousand cash, and I will take the horses, the mules, the saddle horse, and the wagon, and we can call it a trade."

The stranger said, "I will look around a little more." Taking a pick, shovel, and pan, he went up and commenced prospecting again. Towards evening, he came down with a good showing in the pan and a nugget which the boy thought would weigh at least an ounce. Handing the nugget to Walter, the stranger said, "I reckon that is yours."

"No," replied the lad, "what you pan from this claim you can have. I most likely would never have found it." Walter had prepared supper, and it was now about mealtime. Just as the man came back from prospecting, a young man rode up on a fine black horse and the elder gentleman introduced the newcomer as his son. Walter then asked the two to join him at supper.

On coming into the cabin, the elder man introduced himself. "My name is Pierce, John J. Pierce. I am from Texas. Me and my boy John here came out to try our luck in this new country, and he likes it here and so do I. I would like to have this claim if we can trade, but I think your price is more than I can pay. I feel as if the claim is worth all you ask for it, but you see I ain't got so much money. I have got four hundred dollars in gold, and that's all I have got besides the three horses and two mules, their gear, and the wagon. We ain't got much grub."

"What do you hold your mules at?" asked Walter.

"Well, I paid five hundred for the mules. I consider them worth six hundred with their gear. The wagon is worth one hundred and fifty dollars."

"And the saddle horse? What do you hold him at?"

"He's worth two hundred and fifty dollars. I did not think I would part with him, but I will put him at two hundred if you want him."

"And the black horse?" asked the lad.

"He belongs to my boy here," Pierce replied, "and I can't trade him off."

"You can, Father," the son chipped in. "I will, of course, be interested in the claim. And if we can't make it pay, you can give me another colt sometime."

"All right, then, you can have the black horse too, young man," said the Texan. "But I can't spare the gray horses. I am going to keep them to go out of the country with."

"Well, Mr. Pierce," said Walter, "I want to sell the claim, and I will make you an offer. Then I will leave it to you as to whether it is a trade or not. I will take the mules and wagon at your price, seven hundred and fifty dollars; the brown saddle horse at two hundred; and the black horse at the same price. You may pay me three hundred dollars in money. That will make fourteen hundred and fifty dollars, leaving five hundred and fifty dollars due. This you can pay me on bedrock or when you dig it out of the claim."

"But," said Mr. Pierce, "I told you I had four hundred dollars that I would pay you."

"I know you did, Mr. Pierce," replied the boy, "but I will not take all your money. You said four hundred was all you had. You have got to open up your claim, and you may not take out the money as fast as you need it to live on. You will have to pay cash for what you get here, so if you don't take out the balance you owe me for the claim, you need not pay it. If you take it out, pay me."

"John," asked the elder Pierce, addressing his son, "what do you say?"

"I say trade," answered the younger Pierce.

"Very well. We'll call it a trade."

Nothing now remained but to give a bill of sale for the claim, witnessed by a neighbor. When Walter had packed up his effects and was ready to leave the gulch, the Pierces came out to his wagon leading their dog, Lion.

"My young friend," said the elder Pierce, "you have been mighty square with us, and we are well pleased with our trade and with you. We would like to make you a present of this dog. He will be worth his weight in gold to you if you ever go into the Indian country and do any hunting. He will smell an Indian a mile and follow his track forever. He was learned to trail rogues with his mother, the greatest dog for hunting in Texas. If you just let him smell of anything the party ever wore, he will pick out his track among a thousand. We hate to part with him, but he is all we have to give you that we can spare. Will you take him?"

"Yes, sir, I will," said the boy, "and glad to have him for company. Will he stay in camp alone?"

"Yes," said Pierce, "Lion will stay with your horse or stay anywhere you put him. He is a true friend, and you will never regret taking him."

Lion was a large and strong creature. His hair was a dull gray and stiff and coarse like the hair of a Scotch staghound. "He is not full blooded," Mr. Pierce said. "The sire was a large Scotch staghound, and the mother a Scotch terrier and bloodhound mixed. Lion has the nose of a bloodhound, the speed of a staghound, and the courage and grit of the terrier."

"I thank you very much, sir," Walter said, and he started his team forward.

"Hello," cried Pierce, "where will I leave the five hundred and fifty dollars? You forgot to tell me."

"You may leave it with Captain Scudder of Denver, if you will," said Walter, and the team moved forward again. Lion lay in the wagon and seemed contented with his new master, who was very kind to him.

Taking the main Denver road, Walter reached Denver in due time, to find everything in a great commotion. The excitement about the San Juan mines was intense. Fabulous stories were told of the richness of the find, and many were making extensive preparations to go there. Walter, ever ready for a new adventure, was ready to join the San Juan stampeders. He sold his mules and wagon and such of his outfit as he could get along without, only retaining such articles as were absolutely necessary for comfort on an expedition where the only means of transportation was packhorses and mules. Walter kept his fine iron-gray thoroughbred saddle horse, his black Texas horse, and his small pack mule—the latter a perfect pet. He arranged his pack equipment for the mule and black horse, and he rode the gray.

Before leaving Denver, Walter called at Jones & Cartwright's store to learn whether or not the letters he had left the spring previous had been called for by young Hudson. He was informed that they had not been called for and was told that no word had come to them from the young man in New Mexico. "Well," said Walter, "I am going down into that country, and I will try and find him and deliver the letters."

While at Wallingford & Murphy's store, procuring his outfit for the southern trip, Walter met Mr. Sowers, who introduced him to Captain McKee,

Into the West

who was the leader of the expedition then assembling at the head of Cherry Creek. Sowers had told McKee that the young man had been with their big Texas herd the year before and was a good all-around cowboy, and the captain told Walter that he would soon be at the general camp himself and would be glad to meet him there.

Sowers was a medium-sized, quick-moving, positive man, with short red hair, stubby whiskers, and keen black eyes, about forty-five years old and an important dealer in cattle principally from Texas. Captain McKee was a taller man, about five feet eleven, with blue eyes and dark hair reaching in ringlets well down on his shoulders. All in all, he was a fine-looking man accustomed to lead and command. Walter thanked him, saying that he would join the McKee party as soon as he could get his outfit together and then decide whether he would continue in their company or proceed on his own hook.

As Walter approached the Sowers & McKee camp on Cherry Creek, several of the camp dogs rushed out noisily and attacked Lion in a savage manner, two springing for his throat and the others at his hindquarters. Hearing the snarling of the dogs, Walter turned in his saddle. His big dog seemed loathe to engage in a battle, and the lad spoke to some men standing nearby, "Gentlemen, won't you call off your dogs?"

"Our dogs seem to be doing pretty well. You take care of your own dog. If he can't defend himself, he's no business in this camp," said a rough-looking man who seemed to be egging on his dog.

"Very well, sir," replied Walter. "Lion, at them. And take care of yourself." His dog, who up to this time had bounded first one way and then the other to avoid punishment, now changed his tactics. He not only stood his ground, but charged with the swiftness of lightning the whole pack. In less than two minutes, three of the cowardly brutes went howling and limping away, leaving a big half-bulldog to eat up the stranger. For a few seconds, it was an ugly fight. The bulldog got a hold on Lion's neck, but the big dog soon tore him loose and seized the bulldog by the throat and shook him as easy as if he had been a woodchuck. The bulldog's owner, who had given Walter the insulting answer, jerked his revolver from his saddle holster, rushed to the struggling animals, kicked viciously at Lion, and tried to get a shot at him. But the dogs were in such motion that he could not get the opportunity he sought. Seeing that his dog was in imminent danger, the boy sprang from his saddle, bounded forward, and pushed back the big man. He said in a calm tone, "Don't injure that dog, sir."

The man was furious. Holding up his cocked revolver, he kept moving around to get a shot at the boy's dog. Presently he fired. Like a flash, the boy's pistol flew from its holster, and leaping over the struggling dogs, Walter struck the big bully a blow on the head that felled him to the ground. He now saw that the bulldog was nearly done for. With cocked pistol in hand, he patted Lion, saying sharply, "Let go the dog." The big dog dropped the yelping bulldog and sat up panting by his master.

The owner of the bulldog was just struggling to his feet, the blood streaming from his face, swearing vengeance. His pistol had slipped from his grasp when he fell. At this instant, Captain McKee came running up. He stepped to the side of the big bully. "Grant, what do you mean? This is disgraceful." And to the newcomer, he said, "Take off your dog."

"I have already done so, sir," said the young man. "I regret, sir," continued Walter, "having been the cause of this disturbance, but I could not control these brutes, and I think the world of my dog. I could not do less than defend him."

"You owe no apology here," said McKee. "I saw it all. You were in no way to blame. I admire you, sir, for your brave defense of your dog. Walk up to my camp."

"I was on my way to see you," replied the boy.

The captain turned aside and said a few words to the man he had called Grant. Grant turned sullenly toward his own tent, together with his mangled bulldog.

On reaching Captain McKee's tent, Walter said, "I met you in Denver the other day in company with Mr. Sowers, and you said you were going on a prospecting expedition into the San Juan country. If agreeable, I would like to join your party."

"Are you alone?" asked the captain.

"Yes, sir, I am quite alone. My dog and horses are all the company I have."

"Well," replied the captain, "we are going into a dangerous country, full of Indians, and I want only the best of men. We do not care to encumber ourselves with anyone who is not fully able and willing to take his fair share of any and all responsibility. You look very young. What experience have you had?"

"I have not had much experience," said Walter. "I have crossed the plains and have had such experiences as come to one as a herdsman and prospector. I spent last winter with Mr. Bridger and Mr. LeBassett on Green River, and I have spent the summer in California Gulch. While I feel amply able to take care of myself, I do not intend to crowd myself on anyone."

"When did you cross the plains?"

"One year ago, sir."

"Have you been in the mountains all the time?"

"Most of the time, yes. And as I told you, I was with Mr. Bridger and Mr. LeBassett last winter."

"Do you mean Jim Bridger and Joe LeBassett?"

"Yes, sir."

"Why," said the captain, "those are two of the most famous trappers and scouts in the mountain country. A man or even a boy cannot stay with those fellows without learning something. What state are you from?"

"I was born in New York and raised in Michigan," Walter replied. His stock fell some here, as the captain was a Texan and a strong pro-slavery man, as well as a rabid secessionist.

Late that evening, the captain came over to the young man's camp and told him his hunters were going out in the morning and, if he liked, he might go along. "We are out of meat and need some badly. Your gear will be all right here, and I will have the boys look after your pack horses."

"Oh, I will take them along," said the boy.

As the sun came up the next morning, Walter rode out of camp, followed by his dog, pack horse, and mule. The hunters were not yet up. Walter took a southerly direction, and before night, he returned with three antelope on his pack mule. The other hunters returned late, empty-handed.

While loitering around camp that night, various ones got to shooting at a mark. Sowers, Captain McKee's business partner who had just arrived, said to Walter, "There is a mark for you," and he pointed to a buzzard circling over the camp. The boy brought his rifle to his face and fired. The bird fluttered, turned over, and dropped to the ground. Later that evening, the captain told the boy that he could join the party, and if he would do some hunting, he would be relieved of guard duty.

While watering his horses that night, Walter met his old friend, Mr. Collins. The old man explained that he had gotten the San Juan fever, had made an outfit in company with an old friend, and was going to the San Juan mines in hopes of making his fortune. "Now," said Collins, "you come over and make your camp with us. Mr. Coats does the cooking, I do the other work, and you can do the hunting if you like."

"I shall be glad to camp with you," said the boy. "I am somewhat lonesome."

"Was that you who had trouble with Grant the other night?" asked Collins.

"Yes, it seems to be my luck to be always getting into trouble."

"Grant acted outrageously," said the old man. "He is the one troublesome character in the whole camp. The captain handles him, however, and I hear he must keep his dogs away from others or shoot them. I guess they won't tackle that big fellow of yours again."

"No," replied Walter, "they are all badly used up."

It was now the tenth of September. Grass was good, and the animals were fat and doing well, and all hands were anxious to be moving. On the morning of the eleventh, they broke camp and all hands pushed out for the San Juan country. Barring a few accidents, such as rolling packs and bucking mustangs that had to be rebroken every few days, all passed off very well, and the party reached Young's ranch on the Fountaine River about 4 o'clock in the afternoon and camped for the night.

The next morning, Walter rode up to the captain and said, "I believe you told me that you would lay over at Pueblo at least a day. As I told you yesterday, I wished to go to Bent's Fort in hopes of meeting Mr. Bridger and Mr. LeBassett, as I have some unsettled business with them. I will overtake you somewhere on the road."

The captain had no objection to this arrangement, and so Walter pushed on to the fort. On his arrival, he found that Bridger had not been there, but that LeBassett had been there three weeks but had gone away about a week before. He found a letter from Bridger which read: "My dear boy, after we parted with you at Laramie, we pushed on to Westport and had a very good trip. We didn't find any acquaintances at Westport, and so took a run down to St. Louis. It was lively there. We sold our furs for six thousand, two hundred, and ninety dollars. After paying all expenses, your share is two thousand and twenty dollars and fifty cents. This we left with Colonel Hudson, who was glad to hear from you. We enclose his letter to you. I will not go to Bent's now. I am going out on an expedition for the government to the Yellowstone country, which will take me all summer. Joe will go to Bent's, and I hope will see you. You can write to me at Laramie or at Westport, as I directed. I hope you are well. If you get tired of the mines, come to me, my boy. I shall always be glad to have you." Signed—James Bridger.

LeBassett had left this letter, saying simply for himself that he was sorry not to see him and that he hoped one day to find his young friend again.

Returning to Pueblo and going on to the Huerfano, Walter waited for the McKee party, which had traveled by slow stages down the Fountaine, consuming ten days in reaching the Huerfano. The manner in which the McKee outfit was traveling, with delays and other unpleasant occurrences that were constantly coming up, determined Walter and his friends Collins and Coats to leave the party and travel by themselves.

BOOK THREE

The first night on its own, the Collins party was joined by three others, who had asked permission to travel and camp with them, for a time at least. These men were from the North—one from Massachusetts, one from New York, and the other from Maine. They had a good outfit, but had not much experience in the Indian country. The party stopped on the Huerfano for three days, as the weather was rainy and disagreeable. Walter found plenty of game for the party of six. The newcomers were agreeable men and were willing to do anything to help along.

On the fourth day, they started for Fort Garland, camping that night near the summit of the Sangre De Cristo Pass. The trail followed the tributaries of the Huerfano to a point well up towards the summit. The trip was a delightful one. The scenery was outstanding, and occasionally they got a fine view of the valley of the Huerfano and the Arkansas. Passing over the summit, the trail followed down the Sangre De Cristo. Fort Garland was located about fifty miles from Sangre De Cristo Pass in the San Luis Valley, through which flows the Rio Grande Del Norte. There was a settler at Fort Garland who sold the necessaries at extravagantly high prices, but few Americans were there, most of the population being Mexican, with a few Indians.

They passed five days at the fort because the horses belonging to the three newest members of the party had strayed or been stolen. Walter found them at the head of San Luis Park after they had been given up by their owners as lost for good. The joy of the three men knew no bounds. They felt under great obligation to the young man for the service he had rendered them. He had ridden almost constantly for five days before he found their animals.

They then continued their journey to Conejos, where they laid over a day. At Pinos, the three newcomers were again unfortunate and once more lost their horses. The party was delayed three days on that account. Again, Walter found them. His fine horses were wonderfully adapted to covering a large scope of country in an incredibly short space of time. Ordinarily, a pony would soon wear out and the rider be compelled to go on foot.

The travelers now began to meet prospectors returning from the San Juan diggings, with the report that no gold had been found and that the whole story of finding gold was a hoax. Still, they felt, after such a long journey, they could not turn back until they had investigated for themselves.

Turning west to the San Juan River, they soon found themselves in the neighborhood of the place where it had been reported that rich gold diggings had been discovered the fall before. They spent two weeks in this wild region without finding the expected gold prospect. This country had been alive with people from every part of the Union, but they were all leaving. People were stampeding away as fast or faster than they had stampeded into the district.

It was now October, and the Collins party was still together. They decided to turn south along the base of the mountains and go at least as far as the old Mexican town of Taos. They had heard rumors from this direction that very rich diggings had been found at Piño Alto and other places in New Mexico.

One evening, just after dusk, a stranger came into camp leading a lame horse. He asked if he could stay all night. They gave him his supper, and he joined the group, proving to be a most intelligent and interesting person. In the morning, he stated that he would like to leave his horse and get a fresh one, as he had important business in Pueblo. As the Collins party was to lay over for a couple of days, Walter loaned the gentleman his black horse. Upon the stranger's return, on the evening of the third day, he again passed the night with them. He seemed to appreciate their hospitality very much. From him, they got much information, and in the course of the evening, he recounted episodes in his life in New Mexico and some of his experiences among the Indians. He said he had lived many years in the country and apparently had a very wide acquaintance. When they brought their stock into camp for the night, the stranger looked over the animals carefully and took particular notice of the fine saddle horse of the young hunter. He at once proposed to purchase him, and on being told that the gray was not for sale, he expressed surprise at seeing an animal of such value among prospectors. At last he asked where Walter had got the horse. The boy told him he got the gray at Council Grove. The stranger eyed the lad closely, saying that he was acquainted in that country and was not aware that such an animal could be had there. While the boy was absent from the group, the stranger asked Collins if he knew where the horse came from. "That is a thoroughbred of too much value to be so used," he said. Collins told him the boy had won the horse as a prize at a great race. The stranger expressed much surprise, and when the boy returned, the stranger said, "Your friends tell me you won this horse at Council Grove in the great race a couple of years ago."

"Yes," replied the boy, "that is the way I got him."

"I am surprised that you have kept him so long," answered the stranger. "I have heard much about that race. I knew some of the runners, and we have always considered them invincible. I am pleased to meet you, for I feel that I already know you. Colonel St. Vrain told me of that race, and Godfrey, too. My name," said the stranger, "is Carson."

The boy gave the stranger a surprised look and asked timidly, "Are you Mr. Kit Carson, sir?" On being assured that he was, they immediately became fast friends.

Walter told the great scout of his experiences with Jim Bridger, in which Carson was most interested. He said Bridger was, in his opinion, the greatest of all mountain men. "He can," said the scout, "read the redskin like a book and is seldom, if ever, deceived. I have been with Bridger on many occasions and have found him equal to any emergency."

"Why, he says the same thing of you," answered the boy.

Walter was fascinated with the great scout, who was a man of unprepossessing appearance. He was heavyset, about five feet eight inches in height and somewhat bowlegged. His manner of conversation was mild and gentle with a voice as soft and smooth as that of a woman. His eyes were brown, his hair dark and worn at medium length. His chin was heavyset, denoting great firmness and determination. His face and features were quite dark and bronzed from long exposure. His dress was plain and his whole appearance entirely opposite from what one would naturally expect in a man so widely known as one of the most famous mountain men and so celebrated as a trapper and hunter. The mountains, plains, and deserts were as familiar to him as the well-beaten trails and roads of commerce are to others.

In the morning, it was arranged for Carson to ride one of Walter's horses as far as his home at Taos, leaving his lame animal to come along at a more leisurely pace with the pack animals. Up to this time, the party had not definitely decided on its destination. Some were in favor of going one place, and some another, but they now agreed to continue together as far as Taos and there decide on their future course.

About the tenth of October, the party reached the ancient town of Fernandez De Taos. The town was situated in a broad, beautiful valley at the junction of the Rio Taos and Pueblo Creek, north from Santa Fe some eighty miles. Its population was variously estimated at from eight hundred to fifteen hundred, mostly of Indian and Mexican origin. The valley was practically a continuation of the beautiful San Luis Valley, and scattered up and down the valley were several pueblos and ranchos. The valley surrounding Taos was wonderfully fertile, and although the altitude was somewhat high, all kinds of vegetables grew in abundance.

A curious state of affairs existed among these usually hospitable people. At a horse ranch, you could find cow's milk, butter, and beef. At a cattle ranch, if you got milk, it would be goat's milk; if butter and cheese could be had, they would be made from the milk of the goat; and the flesh of the same animal would be served instead of beef.

All habitations were constructed of adobe or sun-dried brick and were usually kept by the housewife in a neat, comfortable manner. The inside walls were clean, the surface being rubbed smooth with stones and the imperfect places filled with clay mortar. The smooth surface was then washed with a solution of fine thin clay mortar about the thickness of good white-wash. The whitish or yellowish-gray clay was put on the walls with a brush made of wild broomcorn.

The people enjoyed frequent social gatherings where they danced and sang. These gatherings were called "fandangos." The Collins party attended several of these dances by invitation and enjoyed them until, on one occasion, three very rough characters made their appearance in a drunken condition. Upon their arrival, some of the best families left the place before refreshments were served. The Collins party had no intimation that trouble was expected, except that they had begun to learn that congregated about Taos were a good many American adventurers of the roughest character, mostly men from Texas. Among these, some really desperate characters—

horse thieves, murderers, in fact, every class of ruffian—were represented. These men cheated the Mexicans badly, and frequent murders occurred. Of law and order, there was none. The brutal acts of these reckless men tended to cause much ill-feeling among the Mexican population against Americans generally.

The Collins party now got together and arranged to go home, but some of the Mexicans, fearing trouble, urged them to stay, as they were sober and could most likely be of some assistance. Several wrangles were started and settled, but finally one of the gamblers struck a Mexican while the dance was in progress. The insult was quickly resented, the Mexican being mortified because he had been struck in the presence of a lady. A general row was thus precipitated, and three Mexicans were shot. Walter, Collins, and their friends assisted in overpowering the ruffians and taking them to a place of confinement. This was simply a sample of what was of frequent occurrence.

Kit Carson had taken a great fancy to Walter and tried hard to persuade him to stay with him. The two were constantly together, and Walter remained the guest of this noted man during his entire stay at Taos. Carson was married, his wife being a Spanish lady of fine appearance and a most excellent cook and housekeeper.

Before Walter left Taos, Carson took him aside and said, "My son, you are going into a dangerous country. You never know how near danger lurks. You may have companions who laugh at the idea of danger. Do not let such men know you are off your guard. Never cease your watchfulness. Take this advice from a man whose lifelong habit has been constant watchfulness. Had I failed to pursue this course, I would not have been here now to advise you. I feel an interest in you, and I have no doubt that Bridger has given you similar lectures."

"He has," answered the boy, "and I shall never forget your kind advice or fail to act on it."

While en route down the valley, the Collins party stopped each night at some Mexican farm or ranch and were always welcomed. They tried to do their part and left every household apparently pleased to have made their acquaintance. The party soon reached Santa Fe, and after several days of moderate travel, they had passed all the other settlements and were again in the wilderness. One evening, they made a comfortable camp on a fine stream. So far, they had experienced no trouble from Indians, although

Kit Carson's Farewell

they were cautioned at every house they passed and had been told upon leaving Taos that, in no case, would it be safe to risk their animals without a night guard. So far, they had not taken much precaution. Just at sundown, however, two young Mexicans rode into their camp and told them that Indians were near and that they must not take any chances, saying that five Americans had been killed but a few miles farther down. The young Mexicans urged the Collins party to turn back, saying, "You are too few. Mucho Navajo," and pointing to the hills. The party concluded to heed the warning and so brought the stock close in among the trees, tying the horses securely and putting two men on guard. Though it was not his night to stand guard, Walter insisted upon making his bed out near the horses, where he slept with his dog,

The night was quiet and mild. There were several scares, but as far as they could determine there was no real cause for alarm. The dog was restless toward morning, but it might not have been Indians that caused it. The company now consisted of ten persons instead of six; four others had joined the party at Taos by mutual agreement. Unfortunately, none of the party were experienced men of the plains. When there was danger, Walter's knowledge and caution came rather from close intercourse with experienced men than from personal experience or a thorough knowledge of Indian methods. He had stored up the information given to him by such men as Bridger, LeBassett, Carson, Godfrey, and others. He therefore advised a close, rigid organization and careful guarding. Some of the party were inclined to think the young man unduly nervous. His immediate friends knew better, telling the others that when trouble came, the lad would not be found wanting and advised the others to withhold their criticism.

It was not long before this advice was remembered by some of the brave critics. The next evening, it looked as though everything was safe and secure. They had just gotten their camp arranged when five strangers rode in and made known their determination to camp with the party. They were a hard-looking lot of men and appeared to be as tough a band of desperadoes as could be found. They made themselves comfortable, taking possession of whatever they wanted, whether it belonged to them or not. The next morning, the party got an early start and moved out before the newcomers had gotten their breakfast. The day passed quietly, and the party made camp early, as they had made a long march in hopes of outdistancing the unwelcome guests of the previous night. To their disgust and regret, the ruffians again joined their camp just as they had finished their evening meal. As they dismounted, the newcomers said they had seen Indian sign and thought it would add to the safety of the whole party to join forces and travel together. To this, Collins made objection, saying that the party was large enough and that too large a party made camp uncomfortable. The strangers pressed the matter in a rather insistent manner and seemed determined to join the party anyway. It looked as if the friends must acquiesce if they wished to avoid trouble.

The strangers had hardly joined up before a party of Indians appeared and made a dash for the horses. Six of the best horses were cut out from the herd, and four of these belonged to the newcomers. It so happened that Walter had his gray saddled and was about to go out in search of game. Four of the Indians took off across the prairie with the captured horses, while the others showered arrows on the camp. Among the stolen animals was the boy's black pack horse. Without a word, Walter spurred in pursuit and overtook the runaways. He shot down the horse of one of the Indians and pursued the others. The black horse saw the gray and heard the boy's whistle, and breaking away, he joined Walter. All the others followed him. The young man then turned them towards camp and followed, keeping the Indians back with his rifle. The men came out to meet him, and not only were the horses saved, but one Indian horse broke away and joined the party's herd. Walter's bravery was applauded by all, and especially did the newcomers compliment the boy for his clever dash. He took his honors with much modesty.

This fracas made the party forget, for the moment, about the newcomers, who were considered by all to be undesirable company. And indeed they were boisterous, profane, and dirty, assuming a familiarity repugnant to all. They helped themselves to anything they wanted without a word of apology or even a thank-you. They were soon in bad odor with the whole party, and how to get rid of them was a question that stumped everyone.

After two days of comparative quiet, a guard of three, well-armed men drove out the horses. A band of Indians again made a dash for the horses, this time from two directions, and it very nearly cost the party its entire herd. This lot of Indians had cached themselves in a small ravine and, at a favorable moment, made a quick dash for the herd. The guards became excited and missed every shot. In this emergency, Walter seized his gun, called four men to follow—telling the others to stay in camp—and by dividing the party, prevented the Indians from getting clear around the herd. Walter and his men finally succeeded in saving all the horses. A man by the name of Bill Travis, one of the new arrivals, was shot dead. His companions paid no attention to him. He would not even have been buried had it not been for the Collins party.

The situation in camp was now worsening. The desperadoes were out of provisions, and they deliberately came into the mess and took the best of everything. Several days, however, passed without incident until, early one morning, they heard firing on the creek below where they were located. There was another trail below them, and Walter said he thought someone on that trail had been attacked. After the firing ceased, they packed up and started out, traveling in a close company line. They had had so many surprises that none seemed to care to take any more chances. About 11 in the forenoon, the flankers sounded an alarm. They had seen a number of horsemen, which they concluded were Indians, some three or four miles away. Walter went out to reconnoiter. He was gone but a short time. He reported that the party was made up of either white men or Mexicans. "They have coats," he said, "and are traveling very fast and are much scattered. There are women in the party." It now seemed apparent that the two trails were gradually coming together, and it looked as if they would join together near a heavy belt of timber a few miles ahead.

As the Collins party reached the junction of the two trails, they came upon a hastily built camp. Sure enough, this party of well-born Mexicans had been attacked by Indians early in the day. Some had been wounded, and a very young girl had wandered away or been carried off by the savages. Collins spoke with the party's leader, Señor Castillo, and learned of his little girl's disappearance. Collins told Castillo that there was a young hunter with his party with whom he would confer.

Returning to his own camp, Collins explained to Walter what he had learned at the Mexicans' camp and asked him if he would go over to see them.

"Oh," said the boy, "I do not see what I can do." But he finally went over to see the gentleman called Señor Castillo, who had been slightly wounded in the encounter. "I have come over to see you," explained Walter, "at the request of my friend here, Mr. Collins."

It was indeed a sad sight. Castillo's older daughter was weeping bitterly at the loss of her sister, the family nurse was beside herself with despair, and an aged priest was praying.

"My young friend," said Señor Castillo, "we are most sadly afflicted. Only in such excitement could such a thing have happened. What to do, we do not know. Our men are reticent. I do not even know whether they could find my little daughter. I would not know what to direct them to do, and I certainly could not force them to carry out my directions."

The young girl came up to the young hunter, wringing her hands, and begged him to find her sister. The bashful lad did not know what to say. The girl—half in Spanish, half in English—cried out, "Oh, I know you will go and find my sister. I know you will go." She moaned bitterly, "My sweet little sister."

The boy paused for a moment or two, and then turning to Collins, he said, "Will you go and see if our party will lay over here tomorrow?" Walter asked Castillo if they had a pair of shoes or stockings the child had worn recently and that had not been washed. Turning to his daughter, the father told her what was wanted. She soon returned with a little pair of moccasins and a pair of stockings that could only have been worn by a very small child. Walter then asked if they were very sure that the shoes and stockings had been very recently worn and had not been washed. After consulting with the nurse, the girl informed him that there was no mistake: The child had worn both shoes and stockings the day before, and the stockings had not been washed. Walter wrapped them up tightly and placed them in the pocket of his hunting coat. He then inquired minutely concerning the exact location where Castillo's party had been camped when they were attacked.

"You cannot miss it, sir," said the old gentleman, "for you will find an old broken cart where we left it among the trees near the road."

The young girl ran to Walter and took both of his hands, saying, "You will find her, won't you?"

"Yes," stammered the bashful boy. "I must hurry." And he rushed away to his own camp.

Walter at once saddled his gray thoroughbred. He took a quantity of dry meat, a good supply of which he always had on hand for his dog. He picked up his rifle, mounted, and was off. He crossed the river and took his course

The Young Scout

down the stream. Upon his return, he gave this account of his adventure:

"When I left here, I crossed the stream and went rapidly down it to avoid any curious Indian who might be watching. I felt sure that the child had fallen into the hands of the Indians. I went down for miles, then recrossed the river and gave my horse the rein. I reached the Castillo camp just before dark. There I took out the little shoes and stockings and let Lion smell of them for a long time. Then I told him to go and find the child. He worked around in a circle and finally began to whine. I examined the spot and found many moccasin tracks. I told the dog to take the trail, which he did. It led down the river. We followed it several miles, no less than fifteen, I should judge. It was a very dark night, yet old Lion never once faltered. Presently he stopped and listened. He smelled the ground near me. I got down, picketed my horse, and tried to examine the trail for footprints, but it was too dark. I finally left my horse some distance from the trail and followed Lion. I proceeded very cautiously and moved inch by inch, Lion crawling ahead. Finally he stopped and would not move. I lay down with him and listened. There was a little wind, just enough to make sound uncertain. I felt sure that we must be very near the savages and perhaps the child, if she was yet living.

"After we had waited long and patiently, the wind shifted. I then thought I saw a human form sitting on the ground fifty feet or more in advance of where we were. I was sure we had not been seen, for we were on lower ground and against a bank. How long I lay there, I do not know, but finally Lion raised his nose. I saw what I was sure was a man rise and move away. He was gone some time, and then I heard a noise that I felt sure was a horse, as in the act of breaking away from a person or straining on a rope—the rope tightening perhaps. Presently I heard a faint snort. I then felt sure that the Indians had but one horse and that certainly there were no more than two. The night air became cool, and I was uncomfortable.

"I revolved many theories in my mind. Little puffs of wind now came up, and when the wind's noise drowned out the sounds of our movements, I forced Lion gradually ahead. It was painful to see him. He would stop, then advance. As soon as the wind died away, he stopped and would not move. I thought I heard a slight moan. I could not see Lion's ears, but I felt them. At each sound, his ears would slightly raise. I began to hope the noise I heard was the moaning of the child. I became eager to go forward, but I was admonished by Lion to have a care. Now I found the ground was rising and felt sure I was near the point from which the man had risen. Up the rise, I could see the dim outline of bushes. I was impatient to reconnoiter before the return of the man. Now a terrible fear seized me. Suppose the absent Indian had mounted his horse and made a reconnaissance. And suppose the horses should recognize each other's presence. My gray, I was sure, would never let an Indian come near him, especially in the night. If he broke loose, what would he do and where would he go? I knew Lion could trail him, yet would I dare risk the effort? How would I carry on without him?

"The wind shifted. I was sure I could smell an Indian. Lion, I was positive, could too. It was the first time that the wind had been so favorable to our purpose. I could now hear the moan and felt I was near the child. I moved when the wind blew, and Lion was a little more aggressive in his movements. He was, however, silent as the grave. I had advanced about ten feet when a sound arrested me. It was simply the snoring or heavy breathing of a man. I moved on, and a cloud moved from over the stars, and I was startled to see a foot not three feet ahead of me. I was on lower ground than the man, who was lying with his head away from me. I could feel Lion moving inch by inch, and he acted as if he wanted to seize the foot. I put my hand on his head and pressed it to the ground, and he did not again raise it. I then heard the little one moan. Just then, the sleeper moved his foot, and his breathing became heavier and now amounted to a snore.

"I began to think over the serious side of the situation and what I was confronted with. I had satisfied myself that the child was alive and sleeping not ten feet from me. I could make out a small teepee-like object ahead. What would I do, or could I do, with the sleeping Indian? Was he alone? It was unfortunate that it was too dark to tell the number of kidnappers. If the other man returned, there would be two against one. I knew that the man who had ridden away had not returned, but he soon must do so. The conviction gradually forced itself upon me that I must slay this sleeper, and that quickly. The life and safety of the child—indeed, my own life—depended upon this. Could I summon courage to do this? Strike down a human being in his sleep? The thought was most abhorrent—it was dreadful to contemplate. Then I thought of the child, of her father and her sister and her sick mother, whom they told me had been left at the family ranch. I then prayed God to give me strength to do my duty. If it was right to kill this creature, an all-wise God would aid me. If wrong, he would not permit it.

"I took my keen-edged hunting knife from my inner belt and took it in my teeth. I took out my hatchet and moved on. Now I could reach his head with my hatchet, and yet I moved on. Now I could reach his heart with my knife, and yet I did not strike. Lion was at my side. He seemed to know that a crisis was at hand and believed it to be his duty to aid his master. It was too dark to strike a sure blow. So, I moved forward, my mind filled with disquieting thoughts, and I still hesitated. Now, a flash of starlight lit up the scene. I could see the face of the sleeper. As I saw it, it seemed to me a brutal and dreadfully repulsive face. Why did I hesitate?

"I heard a movement in the little tent, then a little moan. The sleeper near me moved. I was not ready then. It was only a start on his part. He quickly settled again. The movement of the child and the brutal face seemed to steel my arm and harden my heart. For the little one's sake, I would do this thing. Making careful calculation where the heart lay, I took my knife in my left hand, my hatchet in my right. I drove the knife home. The sleeper started, and I struck him a heavy blow on the temple. He fell back with a heavy groan. I then thought I could hear footsteps. I waited long. I did not want to rouse the child and have the expected one set upon me, thus encumbered and helpless. The child might be wounded or even killed while I tried to defend her.

"Having satisfied myself that I was mistaken, I rose to my feet and moved the blanket that covered the child. The blanket had been thrown over a bush to protect the little sleeper from the night air. I stooped and picked her up, wrapped her in the blanket, and turned to go. I snapped my fingers for Lion. I was much encumbered with my gun, and the child was heavier than I had anticipated. I started on the back trail. I did not like the way Lion acted with his nose in the air. Now I felt sure that what I had feared had happened—that the Indian, after getting his horse, had taken a turn about the camp, and when in the vicinity of my horse, his horse had smelt him, and most likely, upon his close investigation, my horse had broken away, and then of course, the end could not be foreseen.

"The child slept soundly, for which I was grateful. On we went most carefully, Lion constantly sniffing the air. I wanted to go back over another trail, but I found, on reaching higher ground, that my profile would show against the sky. In other words, if my enemy was in the draw or swale on low ground and I should take the high ground, he would have a decided advantage, as he would have the sky for a background and could see me. Had I not been encumbered by the child, I would have taken a far different course. As it was, I must do the best I could. I continued up the draw. Lion began to go slowly. As I moved, I thought I heard an animal snort. I was not certain, for I was moving at the time and, of course, it might have been an antelope. They often trot around an object they can't make out and occasionally snort or whistle during the night as well as during the daytime. Lion began to go slower. Then he crouched. I knew we were near some object or enemy that he did not like. On I moved. Lion now moved faster and with more deliberation. I again heard the same sound. Lion heard it and stopped. Then he hurried on faster.

"We were now nearly opposite where I had left my horse. I felt quite sure he was not there now. I do not know why, but I felt sure he had broken away. I knew we must soon reach high ground. I remembered going in and out of short, deep draws. I now stopped and cast around, hoping to locate the exact spot where I had left the gray. I felt that I had now passed the place. If the Indian had failed to detain my horse, which I felt certain he had, he would surely be watching for my return. I sat down and listened with my ear to the ground. The gray had gone out of my hearing. If near, I would have heard him. He had a habit of striking the ground with his forefoot viciously when he was disturbed or annoyed. I felt quite sure he would not leave me unless he had had a great scare. I tried to remember some place along the trail where there was some protection from the night wind, so I might get the child into a safe place where she would not be likely to awaken during my absence, while I found my horse.

"Passing over a little ridge, I halted. I could see Lion just ahead, standing with his head looking to our left. At that instant, I heard the twang of a bowstring and the hiss and thud of an arrow. I caught a sound from Lion like a half whine, and I knew he was struck. I looked for another arrow. My foot touched a sagebrush. I saw it was large, and I dropped behind it and laid the sleeping child there, close up to the bush. I then moved with great care to Lion, ran my hand over him, and felt the blood, which he was licking. He was struck in the hip by the arrow, which had just grazed his skin. I took my ramrod and handkerchief and ran them through the wound. Lion only flinched. I then bound up the wound, watching all the time in the direction I knew the shaft had come from. I lay there fully an hour. Not a sound did I hear, nor did an object come in sight. And the child slept on.

"The suspense was most intolerable. Presently Lion wanted to raise his head, but I made him keep down. I heard a move, a stealthy cautious movement. I located it to the right of the spot where I was sure the arrow had come from. It was still very dark and I was alert. It began to lighten up, as the clouds parted. I saw directly in front of me, not twenty feet distant, a head and body rise above the grass and short sage. I could have shot him easily. He listened long. Then he lowered slightly and slowly and finally disappeared from sight. I now watched more intently and waited. I could not quite make out why the shaft was not aimed at me, as I was at that time standing—unless Lion was seen and I was not. This could hardly be. I wanted to avoid firing if possible, as I might be surrounded before morning if my whereabouts were exactly located. Yet how to be rid of the prowler was a vexing question. While he lived, I dared not leave the child, and without my horse, my ability to save the child was much weakened. I was very anxious to be moving, I could not find the gray in the dark without Lion, and he might be too stiff and sore to aid me, if allowed to lie too long inactive. And then the horse might stray too far away.

"I felt that a struggle was at hand, and I nerved myself for it. Had Lion not been wounded, I would have waited for light or the clouds to move and let Lion attack and rush upon him, in hopes that between us we could finish him without too much noise and disturbance. I feared his deadly arrows and felt again of Lion's wound. I now was sure the arrow was not poisoned, as the wound did not swell quickly. The brave dog barely flinched. He tried to lick my hand but fearing the noise would betray our position, I made him stop. Should our enemy locate a sound, his trained eye would soon ferret us out. Again I heard a movement, even closer than before. Now I was beside myself for fear the child would wake or even breathe loud and betray her location. Thus, the fatal arrow might find the little one's heart. Laying down my gun, I took out my hatchet and knife. Lion now stretched his neck forward, drawing back his lips as is his custom before attack, and I felt sure he could be depended upon to make the rush. What I now feared was the knife of the enemy. Should he kill Lion, I felt I should be absolutely helpless.

"Again the clouds shifted, and I prepared for the struggle. Placing my mouth close to the noble dog's ear, I waited until he began to tremble with impatience. The light gradually spread over the land. It was not much but enough to enable me to see any object within a radius of thirty-five feet. That is one thing I pride myself on: Nothing can surprise me if I have once surveyed the ground: The least change I can instantly detect.

"Now I saw a man sitting upright, not ten feet distant. Lion must have seen him, for he seemed to gather his forces for the spring. The man looked to the right and left, and I was sure he had not located us. The child was to my right. At this instant, she choked and made a low gurgling sound. I kept my eye riveted on the human form before me. He turned his head and listened intently. I knew he could not identify the sound as coming from a child. He had shot an arrow near that spot. He could not tell at what, although he must have thought he directed the shaft at a human enemy. After hearing the sound that had just come from the sleeping child, I am sure that I would have calculated that the arrow had gone true to the mark and inflicted a death wound. In that case, I should not have hesitated to approach the wounded or dying foe. Sure enough, he turned and moved forward to my right. I waited for the opportune moment, for now there was but one course open. We must attack and destroy him before he could reach the child. He moved on and was passing us. Now he halted, no sound coming from the child. He bent forward as if to creep on.

"I gave the signal to Lion. With a leap and a growl, he flew to the attack. I sprang forward instantly, and we were on him. He threw Lion off and aimed with his knife. I saw it was his only weapon. I rushed upon him. He threw out his left arm and caught my left leg. His right hand was raised. I saw the knife. I struck twice with my hatchet, struck his arm, and Lion came again to the attack. He was a powerful savage. He almost crushed my leg. I had my knife in my left hand and struck him in the shoulder and neck. After this, I scarcely know what happened. I only know that we were engaged in a death struggle. He held my right arm fast, and I could feel that he was trying to strike me with his knife. He cut through my pantaloons, but only once did he draw blood. Lion seized his wrist, and then he must have dropped the knife, for I did not see it afterwards, nor did I feel it. I made a strong effort to reach a vital spot in his body with my knife. He now seemed to realize that he was lost, for he gave an awful yell. Then Lion seized his throat, and he could not call out again. I feared that help might be near and made a desperate effort to relieve myself from his clutches. He now relaxed his hold on my leg, and I was free. He seized Lion by the body, but he was now at our mercy. I ended his life. The child had awakened and was crying in a low, mournful way. She was terribly frightened, and I went to her and hushed her gently. She stopped at once.

"Gathering up my weapons, I shortly left the spot. After I had composed myself somewhat, I tried to get Lion to find the gray's trail, but he did not seem able to do this. I made a complete circle around the spot where we had left him, but Lion could not locate his trail. I then thought of my whistle. Sitting down, so I could quickly put my ear to the ground, I gave the accustomed sound and waited. After some time, I heard the answer. Lion located it and went forward. The child was burdensome, and it was hard to carry her with all I had to carry. I needed my horse. I listened and heard distinctly the tramp of a horse. I sat still and the sound grew plainer. Still, on it came, and presently a horse came into view, and then another. I was now fearful that I might be mistaken, but Lion did not seem to be in the least concerned. It was the gray. He came right up to me, smelt of the child, and then of Lion. The other animal I could not catch, although it had a long rope on it. I mounted the gray, and taking the child in front of me, I turned towards the stream. It was dark again. The gray wanted to go, I thought, too far to the right, but I guess he knew better than I where to go. Finally I saw what seemed to be a belt of timber and went to it. I had struck a dry creek bed far down and concluded to wait for daylight. The child was tired and glad to sleep. It was uncomfortable on the horse.

"We rested and the gray fed on the fine grass. The other horse still evaded me. When it began to get light, I traveled rapidly up the dry creek, and just as it grew light enough to see quite plainly, I saw a number of horses about a half a mile above. Quite a breeze blew down the creek. Taking a careful survey of the place, I felt sure that the horses were being driven in. I backed the gray out of sight, and leaving him behind, I went up the bed of the dry creek as fast as I could. I climbed to the top of a high hill and looked over the country. I saw a man standing on the border of the stream I had just left. He too was looking over the country. I could go no farther, as I would then get on the bench-land and be in his plain view. Presently however, he went down the stream at a point about opposite of where I had seen the horses.

I thought there must be a large camp of Indians where he had disappeared, and I decided that it was best to move fast as I could to the bench-land. I knew they could not see me from the creek bottom. I rode rapidly for about five miles, all the time keeping a close lookout for those Indians.

"This new danger annoyed me, as I was so encumbered that I feared a long pursuit might cost me my dog and perhaps the child and my own head. Coming at last to a depression, I fed both Lion and the child some of the dried meat, and I ate some myself. To my regret, I felt that the country was not favorable to a safe journey in the direction I wanted to go, so I looked for a hiding place where I could pass the day. In the distance, I saw bushes. They seemed to be about in the direction that I thought I ought to travel, and I pushed forward to them. I found a spring, and we all refreshed ourselves. I put the horses in the bushes. The strange horse had continued to follow me, and I now caught him and put my saddle on him. He was small but quite wiry, and I decided to ride him and save the gray, so that in the case of a struggle, I could have the gray fairly fresh.

"About 2 o'clock in the afternoon, I looked over the country and saw, far in the rear, a party of horsemen. I felt sure that they were Indians. It struck me that they might be following my trail. I looked back and located the trail and saw that they were passing certain familiar landmarks. They really were on my trail, and I must move. My pursuers had to go into a ravine about three miles from where I was resting. I could then pass over the summit of the ridge and be out of sight when they again reached high ground.

"Waiting patiently until the last one disappeared, I mounted and made a start. The little horse was not inclined to let me take the child on, but he finally permitted it, and away we went at a rapid pace. My plan was to push the small horse and, when he was worn out, to turn him loose and take the gray for the home run. As near as I could calculate, I was at least thirty miles from our camp, so I gave the little horse the rein and pushed on. Fortunately, it was cool and cloudy. I must have gone ten miles before my pursuers came into view, and they must have been six or seven miles behind. I let the little horse go, and for five or six miles, he held his own. Then he began to lag. I then found that the little fellow had better bottom than I had counted on. I began to think that it might be better to save him so that, in case of an accident to the gray, I would have him as a last resort.

"Passing out of sight over a hill, I quickly changed the saddle to the gray

and led the little horse. He gave me no trouble and traveled up nicely. At
the spring we had come upon earlier, I had washed Lion's wound in the
cool waters, and he had seemed much relieved. Now he was standing the
rapid pace very well. The gray took a long, easy, sweeping lope, and when
my pursuers again came into view, it was plain that they had gained little by
my delay. They now had to go down a hill in single file, and I could see that
they had thinned out and that there were no more than a dozen in pursuit.
But these were riding hard.

"The child was very tired and quite a burden, but the little thing was
brave. She could talk a little English, I could speak some Spanish, and so we
got along pretty well. She was in mortal dread of the Indians. She said that
at first there were many of her captors—she thought twenty—but then all
went away except two, with one horse. I was convinced that our pursuers
were the others in the party that had captured her. I found it difficult to
count them, owing to the compact manner in which they traveled. I told
the child that I had seen her sister and that I had been sent by her father
and sister to find her. She was pleased. She played and chatted in Spanish,
but when she grew too tired, she would go to sleep. Thus it was very tire-
some to hold her in anything like a comfortable position. But I managed
well enough.

"I could now see that our pursuers were crowding me. They had gained
much when they again came into sight. The country over which we were
traveling was somewhat broken, and we were traveling across the breaks. I
took as direct a course as I could. Of course, the country was new to me,
and I only knew in a general way where I wanted to go. I could see far in the
distance a dark range of hills that I had passed the previous day. I knew I
must strike a stream near there, which was many miles ahead. I had no fear
for the gray. I knew his endless bottom, his endurance and matchless courage. No horse that I had ever seen—or had any knowledge of—could touch
him in a long race. Yet, on account of the child and Lion, I was anxious.

"Lion had proved of great value to me on this trip—in fact, it was he that
saved the child—and I was determined to risk much to save his noble life. It
was this that made me travel slower than I would have otherwise. A level
plain now confronted us, and I took a pace that I thought would permit me
to hold my own. I saw a dry-looking stream ahead where I hoped to find
water. I noticed that the Indians, instead of following me, bore well to the

right. This I interpreted to mean one of two things: either that they knew of water and wanted to reach it, or that the stream had cutbanks and they thought I would have to turn down in order to cross. I must now decide whether the first or the second view was the correct one. Being slightly farther to the right, I rode on faster. Presently I concluded that, as I could only see the tops of the trees, they either grew in a depression or the watercourse was very deep. Hence, I so shaped my course as to strike the creek about where I guessed the Indians were heading. I could now see that they were pushing on at about their utmost speed—not caring to be too much behind when I reached the water. I gave the gray the rein, and we forged ahead. I neared the bank. The Indians were still heading to the right of me. Striking the stream, I saw as far up as the eye could survey that its banks were very high and precipitous.

"Directly ahead of me, I saw water below. I searched the opposite bank for a place to get out, and I saw a narrow path that I felt sure the animals could climb. Just ahead of me was a game trail, but to reach it, I had to jump my horse down a perpendicular bank fully eight feet. The Indians were not now in sight. I did not hesitate a second, but jumped the gray down. He struck the soft ground, and we were soon at the water's edge. It proved to be cool and good. I let the child down on the ground and filled my canteen with the fresh, cool supply. Lion plunged into the water. My stray horse would not follow us down the trail, but sped back down the bank for fully a mile and, plunging down, came scampering up to where we were.

"I now began to fear that the trail on the other side might be impassable. But if I could get my horse up the trail, the lead I could gain would justify the effort. The gray having refreshed himself, I led him to the opposite bank and started up the path, letting the child run up ahead of me. The trail was steep, but proved to be very good and had lately been traveled by deer. At the top was a jump-off of about four feet, which the gray made without effort.

"When I reached the high plain, my pursuers were nowhere in sight. I at once divined their movements. There appeared to be a sharp bend in the watercourse. They had entered it lower down, and I thought that they might—not knowing of the pool I had just left—be aiming for some much-used crossing, where there was more water.

"I decided to keep on my original course, and I turned my horse's head in that direction, pressing ahead at a more moderate pace. The tramp horse now joined us. My pursuers did not again appear for more than an hour, and when they did, they were far to the right and fully two miles behind. I was somewhat worried for fear that I might again encounter a cutbank or dry watercourse and be delayed on that account. The one I had just left had been dangerous enough. I was fully satisfied that I had not only been fortunate, but that I had really surprised the Indians by my chance stroke. They had surely expected to entrap me or at least make a great gain.

"It now looked as though there was a long stretch before me without water or timber, and it was growing late. I let the gray go, not caring to have my pursuers too close at nightfall. During the next two hours, I encountered two quite troublesome dry watercourses. Any other horse would have given me trouble, but I did not hesitate to jump the gray down a height of even eight or ten feet, especially where the landing point was soft dirt. By following up or down these steep cutbanks, one was almost sure to find some place where the bank had caved off, leaving a sloping bank of soft dirt six to ten feet from top to bottom, and I found no difficulty in getting down such places. Getting up the other side was worse. After getting down, I usually rode up the stream rapidly until I came to a place where I could get out again.

"As I crossed the last dry watercourse, I encountered fresh horse tracks. These went up the stream, so I went down. I thought perhaps they were hunting water, there being no signs of water at the point where I crossed. Passing down a short distance, I looked over the country as carefully as I could. Leaving my horse and the child at the bottom, I climbed to the edge of the bank and looked around. I could not see my pursuers, and there was no one ahead. The party whose tracks I had seen shortly before evidently had not crossed or at least had not gotten up the bank. I decided to get out on the plain and continue my journey. Just ahead, I found a place to get out.

"Having mounted the gray, I surveyed the country. I glanced back and saw my stray horse looking down the dry run we had just left. He started forward a few steps and looked back as if frightened. Just then, Lion got up and looked back, his hair rising. I looked down the gulch and saw five Indians leading their horses over a steep portion of the route I had just traveled. They had not sighted me. I bent down and moved rapidly away from the bank and out of sight. A moment later, my stray horse followed at a trot. I took my course again and traveled at a good pace. I was more than a mile ahead when the new party came out of the dry cut. I did not think that they at first realized that I was a white man, but presently they gave chase. They seemed to ride good horses and came forward at a very brisk pace. I pushed on in hopes that night would set in and I could find some safe place to rest my tired gray. He had not even shown any signs of fatigue, although he was sweating freely. The child was limp with fatigue and moaning softly. I could see that Lion wanted the day's journey to end.

"The shadows of evening were now falling. I rode very fast for a couple of miles and came suddenly upon a flat watercourse where there grew some scrubby willows. I rode up this in hopes of finding water, which I fortunately found a short distance above. I let the horses drink freely and then pursued my course again, which was almost directly up the stream. Looking back, I saw the five Indians about a half mile distant, riding very fast. I again gave the gray the rein and rode rapidly for a full hour. It was now quite dark, and I made up my mind that I must find a place to rest. I turned square to the left and rode very rapidly for half a mile. I then took a gentle pace until I found myself in a sort of basin at the foot of a steep hill. Here I stopped, unsaddled the gray, and saddled my stray. I tied him short and pulled a lot of grass for him. I made a bed of grass for the child, and I took a little water from my canteen, bathed Lion's wound, and fixed him a smooth bed of grass. This done, I went back on my track a quarter of a mile and remained there an hour. Then I returned to my camp near the hill, and putting Lion on guard, I went to sleep. I must have slept three or four hours when I was wakened by Lion standing by me and looking intently in the direction from which we had come. The wind was blowing quite briskly from that direction. I took my gun and went again to the point where I had been watching earlier. Seeing nothing, I continued my course for a least another quarter of a mile. I was listening and thought I heard a horse making a noise with his nose, which is common when a horse is feeding.

"I then crept up farther and was sure I could see animals feeding. I wanted to make sure, and I ventured closer. I found that I was correct and that quite a number of horses were feeding. I turned back to camp, and catching the stray, I prepared to move as quickly as I could. Once on the road, I kept well to the left to avoid the Indian camp. I had started none too soon, for I had not gone more than a mile when the moon came out and lighted up the whole country. I concluded it must be between 2 and 3 o'clock in the morning. I rode as rapidly as the nature of the ground would permit. Taking my course in the direction of the dark range of hills to the northeast, I found afterwards that I had chosen the right course. At this hour in the morning, it was chilly, and owing to the necessity of moving rapidly and the rough nature of the ground, the child was shaken around considerably. She whimpered, calling for her mother, nurse, and sister.

"I was all the time fearful that I might run upon a camp of Indians. The country seemed to be perfectly alive with them. The larger party that had pursued me the previous day might have traveled late and might be lying in wait for me. Therefore, as soon as day was fairly broken and I could see well in all directions, I thought it wise to change my saddle again to the gray, as I wanted to be prepared for a desperate race.

"Lion was standing the long journey well. He made no complaint and was very watchful, using his faultless nose constantly. I always felt confidence in moving in the early morning, when the wind was favorable. I therefore took pains to travel against the wind as much as possible, even though it took me somewhat out of my course to one side or the other. I could see, far to the right, some big trees and was sure that they were the trees under which was pitched our camp. I headed for them. I calculated that they could not be more than ten miles away, so I told the little one, who continued to moan piteously, that she should soon see her sister. She laughed with delight, but her joy was of short duration as she was tired and hungry. I had no more food for her, and I did not dare stop and find any, as I felt certain that our camp would be watched and that Indians would be hovering near.

"I had not gone two miles before I rode directly into a camp where the men were just saddling their horses. I at once decided that it was safer for me to plunge through them than to be forced back out of my course. I took the desperate chance. Putting the gray to the test, I dashed past them, crossed the stream, and pushed on. They were, of course, at once after me in hot haste, but we got quite a start. I came suddenly upon two scouts.

"I had fixed a seat for the child in front of me, so the horn of my saddle would not hurt her. I had very good use of my gun. I rode directly at the two horsemen with my rifle ready for use. They tried to separate so as to pass one on each side of me, but I put a stop to that by shooting one of their horses and pursuing the other. Him I wounded with my big revolver. Then I scudded away. I now saw the others were after me, and it was a race royal from there to camp. When I got to the point of the hill up there, I thought you had moved camp. I was seriously considering the advisability of taking the back track when I spied the camp—and dashed in, as you know."

"After you left here," Collins told Walter, "we visited back and forth all the next day. On the approach of night, we all thought it best to move down here, as this was the best camp, and one camp could be more easily defended in case we were attacked.

"Señor Castillo was greatly depressed because of the loss of his little girl, and his older daughter wept all the time. The nurse prayed constantly, as did the old father, the priest. The old man is very nice indeed. He asked me all about you, and so did the young girl. Oh, she is a beauty! But her eyes look bad now with so much weeping.

"Well, we kept busy fixing our camp for defense and making a corral for the stock at night. The desperadoes behaved pretty well the first day, but the second, we had a time. One of them, Saxe, was determined to see the young lady. He talks good Spanish. She went into the lodge with her father and stayed there, and Saxe proposed to follow her. But the whole camp was up in arms, and he let her alone after that. The next day, he was determined to travel. He said we would not see you or the child again, that you were crazy to go off alone on a wild goose chase, and that you did not know where to go. In fact, everyone had a different opinion about what the outcome would be. The girl could not understand what you wanted with the little shoes, nor did anyone else.

"We did not see any Indians until this morning. The night you went away they prowled around all night. We saw their tracks the next day, and the horses were uneasy several times in the night. We did not let more than one of the desperadoes stand guard at a time. This morning, the Indians made a rush as we turned out the stock, but they did not get any. We took about half the men and stood them off. I think there were at least thirty. They finally drifted away. We thought that they would watch for your return, as most of the men thought that the Indians knew of your departure, and I guess they must—the way they tried to cut you off. It is well you got so early a start, or they would surely have cut you off and captured you both.

You were very fortunate."

Just at this moment, the desperadoes' leader, Saxe, came out and said, "Guess we had better pack up and go." Several of his men came along with him.

Walter got up and said, "Mr. Saxe, I have had no sleep for two nights, and my horse has had little rest or food. I need to lay over today. I will be ready to move in the morning. Our party seems willing to do this. Of course, we dislike delay as much as anyone else."

"I want to be traveling," said Saxe, "and I don't propose to lay here any longer, so you just get ready to move after dinner, or I will know why not."

Walter said in a cool, calm voice, "Mr. Saxe, our party says they are willing to lay over on my account. It need not delay you and your friends. You are your own masters and can, of course, travel to suit yourselves. I can only speak for myself. I shall not move today."

At this, Graham spoke up, "We have decided not to move. The boy is worn out after his hard trip, and it would not be right to move when he is in such a condition."

Saxe turned around and looked the party over in a silent, sullen way. Finally, he called to Old Tex, "Tex, do you want to travel today?"

"I don't care," answered the worthy. "I'd just as soon lay over if the others want to."

"What do you say, Hank?" asked Saxe.

"Lay over, if they want to," answered Long Hank.

"Well," said Saxe, "see that you are ready tomorrow. I'll let it go this time." So saying, he sauntered away and lay down under a tree.

Collins continued his story:

"Well, every little while, the girl would go to yonder knoll and look over the plain. Coming back, she would ask my opinion as to your prowess and ability to find her little sister. She asked me every day, 'Is he mucha hunter? Has he a good horse? Does he ride well? Has he mucha gun?' And then, she would have me tell her all about you. When I told her you had hunted with Kit Carson, she brightened up and said, 'Señor Carson mucha hunter, mucha hunter. That is very good. If Señor Carson was here, he would get sister quick.' Finally, she would break down and cry. It made me feel so bad to see her grieve so. She blames herself, but Señor Castillo does not. He pets his daughter and talks very sweetly to her. She invariably throws her arms around

his neck and kisses him. Then the tears come to the father's eyes. The old
priest is a most tenderhearted man. He prayed for you and implored the
Heavenly Father to guide and protect the brave boy on his mission of mercy.

"Last night, when the sun went down and there was no sign of your
return with the little one, this was a sad camp. I must confess, boy, that I
lost hope. There was sorrow in every heart. When morning dawned, none
had slept, save that ruffian Saxe. When you came around the point there so
unexpected, we did not see the child until you were within two hundred
feet of the camp. Heard you the shout that went up? When you went to
hand the little one to her father—and the little angel would not go until
she had thrown her arms around your neck—every eye was wet, boy, every
eye was wet."

Collins had hardly finished when Señor Castillo appeared and said that
he would be very glad to have them go over with him, as his daughter was
anxious to extend her thanks. Castillo grasped the hands of the lad and
said, "My son, my son, how can I find words to thank you for delivering my
darling child to me and to my daughter her sister? And my wife—who knew
not of our loss—I could never have told her of her bereavement; it would
have killed her. You cannot, my son, appreciate a father's agony in such a
case. To have her taken by savages to their lodges at her tender age and to be
deprived of the guiding hands of mother, father, sister, friends, the Church,
and the blessed help of the holy fathers, oh, my boy, too well we know
what that means. These relentless, cruel, vicious Apaches would contrive
for her a life of torture, slavery, drudgery, and shame. I shall never through
life forget your heroic action. You, a stranger, to so readily yield yourself to
so hazardous an enterprise."

Collins took the boy aside and said, "You are invited to sup in their
lodge. They asked me to present you as my friend. You will go, I am sure."

"Must I go?" asked Walter. "I had rather not. I don't care for thanks. It is
all over now. We must push forward and make up the time we have lost.
The men are all getting uneasy, are they not?"

"None but Saxe," replied Collins. "He has the whole camp cowed. They
all tremble when he comes near. You must look out for him, lad. He is a
bad man."

When Collins and Walter reached the lodge, they were received by Señorita
Maria Castillo. "Are you quite rested, Señor, after your long, hard ride, and

fast? My little sister tells me you did not eat, but gave her all you had."
Overcome by her feelings, Maria came forward and took the young man by
both hands, the tears running down her face. "Oh, sir, you were so brave, so
generous, so courageous to go on such a mission. Sister says there was blood
on your leg. Were you hurt? Oh, how I thank you, first for my sick mother
at home. Her heart would have been broken. And then to think it was I who
was so careless as to lose my little motherless sister. Mother would not have
forgiven me. But, Señor, it was so terrible, that fight. We were all so excited.
We expected all to be killed, and only for brave, good father, we would have
been. Oh, sir, I will do penance always for my awful neglect. I shall pray for
you every night."

Maria went on, wiping away her tears, "After you left us, we found you
were so young to go so far alone. We feared you might lose your life for us,
for our little one. We prayed, and the good father prayed. Oh, sir, how can
I thank you?"

The young man blushed, stammered, and stood speechless in the presence of the lovely girl. Finding at last his tongue, he said, "It was nothing. It
was only a pleasure to be of service."

At this moment, the old priest entered and was formally presented as
Father Francisco. He grasped Walter's proffered hand with both of his. "You
displayed gentleness," said the father, "that could not be surpassed by loving
brother or sister. Hence, kind sir, each hour, as the child's sweet memory
reveals some new tenderness that appeals to her childish heart, we are
reminded of the great debt of gratitude we owe you—to an acquaintance of
but a few moments."

✳

The night passed without incident worthy of record, and the party made
an early start. Their route led over a country of rough, broken hills. They
kept flankers out all day so that a surprise was practically impossible. Walter
was constantly out. His equipment rendered him the most suitable guard
for dangerous places. They frequently saw horse tracks, but no Indians made
their appearance during the day.

It had been decided that the Castillo party should travel with the Collins
party. Though the increased numbers made them somewhat stronger, their

responsibilities were also much greater. They now had under their protection several noncombatants, consisting of three Mexican women with their children, Castillo's two daughters, the old priest, and Castillo himself, who was wounded. The Collins party included but three fighting men of doubtful courage. Saxe was opposed to taking in the Castillo party, but he was overruled, practically unanimously. While he sullenly acquiesced, it was plain that he was far from pleased.

They made only one drive that first day and camped at a spring in the hills, which Señor Castillo said was the only water in miles. The ground around the camp was rough, with some sagebrush and low, scrubby foliage. At night, they placed a guard around the camp at each of three points, while Walter and his dog slept among the horses. The dog became restless around midnight. The boy insisted that he saw an Indian, but when he cocked his rifle, the Indian at once disappeared. About 3 in the morning, a dreadful scream was heard at the upper end of the camp, where the upper guard was posted. It was too dark to investigate then. Both of the other guards came in, nor did they again go out. There was no sleep after that. Opinions differed as to the cause of the unearthly noise. Most said it was an Indian. Some thought it was the scream of a panther. But the boy said it was the death cry of Long Hank.

As soon as it was light, they found that Long Hank had been shot in the head with an arrow and afterwards tomahawked. He had been sitting on a stone and might have been asleep when he was attacked. His scalp had been taken.

They dug a hasty grave, and Long Hank's body was as decently interred as possible. They said nothing to the women, it being thought best not to unduly alarm them. After breakfast, they moved on rapidly, traveling in the neighborhood of twenty-five miles. The trail led over favorable ground, and they encountered very few cutbank gulches. The stock, and especially the riding horses, suffered less than usual. And there was no disturbance by Indians.

The next morning, they did not make an early start. The party was out of meat, and three hunters were sent out in search of game. Walter went before sunrise up towards the mountains with a packhorse. About 10 o'clock, he returned with three large mountain goats, all very fat. The other two hunters, Charles Saxon and Tim Landor, had not returned, and two others went to meet them. These men met Tim Landor some three miles from camp. He was in a very excited condition. He said that they had gone about five miles when they were attacked by Indians. Saxon had been killed and scalped, and the Indians had pursued Landor and came near getting him. Saxon's horse had escaped from the reds and followed Landor. Upon being urged to return and point out the spot where Saxon's body lay, Landor would not go, saying it was no use—they would all be killed. The three men came back to camp, and a large party went out and found the body of the fallen hunter filled with arrows, and they buried it.

A good deal of unrest now developed in camp, and it was feared that some of the party might desert. Señor Castillo was very much worried for the safety of his family. They started out at 4 o'clock and covered about fifteen miles. They made a dry camp before dark, as it was considered unsafe for so large a party to travel at night.

It was now discovered that Saxe was trying to organize some of the men to take the best horses and push on night and day. Of late, Saxe had beaten several of the men brutally and had threatened to kill Señor Castillo and take his daughter away from him. That good man was in a constant state of alarm. The desperado had also shot at Collins and was conducting himself in a most desperate manner. He took one of young Walter's horses and saddled it, but the animal rebelled and threw him off, whereupon he drew his revolver and shot the creature dead. The boy was not present at the time, and when he returned to camp, he was terribly incensed. It was with great difficulty that he was restrained from going directly to the desperado and chastising him on the spot. All the party felt that the boy would be killed, as the scoundrel would not hesitate a moment to kill the brave boy. Someone was constantly suffering from the bruise or hurt caused by the ruffian. One evening, he had even struck the old priest and hurt him badly. All felt something dreadful was sure to happen soon.

The next day, the party had decided to camp about 2 o'clock in the afternoon at a point where Señor Castillo said there was plenty of water. He also said that the next water was more than twenty miles distant. The stock had begun to show the effects of restraint and needed rest and food. Walter had ventured out to hunt, and as the party approached the stream, they were attacked by Indians in force. Practically surrounded by mounted savages, the entire caravan was panic-stricken. There was no one to direct or lead.

Jake, who was supposed to be in charge, lost his head completely. The river bottom was thickly wooded with large trees. A high, sharp knoll stood up on one side and a steep, rocky bluff on the other, there being some three hundred yards of level bottom between the two.

The women were screaming, and the men running in every direction. The Indians charged down among them. At this moment, Walter came upon the scene. Hearing the firing, he had cut the carcass of a deer loose from his horse and rode into the camp at full speed. Checking his horse and sweeping his eye over the scene, he rose in his stirrups and calmly issued the following orders: "Graham and Dane, go quickly to yonder rock, and stay there. Saxe and Tex, come with me. Señor," he said to Castillo, "take your men and proceed quickly to yonder trees. Nuedo, aid him. Mr. Collins, you and the others follow the señor." Then, putting spurs to his horse, he galloped to the top of the rocky knoll, followed by Saxe and Tex. Springing from his horse, he turned his attention to the howling savages. By this disposition of his forces, he had complete command of the entire field, every portion of which could be covered by the rifles of the three parties.

After a few shots, the enemy scattered, leaving behind several dead. In pursuing the retreating Indians, Walter picked up a fine painted buffalo robe, an exquisite Navajo blanket, a gun, and a beautifully decorated bow with quiver and arrows. Handing these articles to Collins, Walter once more turned his horse towards the plain and rode away. After an absence of three-quarters of an hour, he returned with the fine fat buck that he had cut loose when he heard the firing.

All the men except Saxe took off their hats and lustily cheered the returning boy. Walter did not seem to realize the importance of his dashing achievement, nor, that in the minds of every man and woman, his wonderful command of men, his coolness, and his instantaneous solution of a most desperate and dangerous situation, now made him a hero.

The party gave every attention to preparing a good meal, after which they selected a strong guard and turned the animals out to graze. After Walter's gray had fed on rich grass for a couple of hours, he saddled him and rode out on the plain, saying that he thought it important to look over the country carefully before night. Before going, he advised the men in camp to cut some trees and construct a pen or corral for the stock, which would give them a better chance to defend the herd. He also suggested that a sort of breastwork be built, behind which the women would be safe from arrows and bullets. The party at once turned their attention to carrying out his suggestions.

Taking a wide circle over the plain, the young man examined the country thoroughly without seeing any signs of the enemy until he came upon an Indian, wounded in the pursuit. The boy rode up to the warrior and spoke to him in Spanish, "Hello, is my brother sick?"

The wounded man rose on his elbow and answered, "The heart of La-Ki-Ma-Ha still beats. If the young warrior of the palefaces will aim here," placing his finger over his heart, "his bullet will strike the heart of La-Ki-Ma-Ha."

"My friend," the boy answered, "the warriors of the palefaces do not strike the wounded. I see that my brother has no arrows. He can no longer fight. He is sick. Can I aid you, my brother?"

"La-Ki-Ma-Ha could drink water," replied the warrior.

The young man dismounted and handed the wounded Indian his canteen. After taking a long, deep draught, La-Ki-Ma-Ha handed back the canteen, saying, "The little chief has a good heart. Why does he give his enemy the cool water? La-Ki-Ma-Ha would have killed the paleface warrior. Why did my brother not kill La-Ki-Ma-Ha?"

"Because my brother had no arrows, and you are already wounded. Where is my brother hurt?"

The Indian turned over and exhibited a gunshot wound near the thigh, from which much blood had flowed. The lad fastened his gun on his saddle and prepared to dress the wound of the warrior. It was ugly looking, and particles of cloth from the blanket worn by the Indian had been driven into it. The Indian himself had made two little wads of sweet sage, which he had plucked from a sagebrush growing at hand, and forced them into the wound. The young man took from his pocket a silk handkerchief and got his ramrod and put it through the wound, cleaning it out. Then, taking the same handkerchief, he bound up the wounded leg and stopped the flow of blood. He also gave La-Ki-Ma-Ha some salve made from deer tallow and balm of Gilead buds to apply after the healing process had commenced. He got up and said, "I will come again and bring you meat."

Mounting his horse, the boy rode to the summit of a little swell on the plain and there saw the Indian's horse, which was lame. He caught it and returned to the wounded savage. "I have brought you your horse," he said. "He will carry my brother to the water." He helped the warrior mount the animal, and the two rode to the stream. Here the wounded man indicated that he would like to dismount. He admitted his weakness, and the lad assisted him. The Indian drank of the cool water and bathed his swollen limb. The two talked for some time, until the boy finally asked what he could do to further relieve him. The wounded man said he did not think he could ride far in his present condition, but he said if he had food for two or three days, he could then ride slowly to his camp, which he said was far down the stream.

Walter mounted his horse and rode away, extending his reconnaissance far down the stream. Seeing no Indians, he killed a deer and came back. He again stopped to see his patient. He kindled a fire and put a fine piece of fat deer meat on to roast. He now gathered a quantity of dry wood, placing it in a convenient place so that the wounded warrior could easily rekindle the fire. He left La-Ki-Ma-Ha what meat he wanted and prepared to leave, saying, "I have done all I can do for my red brother. I must go now. I hope the Great Spirit will make La-Ki-Ma-Ha well, so he can ride his horse. I will go to the camp of my paleface brothers and see La-Ki-Ma-Ha no more."

The Indian was a powerful man, fully six feet tall, with immense limbs and a body of equal proportions. He was strikingly handsome, with a keen, kindly dark eye. Slowly raising himself to a sitting posture, he shook the hand of the boy warmly and said, "La-Ki-Ma-Ha is only a warrior, but my father is greater than a chief. La-Ki-Ma-Ha saw the little chief come from his hunt and save his people. He saw him go to the high hills and tell his warriors how to fight. He killed and wounded many of my brother warriors with his two-gun (double-barreled rifle). He has a great heart and a wise dog. La-Ki-Ma-Ha saw him save the little squaw. He killed the cousin of La-Ki-Ma-Ha, who was a great warrior and very big man, strong and brave, but he fell by the hand of the little chief. I fired many arrows at the little chief, but his great medicine turned them away. He is a great warrior. Why does he not destroy me? La-Ki-Ma-Ha will soon be well and will take the warpath again. Then he may kill the little chief and take his scalp. La-Ki-Ma-Ha has been long on the warpath, but his enemies never before gave him water and food and bound up his wounds. It is sad, for La-Ki-Ma-Ha will never again meet the little chief of the great heart.

La-Ki-Ma-Ha will tell his people of the little chief."

The young hunter departed, leaving his new friend to shift for himself. At the camp, night passed without a renewal of the attack, and the next morning, the party made an early start. They covered twenty miles and pitched camp on a dry stream where the water sank, coming up to the surface at intervals, cool and free from alkali. The camp was quite comfortable, and everyone was in good spirits, with the exception of Saxe, who had been surly and overbearing for some time and especially since the last fight. This evening, he knocked Nuedo down and had some trouble with Graham. The latter was much disturbed and feared that he was going to be killed. Saxe talked in a very abusive manner to Señor Castillo, who had the grace to ignore him.

As supper was announced, the old priest was one of the first to obey the call. When he passed near Saxe, the brute struck the old man a terrible blow on the head with his pistol. The old priest came near falling in the fire. Walter was near, and whipping out his Navy revolver, he rushed upon the big ruffian with the fury of a young lion, dealing him a blow on the side of his head that would have felled an ox. The brute fell across the fire, over which the boy bounded and pulled him out by his long hair. He beat Saxe's face into a jelly before he could be restrained. "You ruffianly coward," cried Walter, "will you have no respect, even for the man of God? This brutal practice of beating the innocent men of this party must and shall end!"

Collins and Castillo finally recovered from their surprise and ran to the courageous lad, begging him to stay his hand. Walter then ceased beating the ruffian, but he disarmed him, saying, "I take your weapons, not that I fear them or you, but to prevent your abuse of any more of these good people. Lift your hand against another person of this party, and you shall die like the dog you are."

The brute staggered to his feet, and the boy followed him, kicking him at every step as he went. Tex and Nuedo came running up and remonstrated with the boy, but the lad was terribly enraged and only desisted when the cowardly brute was near his own camp. Nothing more was seen of the desperado that night. The party took the usual precautions to guard against attack, but the night passed without incident. Neither Saxe nor Tex appeared for breakfast.

As the horses were being driven in, Tex came over and said that he had been up all night with Saxe and that he was out of his head and had a high fever and was unable to travel. Tex urged that the party lay over, to which all agreed. As the day wore on, the sick man grew worse. His head was terribly swollen, and most of the time, he had a raging fever. Both Collins and the aged priest were untiring in their efforts to render the sufferer service. The party had little or no medicine, but Señor Castillo and the priest and Collins had had much experience in sickness and their advice was followed literally. Tex was most devoted to the sick man.

Collins prepared a quantity of sage tea, adding sprigs of the spruce tree, and gave it to the patient to drink. The effect was satisfactory, and the fever soon came under control. At the end of five days, the patient was still unfit for travel. The boy, in his daily scouts, had found a most excellent camp about five miles farther on, and slightly above the trail. He thought if the party was to remain longer, an effort should be made to move the sick man to the new camp, where water was much better and grass more abundant. Game was also more accessible. Their provisions were now so low that the party principally depended on wild game, and the young hunter was the only one of the party who was successful enough at supplying meat. All hands were willing to act upon Walter's judgment, and they constructed a travois for the sick man. They soon reached the new camp, and all were much pleased with the change. They made preparations for quite a stay. They built a strong corral to protect the animals at night and constructed a breastwork. They took every precaution to prevent surprise. Any game they found was used, first, for daily food; the remainder they carefully jerked for future use.

On the ninth day after the injury of Saxe, a party of three Americans joined the camp. One of them came up and begged permission to camp with the Collins party. They said they were worn-out with night travel. The party granted their request, and the strangers came into camp. It was at once discovered that the new arrivals were old acquaintances of Tex and Saxe. This the old guard did not at first relish, but Tex told Señor Castillo that he need have no fears, as Bill Salter, the leader of the new arrivals, had once exchanged shots with Saxe and he was sure they were not on friendly terms. In fact, if Saxe were well, Tex said, he would never have consented to Salter joining the party.

One unfortunate thing was that there were no hunters among the new arrivals, and there were more mouths to feed. The strangers, however, had plenty of meal and coffee and also quite a supply of tobacco, an article that had been scarce before they joined the party. People began to manifest much uneasiness because of the delay. Some advocated leaving Saxe. They argued, "He is a disturbing element and keeps us constantly in deadly fear that he will kill some of us, if he is so fortunate as to recover his health and strength."

But the young hunter, whose advice had much weight, said he felt that it would not be honorable to desert even such a man. Walter said, "To leave him at the mercy of the Indians would, to say the least, be an unchristian act. I personally have no fear of him, and I will do what I can to see that none of the party suffers from his abuse in future. Let us stay with him until he is able to care for himself. Then, if you wish to set him adrift, well and good."

On the sixteenth day, it was decided to make a start, and the party covered about ten or twelve miles that day. Saxe grew better and began to be troublesome again. One evening, Tex was taken violently ill and could not ride, so it was proposed to lay over. Saxe objected, "Leave him. The Indians will take care of him. He is no good, no how." Fortunately, the party was more humane. It seemed strange that even after it was known that he was ready to desert Tex, the other ruffians still waited upon him and did his bidding. The man had a strong influence over these rough beings.

One afternoon, the party reached a fine camp early, and all hands proposed to lay over. After dinner, Bill Salter came to the Castillo camp and asked for Walter. Collins called the lad out of the tent, where he was sitting with Señorita Castillo and others of the family. The young man joined Salter, and the two walked out among the trees. Salter then stated the object of his visit, which was a message from Saxe. It was no less than a challenge to fight a duel.

"I am sorry," said Salter, "to have been called upon to do this, but it is the custom in these parts, when a man demands satisfaction, to give it to him. It is considered his right. I believe Saxe has a grievance against you, you having beat him with your pistol."

"Yes, I did," said the lad, "in defense of that kind old priest. Saxe struck the old father with his pistol and nearly killed him. Who could help defending such a helpless man? Saxe has abused or beaten nearly everyone else except myself. He shot down my horse, because he abused and spurred the animal, and the creature threw him off. He drew his pistol and killed him. I was absent when it happened."

"I heard all about that, too," said Salter. "It was wrong, and you had a perfect right to have called him out for it. You ought to have done so, but it seems you let it pass. The other people had the same right, but the whole camp seems afraid of Saxe. But to business. Who will represent you? I want to arrange the preliminaries."

"I have no one here to represent me," said the boy. "Mr. Collins is an old man, a Christian. The father is also a Church man, and Mr. Castillo has his family. I would not ask him to become involved in my quarrel. The other men are all friends of Saxe, and I could not trust them. If Saxe wants satisfaction, let him get his rifle and go with me to yonder pines." Walter pointed to a large clump of pine and fir trees half a mile distant. "I will take my rifle and go there. You can be present, if you like, and see that your man has fair play."

"Yes," said Salter, "but who will see that you have fair play?"

"I am in the habit of taking care of myself," said the lad. During all this time, he was perfectly calm, exhibiting no fear or concern.

"We can't do it that way," said Salter. "There is a right and a wrong way to arrange such matters. You must find someone to act as your second, for this affair has got to come off tonight, and the sooner we get to business, the sooner it will be settled. You can't afford to delay a matter of this kind."

"I think I can think it over," said Walter, "before I decide or act. I am not accustomed to duels and don't know much about them."

"When will you meet me, and where?" asked Salter.

"Here, by this tree, in half an hour."

Just as Walter reached camp, Collins came up to him and asked what was the trouble. The boy at first decided that he would not tell the old man, for fear it would worry him, but he finally concluded to do so, as Collins was the only friend to whom he could turn for advice. He therefore told him all about it.

"So the ruffian has decided to murder you, my son. It must be stopped; it must be stopped. What are you going to do?" asked Collins excitedly.

"I have about decided to meet him. As I see it, I cannot avoid it. If I refuse, he will have an excuse to shoot me down, and in such a case, in this wild place, there would be no redress. And what protection would you have when I am gone? The good father, what will become of him? And Señor Castillo, kind, gentle man, he would be murdered. Then Saxe would take the sweet señorita. Has he not said openly he would have her? Yes, I have decided I will meet him."

"Do not act hastily, my son," pleaded Collins.

"I will not act in haste," said the lad, "but I must decide, I must decide. I must go now."

Collins clung to the lad and begged him to stay.

"I will come back to you, my dear friend," said the boy with much feeling. "I have much to say to you. I want you to take a message for me. Let me go now."

Salter was already standing at the spot appointed for the meeting, and he remarked as the boy came up, "What have you decided upon?"

"That I will meet your man," replied the boy with decision.

"When?" asked Salter.

"You said it had to come off tonight."

"Yes, I said so. Don't you know your rights in cases of this kind?" asked Salter with a lively show of interest in the lad.

"No, sir, this is my first experience."

"Very well, then. Saxe has challenged you to fight. You have the choice of weapons—don't choose rifles—and the right to name the time and place."

"Very well, sir," said the lad. "I do choose rifles at thirty paces. At sunrise tomorrow morning, I will meet Mr. Saxe in yonder grove." He pointed to the grove half a mile up the draw. "Good afternoon, sir," he said, turning on his heel.

As the boy strode away, Salter gave a little whistle. "You are all business and have got the right stuff in you, my lad, but I am sorry for you. Saxe is a dead shot with a rifle and has never failed to get his man. Too bad, too bad," said Salter to himself. He walked quietly into camp to report to his principal.

"Well," said the outlaw, "what news? Has the youngster concluded to fight?"

"Yes," said Salter coldly.

"Well," said Saxe impatiently, "weapons, time, and place?"

"Rifles, tomorrow morning at sunrise in the pine grove above."

"Well," replied the ruffian, "why did you not insist upon tonight? Who is his second?"

"He has none yet, but if I am not mistaken, he will take purty good care of himself. I had rather meet the devil than that brave boy."

Saxe's eyes sought the ground. Gradually there gathered on his swarthy face an expression of hatred. The cruel eyes flashed, and he turned to Tex. "What do you think of it, old man?"

"I think," said Old Tex with caustic honesty, "that this might be your last fight."

"What, you old reprobate, you against me, too? For two cents, I would teach you a lesson," said Saxe, fumbling with his revolver. "I thought you said the young devil was a dead shot with his pistol."

"So I did," said Tex, "but if possible he is a deader shot with the rifle. Why, Saxe, didn't you see him on top of that knoll, knocking off every Injun he pointed his rifle at? Have you forgotten that?"

"No," said Saxe, "but he will surely lose his head when he faces me. Guess he has heard about me."

"Guess he wasn't much scared about what he heard, by the looks of that mug of yours, after he worked you over," replied Tex.

During this dialog, Salter had taken a seat on a saddle in a corner of the tent.

"Well, Salter," said Saxe, "what do you say about this affair? How has it got to be pulled off? I've got to kill that young wolf, and I am going to do it, but it is best to have an understanding and adopt the best plan."

"It's going to be pulled off on the square if I have anything to do with it," answered Salter, "and I guess I have."

Saxe's brow darkened, and an ugly expression took possession of his dark face. "That's all right, Salter," he answered. "I don't want any advantage. I just want to have the details settled."

"Well," said Salter, "them details are settled. You only have a say on one side. You have challenged the boy to fight. He has accepted and named weapons, distance, place, and time. About all there is for you to do is to get there on time with your rifle." A close observer might have noticed a twinkle in the eye of Old Tex. As he glanced at Salter, a smile flitted across his face.

"Look here," said Saxe, "I want to know whether you fellows are going to stand by me or not. I don't like the way you talk, Salter, or you either, Tex."

"Well, Saxe," answered Salter, "I am glad you brought the thing up. It gives me a chance to have one thing understood. I am not going to be mixed up in any murdering match. This fight will be square if I can make it so. I agreed to be your second, and I will be square with you in every way— in fact, that is my style in affairs of honor, but you will get no advantage through me. So far as this boy is concerned, he's got to take care of himself. At the same time, I will not permit any unfair advantage to be taken of him, and of course, a gentleman don't want any. I am acting in your interest— assuming that you don't want your reputation to suffer. You, of course, are looked upon as an expert. You have killed half a dozen men in affairs of this kind and have come out first best in several others. Mighty few men would care to go up against you in any shape. You are considered the best shot with a rifle in all this section of the country. I don't believe your equal lies in the West. You told me yesterday that Jack Snow took water when you went for him. Now, when that feller turns his back on a man, he's got to be a good one. I know Jack Snow myself, and I have had some doubts about Jack showing the white feather."

"Isn't that straight, Tex?" shouted Saxe. "Didn't Jack Snow refuse to fight me?"

"Yes," answered Tex. "Jack couldn't stand the racket. That's straight, Salter. I was Saxe's second, and Jack would not stand."

"Well," said Salter, "so much the better. It shows you are invincible. What would be thought of you, if you was to take advantage of a boy who never faced a man in a duel in his life? No, Saxe, it won't do; it won't do. You must come out with clean hands."

Saxe eyed Salter for some time. It was evident that he detected sarcasm in the latter's remarks, but Salter never flinched. Tex was silent and finally left the tent and started down to the other camp. He met Collins, who asked if the duel could not be fixed up.

"No," said Tex, "I don't think it can. If it was, Saxe would shoot the boy the first time he met him. It's a great wonder he has not done so before. Old man, you don't know that man. He is the most desperate man I ever knew. He has killed more men than there is in this party twice over. He's a desperate outlaw, feared by everyone who knows him. I've got pretty good nerves, and I must say I am in constant fear of my life. I've been surprised that he has not taken that girl long ago. I don't understand it. He don't fear anyone, unless it would be that boy, and it don't seem as if he could care much for him. I never knew him to hesitate about a little thing like that before. Why, he chased the boys out of his tent several days ago and said he was going to bring the gal over there."

"It must be the boy that makes him hesitate," replied Collins. "You know the boy beat him nearly to death."

"I know that," said Tex, "but you see the boy surprised him and got in his first lick, and it is well he followed it up so lively. That blow affected his brain and knocked the sense out of him, but he is himself again, and there will be trouble. If the boy had only finished him on the spot, it would have been better for all. Who is the lad going to have for his second?"

"I don't know," replied Collins. "You see he don't tell me such things. He knows I am a peaceful man and do not like trouble."

"And the old Mexican?" asked Tex.

"He," answered Collins, "is more mild than I, and could only advise. The priest, too, is a man of peace. The good father will pray for the brave lad," said Collins.

"Prayers and advice is mighty poor dependence in a case of this kind, old man, and I'm afraid won't amount to much." So saying, Tex walked away, whistling a solemn air.

As the afternoon wore on, Walter looked after every detail, making sure that the stock were properly guarded and had ample time to graze. He was occupied until late with his scouting duties, and when he rode into camp, he noticed Tex sitting on a stone some distance away. As he came up to Tex, he called out, "Mr. Tex, would you like to take a little ride? If you have time, I would like to have you go with me, for one last scout."

The old man expressed himself as delighted.

"All right," said the boy, "throw your saddle on my horse here, and we will take a spin." Nothing was thought of this, as Walter often asked one of the men to join him for a long, evening scout.

Taking Lion along, the two men rode over the plain and soon passed out of sight over a swell. After riding briskly for half an hour, they brought their horses to a walk and then stopped. The men dismounted, and the boy said to Old Tex, "I have asked you to come out here, as I wanted to talk to you— to advise with you—ask a favor of you."

"Hadn't you better ask advice from the old Mexican, or old Collins, or even the old priest?"

"No, Tex, they are all, of course, kind old men and true, but what I shall ask of you they cannot do. None but a strong, brave man can undertake what I ask."

"How can you trust such as I to carry out your wish?" asked Tex.

"My friend," replied the lad, "you are not so bad as you would have me believe. You have your good side. You may have your bad side. However that may be, I know if you promise me to do what I ask, that you will redeem your promise or die in the attempt. I know this. You are the only one who can aid me."

The eyes of the old mountaineer moistened. Seizing the boy by the shoulder, Tex answered, "Name it, boy. I will do whatever you ask of me."

"Well," said the lad, "you know Saxe has challenged me. I have agreed to meet him tomorrow morning at sunrise."

"And you want me to second you?" asked Tex.

"No, not that," Walter replied. "That might ruin my plans—if I should fall. As I said, I shall meet Saxe in the morning and will probably fall. Do you remember the little cedar grove about a quarter mile below the camp."

"Yes."

"Well, these two horses will be there saddled. My brown horse will also be there. You are to ride your own horse directly to the grove from the field. You will find Castillo, his daughter, the little child, and the priest. My pistols will be in my saddle pocket. Mount immediately and ride for your life. The young lady is to ride my small brown horse; Señor Castillo will ride the black with the child; you are to ride my gray; and the good father will ride your own horse. Take the old man and his children to his ranch. Mounted as you will be, Saxe or anyone else can never overtake you. Will you do this, Tex?"

"I will, yes, boy. I will."

"Will you pardon me if I ask you to swear on this little book that you will save these friends of mine from that merciless villain?"

"I swear."

"Well, Tex," said the boy, "I believe you will carry out your promise. Here is a purse. It contains two hundred dollars in gold."

"I won't take your gold, boy. No, Tex never did such a thing, not for gold, boy, but I will for you. I did not expect you would ask me to do you a favor for gold."

"My friend," replied the youth, "you misunderstand me. I give you the gold because I have no one else to carry out my wishes. Your horse may die, and you must buy another. You must buy food. Take it, take it, or you will offend me."

The old man now quieted down. "What shall I do with your horses?"

"Well, you know I will be dead. They will be yours. Stay at Castillo's place until you are rested. Then take them, as well as my blessing."

The mountaineer stood long with his eyes fixed on the ground. He said, half to himself, "I am disappointed, boy. I wanted to do something for yourself, but I will do this. Yes, depend on it, I will do it."

"Let us go back another way," said the boy, and mounting, they rode away.

An hour later, the boy was talking earnestly to Collins. "I will," he said, "most likely be killed. In that case, I must depend on you to do me a favor. I will come to your tent at the last moment and bid you good-bye, and to bring you a packet to deliver to my friends should you ever reach the states."

As the boy rose to go, the old man broke down and burst into tears. "Oh, my son, my son. I cannot give you up. You are such a comfort to me."

From Collins, the young man went to the tent of Señor Castillo. The old gentleman, whom the young man found pacing back and forth in the tent's narrow limits, was wringing his hands and moaning bitterly. He told the boy he felt powerless to save his daughter from the clutches of the villainous Saxe.

"I came," said the brave lad, "to tell you of my plan to save your daughter and yourself from the villain. Listen, my time is short." He then recounted the arrangement with Tex.

"Can you trust that hardened man?" the old gentleman asked. "I fear him also. He is a tool of Saxe."

"I will answer for him," said the boy. "In any event, this is your only hope. While I live, I think you and your daughter are safe. If I fall, this plan must be adopted with great promptness."

He then directed Señor Castillo in every detail as to the hour and place, saying, "I will meet you at the grove one hour before sunrise. I will guard this side of the camp tonight. Until then, good-bye, my friend."

Going to his own tent, Walter sat down by the dim firelight to pen a few words to his aunt, with the request that she communicate with his other friends, as well as his mother. He now repaired to the tent of Collins, whom he found with the old priest. Handing the packet to Collins, he said, "If I fall, give or send this to whom it is addressed. If I never see you more, my good friend, my effects here are yours. My horses and arms I have disposed of."

It was now midnight. Reaching a sheltered place, Walter lay down with his dog, who curled up near him. He was soon fast asleep. Collins afterwards said that, being very restless, he arose and went out of his tent and wandered over to the tent of the young man. He was startled by a sound in the tent, which he knew to be vacated, as the boy was on guard. He listened. Directly, the tall form of a man crept out of the tent. As the tall man rose to depart, Collins recognized the ugly visage of Saxe. In the pale moonlight, Collins was sure the villain had in his hand a big knife. Saxe moved away, he said, in the direction of his own tent. His visit was believed to have been made for the purpose of murder.

In the very early hours of the morning, the young hunter rose and took his horses to the place appointed and securely tied them to trees. Lion he left with them. He knew that no one could move the animals except Señorita Castillo; she could do as she pleased with the dog. Walter had instructed Señor Castillo that, at the sound of a rifle, they were to mount and await the arrival of Tex.

Before taking leave of his animals, Walter threw his arms around the gray's neck and caressed him tenderly. He patted the other horses affectionately, and then he put his hand lovingly on Lion's head and, patting him gently, said, "Lion, my friend, I now bid you good-bye, most likely forever. It is hard to part with friends like you, the truest and noblest of friends. Be true to your new master, and you will most likely be happy. Farewell, my dear ones, farewell." Shouldering his rifle, he rushed from the spot.

Thirty minutes before sunrise, the lad reached the pine grove by a circuitous route. He entered it from the upper side. Standing by a large pine tree, he waited patiently for the arrival of the others. The first to arrive were two of Saxe's men, Orr and Oakes, and then Saxe and Salter appeared. Presently, Tex rode up on his favorite horse. All tied their horses some distance away from the field. The boy went forward and was greeted by Salter and Tex. "Well, friend," said Salter, "you are here before us."

"Yes," said Walter, "and I am at your service."

"Well," replied Salter, "we will measure the distance and arrange the preliminaries. The sun will soon appear. How shall we measure the ground? Step it off?"

"Yes," answered the lad. "I am quite indifferent as to the exact distance and will take your measurement."

Salter stepped the ground off carefully. "Just thirty paces," he said, making a deep mark with his heel and pressing a small branch into the soft ground at that point. "The sun will rise there," he continued, pointing to the eastern hills. "Owing to the rough ground, one of you gentlemen will have to face the sun, and the lucky man will have it at his back. Shall we throw up for choice of position?" Salter took a Mexican silver dollar from his pocket, placed it on his thumb and finger, and hurled it into the air. As the coin flew upwards, he said, "Heads or tails, son. Take your choice."

"Heads," came the prompt reply.

"And heads it is," said Salter. "The choice is yours, my boy."

I will stand by the tree yonder, sir, with my face to the east," the lad replied without a moment's hesitation.

Every eye instantly turned on the brave boy, as if to inquire, "Why do you surrender such an advantage to the hardened scoundrel you must face?" Tex looked troubled. The others were satisfied. The lad was calm, perfectly composed.

"Gentlemen," said Salter, turning to the three bystanders, "will you examine the weapons of the two principals?" Saxe carried a Hawkins rifle, beautifully mounted. The gun carried a half-ounce ball. Orr took Saxe's rifle, cocked the piece, placed his mouth to the muzzle, and blew a blast of air through it. Oakes held his thumb on the tube, and the air rushed through. "The piece is not loaded," reported Oakes.

"Very well," said Salter. "Load the gun under the direction of Mr. Saxe. He is entitled to have it loaded as usual." This was quickly done.

Then the lad surrendered his double-barreled weapon to Orr, who went through the same process. Saxe, at this point, objected to the use of the double-barreled gun.

"What do you say, boy," asked Salter, "about this objection?"

"That I had the choice of weapons. I chose this gun and will use it or none. Only one barrel will be loaded."

Salter turned to Saxe and said, "Your objection sounds frivolous to me. The boy clearly has the right to the choice of any gun. He naturally chose his own and must use it if he desires. Let us proceed."

"It is now necessary," Salter continued, "to choose a man to give the word, who will instruct the principals when it will be proper to fire and to see that they understand the rules before taking their places. Saxe, I presume, understands the usual form, but this young man will require some instruction."

Quite a period of silence followed, during which it was noted that Saxe was quite nervous. His dark visage had whitened considerably. The boy, on the other hand, was perfectly composed.

Orr finally spoke, "Why can't you, Salter, give the word? You're used to such things." Orr turned to Saxe, "Is that satisfactory to you, Saxe?" The latter nodded.

Turning to the boy, Salter asked, "Are you satisfied?"

"Perfectly."

"Well, gentlemen," said Salter, "we will follow the usual code of rules, which are simple enough. If you will now give me your attention, I will rehearse them with you, after which you will take your places until the sun appears. When we are ready to proceed, I will address you in a voice loud enough to be easily heard, as follows: 'Are you ready, gentlemen?' to which you each respond, if ready to proceed, 'Yes,' in a distinct, audible voice. After the elapse of, say, ten seconds, I will say, 'One. Halt. Fire.' At the word, 'Fire,' you will prepare yourselves. I will then count, 'One. Two. Three.' At the word 'Three,' you are to fire, but under no circumstances before the word, 'Three,' is pronounced. There will be quite an interval between the counts, ample time for you to make easy preparation."

On being assured by the principals that they understood the rules, Salter directed them to take their places. As the principals stood leaning on their rifles, waiting for the sun to appear, those present could scarcely help noticing the great contrast between the two men. Saxe was a man in the prime of life, about thirty-five years old, somewhat above the average in height and size. His shoulders were broad, and his general build was well proportioned. He would weigh about 180 pounds. His eyes were black as night; his black hair was worn long and tied back with a silken cord. His dress, while worn and soiled, was better than that of the ordinary man of the plains. His trousers were of a light-colored corduroy, with buckskin trimmings at seat and knee. He wore heavy, high-topped riding boots and a gray woolen shirt with large collar, around which was a heavy silk tie, knotted in a double bow at the throat. Outside of the woolen shirt, he wore a heavy buckskin coat fringed and ornamented with beadwork. Around the waist, he wore a long Spanish silken scarf tasseled at each end, which he wore in the usual style of Spanish gentlemen. On his left side hung a dirk or Bowie knife in its scabbard, and on his right side was an empty pistol holster. On his head, Saxe wore a broad-brimmed, stiff Spanish hat. His face was shaven except for a heavy black mustache. His black, restless eye never looked anyone in the face. He had a deep, ugly scar on his left cheek, which extended across his nose. His face wore a most brutal expression of fierce hatred, though at times a nervous, frightened expression would appear as he faced the young hunter.

Walter, on the other hand, was a handsome youth, not much over eighteen years of age. Slightly built, he did not exceed five feet five inches in height. Of well-proportioned and well-muscled build, he weighed little over 130 pounds. He had a fine head of black hair, and his face was smooth with not the least appearance of a beard. His eyes were dark gray, with the most kindly expression, and on meeting, he always looked the person addressed square in the eye. His dress was plain. He wore a suit of buckskin in the style usually worn by men of the plains. Moccasins and a broad-brimmed, dark hat, quite soft and well-worn, completed his costume. His leather belt held a knife on the right side and an empty pistol holster on the left. He seemed self possessed and always on the alert.

Collins and the good father, after waiting some time with the Castillo family, finally approached each other. Deciding that the suspense was intolerable, with one accord, they directed their steps toward the place selected for the duel. They approached very near the scene of the affray without being discovered and were actually within fifty feet of the young man's position when he stepped over and took his place. As the first streak of sunlight floated over the hills, Salter broke the stillness, "Gentlemen, the sun has appeared. Come to attention."

The face of Tex had worn an anxious expression all morning. It now

changed as he realized, for the first time, the wisdom the lad had exercised
in choosing his position. Saxe stood in the sunlight yet with his back to the
sun. The lad stood in the shadow, sheltered by the tops of the clump of fir
trees to the left of Saxe. This gave Walter a most splendid view of Saxe, while
he himself stood in a comparatively uncertain light.

"Are you ready, gentlemen?" asked Salter in a cool deliberate voice.

"Yes, sir," responded the young man in clear, ringing tones, bringing his
rifle to his shoulder.

"Yes," responded Saxe in a low, tremulous voice, bringing his rifle into
firing position.

After a slight pause, there came from Salter the words, "One. Halt. Fire."
Then, slowly, the words, "One. Two. . . ."

At the word "Two," a rifle shot rang out on the clear morning air, and a
blaze of flame was seen to pour from the muzzle of Saxe's rifle. At the same
instant, the lad stepped to one side, and a lock of his dark hair fell to the
ground.

"Murder!" shouted Tex, running to the lad.

Salter also ran to where the boy stood. "Are you hurt, sir?" he asked.

"No, sir," replied the lad calmly.

Saxe had started to leave the place on the run.

"Get back here, sir," shouted Salter, drawing his revolver, which action
was immediately seconded by Tex. "You attempted to commit murder, acting contrary to the rules of the field of honor."

"Young man," Salter added feelingly, "the life of your antagonist is yours.
If you wish to shoot him down, do so."

"No, sir," replied the brave boy. "I cannot do that. I will give him a chance
to leave this party forever, or if he prefers, I will give him another chance.
But this time, he must obey the rules."

"I will see to that, lad," replied Tex. "I am from this moment your
second—and your friend."

Saxe had loaded his weapon again. At this moment, the old priest and
Collins came running up, and falling on their knees before Salter, they cried
out, "Sir, do not allow this man to murder the boy." They begged to have
the duel declared off, but all saw that now this was impossible. Saxe had
lashed himself into a furious state and swore that one of the principals
should remain on the field.

In the meantime, Salter had declined to act further for Saxe, stating as a reason that he had acted in a cowardly, inhuman manner, contrary to all rules, and could not be classed among gentlemen. Saxe chose Orr in Salter's place. Tex and Orr now conferred and selected Salter to give the word.

The principals took their places. Salter stepped forward and asked, "Are you ready, gentlemen?"

Both replied, "Yes."

"I shall," Salter continued, "give the word as before. Now, Saxe, you must obey the rules of civilized dueling. A further violation of these rules will be punished by hanging on this tree." Salter touched a large fir that had wide, extending branches. "You will not be entitled to a more honorable death."

Salter then counted with great deliberation, "One. Halt. Fire. One. Two. Three."

At the word "Three," the report of two rifles broke the stillness. A second later, Saxe plunged forward on his face. The boy turned and walked rapidly from the scene.

He had only proceeded a few paces when Tex caught him by the arm. "Boy, boy," he shouted, "you are struck."

"It is but a scratch," said the lad. At this instant, Salter, the old priest, Collins, and Oakes ran to his side. Upon examination, it was observed that the ball from Saxe's rifle had cut a small groove in the lad's throat on the right side. While blood ran freely from the wound, it was of no serious importance beyond a slight discomfort.

After wiping away the blood and looking carefully at the wound, Collins said, "My son, half an inch deeper, and you would have been undone."

The boy now left the field for camp, nor did he again turn his eyes toward the scene of conflict. When the excitement had subsided somewhat, Oakes approached the fallen man and turned him over. On his face was stamped a look of hatred and defiance. On the bridge of his nose, a small wound was visible, from which the blood flowed freely. It told a fearful story which caused a shiver to run through the frames of his hardened companions. It needed no second glance to tell them of the deadly aim of Saxe's youthful opponent, nor of the iron nerve and determination that possessed him.

Tex, as soon as he had satisfied himself that the lad was not seriously injured, mounted his horse and rode rapidly away. Dashing up to the place of rendezvous, where the animals had been left, he shouted, "It's all right! Let's go back to camp. Saxe is dead, and the boy is safe." He found Señor Castillo and his family mounted on their horses ready to move, as the youth had directed. For the first time, Maria became aware that there had been trouble. She would not stir until she had been told the whole truth. Then she fully realized what an obligation she and her father were under to the young hero and how great the sacrifice he had made for them.

At this moment, Collins came up, out of breath, and told the story over again. On reaching camp, the señorita took Collins and Tex into her tent and insisted upon their telling the story in more detail. After they had recounted every detail, she said to Collins, "I could, of course, not expect you, or the good father, or my own father, with his great responsibilities, to defend and second the young capitan, but"—said she, turning to Tex with flashing eyes—"you, sir, how could you stand by and see one so young, so brave and true, put in such jeopardy! Oh, if I had known of his danger, I would have stood by him myself. Go away, sir, go away. I cannot look upon you. I thought you his friend—and yet you desert and deceive him."

Tex rose to his full height and stammered, "You deceive yourself, miss. I wanted to second him, and he refused to permit me, saying, 'If you do this, and I fall, Saxe will kill you, and no one will be left to aid Castillo and his daughter to escape.' Good day, miss." Tex stalked from the tent.

"Yes," said Collins, "Tex did second him at last, and right bravely, too."

"Call him back," said the girl. "Call him back, that I may implore his pardon."

But Tex could not be induced to enter the tent again. He said, "It's no use, for women have too many tears for me."

At this juncture, the old priest and Walter came into the camp. Maria ran out to meet them. She cried, "What a debt we owe you! How could you dare so much for us? I feel so guilty to have been, in part, the cause of such sacrifice on your part."

Lion trotted up to the boy and licked his hand affectionately.

"Yes," continued Maria, "Father has told me about your dog. He was true to your instructions. He would let no one but myself touch the horses. He obeyed me like one endowed with human reason."

About noon, Salter, Orr, and Coates came into camp. Walter took Salter and Tex to one side. He said, "Gentlemen, are you ready to leave this place?

I cannot stay here longer. We must break camp at once and leave this hated scene behind."

Salter answered, "We have buried the man as decently as we could. We are now to dispose of his property. You are entitled to his arms and horse. He killed a noble animal belonging to you, and it is only fair."

Here the lad raised his hand. "If you have any regard for me," he said, "if you care for my feelings, never again refer to this man Saxe. I do not wish to see any of his property, much less accept articles that once belonged to him. They would be a constant reminder that by me he was killed." For the first time since they had known the lad, he was excited. His eyes were wild. He had a haunted look.

Both Salter and Tex tried to pacify him without avail. Finally, Tex motioned Collins to approach. Collins saw at once the excitement under which the lad was laboring and caught the drift of his talk. "My son," the old man said, "what you have done could not be helped. Saxe has been the aggressor all the time. He would have killed you and perhaps others of this party had not he himself fallen."

"What, you tell me this? You, who claim to be a Christian man?" cried the boy. "I am guilty, guilty of an awful crime. Yes, I have committed murder." He rushed away and avoided everyone. He at once occupied himself in preparing to depart. The entire party was greatly concerned with the youth's distress.

It was the middle of the afternoon when camp was broken. As soon as they reached the trail, Walter galloped away with his dog and disappeared. He was not seen again until near sunset. The party gained the summit of a low ridge and saw in the distance the solitary horseman. Both animal and man were motionless. "That's the lad," said Collins, trotting up beside Señor Castillo.

"Yes," replied the old gentleman, "I am sure that is he."

As the party approached, the young man dismounted and began unsaddling his horse. Salter rode up to the boy and asked if there were any signs of Indians.

"No," replied Walter, "I have scouted the country thoroughly and have seen no fresh tracks. There is water over there in those willows. While this place is almost unprotected, it is the best camp I could find. It is a long way to the next water."

The boy's horse showed evidence of having been ridden long and hard, and his dog was panting and seemed to be very tired. The boy ate his supper in silence, after which he took his gun and went among the horses. He did not bring them in until a late hour. In the morning, he was the first to stir and he turned out the animals to graze. Immediately after breakfast, the party got in motion, and as usual, Walter mounted his horse and rode on, as it was his custom to scout the surrounding country. The whole party had come to lean upon him and profit from his judgment and experience, willingly following his lead. The veterans seemed more dependent than those with less experience, because of his knowledge of the dangers that beset the country through which they were making their way.

The day passed without incident. About 4 o'clock in the afternoon, they stopped at a well-sheltered place to camp. Besides plenty of water, there was good grass for the horses. All hands at once set to work to make themselves safe and comfortable for the night.

During the night, one of the Mexican women was taken sick, and it was thought best to lay over. Walter called the men together and advised that close watch be kept on the stock and camp, saying he was going some distance that day and would not be back until quite late. He said that, should he be delayed until after nightfall, he would give three clear, shrill whistles as a signal that it was he who approached. He then rode away, directing his course toward the mountains.

The party had noticed that Walter had prepared for his departure with utmost care, taking the greatest pains with his equipment. He took his best rawhide lasso and a goodly supply of dried meat. No one asked him any questions. Of late, he had shown no disposition to converse with anyone. The whole party noticed this with deep regret, for all loved and admired the boy. He had come to be recognized as the head of the party—although, with the tact and modesty that endeared him to all, he strenuously avoided any show of leadership.

Toward noon, the woman was slightly better, and it was thought the journey could be safely resumed in the morning. A careful watch was kept up, with Tex and Salter keeping horses saddled constantly, one of which was kept on a nearby elevation during the entire day. Sometime before supper, just as the sun was sinking out of sight, a horseman appeared far to the east, and it was soon seen that he was leading a horse. All thought it was surely an Indian, and they made every precaution for defense. They brought in the horses and placed them in the enclosure, and the men distributed themselves around the edge of the thicket. But by the time the horseman appeared on a little ridge near camp, they could see that he was Walter. They were much surprised at his having two horses. When he came into camp, he was riding a beautiful black stallion of powerful build and perfect mold with wonderful muscular development and with a long, sweeping mane and tail. He was broad of chest and forehead, with small limbs and a kindly eye. The lad had obviously ridden over a long road. Both animals showed signs of extreme fatigue, and both the boy and his dog looked tired and worn. The black stallion seemed afraid of the people who came out to see him.

The boy said that, on his scout the previous day, he had discovered a small park over the mountain to the east, in which he saw a small band of wild horses. Among them, he had seen this outstanding specimen, and he had determined to capture him. He had found the horses early in the day and had had no difficulty in approaching them closely. He made careful preparations for a quick dash upon the band, leaving his gun and all unnecessary articles in a safe place. He had been able to dash among the horses while they were on soft, marshy ground. With his lasso, he succeeded in capturing the black stallion but had a long struggle with the powerful animal. The horse did not choke down as he expected and finally turned fiercely on him. He had had great difficulty in saving the gray and even himself. Had he not left his firearm behind, he would certainly have thought it necessary to kill his captured prize to save the gray. And except for his dog, he would have lost the gray. The dog seized the wild horse by the heels and thus diverted his attention. The lasso then got foul, and the animal escaped with the rope around his neck. After a long chase, Walter had again gotten close to the black horse, but owing to the exhausted condition of the gray, he had despaired of again making the animal captive.

In this dilemma, he decided to shoot the horse, using a method sometimes resorted to by the most experienced wild horse hunters. He had taken careful aim at the muscles of the animal's neck, intending to crease them. The shot was successful, and the animal fell, stunned. Before he had time to recover, Walter galloped to the spot, tied the horse's legs firmly, securely fastened a hackamore on his head to keep him from biting, and conquered his prize before he let him rise to his feet again. He decided to saddle and ride the new horse in order to save the gray, and said he, with a little show of pride, "Here I am, and here is he." The horse was quite docile now, but somewhat bruised.

The whole party was amazed at the courage, audacity, and prowess of the young captain. He was looked upon as a wonder. He now gave much attention to the new horse, using great care in handling him. He had little trouble bringing him under complete subjection. The next day, a Sunday, the party rested on account of the animals, the feed being exceptionally good at this camp. The boy was persuaded to defer his scout until after service, which was held by the old father early in the morning.

At the request of all, the old priest, in his prayer and discourse, dwelt on the recent trouble. His sermon was so worded as to bring the boy to believe that he had done no wrong—and that his course was fully justified by the impending danger that had confronted the young man and his friends. The priest laid much stress upon the danger that had confronted Señor Castillo, his daughters, and himself and upon the fact that Walter's valiant act had been a duty imposed by both human and divine laws, which he could not honestly or lawfully disobey.

The good priest prayed earnestly in the following language: "Lord, thou knowest all things. Thou hast watched over us and heard our prayers. Thou didst guide thy servant, this young lad, in his search for our lost lamb, bringing them in safety to father, mother, and sister. Thou didst aid him in saving the life of thy aged servant, bent with age and labor in thy cause, from the wicked man who sought his life. Thou didst save, direct, and protect the brave youth who risked his precious life for those who were powerless to help themselves. We thank thee, O Lord, that you didst shield the kind and noble señor and the sweet and lovely señorita, from the profane and wicked ruffian, who sought their ruin.

"Since you have seen fit to take from this life that profligate and sinful man—known to us as Saxe—and hast called him to his final judgment, we pray thee to be merciful to him. Purify his soul, O Lord, that he may, in the end, be saved and allowed to sit with the pure of heart in thy sacred and heavenly temple. Watch over us, Gracious Savior. Guide and protect us through our journey, and soften the hearts of thy red children, that they may suffer us to pass through thy domain to our several destinations in safety.

"Shed thy divine light upon the soul of the heroic lad, whom thou didst raise up and cast among us to guide and protect thy servants. Thou hast given him great wisdom and discretion—far beyond his years. Console his heart, O Lord, for he is thine own servant. He would, O Lord, do thy will with an honest, faithful heart. Shed thy light upon him. Give him understanding, that he may know that he has done thy will, that even a sparrow cannot fall without thy sanction, and that thou guidest thy creatures in all things. Teach him that thou hast created thy creatures each in thy own form, giving to each such weapons of defense as pleased thee to bestow, and that it is lawful in thy sight for the oppressed to resist the oppressor. Shed thy balm upon this young boy's heart, which is sore, because of his fear that he has broken thy divine law."

After the service, Walter seemed brighter. He got his horse, preparatory to taking the usual morning scout. After a night's rest, the black stallion's spirits had revived, and he was again ready for battle. Walter saddled his gray carefully and led the stallion out into the open, where a lively scene took place. The boy again found it necessary to throw the beast and tie him securely, after which he handled the creature all over, taking the occasion to trim the hind feet.

After an hour's handling, Walter permitted the stallion to rise to his feet. The boy quickly put on the saddle and mounted the powerful beast which, after ten minutes of plunging and bucking, responded to the spur and dashed off over the broad, level prairie. The boy was gone several hours, but upon his return, the horse was quite docile. From that time forward, the stallion gave little trouble. He turned out to be an intelligent creature, of wonderful fleetness and exceptional bottom. Walter was proud of him and rode him constantly, giving the noble gray a much needed rest.

That evening, Maria sent Collins to ask the boy to come to her father's tent. At first, Walter objected to going on the ground that, because of his recent acts, he was not fit to associate with good, Christian people. Collins and the old priest, however, succeeded in getting the lad to comply with the young señorita's request. The visit was a most agreeable one. When the boy entered, the young girl was with her father. Señor Castillo gave him a most cordial welcome, taking occasion to say that he felt grieved that he had not had an opportunity to return thanks for the great service that his guest had rendered both to him and his family.

"What would have become of us," asked Castillo, "had that wicked man been permitted to have his way? You cannot, my son, understand the terrible anxiety of a father who feels himself incapable of defending his child. But," said the old Mexican, crossing himself, "God raised up a champion. Yes, my son, you could not have overcome that wicked man but with the consent and assistance of God." He then shook the lad's hand and left the tent.

When her father had gone, the young girl exerted herself to the utmost to entertain the young man, always addressing him as "Capitan." The youth protested and begged her not to do so, saying that he had done nothing to deserve such a title. But she persisted, saying that she should continue to so address him. She now entertained the lad with a partial history of her family and that of the old priest. Her father, she said, was born in Castile, Spain, and had come to Mexico in his youth, with her grandfather. He had been educated for the priesthood, but upon his arrival in Mexico, her grandfather had died suddenly, and her father was compelled to devote his time almost entirely to the care of the large estate he had inherited from his father. In middle life, he had finally married the daughter of a famous Mexican general and had settled down on his estate, devoting his life to his family and his domain.

She said the old priest was a prince of royal Spanish blood and that he had entered the priesthood in early life, had come to Mexico with her grandfather, and had lived with the family some years in early life. He had finally entered the missionary service and had traveled much among the wild tribes. During their recent visit to Santa Fe, her father had heard of him at a distant mission and had gone there to see his old companion and confessor. Upon arriving at the mission, he found the good father very ill and remained with him, nursing him to health. After the priest's recovery, Señor Castillo had brought him away, having gained his consent to spend the remainder of his days with the Castillo family.

After the long, pleasant call, the lad took his leave of the bright, beautiful girl. The entire party passed a restful night, and all were ready for the road at an early hour in the morning, much refreshed. After traveling twelve miles, the young scout found water and a very good camp. He left a notice, advising the party to camp there and saying that he would look over the country—since he again felt uneasy about Indians.

Noon came and the afternoon passed, and yet the scout did not return. As the evening wore on, much anxiety was felt, and many in the party expressed grave fears for his safety. Daylight came, and still the boy did not appear. He was, by this time, given up by many of the party as surely lost to them. Consternation reigned, and all decided not to make any attempt to move that day, as the parties could not agree as to what course was best to pursue.

Late in the morning, all had given the boy up for lost, save the old priest and the young señorita. Both declared that they felt sure he would return. Their faith was realized when, about 1 o'clock, he rode into camp from the direction of their last camp. He urged an immediate start, telling the party that Indians were in the country, a large band of them, and that they would soon strike the party's trail and follow it. The boy said that thirty miles farther on there was a good camp, well calculated for defense, and it must be reached without delay. The Indians were in great force, and a successful defense could only be made by reaching the point he suggested—or a place with equal advantages. He said that only some of the enemy were mounted, and they had only indifferent horses. In his judgment, the party could not be overtaken before it reached the camping spot he had found. On being asked if he had been to the place, he said, "Yes, I have been there, and farther. The trail is good and can be covered at a good pace. Go on. Follow the trail. When you reach the camp, you will find it well marked. On the summit of a rise about two miles before the spot, you will find two piles of stones, one on each side of the trail, and a mile farther on, you'll find another pile, this one on the left only. Go straight to the timber. You will find water at the edge of the timber. There is a small hill about fifty feet higher than the plain. Camp at the foot of that hill, in the timber. When you get there, you will find a depression easily defended. The hill commands the whole country. On top of it, you will find sufficient loose stones to make a good fort. As soon as you reach there, build a breastwork of stone. Then there will be ample protection for man and beast. I will remain here to rest my horse. I will watch the movements of the enemy and will come to you as soon as I am certain whether they intend to pursue us or not."

When asked if he had not better take the gray horse, because he was better broken, he replied, "No, the black horse is gentle enough now, and he is absolutely tireless. No living thing without wings can overtake him. I feel safe in a chase, even safer than with the gray, because the black is in better condition."

The others urged him to come with the party. "I cannot do so. I must have rest. My horse is worn and hungry, and what is more important, I must observe the movements of the enemy." He now went over the directions to the campsite with Salter, giving a most minute description of the ground and surrounding country. So careful was he that he felt sure that there would be no mistake in locating the place appointed.

The caravan now pushed on at as rapid a pace as possible. As the shades of evening began to set in, the party began to find the landmarks described by the young scout. They soon found the retreat selected by their leader. All set to work to carry out Walter's instructions. Salter took Tex and went to the summit of the hill. Together they began the work of putting it in a state of defense. After supper, the animals were herded until quite late. They were then securely fastened up in an enclosure that had been prepared for them. Three sentinels watched the camp.

As morning dawned, they scanned the plain in all directions. They could see no living thing. They turned out the stock and drove them some distance from camp, in order to save the grass nearby in case of extended siege. As the morning hours passed, much anxiety was felt by all, not only for the safety of Walter, but over the possibility of an Indian raid. Their situation, however, was less dangerous than at any previous camp, because of the openness of the surrounding country. They only needed to keep a close watch on the sparsely timbered approaches above and below camp. To the north and south was wide-open territory, with few depressions that would furnish hiding places for the wily enemy.

As the day wore on, their uneasiness increased. All felt that it was the calm just before a storm. Some of the party even proposed going in search of the boy, but Salter—who seemed to be the most experienced person— said, "No, it would be unwise to weaken our force here. So far as the boy is concerned, he needs no help from us. On the contrary, he looks to us to protect this camp and the helpless ones in it. I know what he would advise were he here. He would say, 'Protect the women and children and the horses.

Guard against surprise. See that your means of travel are not crippled.'"

Tex most heartily agreed, saying, "The boy don't want any hunting. He will take care of himself—if he is in danger, much better than we could take care of him. The chances are that if we went to aid him, it would be more apt to bring him trouble than help. He is not absent on his own account, but on ours. Were it not for us and the women in this party, he would not stay in this country a day. No band of Indians could hedge that lad off or take his scalp. No, friends, be calm and sensible. Let us stay where we are until he comes, which I believe will be soon, for the Indians have now had time to get here themselves if they struck our trail and cared to follow it."

Midday came and passed, and the anxious watch continued. Once, during the noon hour, all thought the Indians were approaching from the south, but Tex rode out to scout and found only a band of big timber wolves which, owing to the peculiar state of the atmosphere, resembled approaching horsemen. The excitement was very great for a time, but it soon subsided when Tex was seen to turn, wave his hat, and ride leisurely toward camp.

The vigil continued without cessation. The old father held a service during the afternoon, which was attended by Collins, Señor Castillo, and the women. After the service, they began preparations for the evening meal. Just at nightfall, the young scout came into camp. He approached to within a very short distance unobserved—a most surprising circumstance, since the most careful watch was being kept. The pickets were quite chagrined that he was able to surprise them. After caring for his horse, which appeared to have undergone great fatigue, Walter called a general council.

*

During his day-long scout, Walter had discovered, to his dismay, that two bands of Indians, one Navajo and the other Apache, were passing through the country, and they both appeared to be "looking for prey." For once, Walter found himself at a "loss to know what to do or advise." After considering the options of remaining in their "especially strong" camp or going into the mountains, the council decided, upon Walter's recommendation, that they would travel down the stream for some miles before turning north. By so doing, they hoped to evade discovery by the two war parties. And if they were attacked, they would be closer to help from white settlements. In any case, by traveling this route, they would not , in Walter's assessment, make their "conditions any worse."

For two days, the caravan traveled down the stream bank, often moving—because the road was so rough—no more quickly than a fast walk. At one point, they passed through a landscape of "great beauty," along a "thickly wooded" stream and among groves of pine, fir, and chaparral oak. Scattered along the hillsides were numerous small parks, and under the cool "shadow of the heavy foliage," the travelers "breathed freely, feeling quite serene." Walter continued to scout the surrounding countryside with his usual thoroughness, finding frequent signs of the war parties, but no certain evidence that the warriors had discovered the caravan.

On the third day, the party began to see Indians in the distance. They were "apparently watching the camp in the hope . . . that an opening might occur that would enable them to make a sudden dash and capture the horses. . . ." The travelers' serenity was soon gone, and the "constant watchfulness and frequent alarms to which the party was subject began to tell seriously on all. . . ."

While it had been unclear whether the Navajos and Apaches knew of the Collins/Castillo party's presence, Walter had counseled against going hunting, for fear the warriors would hear the gunshots and locate their camp. Now that the travelers had been discovered, Walter and Tex went in search of game, taking every precaution.

＊

About 2 o'clock in the morning, the hunters quietly left camp and were soon lost in the darkness. They took their course in a northeasterly direction, passing over the mountains and reaching a point some twelve miles from camp. By the time the sun appeared, they had fortunately killed two large elk. They dressed the elk and arranged them for loading as early in the evening as they thought it safe to travel. During the day, Walter and Tex made a fire on the densely timbered hillside and spent their time jerking a large quantity of the savory meat. The process of jerking was simple. They cut a few small poles and laid them in crutches, about two feet high, driven into the ground. They then collected a quantity of dry willow wood and built a slow fire under the poles. They set the meat, cut into small, thin pieces, on the poles, the object being to smoke and dry the meat quickly. This made it more convenient for packing and less liable to attract flies.

Meat so cured is excellent food, and it will keep—properly protected—almost any length of time.

Tex devoted his time to curing the meat, and Walter acted as guard. The dry willow wood made little smoke, so there was little danger of being discovered, unless the enemy had followed their trail. The young hunter guarded their back track carefully.

As nightfall approached, they loaded their horses and marched back to camp, exercising great care so as to guard against surprise and possible capture. They had packed the horses in such a way that, by cutting a single thong, the animals could be relieved of their burdens. Walter thought it best to approach camp from a different direction than the one they had taken the previous morning, and so by making a circuit partially around the camp, they succeeded in entering without being discovered by the watchful Indians.

The day had not passed so tranquilly at camp. Just after sunrise, as the animals were turned out, some dozen Indians had made a sudden dash on the herd and succeeded in cutting it off from the camp. After a brisk fight, the travelers had driven away the warriors, leaving two horses killed. No Indians were killed, nor was any of the party injured, though the enemy had discharged many arrows and burned considerable powder. They then kept in the horses until after supper, when they were turned out to graze until sundown.

With the return of Walter and Tex, the party now decided to make an early start in the morning and push forward with all speed. Señor Castillo remarked that he was completely lost and that he did not know the country well enough to decide the best course to take the following day. Walter said he thought—from his observation of the country to the north—that they shouldn't experience any trouble for some miles. Now he could see no advantage in avoiding the trails. The enemy was well aware of their presence and would attack when in sufficient force. Now, while the party was well provisioned, they should make every effort to get forward towards their journey's end.

At the first appearance of daylight, the animals were turned out to graze, well guarded by the best men, while the others prepared breakfast and packed the luggage. The good señor was much cast down this morning, saying that he had a presentiment of approaching danger. Every effort was made to rouse him but to no avail. He did not, however, tell his fears to his daughter or the other women. The caravan set out while the morning was cool, and the animals moved forward rapidly, being much refreshed by their long rest. The young hunter traveled in advance, while the other men closely guarded the flanks and rear.

They covered several miles without seeing an enemy. Gradually, heavy dark clouds settled over the heavens to the south, and at about 10 o'clock, Walter rode back and requested the party to close up and travel in close file. He said to Señor Castillo and Collins, "Try and keep them close. I have seen enemy scouts, and we cannot so well defend a scattered group." In the case of attack, they arranged that Castillo and Collins should gather the animals close together in some sheltered spot and stop, so that the defenders could more easily cover them. The party now passed over a country somewhat broken, with no convenient shelter in sight. The weather became more and more threatening, and it seemed almost certain that a storm was approaching. Upon gaining the summit of quite an elevated swell, they saw a dark belt of timber some six miles distant. The route to the timber was over a level prairie, with here and there a deep depression or dry watercourse. Such places were often dangerous, as they could furnish cover for an enemy.

Walter was riding about a mile ahead and approaching one of the dry cutbank coulees when, some two hundred yards from the depression, he suddenly turned at a right angle and galloped west. When he had gained some three hundred yards, he again turned north and quickly approached the stream, a most fortunate maneuver since, on looking eastward, he saw a number of savages who intended to ambush him.

Finding that they were discovered, they mounted their horses and gave chase. The boy galloped back toward the train, just keeping ahead of his pursuers. He finally slackened his pace and dismounted. Taking deliberate aim, he fired and one of the savages rolled off his horse. The Indian's companions quickly picked him up and bore him away.

The boy now signaled the party to hasten forward, and he directed his course to the point where the enemy had concealed themselves. Here, Walter encountered a real wagon trail, and from there on, they made better progress. The advance guard took care to examine every cutbank, while the young scout urged his friends forward with all speed to reach the timber before

Ambushed

the storm. Dense black clouds covered the sky, the wind began to rise, and large drops of rain started to fall.

They now noticed that Tex was missing. The party, however, did not slacken speed. The old man soon made his appearance, riding as fast as his horse could travel. Walter waited for the old man, for it was evident that he had important information. As he came up, he said, "We are in for it now. There is a lot of red devils in the breaks over there. I saw at least fifty. They seemed to be holding a council."

"Yes," said Walter, "I presume they expected us to fall back, and then the large party would fall upon us from all sides. We must get to the timber as quickly as we can. Hurry up the people. Tex, I think you had better stay to the rear. I will go ahead. If they crowd you, get down and shoot their horses."

The party now began to scatter, some animals able to make better progress than others. Walter immediately put a stop to this unruly practice, and the party went forward in a more compact form. Indians now appeared to the west and southeast, and a few were noticed on the east flank, but they did not approach within gunshot.

The rain increased, accompanied by thunder and lightning, which lighted up the heavens on all sides. The young hunter galloped ahead to view the best point to enter the timber. After careful observation, he rode slowly back toward his approaching friends, now some three-quarters of a mile distant. The rain was falling in torrents. An occasional hailstone hit the ground with a heavy thud, and the hail increased with each passing moment. The young man began to gallop, but as the storm increased, he found it difficult to make his black stallion face it. The party now fled before the storm, each intent on self-preservation. The boy dashed on against the storm, touching his spurs to the flanks of his spirited horse.

As he met Collins, the priest, and Señor Castillo, he said, "Gentlemen, keep these frightened people together." A moment later, he passed on, meeting Salter, Tex, and the others. He said, pointing backwards, "Gentlemen, spread out here and protect these helpless ones." The men turned and beheld within a few rods some thirty savages coming forward. "Men," was the quiet, firm command. The Indians halted for a moment as the travelers brought their rifles to their shoulders. They then shied off to the east, and the travelers continued towards the timber.

From then on, it was a race. The Indians gained rapidly on the travelers.

Accompanied by his men, Walter now galloped forward, forming a line between the fleeing party and the Indians. The hail fell so quickly and with such force that a man struck by the icy balls was staggered. Horses seemed determined to drift to the west and turn tail to the storm. At last, with the greatest exertions, the party made it to the timber, taking shelter at once beneath the large trees. They quickly kindled a big fire and put up the tents for the women and children. The storm did not abate, except that the hail ceased to fall—the ground was already white with it. The Indians seemed to have departed.

The party commenced the work of providing shelter and protection for men and animals. No one seemed to care for the presence of the enemy so near at hand and in strong force. They felled half a dozen large trees and placed their trunks so as to form a good breastwork that commanded the entire grove. They set up outposts to the east and north, and with that, the camp was adequately sheltered for defense. They found that good feed was abundant near camp, and towards evening, with the storm somewhat abated, they permitted the animals to feed nearby. As dusk began to settle, they drove in the animals and closed up the corral for the night. After supper, Walter and Orr served duty as pickets, but it soon grew so dark that they could not distinguish anything ten feet away.

The horses grew excited, and Señor Castillo and others ran out to the corral to see what was the matter. While looking around, the good señor was knocked down by some unseen hand. As he fell, he called out for help in Spanish. The señorita and the priest and some of the other Mexicans ran out to the corral. It was not generally known that the girl had left the camp until a piercing scream was heard in the direction of the corral, followed by another scream, partially suppressed. The men made an immediate search. They could not find Maria. A picket was quickly thrown up around the place in hopes of encircling every living creature near the camp, but it was too late. The girl was gone.

Oakes declared that he had heard her captors dragging her away in a northeasterly direction. The outside pickets, Walter and Orr, were called in. Señor Castillo had an ugly wound on the side of his head, but he was conscious. When he was told that his child had gone to aid him and had been captured and carried away, his grief knew no bounds. He mourned and prayed. The good priest was most active. He was doctor and guard, as well as spiritual confessor. It was he who told Walter, when the boy came in, that the girl had evidently been taken prisoner. The youth was greatly affected by the news.

Taking his rifle and calling Lion, Walter started to leave the camp, but Tex laid a heavy hand on his shoulder. "Lad," he said, "cool down a bit. Don't rush off to your death. Consider carefully what you are about to do, and do nothing rash. Remember, all these lives are to be protected. Call the men here, and let's have some plan about what it is best to do."

"You are right, Tex," said the young man. "Tell all hands to come together for consultation."

When all had assembled, Walter addressed them, "Men, we are sur-rounded by enemies, and the señorita is missing. I think it best for two men to enter the corral, one at each end, and watch carefully, while two others watch the camp. It is little use, as we have seen, to try to guard either camp or horses by standing picket so far away, for we cannot see the foe. If you will do this, I will take my dog and locate Maria. Then we may, by united effort, recapture her."

All agreed that the course Walter suggested was wise, and all agreed to obey all orders of the young captain. In his absence, Salter was to take charge. Salter and Orr went to the corral, and Tex and Oakes took the first watch at the camp. The others turned in, with the exception of Collins and the priest, who sat up by the bedside of the señor. They extinguished all fires, and the boy silently withdrew from camp.

Before leaving, Walter said to Tex, "I will find her and come back for you, my friend. We must save her. She is a noble girl."

Tex seized the boy's hand. "Lad," he said, "call on me. I am with you and will follow you anywhere. But, boy, be cautious; be not too rash." Walter promised to exercise every caution.

BOOK FOUR

Walter took Maria's shawl and let the dog smell it. He walked quickly down along the edge of the timber and then turned in among the trees. With the utmost caution and much labor, he worked his way through the undergrowth. He had almost given up hope, when Lion gave a low, scarcely audible whine and turned square to the right, moving forward with his nose to the ground. They went for fully a quarter of a mile when Lion stopped and dropped to the earth. The boy followed his example and listened intently. He felt sure he could hear low voices. At this moment, rain began to fall again, and an occasional flash of lightning lit up the woods. The boy knew well the danger of being discovered now. He at once set to work to cover himself with twigs and leaves. He now watched for each flash of lightning and tried to catch a glimpse of the enemy. The dog soon showed a disposition to go forward, and the lad followed. They had advanced but a few feet when the dog again stopped and rested. Again he moved on. In this way, they gained something like one hundred feet. Then the dog would go no farther. The lad could now hear voices clearly and soon located the camp of the enemy. He could, at times, distinguish figures moving about the camp. A small enclosure made of boughs stood to a height of four feet, and inside the Indians had kindled a small fire. So thick had the boughs been woven that scarcely a ray of light escaped. The rain continued to fall with increased volume, and the lightning flashed more frequently, lighting up the scene.

The lad discovered a log of considerable size but a few feet in advance of his position, and he was about to crawl to it when he saw the dog make a backward movement. The lad just had time to assume a rigid position when a flash of lightning lit up the whole space. What he saw almost froze the blood in his veins. Within twenty feet of him stood a tall, powerful warrior. The Indian advanced, the falling rain shutting out every sound. Grasping his knife and hatchet, the boy awaited developments. The next flash of lightning revealed the form of the Indian sitting on the large log, his back against a small tree. After hesitating briefly, the lad began to move back, his own sounds muffled by the rain. He noticed a large fir tree near at hand and made his way to it with great patience and care. The dog was also able to gain this new position beside his master without exciting alarm. The savage was plainly visible with each flash of lightning, his blanket wrapped closely around him. He had changed his position slightly. He now faced the southeast, while the Indian camp was to the north. Walter's position was to the west of the savage watchman and some thirty feet from him, a most dangerous position, but comparatively safe as long as the rain continued. The lightning flashed less frequently now, and the lad thought he detected the sound of voices, which he thought to be approaching.

He soon learned that he was correct, for he plainly heard voices near at hand. A flash of lightning revealed four more savages joining the first one, and all now stood. Directly they began to move and passed the young man's hiding place, directing their course towards the white travelers' camp. The lad thought it prudent to follow them at a safe distance. After a bit, he came upon them in the act of consulting, but they soon moved on in the direction of his own camp. Believing that no harm could come of their visit, because of the thorough watch that was now maintained, the young man decided to go back to the Indian encampment and circle to the eastern side, where he thought there was less danger of discovery.

Once there, he commenced to advance, but Lion soon halted. The youth then detected the sound of horses and concluded that his present course would bring him to the rendezvous of the Indian horses, which would be well guarded. He retraced his steps, moving to a point farther south. After passing around to the south, he decided to gain a point of observation nearer the camp, in hopes of estimating the number in the party—and the position of the captive. After much labor, he reached a large tree, from which he could see not only the campfire but also a number of Indians inside the bough enclosure and some outside, sitting under a small clump of fir trees, the boughs of which furnished good shelter. He counted fifteen Indians then in camp. With the five that had gone to the travelers' camp and possibly two others guarding the horses, that made a party of twenty-two. He had seen, at one time, a party that he had estimated at thirty, and Tex had declared he had seen fifty. Perhaps, thought the lad, during the excitement of the moment, they had overestimated the number of the party, but it was also possible that there might be others absent that he had not seen. At any rate, the question could not be definitely settled now. The rain continued to fall, and lightning occasionally lighted the scene.

Changing his position to a point farther south, the young man got a better view of the hostile camp and could now, he believed, count eighteen Indians. Near the group of savages outside the enclosure, a small tree stood, to which he believed the captive was tied. He determined to approach closer and, if possible, learn for a certainty whether the young girl was really tied to so exposed a position. His heavy gun was quite an encumbrance in moving forward. It continually came in contact with wet brush and pools of water, which increased the danger of its getting wet and becoming useless. He decided to leave it.

Selecting a rock overhang, he hung his gun and powder horn out of the rain. He moved forward, armed only with a small hatchet and his hunting knife. He also had a small Bowie knife inside his shirt. Moving forward for some distance, he turned to examine the spot where he had left his gun and felt sure that he would know the place, no matter from which direction he was compelled to approach it.

He rose to his feet at the side of a large tree. He then felt the touch of Lion on his leg, in a manner that conveyed to him the impression that danger was near at hand. The dog quickly sank to earth. The youth pressed closely to the tree. In the next instant, a heavy hand grasped his shoulder. "Oh," grunted a harsh voice in broken English, "Catchem little chief."

The lad grasped his knife and hatchet and faced his captor. He was in the act of dealing him a deadly blow when a second hand seized his uplifted arm and a voice exclaimed, "Little chief big fool. No kill Indian." Walter now found himself in the midst of five brawny savages, one of whom said in Spanish, "Come."

Walter told Lion to go, and the dog disappeared as quickly as the savages had appeared. His captors dragged him to the midst of the Indian camp, stopping in front of the improvised lodge and the campfire. The foremost savage faced the captive and asked, "Where gun?" The youth waved his hand to the west, at the same time kicking the water with his foot, as much to say that in the darkness and wet the rifle was of little use. The savages engaged in a general talk, and as the lad glanced back, he beheld Lion in the shadow of the trees, standing at his full height, with his hair bristled up as if about to attack. The lad waved his hand at the faithful creature, and Lion sank to earth and disappeared into the darkness.

The leading Indian, with savage glee, pointed to a form near a tree and said, "You find squaw now. You find squaw now."

"Oh, Capitan," said the weeping girl, "you were looking for me, and these cruel men have captured you."

"Never mind, Señorita," said Walter. "Your friends will try and save you."

The Indian took the lad roughly by the shoulder, saying, "No talk to squaw. She my squaw now."

Walter shook off the hand of the savage and, seizing the big fellow's blanket, tore it from his shoulder. He stepped to the side of the young captive girl and wrapped the blanket carefully around her. The savage shrugged. "Squaw warm now," said the big fellow. He stepped into the wigwam and came out with a robe to replace the blanket of which he had been so unceremoniously despoiled.

The rain had ceased to fall, but it was still dark. After some further talk, two of the Indians led the young man a short distance to one side, placed his back to a good-sized tree, securely bound his hands, and lashed him to the tree. They also bound his feet so tightly that he found it impossible to move—and both his hands and feet were soon chilled so that he could no longer feel them. He found, by letting his body settle on the ropes, that he could rest somewhat. But he had no thought of his own discomfort while the girl was in such an uncomfortable position, so near at hand.

Hours seemed to pass, and the rain again began to fall. It gradually increased until it fell in torrents. The two savages who had settled down by the tree to which he was tied now crawled under a fir tree nearby, where they found shelter from the pouring rain. Walter soon heard heavy breathing, indicating that some of them slept. He was totally unprotected from the rain, and his already wet clothing was now dripping. Presently he became conscious that his dog was licking his hands. Soon that sagacious creature commenced to tug away at the thongs that bound his hands. So diligently did he work that the knots began to give. Suddenly there was a stir under the fir tree, and an Indian came and stood by the boy for a moment. Lion had vanished. After passing his hands over the rope, the Indian went back and rolled himself in his blanket. As soon as the heavy breathing resumed, Lion returned and continued his work. Presently the stretching rawhide cords gave sufficiently to allow Walter to slip his right hand out of the loop. After waiting a moment to let the blood get into circulation again, the lad began trying to reach the small Bowie knife inside his clothing. By shoving up the cords that bound his body at the breast—which had become somewhat loosened by the strain of sustaining his weight—he finally managed to get his hand inside his clothes. And he soon had his knife ready for use. His first act was to cut the cords that bound his feet. He knew that it would take some time for the blood to find its way into his benumbed feet and ankles. Fearing another inspection, he did not disturb the cords around his body. When his limbs were again able to perform their accustomed duties, he severed the bands that bound his body. He was free.

A flash of lightning revealed to him his own hatchet sitting against a tree nearby. He decided to risk an attempt to secure possession of that useful weapon. Lying flat, he moved silently forward and, securing it, at once moved away to a safe distance. He believed that, by going around and approaching the young girl from behind the bough lodge, he might liberate her. The rain continued to pour down in torrents, and he had little difficulty in reaching the tree to which Maria was bound. He found to his surprise that Lion was licking her cold hands. The lad proceeded with the greatest care and freed her feet, her hands, and finally her body and helped the tired girl to her feet. They moved back, making a wide circuit to avoid the Indian horses, for fear they might give the alarm. They soon got far to the rear and halted under a thick grove of fir trees, where they were protected from the rain.

Walter now explained that he had left his rifle behind and must return for it, counseling the señorita that she would be safe where she was. She tried to persuade her young protector that they could get along without the gun, and then, having exhausted all arguments, she said, "Lion will take care of me."

"But," said the lad, "I can never find you again without Lion. He will bring me quicker to your side."

Yet she demurred.

He finally placed his hand on her shoulder and said, with firmness, "I must not delay. Time is precious. Sit here and be silent. Remember, do not speak or stir," and he was gone.

He and Lion retraced their steps and were soon in sight of the flickering fire. The brave dog seemed to understand what had brought them back, and he led his master directly to the overhang where Walter had left his gun. Seizing his weapon, the lad turned and rapidly directed his course to the spot where he had left the girl. They had not gone far when a sound reached his ear from the direction of the camp, and he knew that their escape had been discovered. He urged Lion forward, and they soon found the frightened girl.

Taking Maria's hand, Walter whispered hastily, "They have discovered our flight. Let us go quickly." They soon heard calls in the forest back of them, and they hurried on. The rain had stopped. They came to the bank of a rushing torrent. The young man did not hesitate for a moment. Handing his rifle to the girl, he kneeled down and told his charge to climb on his back. "Oh, Capitan," she pleaded, "we will be drowned."

Taking hold of her firmly, he said, "Señorita, you must obey. We must cross."

She silently submitted. Raising his load as high as possible on his shoulders, he entered the foaming flood. The darkness was intense, and his only guide was the flowing water. Many times he staggered and almost fell, but he struggled on until—totally exhausted—he reached the opposite shore. They had just settled down in the bushes to rest when a call, imitating a whippoorwill, sounded on the opposite shore just a little below where the fugitives had crossed. The youth placed his hand on the girl's mouth, in token of silence. They heard an answering call a short distance above, and shortly two of the savages met and seemed to consult. Then a flash of lightning revealed the enemy in the act of turning back, evidently believing that no sane person would attempt to cross such a torrent and especially not a young girl.

After waiting a few moments, the boy led the way up the stream. They walked for half an hour through an open forest until the youth halted under the friendly branches of a large fir. There he studied long as to the course to pursue, but he could not decide. The storm now resumed with fury. Despite the overhanging branches of the fir, they were soon soaked and chilled. The girl shivered violently, but she did not complain. "What will we do now, Capitan?" she asked.

After a brief silence, the young man replied, "This storm has me turned

around. We ought to be above our camp, but if that is so, the enemy is
between us and our friends. In this darkness, it is unsafe to move in any
direction, since we do not know which way to turn. Will you be afraid to
remain here while I look around a little? Lion will stay with you."

"I am not afraid when he is near," replied the girl.

After helping the señorita wrap up in the big rain-soaked robe, Walter
patted his dog on the head and told him to stay and guard the girl. He then
passed on up the stream, keeping in the center of the timber. After walking
a quarter of a mile, he came to a dense thicket of fir trees, the limbs of
which came to the ground. He at once determined to return and bring the
young girl there and kindle a fire, the light of which could not be seen at
any distance. They could dry their clothes, and the tired girl could get some
sleep. He gathered wood for a fire and then returned to his charge. He cheered
her up by saying that he had found a secure retreat, with good shelter, where
she could rest at least until morning. They hurried on and were soon by
the warm fire. He hung the wet robe close to the flames to dry and cut fir
boughs for a comfortable bed for the girl. He encircled the place with a
dense mass of boughs to form a screen so that no light from the fire could
escape. Maria waited patiently, though violently shivering, until she could
wrap up in the warm, dry robe with her feet to the fire. She was soon sleeping soundly.

Walter now employed himself in making the camp more comfortable
and safe, stopping up every crack where a ray of light might possibly stray.
He dried his own clothes and kept the fire burning. Once or twice, he fell
into a doze, but only for a short time. At the first signs of light, he ascended
a bluff nearby in hopes of discovering a sign of the enemy that might, in
some way, determine his future course. The country was new to him, and
he finally made up his mind that he had, in the excitement of the hour,
traveled much farther than he had at first thought and that he was many
miles from the camp of his friends. He guessed that the stream near at hand
was generally small, but now it had become—because of the heavy rain—a
raging torrent nearly impossible to cross on foot and dangerous on a horse.
He dared not attempt to reach his friends without first knowing where the
enemy was. And he felt that the young girl could not undergo much more
fatigue. He looked for her to collapse when the excitement through which
she had passed subsided.

As he came down from the bluff, he saw a large rabbit crouched under a bush. By a lucky throw with a stone, he stunned the animal and, before it could recover, killed it. Having dressed the rabbit nicely, he commenced to cook it over the fire. It was broad daylight when the girl opened her eyes. She complained that her head hurt her. Walter examined her and found that the savages had struck her a blow on the head with a blunt instrument, a tomahawk perhaps, and it was quite inflamed. The young man gathered some balsam from the trees nearby and put the soft wax on the wound. After bathing her head in cool water, the señorita declared that it felt better. She was much surprised to find a hot breakfast ready for her. Fortunately, the rabbit furnished ample food for the morning, both for themselves and Lion.

Rain continued to fall as the day advanced, but the youth felt quite safe in their retreat, which was completely sheltered from the storm. Toward noon, the level of the stream dropped considerably and the youth determined to try and get some fish. He always stowed away line and hook in his pockets, and he quickly prepared for the effort. He caught several trout and at once proceeded to broil them for dinner. After a hearty meal of the delicious trout, both young people felt much improved. They laid aside the remainder of the rabbit for future use, when they had exhausted the supply of trout. "I would be afraid to use my rifle," explained the young hunter, "for fear it might attract our enemies. I fear, if we were captured again, we might not find it so easy to escape again."

The clouds settled down, and the rain fell more gently. They made no effort to move. "We could not safely go elsewhere," Walter told his companion, "even if the rain ceased to fall, as we might meet an enemy at any moment. I am sure the Indians have every confidence in their strength and superior numbers, and they will be scouring the country in every direction. I am quite sure that the rain has so obliterated our tracks that the enemy cannot trace us, and therefore, so long as we are quiet, we are safe. A horseman could not penetrate this thicket, and I do not look for the enemy to be peering around in this densely timbered glade for lost captives. We will have to content ourselves with staying here one more night. Although we may not like to do this, we cannot help ourselves, Señorita."

"Oh, Capitan," said the young girl, "I feel bad to have been the cause of so much trouble to you. Ever since we first saw you, we have—in one way and another—been a burden to you. My poor father should never have taken this terrible journey without more and better men. My poor mother, I know, is looking for us daily, and her heart would break if she knew what dangers we are subjected to. How grateful she will be to you, and the other kind and generous gentlemen, for caring for us so courteously. Capitan, I do so want you to see and know my dear mother."

"Señorita," said the young hunter, "I am very sorry indeed that you mourn so much about meeting us, for I know that every man in our party feels honored to have made the acquaintance of your good father and yourself. Your presence has more than compensated for the little we have done for you. If we shall succeed in at last escorting you safely to your home and friends, I am sure every one will feel that he has been more than paid for any little service rendered you. More than that, all will regret sincerely the hour when we shall say good-bye. These rough men all admire your father very much."

"Capitan, why do you have to go away? The country where we live is very rich and fine, and we think you might like to live there. There are some Americans in that country who have great ranches like my father. They like the country and our people."

The youth was silent. He found it convenient to replenish the fire and shortly said that he would go out and look around. Leaving Lion, he went out and strolled through the thick underbrush, passing along the sides of a steep bluff. Among the thick bushes and cactus, he noticed a hole in the cliff. Parting the bushes, he found the opening to be a large tunnel cut out of the solid rock. At its mouth, some loose stones had accumulated, and beyond it was open. The youth entered the tunnel and passed within until it began to grow dark. He then gathered some dry twigs and made a torch, which allowed him to further explore the excavation until the torch began to fade.

He retraced his steps, and upon reaching camp, he found the young girl in tears. Gathering a quantity of wood, the wanderers settled down to make the best of their lonely abode. Walter, hoping to divert the young girl from her sad thoughts, asked her to tell him how she came to be captured.

"Oh, Capitan," she answered, "it is only a very short story. You see the horses made a great noise, and my father said something was wrong with them. He ran out to them. He had only been gone a few moments before I heard his dear voice calling for help. The good priest and I ran out. The priest was ahead and did not know I was following—or he would have protected me. It was so dark we could see nothing. I called my Father. As I did so, someone caught me by the shoulder. I thought at first it was Father, but then I felt myself being carried away. I screamed. Then someone put a hand on my mouth, and I pushed it away and I screamed again. Then I felt a blow on my head—which produced the wound you doctored so nicely— and I knew nothing more for some time. When I came to my senses, I was being carried away, and I knew the Indians had me, for I could smell them. I did not speak. When I got to their camp, they sat me down on a blanket. The men were at work making that bough wickiup. They said nothing to me but just let me sit there, and I guess they would not have tied me, had I not tried to run away. Then they tied me to the tree. I did not look up again, Capitan, until you came. My heart was almost broken when I saw you a prisoner, for then I felt sure that our whole party, my father and little sister, the good padre, and all our kind friends would be killed."

After hearing Maria's story, the young hunter spent the evening cleaning his gun. He extracted the bullets and removed their loads, fearing that the continued dampness had penetrated to and wet the powder, which might then fail to go off in case of need, a circumstance to be avoided if possible. In this way, they passed the hours until the young girl began to yawn. The youth suggested that she go to sleep for the night. "I will watch," he said, "with our good, faithful friend here."

"But Capitan," she said, "you watched last night. You must have rest, or you cannot stand the fatigues that might be ahead of us."

"I did watch some last night," he replied, "but I confess I did doze some, even while on watch. I have no fears that Lion will not wake me, should danger come near."

"You will sleep some then, Capitan?"

"Yes, I will after a while."

Heavy breathing coming from the bed occupied by the young girl soon told Walter that she was sleeping soundly. Near midnight, the young hunter dropped off into a sound sleep, nor did he wake until it was quite light— and then only when Lion licked his face. The animal looked intently toward the stream, and the youth felt sure something was moving near at hand. Peeking out through the bushes, he soon saw the cause of the dog's interest. Several deer were feeding nearby. He motioned Lion to lie down, and he himself remained quiet, not caring to alarm the timid creatures. At the same time, he regretted that he could not kill one for food. It would be very improper to do so, he felt, as the enemy was yet in the near vicinity.

The deer soon passed up the stream, crossing it without taking alarm. After cooking the remainder of the savory trout, the youth called the young señorita. He added that it had ceased raining and that it was high time to be on their way. He had not yet decided upon a definite course, and he asked for her advice.

She rose, saying, "Capitan, I am willing to advise, but I have noticed you do not take my advice but instead take your own course. You left me alone against my advice; you carried me across that terrible stream, against my advice—and Capitan, I guess I am glad you did."

After bathing her face and hands in the cool stream, the maiden dressed her beautiful hair as best she could, after which she looked fresh and well. She ate quite heartily of the trout that her handy young companion had so nicely broiled. After breakfast, the young hunter told her of his discovery of the cave or tunnel, saying that he thought it could be entered in such a way that discovery would scarcely be possible. If she would consent to remaining there with Lion, he would carefully reconnoiter the country and look for their people. It would be the best thing for them to do, he said, "for we cannot exist long in this condition."

"Capitan," replied the young girl, "I have no advice to give. You are wise. I shall be guided by your counsel. I have every confidence in you and feel sure that you will do nothing that you do not think is for the best. While you scout, I will pray the good Lord to guide and protect you."

After a search, they found suitable pitch pine from which to make torches, and the young man asked the señorita to follow him. "Should our sagacious enemies visit this spot, they will certainly find our sign. We must hide our trail." Going directly to the bank of the stream, the young man took the girl to the center of the stream and waded downstream some distance to the edge of a deep pool. Then he returned with care, obliterating every sign in the gravel at the bottom of the stream. Again taking the young girl on his back, he waded up the stream to a point where there was a large number of black stones lying in the water and projecting above it. He took hold of Maria's hand and helped her jump from one stone to the next until they

reached a large pile of rocks at the mouth of the hidden tunnel. They carefully made an entrance, so as not to leave any trace of a footprint or broken
twig or other evidence that they had passed therein. To make sure that all
was safe, Walter again returned to the stream, carefully observing the earth
and stones they had lately passed over. He told the señorita that he felt
perfectly sure that their retreat would not be discovered or even suspected.
"And," said he, "the wild growth of bushes has so completely hidden the
entrance that it would be an accident if it was found, even by the savages."

"But Capitan, you found it. Why not the Indians?"

"That is true, Señorita, but what caught my attention would never be
suspected by Indians. I saw in the creek a rock that I was sure had been
taken from a solid bed someplace by the aid of tools used in mining. I
investigated and found others. I then came upon the rocks we have climbed
over. A casual observer might have thought they slid down the hill, but I
did not think so. I searched and was rewarded by finding this retreat."

"If the Indians find our sunny little camp, Capitan, where will they think
we have gone?"

"They will trace us to the water. They will see you have not crossed. They
will see by our tracks on the sand—which I made a clumsy effort to conceal, on purpose—that we passed down the stream. They will, of course,
think we went into the stream to conceal our trail and movements. I hope
they think that we have passed down the stream and possibly reached our
camp in safety. Now, let's go in and explore."

After walking into the tunnel for something like one hundred feet, the
fugitives came to a short crosscut. Here the young man prepared his torches
and decided to further investigate, for he did not think it right to leave his
precious charge so near the entrance. Lighted torch in hand, he said, "Now,
Señorita, if you will stay here, I will go in and find a more secure retreat."

As he turned to go, a well-known rattle—that of the rattlesnake—came
from a shelf on the tunnel wall, causing him to spring back just in time
to escape the stroke of an enormous rattler. The young and frightened
girl was now between the reptile and the end of a short, narrow crosscut.
Quick as thought, the boy whipped out his hatchet and struck the vicious
serpent, severing its head in twain. They soon discovered a second serpent,
which Walter also dispatched. He covered the bodies of both snakes
with loose rock.

"I do not wish to stay here, Capitan. I fear snakes so much."

"No, you need not do so, Señorita. I will go forward. The light will be bright." And the friends walked on.

Presently they came to a wide place in the tunnel. A large stone lay on one side. "On this stone, Señorita, I think you can safely rest until I return. You can see that there is no place for a serpent to hide. To make sure, you had better aid me in making careful search."

Together they searched for some distance each way. After a most rigid examination, they discovered nothing.

Maria said that she would not be afraid to remain with Lion as her guard.

"He will protect you from these deadly rattlers," said Walter. "He kills them whenever he can reach them. He is very watchful, and if they are on the ground, he is never surprised by them. The ones we saw were so high up on the walls that he did not see them."

"Why, Capitan, I saw him acting strangely, looking and smelling up there where the snakes were. He kept pushing me back to the end of the little room, but I could see nothing."

"He must have smelled them," answered the young man.

Walter now left the maiden with a torch and Lion lying at her feet. He walked deeper into the cavern and was surprised to find the air still fresh and pure. Presently, he noticed the smoke of the torch rising, and upon investigation, he discovered a narrow cut that passed far up into the roof of the tunnel. While he could see no light above, he was sure this opening extended to the surface. He estimated that the distance from the air shaft, which it certainly was, to the mouth of the tunnel near the creek was at least three hundred feet.

"I scarcely see the use of further exploration," he thought, "but I do not like to leave the young girl, even with Lion, without satisfying myself that no beast or lurking foe is hidden in the inner recesses of this lonesome place." On he went fully one hundred feet farther when he came to a fork in the tunnel. The branch ran almost at right angles to the main tunnel, and there was every appearance of a vein of some mineral. It was now damp, and the air was less pure. After pushing on fully two hundred feet more, he came to the end of the main tunnel, where there was a large vein excavated from the solid rock. The rock on all sides had the appearance of mineral, in some of which particles of native copper were visible. A light copper hammer lay on the floor. The air being damp and heavy, he quickly left the place, taking the hammer with him.

Coming to the branch, he followed it for 150 feet to its termination. Along this drift, he found mineral here and there, but the air was also thick and heavy, and he at once retraced his steps, finally coming back to where he had left his companion. He handed the señorita the hammer. "I brought this," he told her, "that you might have a weapon for self-defense."

"I need none, Capitan, with this brave dog."

He then held out a leaf-wrapped parcel. "And here is some fish for you. I dislike leaving you in this lonesome place, but it seems best. I will remain away not one moment longer than is necessary. I can assure you that I have explored this place to its termination, at all points, and there is no living thing that could do you harm here." So saying, he patted Lion on the head. "Brave old Lion, I leave you to protect and watch over this young señorita. Let no harm come to her." Taking her hand, he pressed it to his lips and turned to go.

"Oh, Capitan," said the young girl, "you must take food. I do not need all this."

"No, no, Señorita, I shall not want food before I return." Lifting his hat politely, he left her. He mused as he went, "This is a most lonely spot."

Passing most cautiously from the tunnel, the lad entered the stream and made his way, for the most part, by springing from one rock to another. In this way, he covered fully half a mile. As he traveled, he took careful note of all landmarks so that he might recognize them again.

He soon found himself opposite a high cliff, the summit of which he thought he could reach by hard, patient work. Once on top, he would have a broad view for a great distance in every direction. At this point, the stream flowed into a canyon through which one could pass only with difficulty. The youth toiled diligently and finally passed through this gap, sometimes wading, sometimes leaping from rock to rock. At other times, he climbed on the rocky bank or crawled on his hand and knees. He surveyed the situation carefully and decided to make the attempt to climb the bluff on the opposite shore, steep as it was.

On his way up, he came soon to what looked like a rude trail fashioned in the face of the rock. First passing up on a slant to the right, he then turned and went to the left, up the almost perpendicular bluff. He made rapid progress on the switchbacks. "Is it possible that this strange road," he thought to himself, "has been made by humans?" At last reaching a shelf, he sat down to rest. At his feet lay an oblong stone, around which a deep half-round crease was cut. Here was an implement of some kind, formed for use as either a hammer or for defense. Again he climbed forward, now and then finding more articles made of stone or clay, each surely made by human hands.

After passing up in this manner for a thousand feet or more, he saw through an opening in the rock face a spacious room, the floor of which was strewn with broken earthenware. Some of the sherds were gorgeously painted with likenesses of animals and human beings. Amazed, the youth looked around him. This must certainly be the past habitation of a prehistoric people, probably long extinct. There was a kind of fireplace, hewn from the solid rock, the chimney of which passed into the ceiling above. Walter then found a rude opening, partially blocked by stones and rubbish, that led into a dark adjoining room. Removing enough of the debris in the doorway to let in some light, the young hunter found stone arrowheads, more fragments of pottery, and many other articles of great interest to him.

Now he reminded himself that he had other duties to perform before he hurried back to the girl, and he reluctantly abandoned his exploration. Again finding the old trail, he followed its zigzag course toward the summit of the bluff, coming upon other abandoned habitations at intervals. As he approached the top, he discovered the entrance to another room of even larger dimensions. Here, among the rubbish, was a wad of human hair and, in one corner, several human skulls and other bones, probably human. He picked up a stone knife with a rough, sharp edge, and he uncovered several stone hammers. The knife was eleven inches in length, a portion being wound with a kind of flax that served as a handle. Scattered among the debris were a goodly number of arrow points and a slender copper awl. The awl was black, resembling iron, but when the boy scratched it, he found it to be copper, very hard, stiff, and sharp at the point. There were characters painted and carved on the walls. These seemed to relate the history of the strange people who, ages ago, had inhabited these inaccessible quarters. The habitation had been partly hewn from solid rock, while other sections had been constructed of blocks of stone shaped by human hands and placed in position with workmanlike skill. Embedded in clay, yet hard and firm, beams of cedar—still in a fair state of preservation—projected from the masonry walls. In one corner, a large pine tree had taken root in the crumbling wall and had grown to a size estimated by the young hunter to be thirty inches in diameter. This tree had spread the walls and crowded the large foundation stones out of place. How could people, wondered Walter, exist so far from fresh water on this precipitous perch?

The old trail, which in places was really steps formed from the solid rock, led to the summit of the cliff, which opened out onto a broad mesa. The trail led Walter to the left and brought him to a great precipice, from which he had an excellent view of the surrounding country. Opposite was an extensive plateau extending to the south and east. Walter took a position on top of the rock but soon crouched down, having spotted ten horsemen on a ridge opposite. He felt sure that some of them must have seen him, had they turned their eyes in his direction, but they seemed to be looking intently below, at something in the little canyon which he had traversed before beginning his climb past the cliff dwellings. Settling down in a well-protected position, he soon felt satisfied that he had not been discovered.

The Indians now dismounted and stood for a long time on the edge of the plateau, surveying everything within range of their vision. After completing their survey, they mounted and rode away evidently satisfied, for they looked back no more. After they had passed from view, the young hunter crawled around and took a long look down the course of the stream where his friends should be encamped, but he saw no signs of life on the plain where he thought the camp must be.

Directing his attention farther north, he saw another party of savages, four in number, riding in a southwesterly direction toward the stream he had just left. They were heading well down, opposite, and below where he had left the young señorita. He concluded that they were searching for himself and his companion. He made up his mind further that if his friends had not actually been killed, they must be closely besieged, for he could now see the ten horsemen who had lately been just opposite him riding down the plain, miles below, at a point that could not be far from the camp of his friends. He could also see loose horses far below; these were certainly the property of the party of ten. The fact that the savages were so bold made evident that they were strong in numbers. The second party was now some miles down and evidently on its way to a camp. Feeling that he should gain a position from which he could observe the great mesa to the northeast to better advantage, he sought the old trail and made his way up the steep bluff, finally reaching the upper edge, which led to the bluff's highest point. Slowly he climbed to the high elevation, a most laborious task. On reaching the summit, he found quite a level plateau, sloping gently to the north.

Though he encountered horse tracks, indicating that a war party had been there a short time before, the lad felt confident that he had not been discovered. He decided that the only safe plan was to return to the tunnel the same way he had come. It was now past the noon hour, and he turned his face homeward. He decided, however, to hunt for a more covered route to reach the bed of the creek instead of descending the open face of the cliff. Following the rocky ridge of the plateau for a mile or more, he came to a sloping hillside and started down. He finally reached a timbered flat near the base of the bluff. Sitting down under a tree to rest, he soon observed a small band of deer feeding towards him. After some little time, the animals reached a point within thirty yards of the lad. He aimed at a fine, fat buck several times, each time lowering his gun with the thought, "Can the enemy hear my rifle?" He remembered that he had loaded the upper barrel very lightly, with the idea that he might want to kill food. He finally reasoned, "We must have food tonight. Both Maria and Lion will be hungry. I have had nothing, and I cannot safely provide meat any nearer the enemy. I will take the chance."

Leveling his rifle, he was beginning to press the trigger, aiming at the head of the buck nearest him, when one of the does farther down the hillside started and ran up near the buck. Walter watched now and wondered what could have startled the animal. The buck was looking away from him and now began approaching the boy's position, stopping occasionally and looking back up the hillside. The animal was now only ten yards away and still approaching. He then stopped and turned his broadside facing the hill. At that instant, there was a hissing sound and the buck leapt into the air, stumbled forward a few steps, and again looked back. "Whiz" came the same hissing sound, and a fine doe came to her knees. Staggering first in one direction and then the other, the buck presently fell on its side. The doe ran a short distance and fell.

Amazed and petrified, the young hunter did not stir. An Indian had certainly killed the animals. Perhaps several were near. Walter looked steadily in the direction the deer had been looking. There was a small clump of trees about thirty yards from where the buck had fallen. A small fir partially obscured the little thicket, as did a large pine. The youth himself was in the shade of several large fir trees, and against the trunk of one of these, his gun now rested. He dared not move. Certainly the Indian had not observed his presence; otherwise, the savage would have sent his first arrow at the boy instead of the deer. Time passed slowly. It seemed hours. His gun seemed so heavy. Still he watched and waited, his attention riveted to the little grove.

At last, he dared raise his eyes a little higher and noticed, for the first time, a deep ravine just beyond the thicket. Running his eyes down the ravine perhaps a hundred yards or more, he saw the head and ears of a horse. "It must be tied," he thought, "but the enemy is not there. That's too far. He could not have sent those deadly arrows that distance. He is surely in the thicket—and he has now discovered me, and I will get the next arrow." Cold drops of sweat came out on his brow. He strained his eyes toward the dark thicket.

"He is there, certain," thought the lad. "No other place would shelter him, and no other shield is sufficiently near to enable him to send those wicked shafts so straight home. Hold! A twig moves. It surely moves, but I cannot see the hidden enemy." Again the whole pine slightly trembled. "He is surely there."

At this moment, the young hunter imagined he saw something dark just under a limb. The next instant, he heard the same hissing sound, similar to escaping air or steam, and he felt the air of the passing missile on the side of his neck. He did not move. Like a flash, an ugly visage appeared by the side of the pine. It was for but an instant, but it was long enough. The youth covered it and fired. He heard a sound like the falling of a heavy body, and then all was still. Stepping behind the trees at his back, the young hunter reloaded his rifle. Now sliding down the hill, keeping a large pine tree between himself and the thicket, he cautiously approached the spot. He had no fear of the savage whose head he had so quickly covered, but he thought it possible that two Indians might have been there. He waited, making a long, careful survey of the spot. He finally stepped out, his rifle presented, and quickly approached the thicket. Here he found, as he'd expected, the savage lying on his face dead. Turning the warrior over, he found that his bullet had taken effect between the eyes, where the nose joined the forehead, passing entirely through the head. After further investigation, he satisfied himself that the savage was alone. He at once set to work to dispose of the body, together with those portions of the two deer that he could not take with him. Near at hand was a steep crevice, about three feet wide and some five feet deep. To this spot, he carried the body of the savage, taking care that no blood escaped. He then moved the deer to the same spot and quickly dressed them, throwing the offal into the cut. He then deposited the heads and remaining portions of the animals in the improvised grave, throwing first a few boughs on them and covering the top with loose dirt. He then gathered a quantity of old logs and stones and covered the remains completely so that even large animals could scarcely uncover them. He took these precautions so that birds of prey would not hover over the spot and thus enable the friends of the dead Indian to locate the remains.

The ravine where he'd seen the horse was a dry watercourse, cut out by the spring rains. He went to the Indian's horse and found it to be a very good animal. The gelding was a little wild at first, but the young man remembered that Indians approach and mount their horses from the off or right side. He had no trouble stringing the meat cut from the buck and doe upon the horse. His work completed, the young hunter led the horse rapidly from the spot. He was disturbed that he had had to spend so much time away from the señorita, even though he knew Lion was dependable. He directed his course down the creek, and about a quarter of a mile above the tunnel, he halted the horse in the midst of a small grassy park surrounded with high bushes. The grass was rich and abundant. He tied the horse and then approached the tunnel cautiously. About one hundred yards above the tunnel was a very thick grove of trees. In this grove, he selected a camp, well knowing that it would be uncomfortable to pass the night in the tunnel.

The only articles he had taken from the dead Indian, besides the horse and saddle, were a new pair of moccasins, which he had found tied to the horse; a new Navajo blanket of first quality and exquisite workmanship; and an ornamented bow with a quiver of arrows. The bow was wonderfully well proportioned, made from some fine-grained, elastic wood, with its back covered with the skin of a rattlesnake. The bowstring was of the finest deer sinews, and the arrows were models of their kind, made smooth and straight, the feathers most artistically arranged and so beautifully wound with the finest sinews as to be scarcely separate from the wood itself. The points were of flint, fitted perfectly to the wood and so finely and evenly placed and set that the shaft was in perfect balance. Half-round grooves were cut in each side of the long shaft to the depth of some sixteenth of an inch, being slightly wider at the top than at the bottom. These grooves were not straight, but instead waved back and forth on each side in long, graceful curves. The purpose of this part of the mechanism of the arrow was twofold: first, to aid in the turning movement in its flight, giving the arrow a similar movement to that of a leaden bullet, having passed through rifle grooves; and second, in passing into the flesh of the victim, the arrow point cut but a small wound, which the following shaft quite filled up—the grooves allowing blood to escape on each side of the arrow and giving the warrior an opportunity to follow his victim by the red fluid dropping from the wound.

Admiring the weapon, the young hunter mused, "A warrior and hunter may well be known and judged by his weapons. I have never seen such a bow, nor such perfect arrows." On picking up the bow, the young hunter found an arrow near it, which the savage had evidently been fitting to the string for another shot. Walter noticed that the head of the arrow had three deep scars cut with some sharp instrument on each side. These grooves were partially filled with a dark, gluey paste. This arrow he marked and put into the quiver, intending to examine it more closely at a more convenient moment. The bow would certainly be useful to procure food when it was dangerous to use his gun.

The place Walter had selected for a camp was well sheltered and protected by the surrounding chaparral. That settled, he hastened to the tunnel to get Maria and give her an opportunity to breathe fresh air. He entered with much caution, and much to his relief, Lion came bounding forward, followed by the young girl, her eyes wet with recent tears. The señorita said that she and Lion had come out to the point where Walter had killed the snakes in the morning and that Lion had killed two more and had come very near being bitten. "Well," replied the young hunter, "I feel guilty for having left you so long. You look pale. Let us be off." He led the way to the mouth of the tunnel, and they soon reached the retreat he had selected for the night. Returning to the place where he had left the horse, he unsaddled and picketed the animal with a rawhide rope, in such a manner as to enable the animal to feed and, at the same time, not become entangled in the bushes at the edge of the little park. He then fastened the saddle well up in the trees to prevent the rawhide straps from being eaten by wild animals.

Taking the fine Navajo blanket and the two saddles of venison, he returned to the grove. He found the young girl breaking twigs with which to kindle a fire. Her eyes brightened when she saw the venison. "Capitan," she said, "I feared that you would be afraid to fire your gun so near our enemies."

"Señorita," replied the young hunter, "I was far away, so far that I hoped our enemies could not hear my rifle. I knew we must have food. See how gaunt our brave dog is. He needs a good supper, and he shall have it." He now set to work, making the fire and constructing a blind to make the camp more secure from observation. After this had been completed, he went out—it was now dark—to observe the effect from all sides. Returning, he said with satisfaction that they could cook their supper without the fire being seen, unless the enemy happened to stumble right on them.

Maria broiled meat for supper while the young hunter prepared the rest of the venison for jerking. "We must anticipate the worst," he said, "as we may not soon again be able to have a fire. We will smoke the meat nicely, and then we can eat it whether we have a fire or not."

After supper, the youth left the señorita to watch the fire and went out to examine the vicinity, and satisfy himself that no enemy lurked near at hand. Lion went straight to the Indian horse, sniffing curiously. They discovered no trace of lurking Indians. On returning to camp, the young man found Maria in a fever of excitement. Her first question was "Capitan, where did you get the beautiful blanket?" Before he could answer, she cried, "Oh, Capitan, your neck is hurt. It bleeds." The spot where the arrow of the savage had touched his neck had begun to bleed. "Tell me," she said, "what has happened to you." She was now at his side, endeavoring to minister to his injured neck. "Oh, Capitan, you have been shot with an arrow. Here are some feathers through the collar of your coat." They now discovered that when the arrow had slightly cut his neck, it had passed through his buckskin coat and had left some of its feathers sticking in the thick leather. "Tell me, Capitan. Do not try to deceive me. Tell me all you know."

In his calm, quiet way, he told her of the day's adventures in every detail. He discussed the presence of the prehistoric remains in the cliff dwellings, and they also talked of the old tunnel. The señorita, in the most tender manner, dressed the young hunter's wounded neck and bound it up with a small piece of linen from a petticoat. Walter expressed the opinion that the ancient inhabitants had not made the tunnel but that it had been built at a far later date, perhaps by the Spaniards themselves. There were certainly rocks in the tunnel that carried minerals of various sorts besides the copper that was visible to the eye. Maria said that she had heard her father and the old Spanish missionary fathers speak of mines. She had heard the missionaries say that the ancients had evidently made use of the precious metals, for ornaments of both gold and silver had been found in their tombs and the ruins of their ancient habitations. She said that these old ruins were a mystery—not only to the early Spanish settlers but also to the oldest inhabitants of the country. None of the Pueblo Indians could give any account of the old ruins, saying when asked, "They were always there." She therefore thought that the old tunnel had been made by the ancients.

"That is possible," said the young man, "but if it is true, they certainly understood not only the art of mining, but also the art of ventilation, for the air shaft proves this. I would like to explore this place more thoroughly if I had time and it was safe to do so."

"Oh," answered the girl, "think of those awful snakes. They would certainly attack and kill you. I would much rather be killed by the savages, even burned at the stake, than to die from a bite of those terrible reptiles. It makes me shiver to think of them. Lion is a brave creature. He is so quick and expert. He made false motions at the coiled serpent, and when it sprang at him, he quickly caught it and shook it fiercely and threw it down. It was dead and could only move its ugly tail. He is watchful, too. He would go ahead of me. Had he not done so, I would have been bitten, for one serpent was right in the path and I did not see it in the uncertain light—until the noble dog sprang toward me and crowded me backwards. I did not think to strike it with a stone. In fact, I could not, for the cunning dog would pay no attention to me while he was battling the serpents. When they were dead, he wagged his tail and I know he was grinning at me. After that, he would do everything I told him to."

"Lion was charged with a great responsibility, Señorita—that of protecting you. What report could he have offered me on my return, my dear friend, had you been injured or bitten or had accident befallen you?"

"Oh, you are so serious, Capitan," replied the maiden. "But I am glad you have the blanket, for the nights get chilly."

"That puts me in mind," said Walter, "of a more useful article I've brought home. See this beautiful bow and this quiver full of arrows? We may want to use them to provide food when we cannot use the gun. We must both practice with them so we can at least kill birds and rabbits."

The señorita recoiled from the snakeskin cover, but the young hunter told her, "It is dead, and the weapon may be useful." And then he remembered that there was a peculiar arrow in the quiver. Selecting it from the others, he examined it closely. He also found four others exactly like it, tied in a little bundle with a sinew string. He finally concluded that the five arrows were poisoned. And indeed, he found a small buckskin bag tied to the arrows, filled with a dark-colored, gluey, sticky substance.

"This," said the young hunter, "is the fatal bag of poison that Kit Carson so carefully described to me. He said this poison was rubbed into the sharp grooves cut into the arrowhead, it being so stiff and gummy that it would remain there for years—and retain its fatal effect on whatever living creature it came into contact with. The warrior, before using it, usually rubbed the point of the arrow on some rough surface to remove whatever coating may adhere to the gummy substance. It is then ready to perform its deadly mission."

Looking up at Maria, he was alarmed to see a deadly pallor spread over her face. Dropping the arrow, he turned to her in alarm. "You are ill, Señorita. What is the matter?"

But she could not speak. After he gave her some water, she was finally able to say, "Oh, Capitan, you are poisoned." She pointed to the wound on his neck. "Oh, no," he said, "do you not see that so slight a wound, even inflicted with a fatal arrow, would not injure me? Don't you see, the skin is barely cut deep enough to cause the blood to flow? The wound was made with the sharp edge of the arrowhead and is not a finger's length. Had the point touched my neck, the wound would have been longer and deeper. Now, look at the poison on the arrow. Do you see the deep cuts in the arrowhead—on each side? Well, that brown, sticky substance with which the cuts are filled is the poison. To touch the poison, the wound would have to be much deeper. I would never have been able to return to you had I been so poisoned, for the poison acts quickly and most fatally. Therefore dismiss such foolish ideas, Señorita, for there is nothing in them. This one little bundle of arrows contains all that were poisoned. The savage saw that his first shot had failed and that the distance was too great and decided to make sure of me with the second shot. But he failed in his villainous purpose. He had a most brutal and repulsive countenance, and yet he was an able and courageous warrior. Everything of his in the shape of a weapon or implement of the chase is of the very best and in perfect order. See what a great number of arrows—seventy-two in all."

"See here, Capitan," said the young girl, pointing to two arrows stained with blood, "those have been used. They may have been used to slay our friends."

"No," said the youth, "those are the arrows with which the warrior killed the deer. The savage was an accomplished bowman. The deer were stricken down at a distance of fifty yards, and it was fully seventy yards to where I sat. His aim was certainly good. I feel sorry that I was forced, by the urgent circumstances, to kill him." So saying, the young hunter relaxed into deep, thoughtful reveries, which the señorita did not disturb for a long time.

Suddenly, Maria touched him with her hand and signaled that Lion had gone out into the darkness. Walter rose and followed. He returned after ten minutes, saying, "It was only a coyote or some such animal attracted by the smell of the fresh meat. It is most unlikely that we will be disturbed to-night." The señorita now settled into her new blanket and immediately fell into a sound sleep.

In the morning, Walter was up and about long before daylight. From the Indian's saddle, he retrieved a dressed buckskin from which he fashioned a bag to carry pieces of the jerked venison. He then went out and made his way up a high ridge to look over the country. Returning, he crossed a small branch of the creek flowing north. He decided to make a wide circuit up this branch, hoping to locate their party and rejoin it. Having decided upon this course of action, he awakened the girl and urged her to prepare for departure. He put the Indian saddle on the horse and helped Maria to mount. The animal had gotten used to his new master and was quite gentle.

Walter led the horse into the creek, while he went along the bank on foot, taking care to blind his trail as much as possible. They pursued this course to a point where the small creek entered another one, and then the fugitives passed up this larger stream in the same manner. They made slow progress owing to the crookedness of the waterways and the dense growth along the banks. When the creek became too rocky to travel safely, the señorita walked for a time and the young hunter led the horse. Finally they found a trail, and the girl mounted the horse again. After following the stream to its source, they found themselves on the summit of a considerable mountain and continued to travel as fast as possible in a westerly direction.

Walter estimated that they had covered twenty miles over the rough terrain, but that they had gained only a short distance in a direct line. The girl was pale with fatigue, so he looked for a place they could stop with a reasonable degree of safety. He made his way to a place near the ridge top where he saw a thick growth of scrub oaks. He unsaddled the horse and tied him in a sheltered place where he could feed on the few sprouts of grass they found there. He spread a blanket for Maria, and she passed four hours comfortably enough. When she prepared to mount the horse again, she looked quite refreshed. The young hunter, in the meantime, had continued to try to calculate the location of the camp where they had left their friends, trusting that the party had not been ambushed by an enemy. Being on the opposite side of the belt of timber which they had approached on the day of the storm, he could not see a single landmark with which he was at all familiar. He felt sure, however, that he would have to travel some miles before finding their old trail.

After considerable study, he selected a way which he thought would allow them to descend into the valley safely. They would be picking their way among thick shrubs and occasional groves of oak, where he thought he could maneuver so as to stay under cover most of the time. His calculation proved correct, and despite their zigzag course, they made some progress and dusk found them about fifteen miles west of their starting point. Walter believed that they had traveled fully thirty-five miles in a roundabout way. The señorita was tired, and since their position did not admit of making a fire, she was glad to bed down in a couch of leaves and branches. She slept soundly until Walter awakened her.

The young hunter had determined to start about 3 o'clock in the morning in order to cross the valley and gain a broken range of hills on the opposite side. There he hoped to locate the position of the main party. Try as he would to keep such thoughts from his mind, he felt at times that their party must be powerless to move if, indeed, they had not all been captured or murdered. He did not communicate his fears to Maria, but lay down much depressed in spirit.

When he roused the girl, she declared she felt much refreshed, but that it was too early for her to eat anything. She urged the youth to mount the horse also, but he replied, "No, Señorita, the time may come when our horse will have to carry a double burden. We must save him while we can. When it becomes necessary to move forward rapidly, he can—I am sure— carry both of us." He now led the horse, moving forward with such rapid strides that the horse was sometimes forced to trot to keep up with him. As the morning light grew brighter, the young travelers spanned the valley and moved up a long slope toward a small grove of scrub oaks some two miles distant. Walter halted at a spring. The girl dismounted and bathed her face and drank thirstily of the cool water. They moved on rapidly as before, entering the grove in good time, but Walter did not like the position and selected another grove somewhat larger a mile distant. Once there, he made a careful survey of the surrounding country. The grove proved a good place to rest. It was dense, with a small park in the center. Although there was no water, the horse could feed without being observed.

Walter kindled a small fire, and they cooked some meat he had packed in wet leaves for breakfast, after which the señorita lay down to rest while Walter studied the country. He hoped he might discover some sign of their friends who, according to his best calculations, must now be on the opposite side of the valley. After hours of the most attentive watching, he was completely baffled. He had not been able to discover a single sign that encouraged him to believe that their party was near, or even alive. He finally concluded that the camp might be some six miles still farther west, and he determined to move as soon they could safely do so under cover of darkness. Maria slept a good part of the day and, upon waking, was able to eat a hearty meal of the roasted venison. She was quite cheerful.

There were some shifting clouds, and the young hunter decided that, for fear it might rain, he would push on as soon as it was dark enough. After carefully looking over the country, he decided to try and reach a point of timber that jutted up out of the valley. It looked favorable as a place to camp for the next day. "If it should rain," he told the young girl, "our trail would be so plain that it could be seen and followed too easily. We ought to make this short drive early and get plenty of rest after we reach our destination."

At dusk, the young hunter saddled the horse and helped the señorita to mount, and they began the night's march. The route went up over the immediate hills, and they would have to gain two elevations. Walter thought that these landmarks would be plain enough, even in the darkness. The wind blew from the northwest, but this he did not consider a safe guide, as each canyon creates crosscurrents that are often misleading. They traveled as rapidly as a horse could go over the uneven ground, and before it became entirely dark, they were well on their way. In the dark, with no moon, Walter found much difficulty in keeping his course, and he felt somewhat alarmed when he did not reach the second elevation. After some study, he changed his course a bit and soon felt he was reaching the looked-for elevation. Having made the ascent, he believed that the abrupt ridge, bordering on a mesa, would be a guide. In this he was not deceived, for they soon found themselves at the edge of the pine forest where he had hoped to find a safe retreat.

The difficulty was now to find water. At the center of the timber was a dry watercourse. They followed it for some distance until they heard the ripple of water. Walter then unloaded the horse and found a sheltered spot for Maria, where he prepared a bed. He picketed the horse close by, and they passed the night quietly, except for the howl of coyotes. Towards morning, the clouds lifted and the young hunter was able to reconnoiter and secure a more suitable place nearby to pass the day. When the señorita suggested moving on, he said, "We could be, and doubtless would be, quickly observed by our enemies and followed. No, if we are to avoid capture and possible death, we must use the utmost discretion and patience. We shall have to submit to discomforts and perhaps more delays before we can reach our friends—or other refuge of safety."

Rain began to fall, and the young hunter set to work to prepare a shelter, with the aid of boughs and the broad, sheltering limbs of the fir trees. They prepared a bed, laying out the blankets, and Maria made herself comfortable for a long, quiet sleep. Walter and his faithful dog remained on guard. The boy had decided to remain in that secure spot until the storm passed. They were well surrounded by trees and bushes, and no one could see them from more than twenty feet. Near the little camp stood a large fir tree, and

Walter climbed it several times for the purpose of observation. Through the
rain and mist, he failed to find any trace of their friends or, thankfully, of
the enemy. The early hours of the night were made hideous with the howls
and wailings of the coyotes. When they finally got to sleep, the coyotes
came close enough to annoy Lion, but he faithfully kept his silent vigil.

Walter was up at an early hour. The rain had stopped, and they ate their
meal long before it was light enough to travel. He now concluded that the
point where the main party had entered the timber the night of the great
storm was still to the west some distance. At first light, the two travelers
wended their way along the base of the hill, hoping to get a better view of
the valley.

They had traveled perhaps five miles and were looking for a suitable
place to stop, when the girl clapped her hands and cried out in a suppressed
voice, "Capitan, Capitan, Oh Capitan. Look, they are coming. They are coming." About a half mile distant, five savages were approaching from the
west, mounted and traveling at a good trot. Walter did not think that the
Indians had discovered them yet. The young hunter seized the horse by the
bridle and forced him into a thicket. He decided that, as the savages were
likely to pass by on the south side of the thicket, there was a chance to
escape by riding around to the north. He mounted the horse behind Maria,
and the double-burdened animal responded quickly. He saw that the savages were traveling east, at a fairly rapid pace, and the chances now seemed
good to get off unobserved.

After nearly an hour had passed without again seeing the Indians, the
young hunter believed that he had succeeded in giving them the slip. As the
horse was now panting as a result of carrying its heavy double burden at
such a rapid pace, at times up hills, he needed to let the animal rest. When
they dismounted, he gave the rope to the young girl to hold. He ascended a
small hill to look over the back trail and was on the point of retiring when
he saw three savages below, riding at a fast gallop, and then he saw the
other two coming on the trail. He hastened to assist the girl in mounting
the horse, and they hurried to a small thicket situated on an elevated piece
of ground some two hundred yards distant.

The savages saw the movement and, acting with one accord, made a rush
to forestall the fugitives. The girl urged the horse to a gallop, and the young
man ran at the top of his speed. They succeeded in reaching the thicket, and

Walter rushed the horse into it, aiding the señorita to dismount and pushing her out of sight. He waved the pursuers away, but they did not heed his warning. He then made a calculation as to which of the parties it was best to defend against first. The three below him must approach uphill. The other two were on higher ground and closer. He did not hesitate, but brought down one of the two with a dead shot. Without losing an instant, he reloaded. The three from below whipped their horses and continued rapidly up the hill. The remaining savage on the hill was not fifty yards distant and, seeing that their quarry had evidently reloaded his gun, started to ride around him in a circle, while the others stormed up the hill toward him.

At this moment, the young señorita stepped out of the thicket into plain view, a movement that diverted Walter's attention. He called sharply, "Go back, Señorita, go back!"

"No, Capitan," she replied, "your enemies are many. See, I have the bow. I will help. Look, Capitan! They separate! Watch them!"

Walter lost no more time, but covered the nearest savage. Seeing the boy preparing to fire, the rider threw himself on the opposite side of his horse. Noticing that the Indian's head was just visible under the neck of the horse, Walter decided that, if he shot through the fleshy part of the horse's neck, he had a good chance of centering the Indian's head. The moment was now, and he fired. The Indian dropped from his horse, dead. Again, the young hunter reloaded, so as to always have two barrels ready. The three savages dashed on. He fired, and one rolled off his horse. Walter quickly reloaded.

Maria cried out, "They come fast, Capitan. They come fast." But the young scout felt he was the master of the situation, for he still had a ball for each of the last two assailants. They were close enough now to launch their arrows at him. One passed through his garments, but did not draw blood. The two savages were now within forty yards and on level ground. In a quick maneuver, they separated, riding around the two travelers in opposite directions. Realizing that the savages were close enough to send arrows with deadly force, Walter faced them, looking for an opening that would enable him to kill or disable one or the other. Each savage had thrown himself on the opposite side of his horse, and with each lap, the circle grew smaller. Walter waited, for he must not lose a shot, as he had only his knife and hatchet after his gun was spent.

The Chase

The señorita stood frozen to her spot. Unable to withstand the strain, Lion bristled up and was about to charge the enemy when his master shouted, "Go back, Lion. Down!" He knew the brave dog would be mortally wounded by a deadly arrow at such short range. He could not now take cover, as the first step in that direction would be a signal for the savages to rush upon them from two directions, sending a stream of arrows that it would be impossible to avoid. Another reason not to go into the thicket was the fear of fire, as the vegetation was so long and dry and a fire would spread quickly.

The savages continued to circle them with marvelous speed, embracing every opportunity to send an arrow at their unprotected forms. The speed of their horses was so timed as to always be opposite each other. But the young hunter saw an opening and fired, and the horse dropped with his rider. Walter saw that the remaining savage had risen above his horse and was starting to rush upon him, probably thinking that the boy's gun carried only a single bullet and so was unloaded and that the young paleface was at his mercy. Fatal error. In an instant, Walter covered the savage and fired. The Indian sprang into the air with a wild yell and fell to the earth, dead.

At this moment, the one who had been unhorsed rushed upon the young scout, with uplifted tomahawk. The young hunter was surprised. The horse had gone down, but had he missed the savage? And why had the Indian abandoned his bow, which was so deadly at short range? This he could not understand.

"Come back here, Señorita," he called. "Get behind me. Quick! Take Lion with you. The savage has no bow and has only the weapons that I have."

"Watch him, Capitan," she replied. "Your bullet struck and destroyed his bow. I saw him raise up with it, but finding your bullet had cut it in two, he threw it down. Take this bow, Capitan, and shoot him."

"No, Señorita," he answered, keeping his eyes steadily on the approaching foe, "I could not hurt him with it. I am not skillful enough yet. Go quickly, Señorita, to the other Indian and cut his bowstrings before this one tries to get his bow."

"Yes, Capitan, I will," said the brave girl, acting at once.

The savage now ran straight towards the young hunter, brandishing his tomahawk. When twenty feet away, he halted. He said, in Apache, "The paleface warrior will go to the village of the Apache warrior, and the young squaw to the lodge of Tee-Clee."

Walter straightened up to his utmost height. He understood enough to answer, and they continued to communicate in broken English, Apache, and sign language. "Let Tee-Clee first strike down the paleface before he talks of taking the white señorita to his lodge."

"Tee-Clee will soon be a great chief, with much good medicine," answered the savage. "And the paleface is but a boy. He cannot strike Tee-Clee."

The young hunter surveyed his antagonist. He was a powerful savage, about five feet eleven inches in height, and strong and athletic in build, apparently about thirty-five years of age. His features were regular, and though his black hair was unruly and shiny with grease, his countenance was not repulsive. His near-naked body was muscular, and his weight could not have been less than 170 pounds. The savage threw off his quiver of arrows, while the young hunter dropped his buckskin jacket and discarded his powder horn and bullet pouch. Each now stood ready to receive his enemy.

"The paleface is a fool," the warrior signed, "to fight with the son of an Apache chief. The prairie is covered with Apache warriors. The paleface cannot escape. The Navajo dogs are all gone—their horses and many scalps are in the village of the Apache."

Walter understood enough to get the warrior's meaning, and he remained silent while he planned the signs he would use to reply.

The savage asked, "Has the paleface lost his tongue? Is he afraid of Tee-Clee? Why doesn't he speak?"

Walter took a deep breath and signed his reply. "The paleface is traveling through the country of the Great White Father. Why does the Apache cross his path? Why is the Apache so far from his own lodge? Why does he want to make his hands red with the blood of the children of the Great White Father? Why does he tell the warriors of the Great White Father that his people have buried the hatchet, and when their backs are turned, he follows the trail of paleface travelers, not soldiers? Let Tee-Clee go to his village and tell his people to cease telling lies and keep their faith—to fight the white man no more. Let him tell them that the white men are a great people, that one white man has proved as good as five Apaches. Let him tell them that the Great Spirit watches over his white children and turns aside

the arrows of the Apaches. There is a horse. Take him and go. Yonder is the
trail. Go, and save your life."

Understanding but little of this, the Indian answered proudly, "Tee-Clee
will go, but he will take with him the scalp of the paleface boy. It is a lie that
one white man is as good as five Apaches."

The young hunter replied, "Where were you going this morning, with
your horses' heads turned toward the rising sun? Why did you turn back on
the trail of one paleface traveler and one girl? Were you not five men? Where
are your warriors now? Have not four of them already gone to the Happy
Hunting Ground? Let them help you. You need it. You were five. Now you
are one. If you want my scalp, come and take it. You talk much and fight
little. You are big. I am smaller, but my heart is strong. Come on. Come
on!" So saying, he took two steps forward.

The savage began to speak again. The young hunter put his fingers in his
ears, as if to shut out the boastful words.

Presently, Walter continued, "I thought I was talking to an Apache warrior, but I find I was mistaken. I have been talking to a squaw. Go on! I will
set my dog on you."

The savage, with growing anger, said, "The paleface boy has a big dog.
Tee-Clee is going to be a chief. He fights warriors, not dogs."

"Tee-Clee need not fear the paleface hunter's dog," said Walter. "His dog
would not bite a woman."

Beside himself with passion, the savage bounded forward and made a
stroke at the young hunter with his tomahawk. Walter knocked it aside,
and before the savage could recover himself, the lad sprang forward and
drove his knife into the right side of the Indian just below the right breast.
It was a glancing blow and did little harm, but rather seemed to put the
savage on his guard—and to convince him that his antagonist was no mean
one. The warrior slowly backed off, with the young hunter closely following.

"I was not mistaken," said Walter. "I thought you were a warrior, but I
find that you are only an Apache squaw. I prefer to fight warriors."

The Indian sprang forward suddenly, weapon raised, but the young hunter
stepped to one side, avoiding a well-aimed blow at his head. The savage,
expecting a counterattack, sprang back quickly. The two faced each other,
turning slowly, now and then making a feint. Each seemed glad to snatch a
moment's rest.

The savage towered above his opponent more than a full head. His limbs were heavier, and his broad chest and shoulders far outclassed the boy's in size and bulk. The combat certainly looked to be unequal. The boy, while slight, was very compact in build, his limbs well developed and proportioned. His arms were strong and muscular, his chest deep and round. Every move he made proved that he was remarkably graceful in action. His movements were surpassingly quick. His piercing gray eyes he kept constantly on the savage.

The warrior held in his right hand a heavy tomahawk, with a long, narrow back and hammerlike face. In his left hand, he had a long hunting knife, the handle of which he grasped so that the blade was exactly at right angles with his arm, pointing downward. So held, the stroke would have to be downward.

The young hunter, on the contrary, held in his right hand a small axelike hatchet, its blade some three and a half inches wide, with a keen sharp edge, the back not being so long or wide, but more blunt. The hatchet had a long, light hickory handle, somewhat longer than that of the savage. In his left hand, Walter held his Bowie knife, with a blade fully seven inches in length and a sharp, keen edge. This he carried in a very different manner from that of the savage. The buckhorn handle passed between the two little fingers of his left hand, with the end of the handle resting against the palm of his hand, at the base of the thumb. The blade and the small part of the handle extended straight out from the hand, giving the arm a much longer reach and making it possible to inflict a dangerous wound while remaining outside the reach of an arm of equal length.

Kit Carson had told the young hunter, "The Indian always holds his knife at right angles to his arm, grasping the handle with the whole hand. A knife so held can only be used in a standup fight with a downward stroke. It is only effective so held when the combatants are prostrate on the ground or are embraced in each other's clutches."

Thus, Walter had his weapons well in hand, always ready for stroke or thrust. He felt that his safety in this duel depended on his keeping beyond the reach of the warrior's long arm and on watching that the savage did not hurl his tomahawk at him. To avoid this, he kept close to his opponent and watched his every move. He did not fear the knife, as the savage could not reach him as long as he could keep his feet.

Walter moved back and forth, edging constantly around the watchful warrior. He did not for an instant take his eyes from the visage of the savage. Anxious to end the struggle, he moved around in a circle in an effort to keep the savage facing the sun. His agility was remarkable and seemed to surprise the strong aggressor.

Presently, the savage made a rush. The boy dodged, and the warrior's blow landed on the young hunter's shoulder. At the same moment, Walter drove the keen Bowie knife into the shoulder of the Indian. On springing back, Walter avoided another blow from the savage's axe.

Again, the combatants rushed upon each other, and the young hunter succeeded in seriously wounding his opponent in the chest with the edge of his sharp hatchet. Not deep enough to prove fatal, the wound bled freely. Walter's knife thrust to the warrior's shoulder was also serious, and blood was flowing from it. The young man now forced the fighting. They dealt blow for blow, most of which they successfully parried. Some fell heavily, and one gave Walter a scalp wound, from which the blood trickled down his face.

Maria watched the apparently unequal struggle with bated breath. She walked forward and back, almost beside herself with anguish. Then she would raise her eyes toward heaven, in a devoted attitude of prayer. When she saw the blood on the face of the young champion, she ran to the dead warrior and took from his bag a knife. Then she tore one from the bunch of poisoned arrows and, breaking the shaft in two, held the poisoned end in her hand.

The fight raged on with the utmost fury. The youth needed to devote every effort to self-defense, and at times, he seemed powerless to do the savage much harm. Then the heart of the brave girl would sink, almost to despair. She would grasp the knife and arrow and move toward the combatants. But Lion was always near her, and he would crowd her back.

One circumstance gave her hope and that was the fact that, notwithstanding his superior physical strength, the big savage was not able to drive his smaller antagonist from the field. On the contrary, he himself was often forced to give ground. The boy hugged close to the savage giant. Once only was the girl in a position to see the eye of the young hunter. She shrank back in terror. She had never seen it so before. It flashed like the consuming fire of sunlight. Could that be the mild, gentle eye of the young capitan?

No, she knew he was not conquered—and she felt now that he was unconquerable.

The savage suddenly seemed to grow stronger, for he continued to strike most viciously with his tomahawk while his left arm hung helplessly by his side. The young hunter showed that he could use the hatchet, adroitly baffling every effort of the savage to cut him down and end the struggle.

Presently, the Indian stepped back to take a breath, but the young hunter would not have it so. He flew at his opponent with the fierceness of a tiger, hurling blow after blow upon him, which the other was forced to put forth his utmost skill to avoid. The young man dealt the savage a blow that laid open his cheek, and he staggered back. The boy rushed upon him and plunged his knife into the savage's body. This wound was a glancing one and did little harm beyond the letting of more blood.

The savage now rallied and renewed the strife with the fierceness of despair. He succeeded in landing a blow that brought the young hunter to his knees. With a wild yell, the savage threw himself upon his almost prostrate foe. The señorita screamed, for she thought the battle over. And indeed, it was—but the result was different from what she expected.

As the infuriated savage rushed upon his enemy, expecting at once to brain him with the tomahawk, the young hunter sprang forward and gave the warrior a deep thrust with his knife. A second later, with a stroke of his hatchet, the boy nearly severed the savage's right arm above the elbow. The big Indian reeled, staggered, and fell heavily to the ground, bleeding from many wounds. The young hunter tried to speak, but his tongue seemed to cleave to his mouth, and he, too, sank down, first to one knee and then on both to a kneeling posture.

Maria rushed to his side, crying, "Oh, Capitan, he has killed you." The exhausted boy shook his head in the negative. The girl seemed to have lost her head, and afterwards, she said that she heard him say one word, "Water." Rushing to the horse, she seized a leathern bottle and ran back down the trail to a spring in the rocks that the dog had discovered. When she returned, the young defender had fainted and Lion stood over his master, licking his face. The girl dashed some water in the face of the youth, and then, placing the bottle to his lips, she poured some of the cool water down his parched throat.

After a few moments, the youth recovered so far as to breathe naturally and open his eyes. The señorita had now begun to investigate the nature of his injuries. She found a nasty cut in his breast, just below the left shoulder, and others on the shoulder and the left arm. Some of these seemed dangerous. She asked him which he thought might be the worst. He shook his head and pointed to the savage. Presently he found his voice and said, "The Indian is seriously hurt and needs attention more than I. Attend to his wounds first." Walter would not listen to any protest, much to Maria's disgust.

She turned finally to the enemy and found that the most serious wound the savage had sustained was that on the right arm. The blood streamed from it as though an artery had been severed. Tearing some strips of cloth, she applied a tourniquet and bound up the wound, effectively stopping the flow of blood. Upon turning around, she saw that the young hunter had fainted again. She was now thoroughly alarmed and turned her entire attention to him. She found an ugly wound on the back of his neck, which she had not noticed before. Doubtless the blow had been aimed at his head, and he had dodged forward and received the force of the blow on his shoulder and neck. She now applied herself to the dressing of his wounds. When she had gotten the bleeding stopped, the young man seemed to revive and soon felt strong enough to move about. He assisted in caring for the wounds of the savage and in placing him in a comfortable position where he could rest easily.

When Tee-Clee returned to consciousness, he was sullen and had little to say. He was surprised that he had not been killed at once and scalped. As he was weak and helpless, he now seemed to await the final issue with indifference. Walter and the señorita had dressed most of his wounds when he was unconscious, and when he realized that his late enemy was really trying to save his life, he expressed great satisfaction. He offered his captors all the horses that he and his late comrades possessed.

"No," said the young hunter, "the white man does not want the horses of his red brother. If he did, he would take them without asking. He does not come into the country to do injury to the children of the prairie and mountains. He only desires to peaceably pass over the land that now belongs to the Great White Father. My red brother is sick. He cannot stand on his feet. His warriors are all dead, and they are now in the Happy Hunting Ground. We will stay here tonight and give our red brother food and water.

Tomorrow, we will go. We will leave the red warrior food and drink. We will picket a horse near him to ride when he is strong enough to go to the village of his people. Let him tell his people that the white men are not all killed, and it is better to make peace with them."

Tee-Clee responded, "What my white brother says is good. My heart is warm towards him. He is a very small and young warrior, but his heart is strong and very big. Tee-Clee could not keep meat in his lodge now, for the arm of his white brother has made him weak. His wounds are very deep, and he may never again ride his horse or bend the bow. If he cannot follow the trail of his enemy or hunt the buffalo, Tee-Clee wishes to die. He would go to the Happy Hunting Ground and be strong again and follow the warpath with his father and brother, who are there already."

The wounded savage relaxed into a gloomy silence. Maria cut the boughs and prepared the beds, and they placed the savage upon his blanket on a bed of boughs. He seemed to rally and accepted some of the jerked venison.

Walter again made known what he wished to say in sign language. The señorita knew a little Apache. She had learned it from an Indian boy who had been brought to her home by Mexicans who had captured him from the Apaches. She had played with him when they were youngsters. When he grew older, he disappeared. They thought perhaps that he had returned to his people. With Maria's help and his own knowledge of sign language, Walter said, "I would like my red brother to tell me if any of his people are now on the prairie near us. We do not wish to fight, but would like to rejoin our party."

Tee-Clee responded with signs and a few words that the girl understood. He said that many Apaches were on the prairie and that they had not captured the white men and women who were encamped one-fourth of a sleep, or ten miles, distant. He conveyed to them that both the Navajos and Apaches had come to get the horses and scalps of the white men, but that they were at war with each other. If it had not been for a battle that had taken place between the Navajo "thieves" and the Apache warriors, the whites would have fallen long ago. The Navajos had now been driven away, having lost many of their braves. The field was now open to the Apaches, and he felt sure that the white men and women would soon die. Their property would be taken to the Indian village, and if any prisoners were taken, they would be tortured and put to death.

He assured them that he would save them if he could. "But," he said, "I have many wounds, and I have lost four of my best warriors by the arm of the little chief, whose heart is good but medicine strong. My brother is a great chief, and he will be very angry with me. He will say, 'You have lost four warriors. For them, white man must die.' My white brother is in great danger. He and the young squaw will certainly be killed or taken. If he leaves the young squaw, he can save himself, for he could go over the mountains and ride very fast. He has a good horse. He is young and strong and very brave. Let the young chief go before the sun can be seen. The Apaches will not kill the young squaw. They will give her to a chief, and she will go to his lodge to keep his fire bright. She will cook his food for him and be very glad."

During this recital, the girl had sat motionless, with her eyes on the ground. She had understood every word, and they had chilled her heart. Her face was white as death. Several times, her eyes had sought the face of the young hunter, but she could not read that impassive face. His keen eyes seemed fixed on some distant object far to the west. So intent was his gaze that she first thought that he had not understood the chilling words of the savage—which had in them no gratitude for her, or expression of sympathy. It is true that he had intimated that she would be spared death, but at a cost so great that she would prefer death, even by the poisoned arrow still concealed in the bosom of her dress.

The young hunter was so long silent that the savage asked, "Are the ears of the little chief closed to the words of Tee-Clee? Why does he not speak? Have his little wounds made his heart weak?"

"Let Tee-Clee have no concern for his white brother, who has heard his words. The heart of the white hunter does not change like the shadow of the forest tree or the winds of the prairie. He loves his friends and pities his enemies. When he left the camp of his friends, they were strong, watchful, and brave. The Apaches may capture their horses and kill the white men, but many warriors will fall, never to see their native village again. The little chief will go to the camp of his friends. He will not leave the señorita. No Apache hand will touch her while the white chief lives and can use his rifle. He will take the young girl to her father, who mourns her as lost. Her little sister waits for her with red eyes. Why should Tee-Clee wish the young girl harm? Has she not bound up his wounds? Has she not saved his life? If he ever sees his lodge again, it will be because she stopped the flow of blood that soon would have sent Tee-Clee to the Happy Hunting Ground to keep company with his four warriors yonder on the prairie."

"The white chief is wise," answered the sick warrior. "His words are loud, and Tee-Clee heard him speak. The Manitou, whose voice the Apache often hears in the clouds, teaches the wise men of the village that women are made for slaves of warriors—to care for their lodges, cook their venison, and keep their lodge fires bright. She is the warrior's to keep, to kill, to sell or give away, like his horse. When she is gone, he gets another. He can have many. The Manitou of the white man, and the Manitou of the Apache, do not see with the same eyes or teach the same things. One of them has lying eyes and a forked tongue. Some things that are good for the white man would be good for the red man—but not all. Tee-Clee has sharp ears. He can hear quick. He heard the young white chief tell the white squaw to bind the wounds of Tee-Clee. She did what the white chief told her to do. Tee-Clee is glad. His heart is warm for the white chief. If Tee-Clee gets well, he will give his life to save the little white chief. He would save the white squaw so she can serve his friend, the brave white chief. Tee-Clee has spoken. His eyes are heavy. His heart is sad. He will sleep."

Walter walked away, giving a sign to the girl to follow. When at a safe distance, he said, "Señorita, the savage has said that there are many Indians. We must have another horse. I will wait until dark, then try and get one of those left by the dead enemy. We can then travel faster, and if we get another horse as fast as this one, we might give a good account of ourselves in a chase. I feel weak now, but if I can rest some before starting, we can then go with safety. I have decided as to the route we will pursue, and I hope we will succeed in reaching our friends. We have wandered away from them farther than I supposed."

"Now, Capitan, you rest and watch, and I will try and catch the horse. Which one shall I get?"

"No, no, Señorita," said the boy. "I will take an Indian blanket and go without a hat to catch a horse, and I think I can succeed. The odor of the blanket will deceive the horse, and he will scarcely think it covers a white man."

Summoning a last cache of strength, Walter acted upon his own suggestion, which proved to work, and he soon returned with a good horse with a fine Mexican saddle still on its back. They then securely tied a horse for the wounded savage near the spring, where it could get water and grass in the event that the Indian should be laid up for several days. They also gave Tee-Clee jerked venison and water. After resaddling the horses in case of sudden surprise, Walter lay down to sleep. He stayed wide awake for a long time on account of his sore wounds, even though Maria had greased them with deer tallow. He finally slept, until he was awakened in the night by Lion licking his face. The wind was blowing from the west, and the dog seemed to find something in the air that made him uneasy. Walter listened intently until he heard in the distance the cry of a coyote, with the answering call of an owl far to the left. These sounds did not seem natural. He roused the girl, and they left immediately. The savage seemed sorry to be left alone, but did not complain. Each of the young people shook hands with him.

They started away in the opposite direction from that which Walter had intended. Passing down the slope some two hundred yards, they made a complete half-circle around the camp and passed up the slope of the hill for about a half a mile. Then they turned to the west and traveled rapidly forward for something like an hour. When they halted, Walter said to the señorita, "I think we have traveled some six or seven miles. We cannot be far from the camp of our friends. I have a mind to stop here for a while, until the gray of the morning. Then, if the way is not blocked, we can make a dash for our camp. It is now so dark that we move at great risk; we may, at any time, stumble on a lurking foe. The wind is blowing strong from us to the very point where we want to go. You lie down, Señorita, and I will watch with Lion. His nose is of no use to him except to scent danger from up the hill, and I do not look for it from that direction."

So saying, Walter at once prepared a place for Maria to rest, and although sore in need of sleep himself, he assumed the task of guarding the party. Lion was already asleep. Walter sat at the edge of the bushes, holding the horses and permitting them to feed until it began to be a little light in the east. He could now see that there were many thickets on the slope of the hill below, but he could not discern a living thing anywhere. He helped the señorita mount, and they moved down the slope. After about a half a mile, they were about to enter a small, open park when Lion bristled and faced the northwest. A moment later, a dozen savages came into view, with

evidently full knowledge of their presence. The young hunter instantly lev-
eled his rifle and having covered the leader, was about to press the trigger,
when the young señorita spoke quickly, "Hold on, Capitan. Many are behind
us. We are surrounded." The young hunter quickly took in the situation
and said, "It is as you say. It is wisest to surrender, as we cannot defend
ourselves against such odds."

The leader now rode forward, and with a few words of Spanish, some
broken English, and sign language, they communicated. "Where is the young
paleface going?"

The young man, with great composure, answered, "To the village of the
Apaches."

This quick answer created a general laugh. All began to dismount and
remove the trappings from their horses. The captives were told to do the
same. Walter spread a blanket for Maria, who now began to weep. He said
to her kindly, "Do not exhaust yourself, Señorita. We will hope for the best.
I presume they will take us to the village. We may yet escape."

"Oh, Capitan," said she, now drying her eyes, "where is Lion?" He was
nowhere to be seen.

"He does not like savages," replied Walter. "Depend on it; he will remain
near us."

The chief now came forward and asked if they had food. The boy told
him they had. The chief then gave them some parched corn to eat with
their meat, and they finally had a good breakfast. The señorita could not
keep back her tears. The chief came forward, saying kindly, "Young squaw
no cry. No good cry." This she understood. The chief asked the young hunter
where he was from, to which Walter promptly answered, "Taos." The chief
then asked if there were others in their party. The young hunter answered
truthfully. The chief asked how many whites were in the party, and again
Walter answered truthfully.

At this moment, an Indian picked up the bow and arrows carried by
Maria and looked them over. The leader then took them and, after a careful
examination, said, "Navajo. Navajo." The young hunter nodded assent. An
Indian then led up the horse which the señorita had ridden. The saddle,
they also noted, was Navajo. The chief wanted to know where the horses
came from. This the young man also answered truthfully. The Indians were
now more familiar and friendly. Presently the girl asked for water. Walter

took the leathern bottle and walked through the camp to the small stream some distance beyond. He filled the bottle and returned, handing it to the young girl. The Indians paid no attention to this liberty taken by their prisoner. They soon gathered, as if in consultation, and seemed much interested in the subject under discussion. They were enough away from the prisoners so that their words could not be understood.

The young hunter asked Maria if she did not think it best to tell the Indians where the wounded Tee-Clee lay. "They cannot fail to find him," he said, "for they must discover the loose horses near him and will, I feel certain, investigate the cause of their being there. It may be best for us to be frank about this matter. Should Tee-Clee be found alive and recover from his wounds, he might do as he promised—aid us—and perhaps save our lives. He might die, if neglected, and I should feel better if he had timely assistance. Should he then fail to recover, we will be conscious of having done our duty, and his blood will be upon his own head, for he was the aggressor."

"As you think best, Capitan," replied the girl. "If you feel sure he will be discovered, it is surely the best course to pursue, as he will know that you alone saved him. But think well, Capitan, I am sure he is a cruel, wicked Indian and will, if he recovers, be more likely to do us injury than good."

"And I think," said the young hunter, "that he would be more apt to injure us if we fail to point out his whereabouts and let his friends care for him."

Walter rose to his feet and approached the Indians. When he had reached a point near enough to attract attention, they ceased their conversation and looked at him. He motioned the chief to follow him. The two now became the center of interest. Taking the chief to one side, the young hunter indicated that he wished him to go to a small hill nearby. The Indian motioned to him to lead the way. On reaching the hill, which commanded a good view of the mountain slope, Walter soon located the spot where the wounded warrior lay, and he pointed it out to the chief, explaining that the Apache, Tee-Clee, lay there injured and helpless. The Indian started as Walter mentioned the name of the injured man.

"My brother," he said. They quickly walked back to the camp, and the chief called his warriors together and prepared to depart. The young hunter joined the señorita, noting that there were thirty-seven of the savages. Ten

Indians caught their horses and accompanied the chief. As they were about
to ride off, the young hunter again took the chief to one side, suggesting
that they should make a travois to carry the sick man. Walter added that
they would find no suitable timber in the vicinity of Tee-Clee. The chief
promptly acted on this suggestion, and in a few moments, the warriors had
cut two long poles and tied one to each side of a gentle horse. Then the
party moved rapidly away.

During their absence, the prisoners caught up on some much-needed
rest. When they woke, the girl urged the young man to tell her of his past
life, which he did. She was genuinely interested, and in turn, she told him
much about the early hardships endured by her great grandfather and his
neighbors in the fertile valley where they made their home. The Indians did
not pay any attention to their prisoners and permitted them to go anywhere they chose about the camp. And so far, Walter had been permitted to
keep his gun and sidearms.

Just past the middle of the afternoon, there was quite a stir, and most of
the Indians left the park, doubtless attracted by the approach of the party
that had gone to search for Tee-Clee. Presently, they all came back, followed
slowly by the chief with his escort and the sick man. They soon decided to
remain at this camp for the night. Both the young hunter and Maria went
forward and greeted the wounded man. They were surprised to find him so
much improved, though still weak from the loss of so much blood. He was
mending fast and would soon be able to ride a horse.

During the night, Lion came like a shadow, silently and cautiously. He
visited both the señorita and Walter and took away with him a good supply
of the jerked meat. The young hunter slept near Maria, and both slept quietly and well. As daylight broke, a young Indian came to the bed of the
young man and indicated that he was wanted. Walter immediately arose
and followed his guide, who led him across the meadow to a grove on the
opposite side. The chief was sitting near a small fire, under cover of some
bushes that had been arranged to keep off the night dampness. The chief
motioned Walter to a seat beside himself. The chief now spoke to the young
Indian guide, who had come and sat on the opposite side of the fire. He
discoursed with the young Indian for some time.

Then the young Indian spoke to Walter, speaking in very good Spanish.
"Our chief wishes to talk with the little chief. He says the young capitan

much kill Indian. Fight hard with Tee-Clee, his brother. He says young capitan
very brave to kill all the Indians. The chief wants you to tell him how you
killed them on the hill with the young Spanish girl; where you came from;
and where the main party is."

The young hunter decided that it was best to tell a straight story, and he
detailed, as best he could—not being a perfect master of either the Spanish
or Apache language—the capture of the señorita; his attempt to liberate
her; his own capture; and their subsequent escape during the great storm.
He left out all reference to the brave dog, Lion.

The young Indian, as the narrator paused in his recital, asked how he got
the horse and saddle, bow, and blankets. The prisoner then related the circumstances of the killing of the Navajo hunter. He wound up by saying that
he was on his way to join his friends again, when he was attacked by
Tee-Clee and his companions. The chief insisted upon his giving a full and
accurate account of the fight, which he did in a modest way. After the recital,
the chief expressed great satisfaction that his young prisoner had killed the
Navajo.

He said with reference to the later fight, "Injun big fool. Five big Injun,
one small chief kill all. Now Tee-Clee, him die, too."

The prisoner protested that Tee-Clee would get well.

The chief smiled grimly, adding, "Maybe so."

The young prisoner was then questioned about the main camp of the
travelers; the number of horses they had; and their condition. The prisoner
told all he wished to tell, declining to answer some pertinent questions. He
maintained that the members of the party were very strong and brave and
that they could not be taken without great loss on the part of the Indians.

The chief listened respectfully until Walter had finished. He then said,
"Apache very brave. Heap fight. Want horses, scalps. Me kill all travelers. Me
take you to Apache village. Maybe burn, maybe kill. Paleface no good."

In answer, the prisoner said, "Are you the head chief of your people? If
you are, tell me why you make peace with the white chief and promise to
bury the hatchet, and then, without warning, you break forth and go upon
the warpath, fighting, killing, and stealing from the children of the Great
White Father."

The chief looked upon his prisoner with a dark, lowering brow, his fierce
eyes flashing. He sat some time in silence. Finally he asked, "Where did

Tee-Clee strike the young paleface?" The prisoner removed his coat and pointed out his various wounds. After looking at the wounds a moment, the chief said, "Not much hurt."

He then said to his prisoner, "Stay here for Tee-Clee to get well. Hunting is good. If you will promise not to try to get away, you can have the liberty of my camp, as you have had since you've been here. You no promise, I tie up fast."

The young prisoner, after a moment's hesitation, gave his promise.

The chief then raised his hand, saying, "Go and eat."

The prisoner followed his guide back to camp. Maria was now up and weeping bitterly, but dried her eyes at the approach of the young hunter. "Why, Capitan," she said, "I could not see you. I thought they had taken you from me."

The young Indian guide now departed, but came back presently with more corn and some nice fresh venison. As he set it down, he spoke to the young girl in Spanish. She gave a little scream of surprise, but quickly suppressed further emotion at the request of the young Indian, who quickly departed. When she and Walter were alone, the young girl explained that she knew this Indian lad. When she was a little girl, he had been captured by Mexicans and her father had saved his life. Her father had taken the boy into the family and partially raised him. She had often played with him, and it was from him that she had learned much of the Apache language. He had lived with them for six years and had only returned to his tribe two years ago.

When the Indian lad returned with some gourds full of water, he and the señorita talked together. He urged her to seem not to understand the Apache language and not to notice him any more than the others. He would keep her informed and would aid her when he could. If necessary, he would desert his people, for he had a great affection for her father, who had been so kind to him.

Maria told Walter that the lad, Antonio, had been a disciple of the old priest and would, she thought, die for him. "Capitan," she went on, "you have promised not to try to escape. Antonio says that a very careful watch is being kept on us, and kept in such a way as to not attract attention. He says we will not escape until the dark nights come. He will take a message to my father when he can get away and not be discovered. He says he is a favorite of the chief, who is very good to him, and that he will try and get away. He says for us to write a message, and he will take it to my father's camp. If only I had a pencil."

"Never mind," said Walter. "I will make you one." So, taking a bullet from his pouch, he pounded it out and formed a short, sharp pencil. He then gave the girl some leaves from a small book that he carried in the pocket of his rawhide coat.

She wrote her father the following: "My own dear father, I have found Antonio, our Indian boy, and send this by him. I am nearly distracted for fear you have all been murdered. Antonio is in great fear about being able to enter your camp without being shot, as he cannot speak English and some of the Americans would be on guard, most likely. He will find some means of leaving this note. He says, if you will listen, he will return at night, giving three hoots in imitation of an owl, and upon your giving a return signal, three shrill whistles, he will enter camp and get a note in reply. It must all be done very quietly as the Indians are watchful. I shall be beside myself with fear until I hear from you.

"I was taken the night of the storm, when you were knocked down. In trying to help me, the capitan was also captured, but before morning, he escaped in the midst of the terrible storm and released me. We have been trying to get to you ever since. We were captured again yesterday morning by a party of thirty-seven Apaches. I cannot tell you all now.

"The capitan has been so good and kind and so very thoughtful of my comfort. He is a most noble young man, father, and so brave and true. Kiss little sister, embrace the dear father, and give all my love.

"We do not know what may be done with us. The capitan says to tell you to use great caution, for you could be attacked by strong force. Look carefully to the stock. Graze them only under a very strong guard. Do not, under any circumstances, separate.

"So far, we are treated well enough, but how long it will last, we know not. Adieu, dear father."

At this moment, Antonio came up and said, "Put paper under stone at fire quick. Injun talk and look. I come again and get paper." The girl obeyed the command without looking up or paying any attention to the young Indian. He gave the prisoners some water and then departed. Three savages came up and examined every article about the prisoners. The girl had had the presence of mind to bury the little pencil in the sand nearby. The Indians conversed some with the young hunter concerning his gun which, with its two barrels, was a great curiosity to them.

The day passed quietly. No more than four Indians stayed in camp. One was left to guard them when the other three took their departure. They took with them the young hunter's rifle and hatchet, even his Bowie knife, leaving him only a dull butcher knife. He was, however, left at liberty. Towards evening, the chief and his party came back to camp. The señorita counted the warriors and told the young hunter that none were missing.

At nightfall, young Antonio came and told Maria that ten of the savages had gone off to prowl around the camp of her friends—and so he would not be able to go that night. Finally, however, on the third night, the note was missing from under the stone, and in its place, she found a long note, written in the plain, bold hand of her father.

Her father's note read as follows: "Blessed daughter, your welcome note was found near our camp, suspended to a bush, by Tex in the early morning. The news of your safety has given us all new life and hope. We had long since given you up as dead and have mourned bitterly. We have many times discussed the propriety of moving on, but these hardy men could not be made to believe that the young capitan had been killed. They care for his horses more carefully than for their own. Tex, especially, could hardly be held in camp. He has wanted to go out and search for his young friend. When your note was read, all shed tears of relief. All wish to be remembered to both of you. The reverend father prays constantly for your safety, and little sister sends her kisses."

During the fourth day after the arrival of Tee-Clee, the young Apache Antonio remained in camp as one of the guards and found time for a long talk with the young Mexican girl. He said he often went with the parties that watched the travelers' camp by night and day and could then exchange messages. He did not want his name mentioned in any further notes, as there was another party nearby, among whom was a Mexican, and he feared that some accident might happen and one of the notes would be discovered. He also mentioned that a large party of Navajos had made their appearance nearby. While their presence was a new menace to the besieged travelers, it was a threat to the Apaches.

Antonio said that the prisoners would soon be sent to the Apache village, as the Navajos were the larger party, and the chief did not want to lose his prisoners. He had sent scouts ahead to look over the trail and ascertain if it was safe to send Tee-Clee and the prisoners on to the village of the Apaches. When they returned, it would be decided. Maria wrote down this important information, in hopes of being able to send it to her father. She said she thought it might be the last time she would be able to write, and sure enough, it so transpired.

On the night of the seventh day, they were hurriedly informed that they would march immediately in the direction of the Apache village. They were mounted on the horses with which they had been taken. The young hunter was given no weapon. He asked to see the chief. When the latter approached, the young prisoner protested that he should be allowed his gun to defend himself against the "cowardly" Navajos.

"But," the chief remarked crustily, "gun no good for paleface boy. He killed five Apaches." He finally gave Walter's gun to the young Antonio, with instructions that he should return it to Walter only if the party were attacked by a superior force of Navajos. Tee-Clee was now able to ride his horse. Since he had recovered, he had been very sullen. This, the boy discovered, was on account of his being unmercifully guyed and laughed at by his companions because he had lost all his warriors and he himself had been worsted by the young paleface.

Antonio dropped a suggestion that had greatly worried the señorita, which was that Tee-Clee might kill Walter. "Heap mad, Tee-Clee." But so far, the disgruntled warrior had kept aloof from the prisoners and traveled as much by himself as possible, having no word to say to anyone. However, having apparently recovered his strength, he was now given charge of the party, composed of the prisoners, four warriors besides himself, and young Antonio.

The party traveled very rapidly and silently from the first watch at night to the first gray streak of day. Morning found them on the summit of a high range of hills surrounded by thickets of piñons. Here they stopped to graze their horses and take much-needed rest and food. Maria was much worn. The hard night's ride had almost overcome her. As a precaution, one of the savages was left some four miles behind to watch their back trail and report if he saw pursuers. Another savage watched on a high point near the camp.

Among the warriors who accompanied Tee-Clee was a large, good-natured savage who was quite a wag. He took special delight in constantly nagging Tee-Clee about the wounds he had received at the hands of the young hunter, and on several occasions, Tee-Clee was worked up into a terrible passion.

In one of these fits of wrath during the day, he had not only threatened to kill the young prisoner, but said he would take the young squaw to his teepee tonight. This fell on the ears of the young girl, and she wept much of the day. Walter felt he was in a defenseless position and that his responsibility was great. He managed to ride near Antonio, to whom he said, "Do you know the father of the señorita?"

"Yes," replied the Apache boy.

"Do you like him?"

"Yes."

"Do you like the señorita?"

"Yes, much like white squaw."

"Do you know what Tee-Clee said today?"

"No," came the quick response.

Walter then related what Tee-Clee had said.

"He say he kill you, too," the boy responded.

"Never mind what he may do to me," replied the young prisoner. "He must not touch the señorita."

"No, he shall not," answered the boy. "Señorita good to Antonio. Antonio save her."

"But Antonio," asked Walter, "will you give me my gun now?"

"No," replied the Indian boy.

"Will you give me my tomahawk?"

"No."

"Will you give me my knife?"

"No."

"How, then, can the señorita be saved?"

"I will sleep near her," answered Antonio.

"Would you kill Tee-Clee?"

"Yes," responded Antonio. "Then give girl knife. Injun all glad. Tee-Clee no good. Him heap bad. You no good. He ought to be dead now. You no good to save him. Antonio watch close. Tee-Clee no hurt señorita."

Tee-Clee interrupted their conversation, riding for some time in silence near Maria. He finally said, "I want squaw. You my squaw now." The young hunter rode between them, and the savage struck Walter several times over the head with his bow. The prisoner paid no attention to the assault. The other savages laughed. Tee-Clee was much enraged. He took his tomahawk from this belt and grasped its handle. At this point, Maria screamed, and Antonio rode up near Tee-Clee, but said nothing. Walter slipped his hand inside his hunting coat and rode on in silence. He, however, never changed his position, which soon became the subject of another sally on the part of the big, good-natured Indian. Presently, a savage who had been in the rear rode up, and Tee-Clee fell back to talk with him. Nothing further transpired during the afternoon to disturb the prisoners.

As soon as they halted, Tee-Clee lay down under a tree, as he seemed fatigued. The young hunter quickly provided a bed upon which the señorita could rest. She soon slept soundly. About 9 o'clock in the morning, the Indians kindled a fire and began to cook their breakfast. Antonio brought the prisoners some venison, which Walter proceeded to roast. Tee-Clee soon announced that they would resume their march in a short time, and Walter roused Maria. She hastily washed her face and ate some of the venison. The young hunter secretly left behind a good portion of food for Lion.

They continued their march until late in the night when they halted until daylight. At dawn, they pushed on a couple of miles farther to a protected spot, where the horses could be turned out to graze.

While the party was preparing some food, a young grizzly bear came running into camp—and immediately turned tail. The warriors shot it with several arrows. Tee-Clee was the first to launch a shaft into the body of the fleeing cub. It instantly began to scream and squall to the great amusement of the savages. In the midst of their fun and merriment, the mother bear, a huge grizzly, sprang among them, followed by a big second cub and a third large-sized grizzly. Immediately there was consternation among the savages. Tee-Clee ran to a tree, dropping his bow as he scud up among the limbs. All the savages scampered for places of safety. Their horses were much disturbed and would have stampeded, but for being securely tied with strong ropes. The mother bear, after charging about for some time, went up to the wounded and howling cub and cuffed it, apparently in an effort to make it follow her. The little one, now nearing death, staggered around and finally fell, moaning piteously. Again the mother bear charged at the savages, all of whom had now taken refuge in the limbs of the surrounding trees. The old bear would first run up to the dying cub and then to the fir tree in which Tee-Clee had taken refuge. The huge beast would rise up on her hind feet and crawl among the bottom limbs of the tree, where she would tear out great mouthfuls of the soft wood. She would fume around the tree, glancing fiercely with her fiery red eyes at the shivering savage, who now began to fear that the maddened brute might succeed in gnawing down the tree. He began to call out loudly to his fellow Indians, all of whom had looked out for themselves.

At the first appearance of the enraged bear, the young hunter had seized the terror-stricken señorita and dragged her behind a bunch of bushes. He helped her climb high in a fir tree, telling her to remain quietly. He stood alone under another tree near the Indian boy, the only savage not to lose his head. He was among the horses, apparently perfectly cool, while the old mother bear thrashed around. The other cub walked up to the campfire and began to devour the roasted meat. He made short work of what remained and then pranced around with his angry mother, seeking what else he might devour.

At this moment, the señorita spoke to the young hunter in a low voice, saying, "The savages are talking about you and your gun, Capitan."

And the Indian boy rose from the grass and bushes, holding Walter's gun. "You take gun," he said. "Kill bear. Give gun back. This good."

Before Walter could reply, Maria said, "Capitan, take the gun and let us join the bears. They are safer and more merciful than the savages. I had sooner risk that savage mother beast than the more dangerous beast yonder in the tree—Tee-Clee."

The young Indian smiled grimly and laid his hand on the young prisoner. "Shoot bear. Give back gun. Tee-Clee no hurt señorita."

The old bear now presented a broadside, and the prisoner brought his gun to his shoulder and fired. The mother bear fell dead, the ball having entered her ear. With the other barrel, Walter brought down the second cub. The third grizzly galloped away. The young hunter reloaded the rifle and handed it back to Antonio. The señorita asked her friend if he had had any thought of turning his gun against the savages.

"Yes," he replied, "but Tee-Clee was the only one I could make sure of.

The others were scattered around and would have run us down. Had we been encamped on the prairie, where I could see all, and had a chance to kill two, I would have taken the chance."

The young girl laid her hand gently on his arm. "Capitan, nothing seems to appall you. How could you engage in such an unequal contest?"

"I would fight the whole tribe for you, Señorita."

The savages skinned the bears, saving the flesh of the two young bears, and prepared to move ahead without breakfast. Tee-Clee announced that they would no longer travel at night—the danger from Navajos had passed. The day passed in a monotonous tramp through the broken hills. About sunset, the party halted and prepared for their night's repose. The camp was pitched among scrubby pines, near a small spring in the mountainside. All the party camped near together. Tee-Clee had the Indian boy help him construct a hut, built in circular form. In this, they made two beds of boughs.

As soon as they had finished the evening meal, the party made preparations for the night. The young prisoner was taken to a tree and firmly bound with his back to it. He made no protest, but Maria wept bitterly. As soon as Walter was bound, Tee-Clee approached the young girl and dragged her to his lodge. He told her to spread her bed in one corner, which she did. One by one, the savages lay down, no effort being made to keep a watch. All appeared to fall asleep, save the young white prisoner, whose bonds were so tight that he could not sleep even if he wanted to. He watched the stars and the moon sink behind the mountain top.

It must have been midnight when he thought he saw a shadow near the lodge. At first, he thought it was a man creeping along. "Is it," he thought, "Tee-Clee coming to finish me?" He felt sure that the savage meant to do this, and he had seriously debated if he had not made a grave mistake in not shooting the villain when he was in the tree, before he shot the bears. Now he felt his chance was gone, for he would doubtless be bound, even on the road, from this time on. At this instant, a dark form glided to his side, and the next moment, the cold nose of Lion was on his cheek. Walter gave a low, scarcely audible hiss to put the happy creature on his guard. Lion instantly sank to earth and began to smell his master's hands. He commenced to chew the leather thongs, but Walter stopped him, thinking it better not to allow his faithful dog to release him at present.

Walter detected a movement in the lodge. He believed it was Tee-Clee stirring. He was near enough to hear heavy breathing all around him, which told him that all the others were sleeping soundly. Again, a twig broke, and he touched Lion's foot. The faithful dog arose, and a sign from his master directed his attention to the sound within the lodge. Then, in response to a motion of his master's head, the dog dropped and moved stealthily toward the lodge. Like a fleeting shadow, he crept away and disappeared around the corner toward the opening.

For some moments, all was still. Presently, the quick ear of the young hunter detected another movement inside the lodge—and then a shrill scream broke the midnight stillness. Another, and then another. The señorita cried out, "Capitan," and the young prisoner nearly tore the flesh from his wrists, as he tried in vain to break the rawhide bonds. At this instant, another sound reached his ear. It was a muffled growl, as fierce as that of a lion. Then there came a savage yell followed by a fierce struggle. Maria bounded from the lodge to where the young prisoner was bound. She whispered, "Lion saved me."

A terrible struggle was now going on in the tent. A gurgling sound reached them. "He has his throat," said the young hunter. "Do not let it be known that he is our dog."

The sleeping savages were now astir, running around every which way.

"I guess he has finished him," whispered Walter. "I will call him off." He gave a suppressed whistle, and the struggle in the lodge ceased. Lion appeared on the outside. Another sign from his master, and he glided away among the trees and disappeared.

"What will we tell them, Capitan?"

"Say that it was a mad wolf. The Apaches are superstitious and will think it was sent by the Great Spirit. Go, and tell Antonio to spread that story."

Finding the boy, the señorita did as she was told.

"Now, Señorita," said Walter, "have the boy unbind me, and we will see what Lion has done." In a few moments, he was free. Taking a light from the dying fire, he entered the lodge, together with the savages. They found Tee-Clee on the ground, with his throat terribly torn. He was entirely naked and bloody from head to foot, showing several ragged wounds. He was unconscious. Near him was a knife, which he had likely tried to use against his unknown foe.

The savages collected around the wounded Indian, each inquiring what

animal could have made the attack. When Antonio suggested, "Mad wolf,"
they all started. There is a superstition that mad wolves are the instruments
of evil spirits. Not one of the savages would touch the wounded Indian.
Even Antonio could not be induced to remain in the tent alone with the
mortally wounded Tee-Clee. There was consternation among the Indians,
and yet they soon pulled themselves together and were all on guard.
Antonio prepared a bed for Maria under the pine tree nearby and, under
the pretext of guarding against her escape, planted himself near her, indicating to both her and the young hunter that he would die in her defense,
and that no man should touch her.

Walter now addressed himself to the Indians, inquiring as to who was
the new leader now that Tee-Clee was disabled. The large, good-natured
savage, who had so tormented Tee-Clee, came forward and said he was in
charge. The young prisoner told him that the wounds of Tee-Clee should be
washed and bound up, but the savage said that none of the Indians would
touch him, adding, "Mad wolf no good."

Walter answered, "The teeth of the mad wolf are sharp and have cut deep
into the neck of Tee-Clee. His blood is flowing, and if his wounds are not
bound up, he will surely die." He also pointed out that the party could not
travel, as Tee-Clee could not ride his horse. He wound up by suggesting that
the leader dress the wounds made by the mad wolf so that the wounded
savage would not die. But the big Indian shrank away, saying, "Mad wolf
heap devil." He wanted to move the camp away from the spot for, said he,
"The mad wolf will come back. I saw him with my own eyes. He was so
big." And he indicated its height to be about five feet above the ground,
and nearly as long as a horse. Two others insisted that they had also seen
the wolf, and his teeth were long—they indicated a length of five or six
inches. Some said he was very black. The prisoner suggested that it was a
bear, but nothing could shake their belief that the creature was a mad wolf
and that it was possessed of evil spirits.

The young prisoner, fearing that Tee-Clee might die, saved the life of the
helpless heathen. He would not have hesitated to put an end to his life with
his own hands to save the young girl or himself, but now he felt that all
danger was past for the present. He told the Indians to bring him some
water, bear's grease, and strips of cloth, and he would bind the wounds.
This being done at once, he soon had the wounds dressed and the flow of

blood stopped. Walter feared that the savage had wounded his noble dog, and he was anxious to find him. He went to the fire, which was kept bright to fend off another visit of the vicious brute, and proposed to take his gun and go into the forest and try to kill the beast. The big Indian hesitated to let him have so formidable a weapon, but he finally gave the young hunter his own hatchet and knife. With these, Walter stole into the woods, taking some jerky for the dog. He gave a low whistle, and Lion almost instantly joined his master. The boy searched carefully for a wound, but he found none, except for a small cut on his hip. He gave the meat to the dog, who buried it at once. The hunter then became convinced that the dog had found the dead bears and had laid in his own meat supply. He patted the dog for a time, much to the delight of the faithful creature, and finally rose to depart. He told the dog he must not follow. After making a circle around the camp, the young hunter returned from another direction. He could easily have secured a horse and made his escape, but in his unarmed condition, he could scarcely be of much help to the señorita from the outside. He determined to stay near her and guard her as best he could, let the consequences be what they might. His wounds were now healed, except the one on the back of his neck. He slept long and soundly the rest of the night and did not wake until morning was well advanced. Maria seemed much refreshed, and the savages showed little disposition to move.

Tee-Clee was in a frightful condition. His face, neck, and limbs were fearfully swollen, and his eyes entirely closed. He could not speak, and it seemed impossible to move him. And yet the savages seemed determined not to remain another night in this place. They finally decided to find another camp in a more favorable place and move to it. For this purpose, two Indians went ahead. They returned shortly after noon with the information that a good camp lay a short distance ahead. After eating a hasty meal, they constructed a travois and placed the helpless Tee-Clee upon it. He groaned fearfully as the poles jolted over the rocky ground. After two hours of toilsome travel, they pitched a camp on the banks of a little stream in the midst of a small grove of fir trees. Here, the leader said, they would remain two days, if necessary, for the recovery of the sick man.

They spent the remainder of the day in making the camp comfortable. The leader of the party proved to be a good soldier, for he kept scouts all the time. Walter offered to go and get some deer meat, as Maria did not like the bear meat. The leader hesitated, saying that the gun might alarm the Navajos. He went himself and got meat, which he divided most liberally with the prisoners. They were grateful and so expressed themselves to him, which seemed to give the savage pleasure.

The night passed without any special occurrence, except a visit from Lion, who first went to his master and then to the señorita. The girl suggested that they tell the young Indian about the dog, fearing he might shoot the faithful creature with arrows. But the young hunter hesitated and said, "No, I have not known the Indian boy long enough to place full confidence in him."

However, an incident occurred that somewhat strengthened the young hunter's confidence in Antonio. Before retiring for the night, they discussed the attack of the mad wolf on Tee-Clee. The young hunter spoke of Tee-Clee's efforts to defend himself with his knife when the beast had attacked him. Antonio spoke up quickly and asked, "Where Tee-Clee's knife?" Walter produced the knife. The boy said, "No Tee-Clee's knife. That my knife." Both prisoners were surprised. The boy then told his story: "Me lay down on dark side of teepee. Me no sleep. Me all time wait. Me hear little noise. Me listen, then me hear Tee-Clee crawl on ground to girl. Me get up, me look in. Tee-Clee creep close to girl. Me stand ready with knife. Girl scream. Me jump in with knife. Then wolf jump in, catch Tee-Clee by arm, knock me down. Me get up quick. Wolf have Tee-Clee by throat, much growl, big wolf, pull Tee-Clee all around in teepee. Knock me down again. Me lost knife, girl run. Me follow. Wolf run away. Tee-Clee all still. Yes, that my knife."

Antonio told this in a straightforward way, and both prisoners believed he spoke the truth. The young hunter still declined to tell the boy about the dog, for should he be told the whole truth, he would lose his superstitious fear about the mad wolf.

They passed three days in the new camp before Tee-Clee began to rally. Told that he had been attacked by a mad wolf, Tee-Clee was seized by a deadly fear and begged to be taken to the Apache village where he might be under the protection of his family. He knew that, at the least unfavorable symptom, he would be abandoned by his fellow savages and allowed to die alone. And so, literally paralyzed with fear, he resolved to make friends with the captive hunter. Accordingly, he sent the Indian boy for the young prisoner. When the two boys entered the teepee, Tee-Clee sent away Antonio and motioned to Walter to sit down. This his visitor declined to do, saying, "Let Tee-Clee speak, if he wishes the little chief to wait to hear him."

The sick savage replied that he wanted the white hunter to aid him in reaching the Apache village, that he feared the Indians would abandon him, and that he could not help himself.

The young hunter answered, "The ears of the white prisoner are closed. They will only be open when Antonio is present."

But Tee-Clee tried to talk, saying that the boy was no good.

The young hunter turned on his heel and strode from the teepee. Tee-Clee tried to call after him, but Walter did not look back. Presently the Indian boy came to him again, saying, "Tee-Clee want white chief."

The two repaired again to the sick man's teepee, and this time Antonio interpreted their conversation. The wounded savage began, "Tee-Clee very sick. He cannot walk. He is far from the village of his friends. He wants white brave to help him." He added, "If white brave help, Tee-Clee set him free at Indian village."

The white prisoner answered, "The little chief saw Tee-Clee, the Apache warrior, on the mountainside far back toward the rising sun. He came with four warriors. They fired arrows but did not strike the white warrior. His warriors all died, and Tee-Clee was alone. He could not shoot his arrows because the bullet of the paleface had destroyed his bow. He fought the white hunter with his tomahawk and knife, but the paleface struck him down. His wounds were many. The young señorita bound up his wounds and saved his life. He told the white hunter that he was now his friend, that harm should not come to him, and that he would also save Maria. Then they left Tee-Clee, left him with food, water, and a horse to ride. Also weapons to defend himself from his enemies. When the white hunter and the señorita became the prisoners of Tee-Clee's brother, they told the brother where the wounded Tee-Clee lay, and he was rescued and brought among his people. Then the prisoners were sent away to the Apache village. When the bears drove Tee-Clee into the tree, Tee-Clee begged the white prisoner to drive them away with his two-gun. But then, Tee-Clee bound the white prisoner to a tree, making his bonds so tight that he could not reach the teepee of the white girl to defend her from the coward Tee-Clee."

"See," Walter continued, exhibiting his lacerated wrists, "the wounds that the tight bonds made, which Tee-Clee placed on his wrists. When the white prisoner could not break his bonds and could not go to the teepee to help the white girl, he looked up to the clouds where the Manitou of the white man dwells, and the mad wolf came to the defense of the helpless white girl. Are the ears of the Apache warrior Tee-Clee open? Has he heard the words of the paleface prisoner?"

"Yes," answered the savage.

"Has the paleface spoken the truth?"

"Yes," answered the terror-stricken savage.

"Then Tee-Clee," continued the young hunter, "has two tongues. He is a liar. He has broken his promise to the little chief and to the white girl."

The wounded savage was silent. The interpreter waited. The young hunter finally continued, "Are the ears of Tee-Clee open? Has he heard the words of the paleface?"

"Yes."

"Then," replied the young hunter with flashing eyes, "where is his tongue?"

The savage, with apparent effort, answered, "The ears of Tee-Clee are open. He has heard the words of the white chief. They are good. The white chief has spoken truth. The heart of Tee-Clee is bad."

"Yes," said the youth, "the Manitou read the heart of Tee-Clee. He saw it is bad. The Manitou of the paleface heard the cry of the young girl and said she should be saved. The Manitou of the red man said that was good. The Manitou sent the mad wolf to the teepee where the girl slept—to save her from the cowardly midnight prowler. There the mad wolf found Tee-Clee. The mad wolf tore his body and throat and could have killed him, but the Manitou said, 'No, let him live. He is an Apache warrior.'

"Does Tee-Clee know what the bite of the mad wolf means? It means that the poison of the mad wolf's teeth has gone into his blood, and after many days, his head will burn like fire; his eyes will turn red; white foam will come to his mouth; and he will go mad. He will run to the forest and the mountains and sleep in the den of the mad wolf.

"His friends will turn their backs on him; his wife will flee from him; his father will avoid him and drive him away. The paleface does not fear the mad wolf, and he does not fear Tee-Clee. The Manitou of the paleface protects his children. Tee-Clee has seen that this is true. Let Tee-Clee ask the

Great Manitou for forgiveness. The little chief is in the camp of the Apache warrior, a prisoner. He has to obey the leader of his captors, but if he can, he will help Tee-Clee reach the village of his people, that his father and mother may see him before his eyes go red and he leaves them for the den of the mad wolf." Saying this, Walter stalked from the teepee.

The young Indian bounded past Walter in his haste to get from the presence of the afflicted warrior. Soon after, all the Indians knew of the meeting in Tee-Clee's teepee, and it was with great difficulty that they were induced to aid the wounded man in his homeward journey. However, they gladly agreed to the captive's suggestion that he sleep near Tee-Clee's lodge to keep away the mad wolf.

The journey to the Apache village was very tedious, and as the road was rough and rugged, it was very hard on the wounded savage. At times, his mind would wander. During such periods, the Indians would not go near him. The entire care of the wounded man thus devolved on Walter. He told the Indians that he would tell them when the sick warrior would go mad, and he said he would defend them from the mad creature on condition that his rifle was returned to him. They then volunteered to let him keep his rifle at night so as to better defend the camp from the mad wolf.

One night, while on guard, the young hunter called the Indian boy to one side and sounded him out about making their escape from the camp. But the boy would not listen to the suggestion. He said that they must go to the village and that he dare not be party to the escape. He said his uncle was a great man among the Apaches. He insisted that his uncle was greater than the chief, and he felt sure that his uncle would take the young señorita under his protection. "But," he told Walter, "I do not know how it will be for you. Injun maybe kill hunter."

The next morning, the leader of the party told the young hunter that they should reach the Indian village that night. They kept up the march the entire day, and the young girl begged to have a halt made so that she might rest. But the leader, who kept well in the advance, would not hear of it. He pushed on with greater rapidity than before, and it was with difficulty that the poor girl kept her seat in the saddle.

Night settled down, and yet there was no sign of the village. Finally, the leader halted and rode up to the side of the young hunter. The village was near at hand, he said, and he must now take the gun of the prisoner. The youth gave up his weapon. The leader said that he must now bind the prisoner. The young man submitted to having his hands tied.

While this was done, Maria sat by in mute despair. She said, "Capitan, it breaks my heart to see you bound."

The youth cheered her up with kind, gentle words, adding that he hoped they would soon be at liberty. He now called the Indian boy to him and asked, "Are you going to remember the kindness of this brave girl and at once see that she has good care?" The boy said he would go at once to his uncle. He spoke to the leader, who told him that the captives would have to go first before the chief.

The village was situated on the west bank of a considerable stream at the base of a high mountain. The village contained several hundred lodges. The party crossed the stream and entered the village at the lower end, slowly making their way to the center. The lodges, pitched in irregular formation on both sides of the "avenue," extended in a southerly direction for nearly a mile up the stream. About halfway through the village, they came to a very large, skin lodge, pitched in the center of the avenue. Around this lodge, a large space of open ground had somewhat the appearance of a public square. Near the lodge, a considerable group of warriors had gathered. One was speaking. Quite an assembly of men, boys, and women began to gather on either side of the newcomers. They indulged in many abusive remarks. The warriors escorting the captives paid no attention to the mob.

As the party halted in front of the big lodge, the mob howled and fell back. The leader made no effort to attract attention, but sat quietly on his horse. The council of warriors seemed to be giving close attention to the speaker, who continued his discourse some ten minutes. When he sat down, another spoke, and so on, until nearly an hour had been consumed. Then the council began to disperse. Not one of the passing warriors paid the least attention to the newcomers. Finally, three Indians who had been in attendance at the council came to the front of the lodge and, without noticing the party, entered. Still the leader sat quietly on his horse. Presently a young savage came out of the lodge and approached the party's leader and spoke a few words to him.

The leader at once dismounted and entered the lodge. At this moment, the Indian boy slid from his horse and approached the young girl, saying, "Me go now. Me come back quick." And he at once disappeared among the lodges. The señorita was distraught, not only by the long, fatiguing journey, but also because of the tedious delay in not being allowed to dismount. She wept bitterly. After an absence of ten minutes, the boy returned, accompanied by three persons. One was a savage of gigantic stature, with a large head and a most kindly expression of the face. He was followed closely by two others: a tall young warrior with a slight limp in his walk, who resembled the larger savage so much that he would at once be set down as his son. He approached close to the prisoners and, for a single instant, fixed his eyes on the young hunter. They then sought the face of the weeping señorita. The third person was a tall, slight Indian girl, with long dark hair and a kind face, who was dressed in neat and comely attire. The large savage took Maria in his arms and lifted her gently, as easily as an ordinary man could lift an infant. As he set her on the ground, he said kindly, "Little squaw much tired. Go to the lodge of White Fawn. Eat and sleep."

The girl wiped away her tears and stepped quickly to the side of the young hunter. "Oh, Capitan," she said, "my heart is breaking. You are in this terrible situation because of me, for whom you have suffered so much already. We may never meet again. Capitan, my tongue refuses to say to you what I would." She seized his bound hands and pressed them. "I shall pray for you constantly. Farewell, Capitan, farewell."

The young hunter was choked with emotion. "Señorita," he said, "I have done nothing to deserve your prayers. I am your debtor and would that my life would suffice to place you again under the protection of your noble father. My dear friend, God will protect you."

The young prisoner sat on his horse for a long time. Finally, three warriors came from the big lodge. The leader of the party, who had brought him to the village, was with them. He seemed surprised by the absence of the girl and asked what had become of her. One of the savages answered, and the name of Sehi-Za-To-On caught the ear of the prisoner. No further questions were asked. They told the young hunter to dismount, and he was ordered to follow one of the savages. In the meantime, Tee-Clee had been taken to his own lodge, to be cared for by his family.

Walter followed his guide for some distance among the many lodges, and they finally entered one. The savage was soon joined by several others, who securely bound the prisoner and left him lying on a bed of skins.

His tight bonds kept sleep from his eyes, and he lay long and suffered much discomfort.

Late in the night, the young hunter heard dogs fighting. This seemed to commence at a point far down the avenue, and it continued to a point just opposite where he was confined. He guessed that Lion had boldly entered the village in search of his master and had been set upon by numbers of the village dogs, whom he had managed to disperse. No dog would make a second attack, for the powerful Lion only needed one chance at a dog to maim him. Presently all was silent. Evidently, Lion had taught the belligerent creatures that it was dangerous to meddle with this powerful stranger.

Half an hour elapsed before the prisoner heard a slight noise just back of the center of the lodge. It was the sound of a body inserting itself under the side of the lodge. Presently Lion crept to the side of his master and licked his hands and swollen wrists. Walter encouraged Lion to cut his bonds with his sharp teeth, which the noble dog soon did, and the young hunter was greatly relieved. He decided not to remove the bonds at his ankles. After fondling the faithful animal for a long time, he took up the pieces of rawhide used in binding his wrists and put them in the dog's mouth. Then, with a big hug, he motioned for Lion to go. With reluctance, the animal turned away, passed out of the lodge, and disappeared.

The young prisoner now slept soundly, nor did he waken until the sun was well up. When he did wake, he was joined by several of his captors and was the subject of active discussion. He understood enough to satisfy himself that they were debating how he had succeeded in freeing his hands. Finally, two of the savages left the lodge. They could be heard all around the outside of the lodge. When they returned, it was evident they had discovered nothing that threw light on the matter. They questioned Walter closely. He explained, with grimaces and gestures, that the bonds had been too tight and hurt his wrists. He had not been able to sleep, and so he had worked the bonds loose and threw them out of the lodge.

For the first time, they missed the leather thongs and made another search, again without success. They were much puzzled, but could get no further light on the subject.

The day passed without his leaving the lodge. His ankles were still tied. As evening came, they again tied his wrists, and it was evident that they were determined to learn how he had succeeded in liberating himself. Lion had no further opportunity to enter the lodge, but toward the last watch of the morning, the measured breathing of the guard satisfied the young hunter that he was asleep. Walter knew that Lion was near. He slipped his wrists under the edge of the lodge, and the brave dog soon cut the bonds and set his master at liberty. With his hands free, the hunter untied his feet and passed the thongs to Lion and dismissed him. He now arranged the bottom of the lodge as it had been and moved himself as far from the side as he could. Drawing a buffalo skin over himself, he was soon sound asleep.

As soon as the savages found that he had again been able to free himself, consternation reigned. They expressed the greatest surprise, and many warriors came to see him. The Indian girl, the daughter of Sehi-Za-To-On, White Fawn, came to him with some boiled corn and meat in an earthen dish. She sat down, and the guard got up and left the lodge. The girl rose and gave him a small note, written on a piece of buckskin. It ran thus: "Dear Capitan, I am well. The bearer of this is so kind and good. Her father is also kind. Her brother knows you and will aid you. I do not know how. I send a pencil by the girl. Adieu, Capitan. From your friend."

He quickly wrote an answer: "I am well. Lion is a comfort. Your bright note gives me much happiness. Hastily, I am your friend." He handed the pencil and note to the girl, and she rose and left the lodge. As she departed, the guard entered. The limbs of the hunter were not again bound that day. The friends found no opportunity to communicate for several days, but the young hunter felt easy, for he now had little fear that the señorita would be harmed. Daily, the young Indian girl came to him with food, corn and the choicest pieces of the buffalo and other game. He noted with much satisfaction that all the savages treated the Indian girl with the utmost deference. In turn, she treated him with great kindness. This the guards did not seem to notice, and as soon as she was gone, they were often rude and even brutal.

One day, while he had been left unbound, he went to the door of the lodge and observed a very old warrior at work grinding on a stone a peculiar gluey substance. His curiosity was aroused, and he asked the old Indian what he was doing. At first, the savage was not communicative, but the young hunter gave the old man a small steel awl, which he carried in his pouch. After the Indian had examined this useful article, he motioned for the prisoner to follow him. Presently the savage stopped and took a piece of buffalo robe from the ground. The robe covered a hole some three or four feet deep. In this hole were a half a dozen rattlesnakes. The hole was considerably larger at the bottom than at the top, making it impossible for the reptiles to escape. Taking from a stake near the hole a piece of skin—in which was wrapped a piece of fresh deer's liver attached to a long string—the old man let the piece of liver down into the hole near the serpents. They at first paid no attention to it. The savage then took a stick and annoyed the reptiles until they began to strike the liver. When they tired of paying attention to it, he took the liver away. He carefully covered the hole and returned to his work place. He hung the liver up in the sun, explaining that, when it was dry, he would grate it to powder on his rough stone. He then dampened the powder and made it into a cake, which he dried on a slow fire or in the sun. When it was thoroughly dried, he again pulverized it on the stone. He continued this process until the mass formed a pasty, gluey substance of a dark brown color. He put this in a small skin bag and sold it to warriors. He said the substance was very poisonous and produced death quickly. He showed how it was used, by roughing the arrowhead on its sides and then inserting it into the bag. He pressed the arrowhead between his thumb and finger on the outside of the bag, forcing the gummy substance into the rough scratches on the arrowhead. When he drew the arrow out, it was ready for use. The poison soon dried, and when it came into contact with the warm flesh of the victim, it took immediate effect and was always fatal, he declared.

The old man said not all warriors carried the poison, but some did. He explained that all tribes used this kind of poison, more or less. Walter could not help but shudder as he reflected on the loathsome methods adopted by the savages. He was afterwards told that poison was not often used and that warriors only used it in desperate cases. Savage animals were sometimes poisoned in this way, he was told.

Growing increasingly impatient, the young hunter was anxious to know what his probable fate would be. He failed to secure any information from the savages who had immediate charge of him. From many sources, he learned that the savages were very bitter against the white men, and there was a strong feeling in favor of putting him to death by slow torture. Of late, the savages seemed to delight in telling him that he would be burned.

They told him that all white men were women and that, when the fire touched their flesh, they would scream. They discoursed often on this subject, doing their best to make an impression on the young prisoner. But they utterly failed. One day, Walter challenged one of his guards, much larger than himself, to fight with knives or tomahawk. The savage refused, and Walter called him a squaw, which the boy's tormentor did not relish.

One day, two Indians entered the lodge with food, including some hot soup. Walter's savage tormentor was present and continued his ugly treatment. Without hesitating, Walter seized the dish and hurled the hot contents into the Indian's face. The boy then felled the big savage with the heavy earthen vessel. The young hunter seized the prostrate Indian by the hair and quickly dragged him from the lodge. Having done this, he returned and ate what was left of his dinner. The savage was badly hurt and was soon the laughingstock of the village. He offered no further indignities to the prisoner.

Walter often expressed a desire to go through the village, but his wish was not granted. Lion had not visited his master in several days, and the young man grew anxious concerning the dog's welfare. When he had about given Lion up as dead, he was agreeably surprised one night to be awakened by the kind-hearted creature licking his face. When Walter opened his eyes, the dog picked up something, placed it in his master's hand, and disappeared.

In the morning, he found the package to be a small piece of wood to which a note was tied. He was not immediately able to read the note. Lion now came frequently. The young Indian girl White Fawn ceased to come to the lodge, and his food was brought by a warrior. He was now bound nights, but he protested so strongly against tight bonds that they were only tied sufficiently tight to prevent his escape. He learned that there was much speculation concerning his having been able to release himself when it pleased him to do so.

His captors made some experiments. His hands were bound tightly behind his back, and the Apaches kept a close watch. The first night this happened, the dog came and Walter took a position as near the edge of the lodge as possible. He forced his wrists out under the lodge's covering skins, and the dog soon released his master. Walter then untied his own ankles and gave the bands to the dog to take away. In the morning, there was consternation among the savages. During the day, Antonio came to see Walter and told him that the savages were not only very much surprised, but alarmed at not being able to account for this strange occurrence. He said that a great medicine man was going to look into the matter.

Walter answered that the Great Spirit of the white man would not let his children suffer, and he intimated that it would not be safe to tax the Great Father's patience too far—that the guards might fall dead, by knife or hatchet. He added that there was no danger of his escape, that he would not leave the camp unless the Mexican girl was released. Antonio now told him that his uncle had bought Maria from Tee-Clee, giving a horse for her, and that she would now live in his uncle's lodge as one of the family and would not be abused or killed. This news greatly lightened the heart of the captive. He now thought it likely that the note Lion had brought him conveyed this and other important information, and he longed for an opportunity to read it. But so far, he had not been left alone for a single moment.

Antonio also said that the Indian guards were afraid to stay in the lodge with Walter. He ventured to ask the prisoner what had become of the thongs that had bound his hands and feet. "This I cannot tell you," answered Walter, "but you need fear nothing. You are a friend of the señorita and my friend. Come to me when you can. I am glad to see you. Do you know when I am to be killed? Do not fear to tell me; I shall always be your friend."

"I do not know," replied the boy. "Injun have great council soon. Don't know how many days. Then Injun talk—maybe kill with knife—maybe burn—maybe sell to other Injuns for slave; heap work then."

Antonio now told his friend that he must go. "But," said the prisoner, "you will come again, will you not? Tell the señorita how happy I am that she is free and no longer in danger of death or slavery. Tell her I can now sleep."

When he was alone, Walter took the piece of skin from his sleeve and read as follows: "Dear Capitan, my kind benefactor informs me that he has purchased my freedom, that he has adopted me into his family, and that, whenever I can go in safety to my father, I am at liberty to go. He had a stormy time to accomplish my release. He is so good and kind, and his daughter is the sweetest and most loving creature living. She is very kind to me. I want for nothing that is within their power to furnish me. But Capitan, I grieve for you, and my heart almost breaks when I think that, only for me, you would not be a prisoner. I have ceased to fear for myself. I pray for you constantly. Capitan, there is great commotion in the camp. White Fawn seems to fear something, but she does not tell me. She says I am safe, but she does not know about the white capitan. I have learned that captives are treated with great cruelty and have often heard of their being killed outright. White Fawn tells me her father is always kind. He is not a chief, but is much beloved. Many warriors come to his lodge to talk to him in private. He seems to have great influence. Adieu, Capitan."

Thus the note abruptly closed. Going to the edge of the lodge, Walter dug a small hole and, after chewing the buckskin to a pulp, buried it in the ground, covering it deeply and tramping the loose dirt around it. He had scarcely finished hiding the note when several warriors entered. Among them was an aged savage whom the prisoner at once concluded was the medicine man.

The warriors treated this old man with the utmost deference. The old savage fixed his snake-like eyes on the young prisoner and gazed long into his eyes. The other Apaches searched the lodge. The young man never flinched, but returned the gaze with equal steadiness. The savage finally looked the other way and began his own careful inspection of the lodge and its surroundings. The Indians turned over and shook every article to see that no hidden object was about the lodge. After they had consumed a half an hour in fruitless search, the party withdrew for consultation. When they returned to the lodge, some of them attempted to talk to the prisoner, without avail. Finally, one left the lodge and, after an absence of some twenty minutes, returned with the young Indian boy, with whom the savages conversed for some time. Finally, Antonio turned to the prisoner and said, "Injun want to know where straps that bound hands."

"Tell them to bring their wise men and let them answer,"

"They say, 'You answer.' You no answer, they cut off your hand."

"Tell them they had better talk to the Great Spirit."

The old Indian now came forward with a great knife and, after many flourishes and mumbling something in a low voice, addressed the boy in Apache. Antonio told the prisoner to hold out his hand—that the medicine man would now cut it off. The prisoner promptly stepped to the center of the lodge, raised his eyes toward heaven, and said, "Father of Spirits, watch over and protect thy children." He then stepped back to where the Indian stood, in an attitude of listening, with his eyes and ears averted. Turning to Antonio, he said, "I am ready. Let the wise man proceed."

While the savages had been outside the lodge in consultation, Walter had taken his Bowie knife from his inside pocket and concealed it in his right sleeve, with the intention of slaying the old Indian should the latter offer violence to his person. But while in the act of prayer, an idea had occurred to him, which he now determined to put into execution. Letting the heavy Bowie knife drop forward into his hand, he held the blade in his palm and turned his hand over, presenting the back of the hand to the blade of the savage. The light in the lodge was somewhat dim, which was favorable to his bold project. Now, watching the Indian closely, he waited calmly for the expected blow. He noted that the old savage was somewhat unsteady. As the knife descended, Walter quickly turned his hand—and the knife of the savage encountered the side of the blade of the thick Bowie knife. As the two pieces of steel met, sparks of fire streamed from them and were plainly visible. Walter quickly threw up his arms, and the Bowie knife dropped back into its place of concealment in his sleeve.

Seizing the medicine man by the arm with his left hand, he presented his unharmed wrist to the astonished savages, none of whom had noticed the trick. The old man looked at the smooth white wrist of the prisoner for a single moment—dropped his knife and darted from the lodge, followed by all of the others, including the Indian boy. Walter picked up the knife that the savage had thrown down and found that the edge of its blade had turned, the material being somewhat softer than the keen edge and better tempered blade of his Bowie knife. He now concealed his knife as before and calmly waited the pleasure of his captors. What he feared was that some incredulous one might repeat the experiment of the old medicine man and that he might not be so successful a second time in deceiving them.

Darkness fell, and yet no guard returned. He did not doubt, however, that they were stationed at a safe distance, keeping a close watch on his lodge. When Lion came, the young man wrapped up the old Indian's knife in dirty scrap of cloth and gave it to the faithful dog to hide. Afterwards, he was sorry he had done this—he feared that a close search for the missing weapon might result in the savages' discovery of his Bowie knife, leaving him weaponless and, in a measure, helpless. With the trusty Bowie knife, he felt that he could defend himself.

He decided to keep alive the superstitious belief among the Indians that
something was wrong with their prisoner—or at least that his medicine
was very strong. Whenever the savages were near, he went through as much
ceremony as he could, like making crosses and looking toward the sky from
the opening in the center of the lodge. He also made strange marks on the
floor, all of which the Indians looked upon with more or less awe.

In the morning, the boy came to him. He entered with apparent reluctance, handing the prisoner a chip upon which was written: "Capitan, a
great council is to be held, and you are to be tried. I will pray for you.
Hastily."

Having read the note, Walter returned it to Antonio. "I give it back," he
said, "that the Indians may not see the writing and watch." The boy nodded
and took the piece of wood, concealing it in his robe. He was about to leave
when the hunter laid his hand on him, saying, "Do not fear. I am your
friend. My great medicine may some day save you. Why do you not come
often?"

"Injun no come," said the boy. "Injun no like great medicine of white
man."

"When is the council?" asked the prisoner.

"Today," replied Antonio. "Injun come soon. Heap talk. Maybe kill with
knife, or spear, maybe hatchet, or maybe burn. You heap kill Injun. Injun
heap mad warrior—lost boy, squaw cry. Much talk. Many warriors dead.
Maybe no come back to lodge—maybe no see girl."

For one brief instant, the prisoner lost his admirable self-command. As
Antonio said, "Me go. Injun come now—you go now council," Walter
grasped the boy's arm and said quickly, "Wait." Then, in a voice quite unsteady, he said, "Go to the señorita. Say good-bye. Say the Great Spirit watch
her and bless her. Say the capitan does not fear death." Then, remembering
his weakness, he nerved himself and was calm. Grasping the boy's knife, he
cut a lock of hair from his head and handed it to Antonio, together with the
knife. "Give it to the señorita," he said.

Walter then walked to the center of the lodge and, raising his eyes to
heaven, began a short prayer, "Strengthen thy servant, Oh Lord, for the coming ordeal. Give me power to sustain my dignity. Amen."

Several savages now entered and motioned to him to follow. He had
previously made his toilet as best he could, straightened out his long, dark

hair, washed his hands and face, and gave such touches to his face, body, and clothing as would enable him to make a creditable appearance. The warriors indicated that he was to walk behind them, except for two guards who followed. The main avenue was deserted, with the exception of a few dogs and now and then a horse tied near a lodge. Walking some distance, the party reached a slight elevation and moved toward a grove of trees. They continued rapidly through the timber and then came into full view of a vast congregation. The area had been cleared of underbrush, with only a scattering of logs remaining that served as seats.

Toward the east ran a mountain brook. To the north and south, the ground receded for a distance of some two hundred feet. To the west, it inclined gently for about one hundred feet. Then it began to rise rapidly. Back of the council ground, at a distance of something like a quarter of a mile, rose a high rocky ridge, the mountain rising abruptly with precipitous sides to a height of some three thousand feet, which gave the general surroundings a picturesque grandeur. The rays of the sun lighting up this scene of indescribable beauty gave one the impression of castles and battlements of grand and imposing proportions. Towering above all was a massive belt of perpendicular rock. It was an impressive setting for the gathering of a multitude such as this.

As the guards approached with their prisoner, the crowd fell back, and the prisoner was conducted through the vast concourse of these wild people. It was certainly a gathering of the entire camp. The warriors, seated together on a slightly elevated ground, took no notice of the arrivals. They were talking and gesticulating in a most excited manner. The squaws and children pushed toward the prisoner until the compact mass of humanity was wedged in around him so tightly he could hardly breathe.

A warrior now rose and, turning to the spot where the prisoner stood, spoke a few words in an authoritative tone. The squaws and children immediately fell back and took up their position on a designated hillside.

The prisoner had been left near a low-burning campfire and in front of a small pine tree, some eight or ten inches in diameter, to which he fancied he would eventually be bound. Now there was silence. The hour was just past the meridian, and the sun shone out clearly, although a few heavy clouds hung on the northwestern horizon. The prisoner raised his eyes to take in the awesome scenery.

A low murmur now disturbed Walter's meditations. All heads turned towards the village to watch the rapid approach of a number of savages. They strode forward in silence, looking neither to left or right, and they passed through the circle of the warriors and climbed to a higher ground. One of the newcomers took a position to the extreme east, five others took positions some ten feet farther west, each seating himself at a uniform distance from the other, forming a frontage of some forty feet extending from north to south.

The young prisoner eyed these arrivals closely. The leader was a man of some forty-five or fifty years of age. His hair was long and black, arranged carefully in two braids. At his forehead, the hair was cut square across, which seemed to be the fashion of the men of the tribe. A reddish-yellow paint was lavishly daubed on his savage face. Above his eyebrows was a deep line of black, and he wore stripes of black on each side of his face. Red seemed to be used on the tips of his hair, and just below his eyes, and on his chin. This savage was lightly built, about five feet, ten inches in height. His head was small, with the forehead receding, and there were large brass rings in his ears. On his head, he wore a sort of helmet, painted and made of buffalo hide, which shaded his eyes. He wore a shirt of deerskin, ornamented with porcupine quills, beaded, and enhanced with silver ornaments. The shirt came down below his abdomen. He wore a breechcloth of softened leather, ornamented with beads. His feet were covered with moccasins of elk skin, and his leggings of the same materials were fringed at the side. Both moccasins and leggings were decorated with quills and beads in the most elaborate manner, and his belt was also decorated with beadwork. He wore a blanket, striped with brilliant colors, thrown over his left shoulder. He carried a knife, a tomahawk, and a bow with a quiver of arrows, and a Navy revolver was visible under his belt at the left side. His countenance was repulsive. He had high cheek bones, a thin face, and dark, snake-like eyes. He was No-Tok-Ho, the ruling chief of the village. He had the reputation of being a brave and successful warrior, formidable on the warpath, acquiring horses, scalps, and prisoners without mercy. His father had been a distinguished chief whose memory gave the son additional weight and influence. No-Tok-Ho, cruel and feared by most, was also called Soldier-Killer, a name of which he seemed extremely proud.

His companions, all of whom were more or less lavishly attired, were lesser chiefs and had taken seats with reference to their rank, the highest being in the line nearest the chief.

There was an uneasy silence as the chief entered the circle, and then a murmur of approval issued from many warriors as they greeted No-Tok-Ho with signs of recognition. There were others, however, who remained silent. Walter now took time to appraise the assembly. On the hillside above, he saw a sea of faces—mostly women and children—in whose visages he could see no sign of pity or hope. Many of them were old hags or crones. Between them and the warriors were the young warriors, from sixteen to eighteen years of age. Many were fine specimens of their kind. They carried bows and arrows and expressed eager expectancy as they cast furtive glances at the prisoner and whispered to one another, apparently discussing the prisoner's chances.

Walter's eyes wandered over the assembled savages—in search of some familiar face. There, they fastened their eager gaze upon a group of young women who stood by a large fir tree, between the warriors and the young men. The prisoner was surprised that females were allowed to occupy such a prominent position so near the privileged warriors. He recognized the well-known form of White Fawn and, near her, about the same height and size, a familiar figure whose face he could not see. He felt certain it was Maria. She was covered with a large blanket, and White Fawn held one of her hands. She seemed restless. Several other young women stood in the group. The eyes of the prisoner now dropped to the face of a warrior sitting very near White Fawn, and Walter at once recognized La-Ki-Ma-Ha, the Apache whose life he had saved on the prairie. He was White Fawn's brother, Walter had learned, and he now understood the presence of White Fawn so near to the inner circle.

The prisoner had noticed the chief look many times at the sun, as if impatient to begin. He also noticed White Fawn and her brother turn their eyes repeatedly to the village. The chief now rose and began to speak. As he did so, Walter heard the name, "Sehi-Za-To-On," murmured on many lips. The chief stopped talking abruptly. At this moment, the prisoner saw, on the elevation beyond the edge of the timber, the imposing form of a tall, powerful-looking warrior. Walter guessed that he must be the father of White Fawn and La-Ki-Ma-Ha.

A moment later, the gigantic form of Sehi-Za-To-On strode to the center of the circle of warriors and halted. He looked at the sun a single instant, then said, "Why is No-Tok-Ho in a hurry? Why does he open the council before the time?"

The chief answered, "Sehi-Za-To-On is late."

The old warrior faced the chief and said in a calm voice, "Sehi-Za-To-On is never late." Then stepping back and facing the sun, he stood his ponderous bow in front of him, and with his foot, he marked the line of the shadow. He said, "When the sun is there, let No-Tok-Ho begin." He then sat down. This action was watched by the warriors, and a murmur of approval followed. The chief sat down. Silence prevailed.

A pipe was now produced, and the prisoner watched as it was lit by a burning stick from the campfire near him. It was passed from one warrior to another, to the older and more distinguished men first and finally to the young men. When the last man had taken the pipe, all looked at the sun. During the smoking, which took some time, not a single word had been spoken. Now it seemed that all knew the time for opening the council had arrived. Now Sehi-Za-To-On took from beneath his robe a large stone pipe, lighting it with a coal from the fire. He raised it before him and pointed the stem to the sun, then to the earth, and began to smoke. After a few puffs, he passed the pipe to a warrior near him, and it passed to the first line of sub-chiefs and so on, until it was finally handed to No-Tok-Ho, who drew a few puffs. Each savage, as it was handed to him, went through the ceremony of pointing to the sun and to the earth before smoking.

The chief rose and, after looking over the vast assembly, said, "Warriors, we are in council. A paleface dog has been taken and is before you. Why have his guards not bound him to yonder tree? Let him be bound tight that my warriors and my people may know that he is a prisoner and awaits death, which all paleface dogs deserve."

The prisoner was then told to remove his coat, which he reluctantly did, remembering his knife hidden therein. Upon removing his garment, he placed it carefully on the ground at the foot of the tree, stepped on it, and placed his back to the tree, at the same time motioning to his guards, who bound him to the trunk.

At this moment, a young Indian stepped forward and took hold of the coat, attempting to remove it. The prisoner, quick as a flash, administered to the would-be thief a swift kick that sent him sprawling on the ground, to the amusement of all present. When the culprit rose from the ground, his nose was bleeding profusely. Exasperated beyond control by the force of the blow and the derisive laughter of the warriors, he drew his knife and darted at the now bound and helpless prisoner, with the evident intention of killing him on the spot. But just as he was in the act of plunging his knife into the heart of the captive—whose bonds deprived him of the means of helping himself—a tall, powerful warrior nearby dealt the would-be murderer a blow on the head with the side of his tomahawk and felled him to the earth. Then stooping over the prostrate form of the culprit, the warrior disarmed him. The cowardly creature lay some time on the ground. Presently, he arose to his feet amidst the laughter and jeers of those around him. Stepping up to the captive again, he aimed a crippling blow at the face of the helpless prisoner who—quick as thought—threw his head to one side, and the clenched fist of the infuriated savage came in contact with the tree. This last act was greeted with roars of laughter, and the discomfited assailant withdrew amidst the universal derision of the multitude.

The chief now invited the lesser chiefs and warriors to express their views as to the best means of disposing of the prisoner. For some time, no one seemed to care to open the question, during which interval the presiding chief stood looking over the assembly. He finally called upon one of the sub-chiefs near him to give his views. The person addressed, a splendidly attired savage, rose and said, "Warriors, I have been on the warpath many times. I have helped destroy many palefaces. They are bad. They should all be killed. Their women are weak and only fit to be slaves. This man is as small as a boy, and his flesh would burn quick. It would be better to see if he is as brave as we have been told he is. If his tongue were cut out, he would shed tears like a woman. Let the young men see if he can face death. I have spoken. Let us begin."

Another chief immediately arose and delivered a similar address. One followed another in rapid succession until every chief, save one, and many warriors had spoken. Not one word had been said in the prisoner's favor, and the views advanced by the chiefs and warriors were quite universally applauded by the multitude who, as each speaker concluded, gave vent to howls of general approval.

One savage, sitting in the second circle among the lesser chiefs, had kept his blanket over his head in such a way that his face was hidden all the time from the eye of the prisoner. Walter watched this Indian closely, believing that this was no other than Tee-Clee. The eye of the presiding chief now rested upon this worthy, and he called his name. Tee-Clee rose and glanced over the assemblage. For a brief moment, he was silent. Then he spoke. "Warriors," he said, "I know this paleface. He is a coward and should die. All palefaces are cowards. They bow their heads before the Apache warriors. He belongs to a party of palefaces who came from the north into our country, going south to the land of our enemies, the Mexicans. They would rob us of our horses, burn up our grass, and destroy our country. Should an Apache hesitate to kill his enemies, the paleface and the Mexican? No, let them all die the death of dogs. The paleface is like the coyote. He barks much and does little. Let this one die. He is a dog. Tee-Clee has spoken."

During this harangue, the savage had never once turned his eyes to rest on the prisoner, but steadily looked beyond him. As Tee-Clee ceased speaking, Walter felt a touch at his elbow. Glancing to his left, he saw that the Indian boy Antonio had approached so close as to almost touch his cheek. The lad said, in good Spanish, "Little capitan now talk. Talk loud, all hear." What to make of this advice, the prisoner could not, for his life, divine. He had, in the first place, not expected a hearing, and if he were granted one, how could he speak to the people so that they understood? He only knew small fragments of their language, and as to Spanish, he could understand it but did not speak it fluently or with sufficient accuracy. Before he could come to his senses sufficiently to make up his mind what to ask the boy, it was too late. Antonio was nowhere to be seen, and he saw that No-Tok-Ho was on his feet, preparing to speak.

The hum of voices that followed the speech of Tee-Clee had ceased, and all eyes turned toward the chief. "Warriors," he said, "I am your chief. My father was your chief before me. He was a great chief. He led his people to victory. He was the foe of the paleface; many died at his hand. While he lived, the Apaches were never hungry. His heart was big and his arrows sharp. Shall No-Tok-Ho be different from the great chief, his father?" He here recounted the principal exploits of his father and himself at great length, dwelling upon the bloodthirsty deeds of each. There were many demonstrations of approval, especially from the warriors gathered on the hillside.

By this time, No-Tok-Ho had wrought himself up to the highest pitch of ferocity, and he walked back and forth flourishing his knife and tomahawk, shouting and hurling threats at the helpless prisoner and demanding his blood to atone for the savages whom the young hunter had slain in his own defense. He closed his speech, "Warriors, you have heard the brave Tee-Clee tell you about the paleface prisoner. You have heard your chiefs speak and tell you more about our enemies, the paleface dogs. No-Tok-Ho is an Apache. He has no other blood in his veins. Shall he wait to be told what is good for his people? There is another prisoner among us—a girl— the daughter of a Mexican dog. She has not been in the prison lodge, nor has she eaten prison fare since she came here. Shall she go free, while the blood of our warriors is not yet dry, blood that was shed making her a prisoner? No-Tok-Ho says, 'No, let her die.' Warriors, can one prisoner atone for the blood of many warriors? Is it not best to shed these prisoners' blood when we have them? If we let these prisoners go free, the Great Spirit will curse us, and we shall go hungry. Yes, our women and children will die of starvation. Who will say that our prisoners shall not die—when the blood of our dead warriors is not yet dry, and their bones are on the far-off prairie, being torn by the sharp teeth of the wolf? No, warriors, it must not be. Let us decide how their blood shall be taken. The hour has come. No-Tok-Ho has spoken. He is done."

The chief concluded his speech amidst great applause. Several of the lesser chiefs and warriors advanced and greeted him. Presently, all subsided and sat down. There was now a hum of voices, conversing in excited tones. After the lapse of some five minutes, a minor chief rose and addressed No-Tok-Ho, "Are we done, or are we to sleep here? Shall the prisoners be sent away?"

When the speaker sat down, La-Ki-Ma-Ha, White Fawn's brother, addressed the presiding chief with great dignity, "Who is the prisoner? La-Ki-Ma-Ha has not heard his voice. La-Ki-Ma-Ha does not know whether he is Mexican or a northern paleface. When La-Ki-Ma-Ha has heard his voice, he will know. Do the Apaches kill their prisoners without a hearing? La-Ki-Ma-Ha will listen for the words of the chief No-Tok-Ho. La-Ki-Ma-Ha will wait." And remaining standing, La-Ki-Ma-Ha assumed a listening attitude.

Tee-Clee turned and spoke to No-Tok-Ho in a low voice. The latter rose and said, "The prisoner has not asked permission to be heard." La-Ki-Ma-Ha turned and beckoned to a man who was sitting some distance back in the outskirts of the gathering, among the old men. When that person came near, La-Ki-Ma-Ha spoke to him in the Apache language. The man was an interpreter who, in turn, addressed the prisoner in plain enough English. "Do you wish to speak?" he asked the young hunter. "Some of the warriors wait to hear you tell your story."

"Yes," Walter answered, "I would like to speak, but can a man speak when his bonds cut his flesh and his arms are bound?"

The interpreter translated Walter's answer in a loud voice.

The chief hesitated. Noting this, La-Ki-Ma-Ha strode to the side of the prisoner and, with quick strokes of his knife, set him at liberty. Turning, he returned to the center of the circle of warriors. Pointing to a spot that was vacant, he said to Walter, "Stand there. Stand there and talk."

The interpreter was an old man, much crippled. He spoke the Indian language with much fluency and was also master enough of the English language. He was dark skinned and dressed shabbily in skins in the manner of the common Indians. His face was scarred and wrinkled and covered with a stubbly beard. If he was an Indian, he belonged to another tribe. If he was a white man, he was no doubt a criminal. It was evident that explicit confidence was not placed in him by the Apaches, because both a Mexican and Antonio were called to listen to the speech of the young prisoner and to its interpretation.

Up to this point, Sehi-Za-To-On had not moved. Instead he sat silent and motionless, watching each speaker and seemingly deeply absorbed in everything that transpired. He now rose and moved to one side, facing the prisoner. He sat again, within easy reach of the young speaker and in such a position that he could watch his every motion and gesture.

All was now ready, and an impressive silence reigned throughout the assembly. Each auditor drew nearer with eager expectancy to hear what the prisoner had to say. Even the warriors who did their best to look and act unconcerned could not conceal their deep interest. Walter found his limbs numb and stiff, so much so that he found it quite impossible to put on his coat, which he now held in his hand. Straightening up to his full height, unimpressive as it was, he looked over the assembly. He saw the young Indian girl sitting upon the ground, leaning against the big fir tree, where he had seen her hours before. Near her, and reclining lightly against her shoulder, was Maria. He could not see her face, but he knew her form and recognized her carriage. Around them were several young women, making as attractive a presentation as a bouquet of blossoms. He next saw the tall form of La-Ki-Ma-Ha standing a few feet from him, and he saw Sehi-Za-To-On, also known as Eagle Feather. The old man's eyes were riveted on him. He thought he could detect a kindly expression on the otherwise stern face. This encouraged him, and he turned his eyes toward No-Tok-Ho.

He began by saying, "No-Tok-Ho, Chief of the Apaches, and warriors of the wilderness, I am your prisoner. You have asked me to speak to you. Those of you who have spoken here today are older than I am, and therefore know better what to say. You can see that I have not long been away from my father's house, and you cannot expect a great speech from me. My ears are full of what you have said, but I did not fully understand your words. Therefore, do not expect me to answer your speeches. You can see that my skin is white. I am one of the children of the Great White Father who lives beyond the mountains, on the banks of the Great Water. Why have you taken me prisoner? Why have your warriors made war upon the children of the Great White Father? Do you not know that when he hears what you have done, his anger will be great? Do you not know that his soldiers are as numerous as the sands of the desert?" He stooped and picked up a handful of sand and raised his hand and let the sand sift out between his fingers, little by little, until all was gone.

"He will send them to destroy your people," he continued, "but you may say that he will not know that you have spilt the blood of one of his children. Here, let me tell you," and his voice rang through the air like a trumpet, "for every drop of white blood you shed, a hundred white men will rise and avenge the murder. The Great Spirit has told you that you must not kill, the black gowns have told you this. Why do you close your ears to their words? They are wise and good. The white man does not attack you. He wants you to be his friend. You ask me why I fought your warriors and slew them. I will tell you. My friends were traveling on the Great Trail built by the Great White Father's soldiers. A great storm came, and the Navajos came to our camp and took yonder girl. I went to their camp in the night and set her free and was trying to get back to the camp of our friends when yonder coward and liar"—he pointed at Tee-Clee—"attacked me. I was one. He and his four warriors were five. Has he told you what happened? For fear that he has forgotten, I will tell you. I want you to open your ears wide and hear what I say, for it will be true.

"The Great Spirit in the clouds saw yonder coward come upon me. You could not have sent him, for you know that you have no right to disturb the people of the Great White Father in their peaceful pursuits. I was there upon the trail that belongs to the Great White Father, and Tee-Clee came upon me. He divided his warriors—two upon one side and three upon the other. They came fast, for they had swift horses. They all had many arrows. The Great Spirit of the white man teaches his children that they must defend the weak and helpless. Is there a warrior here who is so big a coward and so mean that he would not risk his life to defend a woman or a wounded warrior? If there is, let him stand up for I want to see his ugly face. I want"— Walter stooped to pick up a stone—"to strike his cowardly body with this stone, for your guards have taken my tomahawk and my gun. A coward should be killed with a stone. Where is that man? Let him stand, I say, that all the women here may see him."

Walter turned around and looked calmly over the vast assemblage. "Where is that coward?" again asked the prisoner. "I am glad he is not here. I am glad there are no warriors among the Apaches who are so cowardly and mean. I ask you, No-Tok-Ho, did you send Tee-Clee upon the trail of the Great White Father to strike his people? You do not speak, but I will tell the captains of the Great White Father and he will punish your people and if they fall by the long knives of the white soldiers, their blood will be on your head—for you are their chief." Shouting, Walter shook his finger at No-Tok-Ho. "Did you not violate your treaty? You are a liar. It is your duty to teach your warriors to do right. It is your duty to tell them that they must not disturb the Great White Father's people when they are upon their own ground and do you no harm. Well, the warriors of Tee-Clee all fell, and Tee-Clee was there alone. There was no bullet in my gun to strike him. My last bullet was guided by the Great Spirit, and it struck Tee-Clee's bow. Did he tell you that he came upon me with his knife and his tomahawk? Well, he came, and he fell with many wounds. Look at his breast, look at his side, look at his arm, and look at his mutilated face—and you will find that the knife of the paleface has been there. He is big; look at me." An involuntary expression of admiration swept over the throng of warriors present.

"Ask him," Walter shouted, pointing at Tee-Clee, "who gave him his life. Has he told you that? He told me that I should not be killed, that he was chief and he would save me. Has he told you this? My ears are open wide, and I am listening for your answer. You do not speak, but it matters not. The Great Spirit saw the wounded Tee-Clee, who had no food, no water, no weapon, and no strength to use them. He knows his heart as he knows mine. I know that No-Tok-Ho is your chief. I know that he is the enemy of the Great White Father. I know that he will take my life. I know the eyes of the Great Spirit will see my blood flow out upon the sand. Does he think a son of a white chief is afraid to die? If he thinks so, let him see. But when I am dead and my blood has made these sands red and my spirit rises up, up, and up to the clouds, the home of the Great Spirit, let No-Tok-Ho beware. The Great Spirit will be angry, and if he strikes the Apaches, they will know it was because their chief No-Tok-Ho has a lying heart. He has broken his treaty and offended the Great Spirit.

"Warriors, I have spoken. You will hear my voice no more. Let my words stay in your ears, but I want to tell you that I shall die happy because the Great Spirit opened the heart of a great warrior who has taken the white prisoner, the paleface girl, to his heart and his lodge and given her food, shelter, and the protection of a father. I am done."

As the last words of the young prisoner died away, a murmur of approval swept over the assemblage. Walter folded his arms and straightened up to his utmost height and fastened his eyes on the chief No-Tok-Ho, who acted uncomfortable and ill at ease under the searching gaze of the brave young captive.

Following the speech of the young captive, silence prevailed until White Fawn glided to the side of her father and whispered some words to him. Walter was led away and again bound to the tree. The chief now rose and said, "We have heard the voice of the paleface. Let us see if he is a warrior." Tee-Clee, in the meantime, had approached No-Tok-Ho and held a moment's conversation with him. Several young men gathered in the vicinity of the captive. Presently one stepped forward and threw a peculiar missile which struck the tree, just grazing Walter's cheek. This little instrument of torture was a slender piece of wood, on the end of which the quill of a porcupine was neatly fastened with small shreds of sinew. Fastened to the shaft in the same manner were delicate feathers in three rows, beginning about four inches from the point of the quill and extending to the end of the shaft, the whole being about nine inches in length. These little missiles could be thrown with great accuracy. Hurled at the victim, they attain great velocity and sink into the flesh from one to two inches. When withdrawn, they cause the victim great pain as they have delicate barbs and, if left in the wound, will constantly work in deeper. In practice, the points are made of the long, sharp barbs of the cactus, but the quill points are reserved for hurling at the unfortunate victims who fall into the hands of these cruel people.

All attention was now given to the prisoner and his tormentors. A woman approached and struck him a blow with a club. It was said that she was the mother of one of Tee-Clee's followers whom Walter had killed. She was driven away and did not return. Most of the young braves tried their skill with the miniature lance, until the missiles were thick all around the head of the prisoner. It is said that captives have been stripped, bound, and put to death with these terrible instruments of torture by literally having their bodies filled full of them, the last one being poisoned.

The interpreter now approached the prisoner and spoke to him. As Walter turned his head, a young brave hurled one of his lances, which buried itself in the captive's cheek. In less than a minute, the painful missiles filled his face and forehead, somehow missing his eyes but one being driven through his nose. At this moment, the señorita—who had turned her eyes away— looked at her friend and was so horror stricken at the sight that she gave a terrible shriek and fainted in the arms of White Fawn.

For a few moments, the torture abated, but was again renewed. The tormentors now stopped throwing at the face. They hurled their missiles at Walter's body, arms, and breast until they were literally full. Now and then a warrior would give expression of admiration at the wonderful self-command and patience of the youthful captive. Not once was he taken by surprise or caught off his guard, nor did he flinch under the most excruciating torture.

During this ordeal, both Sehi-Za-To-On and La-Ki-Ma-Ha had been the most attentive watchers of the progress of affairs. The latter stood motionless. He was fully armed and never took his eyes off the prisoner for a single instant. Presently, for no apparent reason, the young braves discarded the little missiles and took up their bows and arrows. Stepping back twenty feet or more, they sent their arrows with the greatest velocity at the head of the prisoner, but though every arrow grazed his skin, not one gave further injury. Finally, Sehi-Za-To-On called the Indian boy, Antonio, to him, and after a few words, the latter disappeared. Sehi-Za-To-On then turned to the chief and said, "Is not No-Tok-Ho satisfied?" The chief was silent. The old warrior then said a few words to the young tormentors, and instantly the torture ceased. The young men approached their victim and, one by one, withdrew the darts from his face and body. La-Ki-Ma-Ha also went close to the sufferer and appeared to superintend the operation. When the last arrow had returned to the quiver of its owner and every dart had been extracted, La-Ki-Ma-Ha leaned against a nearby tree and was silent as a statue.

Sehi-Za-To-On stepped to the center of the circle of warriors and stood upright, looking over the great assemblage. Every warrior resumed an attitude of attention. Profound silence reigned. Every eye was riveted on the gigantic form of the old warrior. The silence deepened into awe, each person seeming to realize that the great Sehi-Za-To-On had something of the greatest moment to impart. Yet he said not a word but stood silently and as motionless as a statue of brass. The strain grew to be oppressive. It affected even the prisoner, notwithstanding the great agony he suffered from his many wounds. Women nestled closer to each other. Young men huddled together. All now strove for a position that would better enable them to hear every word of the speaker, for they realized that grave questions of vital interest to the entire tribe would be discussed, for this great man never meddled with minor affairs. He was the one man to whom all turned in time of private distress or tribal disaster. In fact, he was a warrior, general, diplomat, and matchless leader in either war or peace. In an incredibly short time, the vast audience had come together and now occupied less than half the space that it had previously. Lads and young men who could find no room nimbly climbed to the first limbs of the adjacent trees. Gradually the people settled down.

Sehi-Za-To-On was fully six feet, seven inches in height in his moccasins. His shoulders were broad and massive, his breast of tremendous girth, his limbs sinewy and powerful. His head was large in proportion to his stature. His forehead was broad, high, and of an intellectual type. His nose was large, his face broad, and his chin and mouth denoted great firmness. His brows were heavy, and he had large, dark, kindly eyes that flashed like diamonds. His hair was long and heavy, parted in the middle, and hung in two large braids far down his back. His skin, while dark, was different in color from that of the common Apache. He did not have the high cheekbones of the Apache, though he possessed a noble, handsome face, and if no white blood flowed in his veins, he was of a different nation from those around him. On his head, he wore a skullcap of rawhide, and he wore a plain buckskin shirt, moccasins, and long leggings, together with a buckskin breechclout. Over his shoulders and fastened to his waist by a rawhide belt, hung a large robe of dressed buffalo skin. No ornament of any kind adorned his apparel. He secured on his belt an ordinary knife and a large tomahawk. He carried, too, a ponderous bow with a quiver well filled with arrows of immense length and the most exquisite workmanship. The only things that might be called ornamental about the person of this giant were two eagle feathers fastened in his hair.

He now spoke, "No-Tok-Ho and warriors, Sehi-Za-To-On is here. He comes to speak to the people of the Apache nation. Let the young men and boys who have never seen the warpath open wide their ears—for the words that Sehi-Za-To-On speaks are for them also. When Sehi-Za-To-On is gone, he wants his words to ring in their ears for many sleeps. His words are for the maidens and mothers of the nation, and he wants them to remember them. When a young man forgets the words that Sehi-Za-To-On shall speak today, let his women remind him that he may again remember. Mothers speak first in the ears of the young boy. Each mother must tell her son what she heard today. All must live. The nation must not die.

"Who is Sehi-Za-To-On, also known as Eagle Feather? Who is Eagle Feather?" again demanded the old warrior in deeper, louder tones than before. "Where are the old men and women who were here when Eagle Feather came?" He looked back to where the old ones had congregated. "Will you not answer? Who is Eagle Feather?," he demanded for the third time, in tones of thunder. His words echoed and re-echoed from the adjacent hills and came back as if in answer to his fervent demand: "Who is Eagle Feather?" Stretching forth his mighty arm and pointing toward the towering cliffs, the speaker said in softened and subdued tones, "The Great Spirit does not know." He stood for a moment looking over the assemblage, which seemed awed into deathly silence. Folding his massive arms across his breast, the old warrior said, "Sehi-Za-To-On will tell who Eagle Feather is. When he was a little boy, when he first remembers the sunshine, he was here among the Apaches. He was in the lodge of a warrior who gave him food and shelter. Eagle Feather remembers the warrior who was not his father and the woman who was not his mother. The warrior had many children in his lodge. Sometimes Eagle Feather was hungry and cold. The other children shivered and cried out, but Eagle Feather did not complain. Once he received a bow and some arrows for bringing a warrior's horse to his lodge. Then Eagle Feather hunted the rabbit and the squirrel. He grew larger, and he hunted the turkey and the deer. Eagle Feather was strong then. He climbed to the top of yonder rock and killed the eagle that lived there. He put two big feathers in his hair, and when he came to the lodge, the warrior who was not his father gave him a name. He called the young hunter, 'Eagle Feather.' When any Apache climbs to the top of yonder rock, he will find a pile of stones there and the eagle claws in the bottom. The warrior who was not Eagle Feather's father died on the warpath, and the woman who was not his mother was poor. Eagle Feather hunted the buffalo, the elk, and the deer, and her lodge was never empty. Meat was always there. Food, skins, robes, and furs were always there. When the woman who was not his mother died, she left many children, but they were never hungry. When they had all grown to be men and women, Eagle Feather went to a lodge of his own.

"When he was a very small boy, lying in his lodge covered with skins, a voice spoke to him and its words have never left the heart of Eagle Feather. When his eyes were closed, he saw the face of a woman. It was fair as the morning sun. She had long black hair and beautiful eyes. She wound her soft arms around the neck of Eagle Feather and gave him many kisses. She wet his cheeks with her tears. He always believed that she was the mother of Eagle Feather. Her voice told him it was always good to love the Great Spirit and ask his protection. The voice told Eagle Feather that he must not lie. It told him he must not steal. It told him he must never break his word. It told him he must not scalp his enemies and he must not be cruel to them. It told him he must be merciful to his prisoners and kind to the old and destitute. It told him he must feed the poor. That voice is here still"—and Sehi-Za-To-On struck his broad breast.

"When Eagle Feather had seen eighteen winters, he went on the war trail with the Apache warriors. When he had seen twenty winters, he was made a warrior, and warriors young and old asked him to lead them against their enemies. Where are the Apache warriors who followed Eagle Feather over the mountains to the land of the Comanches, their enemies, to bring back the horses and prisoners taken from us? Are there any left who fought against the great Comanche chief? Nash-Nish-To was chief of the Apaches then. Did he fight the great Comanche chief when he rode out on the plain and gave him the challenge? Who met the Comanche chief and saved the Apache warriors from being called cowards?"

"Sehi-Za-To-On," shouted a dozen warriors.

"Did Eagle Feather slay the great chief and bring his body, horses, and arms to the camp of the Apaches?"

"Yes," came the answer.

"Did not the Apaches gain a great victory and bring home many horses and prisoners? Where was Nash-Nish-To when the Mexican soldiers came and took the Apache village? Did he stay and fight the enemy, or did he and his son run away to the mountains? I will not speak of the battle which the Apaches fought with the Mexicans and the Mojaves, their allies. That is many years ago, but I see there are many warriors here who fought on that bloody field and saved this nation from destruction. Warriors, these things happened when Eagle Feather was a young warrior, too young to have great wisdom, and he will speak of them no more. Did any Apache ever hear Eagle Feather speak of the warpath and his battles before? Well, he will never hear him again. His heart is sad that he cannot speak of a father, of a mother, and of his Apache blood. Warriors, Eagle Feather did not know his own father or mother, but what he does remember is that he first saw sunlight from the door of an Apache lodge. No one will tell him of his father or his mother. An Apache warrior gave Eagle Feather shelter and a home. Eagle Feather gave his blood and service to the Apache nation. Will she take Eagle Feather for her son?"

"Yes!" came the reply from hundreds of warrior throats.

"Then let not Eagle Feather again hear that he is not an Apache. Eagle Feather is now old, but his limbs are strong. He is old, but his ears hear everything. He is old, but his eyes are not blind. Age has not chilled his heart. Did ever an Apache warrior go ahead of Eagle Feather on the war trail, or return behind him? Is there a warrior living in the nation who ever saw him turn his back on the enemy when a living warrior was by his side? Who ever saw Eagle Feather retreat when a wounded comrade was left behind?" A wave of approval and admiration swept over the assemblage. Warriors almost universally applauded.

"Sehi-Za-To-On is a warrior. He is not a chief, but where is the Apache who has seen him follow any chief on the war trail of the enemy? Sehi-Za-To-On has been on the war trail many times with No-Tok-Ho and Nash-Nish-To, his father." Looking down on an old warrior at his side, he asked, "Who led the Apaches then?"

The answer came in a loud, firm voice, "Sehi-Za-To-On."

"Eagle Feather will tell you more. When the children of the warrior who was not his father were all gone and his lodge was lonely, an Apache maiden came to the lodge of Eagle Feather. She was the daughter of a great warrior who was not a chief. This great warrior was brave and true. He followed Eagle Feather many times on the war trail and never left his side. Who has forgotten Great-heart, the father of Star-eyes? When Star-eyes came to the lodge of Eagle Feather, she was tall and beautiful as the sunlight. Her step was quicker than the young doe's. She had never bent her fair shoulders with heavy burdens. Her eyes and face are always in the heart of Eagle Feather. She has been a mother to his children and has kept his lodge clean and bright. When Star-eyes came to his lodge, Eagle Feather told her of the voice he had heard when a child. She listened and said it was good. Warriors, has Eagle Feather done right to listen to the voice of the woman who might have been his mother?"

A general expression of approval followed.

"Warriors, Eagle Feather has seen sixty-two winters come and go. All these winters, he has been with the Apache nation. When he first went on the war trail, the Apaches were like the leaves of yonder trees. There were too many to count. How many are there left? White Fawn can count them here now. What has become of our warriors? Where are the Apache people? When you turn your horses onto the prairie to feed at night, are you sure that you will find them in the morning? Where are the allies of the Apaches? What neighbor among all the tribes would pass them by and say, 'Those are the horses of our friends, the Apaches'? Would the Utes leave them for you to drive back to your village in the morning? Are the Comanches your friends? Would your young men find them again if the Yumas should see them? Why do you guard them at night? When the Apache meets any of his neighbors, can he greet them as friends? Can the Apache trade with the Mexicans?

Let No-Tok-Ho tell Eagle Feather where the friends of the Apache are. If he is a chief, let him tell his warriors and his people how many winters will pass before the Apaches are all gone. Is it good to live without friends?

"And yet No-Tok-Ho tells his people to make another enemy. He tells them to shed the blood of the children of the Great White Father. When has the white man come to the village of the Apaches to take their property and kill their people? Never, since Eagle Feather came, and he was here before No-Tok-Ho was born. Warriors, you have told Eagle Feather that he did right when he listened to the voice that told him he must not steal, he must not lie, he must not kill his prisoners or treat them cruelly. He must not break his word. If it was good for Eagle Feather, it is good for No-Tok-Ho, it is good for all the Apaches.

"Many years ago, when the white chief sent a messenger to the Apache village to ask the chiefs and warriors to go to his teepee to smoke and talk, No-Tok-Ho called a council. Many Apache warriors were there. No-Tok-Ho said, 'Let us go and get presents, and flour, sugar, and coffee.' The warriors and the chiefs said, 'Yes.' Eagle Feather said, 'No. I do not like the White Father and his children. His people destroy the Apaches. They sell them firewater that makes them mad. They kill their own women. They give away their horses, their wives, their children, and become beggars. They wander away and die. It is not good to go to the council. Neither is it good to fight them.' My son was a young warrior then. He said, 'Father, let us go. All the warriors and chiefs say it is good. I have said it is good, but I want you to go.' Eagle Feather said, 'I will go, but I will talk to the white man and tell him not to give the Apaches firewater.'

"Eagle Feather went with his people. When they came to the fort of the white chief, No-Tok-Ho got firewater quick—and what did he do? Did he not kill his squaw with his hatchet? Did he not wound a young warrior with the same bloody hatchet? Eagle Feather went to the white chief and told him that the Apaches must not have firewater. The white chief did not believe Eagle Feather when he told him what had happened. Then Eagle Feather told the white chief that he must come to the Apache camp and let his own eyes see the wrong that had been done. The white chief got some warriors and came to the camp of the Apaches. He saw the dead woman and the young warrior who was wounded. When the white chief saw this, he said to Eagle Feather, 'Come with me. Some bad white man has given your people firewater. I will find him.' He did find him and put him in the strong box, but much wrong had been done and much firewater was already in the Apache camp. Did Eagle Feather let the warriors drink the firewater for which they had given horses? No, he went to the lodge of No-Tok-Ho and found him mad. No-Tok-Ho had his bloody hatchet and he tried to kill Eagle Feather. Look on the side of his head and see where the hatchet of Eagle Feather put No-Tok-Ho to sleep. When he was asleep, Eagle Feather had his hands and feet bound. Other warriors ran away.

"When No-Tok-Ho was well, we all went to the council of the white chief. No-Tok-Ho took presents and told the white chief he would never go on the warpath again. He made peace, and he touched the pen. All the Apache chiefs did the same. Eagle Feather did not touch the pen, and his son did not. Eagle Feather sold skins and bought goods for Star-eyes, White Fawn, and La-Ki-Ma-Ha. The white chief did not like this, and he thought that Eagle Feather was angry because he made no speech. Eagle Feather made a speech then. Listen, and Eagle Feather will tell you what he told the white chief. You were there, and you will know if Eagle Feather has forgotten or has two tongues.

"'I have come to your council not because I wanted to come, but because all of the Apaches came and my son, who is a young warrior, wanted to see the white chief and his council. I told the Apaches it was not good to come here for the Apaches would get the firewater of the white man which makes them mad. You see my words were good. When our chief No-Tok-Ho got firewater and killed his squaw and wounded yonder young warrior, Eagle Feather told the white chief who came to the Apache village to see with his own eyes. The words of the white chief made the heart of Eagle Feather glad. Eagle Feather then knew that the white chief did not want his red children to have firewater. This is good. Eagle Feather is glad. Eagle Feather has taken no presents because he has nothing to give the white chief in return. He does not touch the pen because he does not know about the talking paper and he does not know the man who makes it talk. Eagle Feather has been told that the white chief gave firewater to the red man. Now he knows that is not true, but that bad white men give the red men firewater and they do not tell the white chief what has been done. Eagle Feather now knows that the horses that the red men gave for firewater were not given to the Great White Father or the white chief. The white chief was sent to talk to the red men. This is good. Eagle Feather is not a chief. He is only a warrior, but when he goes upon the war trail, some chiefs and many warriors follow him. He will not tell the white chief that he will never go on the warpath against the white man. Eagle Feather does not lie. If he told the white chief that he would never go on the warpath against the white man, and the white man gave the red men firewater and sent the white soldiers to fight the Apaches, then Eagle Feather would have to sit in his lodge and see his people killed and his family murdered—for he could not use the bow or the hatchet because the Great Spirit has told Eagle Feather that he must not lie. If the white chief should go away and the Great White Father should send another chief with a bad heart who would sell the Apaches firewater and send soldiers to the village of the Apaches to take their property and kill their people, then Eagle Feather will go upon the war trail with many warriors and he will kill the white soldiers, but before he goes on the war-path, he will send the white chief word and tell him that Eagle Feather is no longer at peace with the Great White Father or his people. Eagle Feather, when he came to the council, believed that the white chief was bad, that he did not care for the red men. He knows better now. He goes away your friend. He does not want your blankets, your beads, or your cloth. The Great Spirit made the buffalo for his red children. Its skin is warm and good for Eagle Feather. He has the skins of the wolf and the beaver to give to the white trader for beads and calico for Star-eyes and White Fawn. He does not want your black dirt called coffee, sugar, or firewater. The Great Spirit has made the bees. There is plenty of honey in the lodge of Eagle Feather. When he wants to drink, the Great Spirit has made the rivers and springs for his red children to quench their thirst.'

"That was what Eagle Feather told the white chief at the council. Eagle Feather has not been on the warpath against the white man. My son did go once. He is a man now, a wise warrior. He is no longer in the lodge of Eagle Feather. He went on the war trail against the Navajos with a chief. They found some white men and attacked them. They killed some of the white people, but a little white chief—who was hunting when his friends were attacked—came and saved his people. Many Apaches were killed. The little chief was a brave warrior. He drove the Apaches away. When the chief gathered his warriors together to come back to his village, my son was missing. No-Tok-Ho did not look upon the prairie for La-Ki-Ma-Ha. He came here and told Eagle Feather that he was dead and that his body was taken by the white man. This was a lie.

"This little white chief here found the son of Eagle Feather wounded upon the prairie. Did he kill La-Ki-Ma-Ha and take his scalp? No, he came to my son and asked him if his heart was alive. My son is a brave warrior. He put his hand on his heart and told the little chief that, if he struck him there, he would find the heart of La-Ki-Ma-Ha. What did the white chief do? Did he strike the wounded warrior? No, he said the white man does not kill women and wounded warriors. He gives them food and water. He gave La-Ki-Ma-Ha water. He put him on his horse and took him to the brook and to the shade of the forest trees. He bound up his wounds with the white man's medicine. He gave him food. He made him a soft bed and left La-Ki-Ma-Ha's horse nearby where he could eat grass and drink of the cool water. When his wound healed, my son came home. You see him here. He is lame, but he is here. Yonder is the little white chief who saved his life. More Apaches went after the white men. They took the little white chief and the white maiden and brought them to this village. Eagle Feather took the maiden to his lodge. She is there with my daughter, White Fawn"—and he pointed to the young Mexican girl.

"No-Tok-Ho has said that she has not been fed on prison fare. That is true, for she has been in the lodge of Eagle Feather and has eaten from the same dish with White Fawn. No-Tok-Ho has asked, 'Who shall say that she shall not die?'" Taking from his hair one of the two eagle feathers, the old warrior stepped to where White Fawn sat and, throwing back the blanket that covered the head and face of the beautiful young señorita, placed the eagle feather in her hair. Stepping back with flashing eyes, he shouted in a voice of thunder, "Eagle Feather says she shall not die. Who shall dare touch one hair of the head of the friend and companion of White Fawn?

"When Tee-Clee went on the warpath, he said that he was going to the Navajo country. He was one of the Apache chiefs who told the white chief that he would never again go on the warpath against the white man. He took blankets and flour, sugar and coffee. He has told a lie. He found the little chief and the white girl. He had four warriors. Did he take the little chief? When his warriors had all fallen, did he kill the little chief? No, he did not. He fell. The little chief gave him his life. He gave him food and water and left a horse for him to ride.

"So-Sash-To captured the little chief, who was wounded. Did the little chief tell So-Sash-To where the wounded Tee-Clee was? Yes, he told him and So-Sash-To found Tee-Clee and sent him to the village. He sent the little chief and the white girl. Tee-Clee was almost well when the bears came to his camp. Tee-Clee climbed the tree and asked the little chief to shoot the bear with his two guns. The little chief gave Tee-Clee his life again. When Tee-Clee went to the couch of the white girl, the Great Spirit was angry and sent a mad wolf to attack him. Look at his neck. Look at the coward's body. Where is Ma-So-To, the leader of the party when Tee-Clee was wounded by the mad wolf? If Ma-So-To is here, let him stand up. I see he is here. Has Eagle Feather spoken the truth?"

Rising to his feet, the savage answered, "The great Eagle Feather has spoken true."

"Did Ma-So-To and his warriors save Tee-Clee?"

"No," answered the savage, "the mad wolf left the devils in him."

"Who dressed the wounds of Tee-Clee?"

"The little chief," replied the savage, pointing to the prisoner.

"Did he save his life?" thundered the old warrior.

"Yes," answered the frightened savage. "He had great medicine and he drove the devils away and Tee-Clee lived."

"Warriors," said the orator, "you have heard Ma-So-To speak. The little chief gave Tee-Clee his life three times and yet the coward Tee-Clee would take the life of the little chief. No-Tok-Ho has said that Eagle Feather is the friend of the white man because he took the little white squaw to his lodge. He is her friend and has given her food, but has he not given food to the Apaches also? Eagle Feather has spoken long, but he is almost done. The Great Spirit will soon send the darkness. While the little chief was in the prison lodge, Eagle Feather did not see him. He did not hear him speak until he talked at this council. Eagle Feather heard all the words of the little chief. At first, they were only in his ears, but now they are in the heart of Eagle Feather and will never go out. The words that the little chief has spoken are wise. They have so much wisdom that Eagle Feather does not believe that a warrior who has lived so few years could have thought of them. Eagle Feather believes he speaks the words of the Great Spirit.

"When these Apache warriors are all gone, Eagle Feather wants the young men who come after them to know where their fathers lived and shed their blood for their country. Warriors, look at yonder rocks. See far up the steep, rocky sides of yonder cliff the stone lodges of warriors who are gone (the cliff dwellers). Let our old men and women who were here before Eagle Feather came stand up and tell you who made those stone lodges. Where are the warriors who lived there and died for their homes? They are gone, but their axes, war clubs, their bows and arrows and arrowheads are there. Their bones are there, but where are their children? Where is that nation?" Stooping to the earth, the old warrior picked up a fragment of broken and painted pottery. "Will our old men tell us who made this? It is made of earth burned with fire. It was not made by the Apaches. Who, then, made it?"

Stepping to one side, the speaker took from the arms of a young mother an infant boy and held him aloft, saying, "This mother has this child. If he becomes a warrior and grows old as his grandfather there, Eagle Feather wants him to know, and his children to know, where the Apaches lived. He wants them to make peace with their enemies and make lodges of stone and wood. Soon the buffalo, the elk, and the deer will be gone. Look yonder where the sun is first seen in the morning. You cannot go there—for your enemies live there. Look yonder where the sun goes to sleep at night, look there where it warms the earth and yonder where it does not go, and you will find no home. No, you must stay here. When the buffalo are gone, you must get goats and plant corn, but you must make peace first, for when you have many enemies they will drive away your goats and sheep and burn your corn. Yes, it is good to have friends. We will not fight the white man. We will not kill the little chief." Stepping to the captive, he cut his bonds and led the young hunter to the midst of the warriors and seated him among them, saying, "Eagle Feather has but one son. He wants two. He will take the little white chief and send him back to his white brother, the Great White Father, and tell him that the Apaches will fight the white man no more. Eagle Feather has spoken. He will go to his lodge." Looking kindly down to where the young hunter sat, he said, "Let the little chief come to the lodge of Eagle Feather, his father. If he is hungry, he shall eat with Eagle Feather, his father."

Eagle Feather's great speech had produced a profound impression on the minds of the Apaches assembled. The instant he ceased speaking and started to leave the council grounds, the assemblage broke up. The old men,

women, and children flocked toward the village. The warriors rose with
more dignity and deliberation and left the grounds. No-Tok-Ho made no
attempt to call the council to order, nor was any further business attempted.
No effort was made to further discuss the disposition of the prisoners. The
course pursued by the old warrior had taken all by surprise, and his action
was quietly acquiesced in, at least for the time, by the entire village. Nor
was there any outward demonstration or protest. The name of the great
warrior was on every lip, and there seemed to be an overwhelming majority
of the people who supported his action. As he left the ground, he was followed by the young hunter first and then the women of his household.
Following these were a number of warriors, the friends of Eagle Feather,
and following these came La-Ki-Ma-Ha, the son of Eagle Feather.

The young prisoner followed the gigantic leader with an uncertain step.
His face was fearfully swollen. His whole system seemed to have undergone a great strain, and it now looked as though he would collapse. He had
been half-starved for many days, and when food was brought to him, it was
often unfit for a dog to eat. When Eagle Feather arrived at his lodge, he
stepped aside with courtly grace and motioned his guest to enter. As the
young man stepped in, a tall, fine-looking Apache woman stood before
him. Star-eyes, the wife of Eagle Feather, put forth her hand and said in
Spanish, "The white chief is welcome." She saw at once the sad condition
of her new guest. His eyes were bloodshot, his face a mass of blood and so
badly swollen as to be almost beyond recognition. At the door of the lodge
stood the young Indian boy Antonio, holding the horses of the prisoners
saddled and bridled and ready to mount. Behind the saddle of each was a
saddlebag made of the skin of the buffalo, filled with provisions. As the son
of the old warrior entered, the old man began to explain that he thought it
best for the prisoners to depart at once. He evidently looked for a reaction
on the part of the savages and perhaps trouble, but it was soon evident that
many days would elapse before the young prisoner would be able to take
the trail on his homeward march.

Walter stood at the center of the great lodge. He staggered a little. This
was only noticed by Star-eyes. She moved toward him but was not quick
enough to prevent him from plunging forward and striking the ground
with great force. She sprang to his side and raised his head, but his eyes
were closed and his body was limp and motionless. White Fawn and Maria

were at the side of Star-eyes in an instant. The latter gave a scream as she saw the white face of the young captive. The men left the lodge, and the women attended to the needs of the young hunter. Tenderly they bore him to a soft bed of furs arranged by Star-eyes. His face was bathed, and the blood washed away. He was unconscious, and the breath of life seemed to have left his body. Maria was distracted. She ran to Eagle Feather and La-Ki-Ma-Ha, who both came in quickly, but neither seemed to know what to do. Star-eyes bathed Walter's fevered brow, and others rubbed his hands and feet. The patient did not gain consciousness until morning dawned. Then he was able to take a little nourishment from a cup of broth. They took every care to keep the fact that the young prisoner was ill from the Indians of the village. Eagle Feather said that if the Apaches knew he had sickened, they would attribute it to a weakness of his medicine and there might be a general clamor for his life.

For days, the sufferer tossed and rolled on his bed with a burning fever. The three women were constant in their attention. At no time were all of them absent from the bedside of the sufferer. Star-eyes—as soon as she found that fever had taken hold of the young captive—gathered a number of herbs, among which were common sage of the prairie and the young green twigs of the mountain spruce. She cut these up very fine and boiled them for hours over a slow fire. When the fluid was ready, she gave it to the patient every two to three hours. His head was often cooled by bathing with cold spring water. The señorita and White Fawn carried out the directions of Star-eyes with thoughtful and touching tenderness. Star-eyes moved everything into another lodge near at hand, so that the lodge of Eagle Feather could be turned into hospital quarters.

One night, the quick ear of White Fawn heard a noise at the edge of the lodge. She was all attention. Seizing a hatchet, she stood in an attitude of defense. For a long time, the brave girl stood motionless. She had covered the face of the sick man so that no prying eye could see who was on the bed. Presently an ugly face appeared in the dim light of the lodge and in the next instant a head. As the face turned toward White Fawn to make a more careful survey of the interior, she recognized the face of She-She-Note, the "Rattlesnake," her father's most deadly enemy. Why this savage had come to the lodge of her father, she knew not, but she certainly knew it was for no good purpose. He was a powerful man. She knew she could not for a single

instant defend the sick man against this terrible Indian, and she knew that
if he was there for mischief, he would not hesitate to carry out his design,
whatever it was. Quickly, the body of She-She-Note moved forward. If she
called to her father, she must leave the sick man—and a movement on her
part would reveal that only a woman stood between him and his victim. He
would not let her live a single instant lest he be recognized by her. White
Fawn was no coward. She had first seen the light of day in the Apache village and she had been reared in the presence of danger. She did not hesitate, but gathered her strength to make the attack. The light was uncertain,
but she felt she was equal to the occasion. With as much force as she could
command, she dealt the stealthy invader a blow on the head. It stunned
him but only for an instant. Had she stepped back out of his reach, she
could have yet defended herself, but she had not thought to do this, placing
her whole dependence on herself and her weapon. She dealt him another
blow. The assassin seized the brave girl by the hair and raised his knife to
plunge into her breast. The noise awakened the sick man. He took in the
situation and raised from his bed, but before he could make a move, the
gaunt form of Lion shot past him and, with a bound and a growl fierce as
the lion for whom he was named, fastened his teeth in the throat of the
would-be assassin. Lion attacked with such swiftness and fierceness that
the savage had to let go of White Fawn. The brave girl ran directly to her sick
charge and stood over him, ready to die in his defense.

The savage at last drove the dog from him, receiving many terrible wounds
without being able to inflict any harm on his assailant. Lion dashed between the savage and his master. There he stood at bay, apparently conscious that the assassin—for the moment—had the advantage, since he had
regained his feet and had his knife and tomahawk ready for use. Taking in
the situation, Walter whispered to White Fawn, "Let my sister go for her
father. The Great Spirit will protect your brother, the white chief." The bleeding savage was endeavoring to watch the animal that had so lately torn his
flesh and did not see White Fawn glide from the couch toward the door of
the lodge—or if he did see her, he felt that he had his hands full in looking
after the powerful beast that confronted him. Meanwhile La-Ki-Ma-Ha had
heard the struggle, and he met White Fawn at the door of the lodge. He was
fully armed and ready for any danger. White Fawn told him of the assault
by She-She-Note and that he was still in the lodge near their sick friend. She

cautioned him, "Don't hurt the animal." As her brother leapt forward, the savage She-She-Note quickly slashed the lodge with his knife, but when he bounded through the opening, the dog caught him by his bare leg and threw him to the ground. Before he could regain his feet, La-Ki-Ma-Ha was upon him and beat his weapons down with a heavy blow from his hatchet.

White Fawn passed on the alarm to her father, who now appeared to find La-Ki-Ma-Ha standing over the prostrate villain. Just as Eagle Feather reached the spot, an arrow shot past his temple and passed through the lodge. The old warrior instantly strode forward in the direction from whence the shaft had come. As he did so, he told his son to remain and be on his guard. A second later, a plaintive call, the war cry of Eagle Feather, was heard on the still night air. Calling some trusty friends to his side, he sprang after the shadow gliding away in the gloom. An arrow sped from his deadly bow, and the shadow went down. In a short time, dark figures were seen approaching from all directions, and soon some dozen husky warriors were at the side of Eagle Feather. The old warrior now scattered his men and warily approached the spot where he had last seen the shadow at which he had strained his bow. As the circle contracted, Eagle Feather stooped and disarmed the fallen savage, directing his men to bring the wounded warrior to his lodge. On arriving there, he found all his family astir. Star-eyes appeared and hastily repaired the rip in the lodge cut by She-She-Note.

Not knowing the extent of the conspiracy, Eagle Feather placed trusty guards around the lodges. Now there was great astonishment when they discovered that the wounded man was none other than Noh-Noh-Co, also a deadly enemy of Eagle Feather. Both Noh-Noh-Co and She-She-Note were confidential friends of Chief No-Tok-Ho. Eagle Feather now had some twenty loyal friends around him. He told them of the assault by these two warriors and asked his friends what they advised. They offered a variety of opinions. As none agreed as to a plan to be pursued, Eagle Feather said, "My friends, I think it best to send for the chief." So saying, he selected three of his best and most trusted men and said to them, "Go to the lodge of No-Tok-Ho and say that Eagle Feather waits for him at the lodge of La-Ki-Ma-Ha." The warriors turned and left the spot. After an absence of some thirty minutes, they returned with No-Tok-Ho. As the chief stepped into the lodge, he saw that something unusual had transpired.

The chief turned to Eagle Feather and said, "No-Tok-Ho is here."

"The eyes of Eagle Feather are sharp," answered the old warrior. "He sees the chief."

"Why has Eagle Feather sent for No-Tok-Ho?"

"Let the chief look around the lodge. Look into the faces of the warriors he sees upon the ground, then let him tell why he sent these men to the lodge of Eagle Feather with arrows, tomahawks, and sharp knives. Let him tell whose blood he told these men to shed. Did he send them to take the life of Star-eyes or White Fawn, or has Eagle Feather been too long in the village of the Apaches? If his love for Eagle Feather and his family has not grown cold, let him say if he sent these men in the dark hours of the night when only the wolf and the panther are abroad—to take their lives and shed their blood. Eagle Feather awaits an answer, oh chief of the Apaches."

Having examined the fallen men carefully and noting that these two desperate characters had sustained near-mortal wounds and were in no condition to stand by him—and knowing that none could take their places—No-Tok-Ho was visibly affected. Notwithstanding, he used every effort to preserve his self-control. Stepping back, he answered with a show of authority, "Who has struck down the great warriors, Noh-Noh-Co and She-She-Note?"

Eagle Feather stepped forward and handed No-Tok-Ho an arrow, saying, "Let the eyes of the chief look at this and he will know whose bow sent it after the fleeing coward."

"Eagle Feather has shot down the Apache warrior," answered the chief. Looking around the assembled warriors, who were now equally divided among the followers of the chief and Eagle Feather, he said in a loud voice, "Yes, Eagle Feather has shed the blood of an Apache warrior."

While waiting for the arrival of the chief, Eagle Feather had taken advantage of the interval to investigate the case of She-She-Note. He had found Star-eyes, White Fawn, and Maria in the hospital lodge, sitting around the sickbed of the young hunter. He asked White Fawn to tell of the attack by She-She-Note. When she came to the point where the savage was attacked by the brave dog, she hesitated to give the creature a name. Remembering the superstitious dread that had followed the attack on Tee-Clee by the mad wolf, Maria laid her hand on White Fawn's arm and asked with assumed excitement, "Was it so high?" indicating the height of the big dog.

White Fawn said, "Yes."

Snatching up a piece of the skin of the mountain sheep, the señorita asked, "Was it this color?"

White Fawn again said, "Yes, as near as I could tell."

Rising and looking around with apparent alarm, Maria exclaimed in a suppressed voice, "It was the mad wolf. It was the mad wolf."

Both Star-eyes and White Fawn shrank back from the señorita, but Eagle Feather stepped forward and said, "Let not my children fear the mad wolf. Eagle Feather will not sleep tonight."

White Fawn finished her story to the point where the would-be assassin had tried to escape from the lodge, and La-Ki-Ma-Ha now joined them, corroborating her account of the wolf. Eagle Feather and his son now left the hospital lodge and returned to La-Ki-Ma-Ha's lodge, telling White Fawn that they would soon send for her.

Later, as the chief No-Tok-Ho accused Eagle Feather of shedding the blood of an Apache warrior, the old warrior asked, "Have the eyes of the chief seen the wounds of She-She-Note? If he has, let him tell the warriors here what has made them."

"Some of the wounds were made by the hatchet of Eagle Feather," replied the chief, "but the others are strange and No-Tok-Ho cannot tell what made them."

Eagle Feather sent La-Ki-Ma-Ha for White Fawn. She now stepped forward and stood close to the side of her father. Every eye was upon the graceful girl for she was a great favorite of the village. Her father now raised his hand. "Warriors," said Eagle Feather, "White Fawn is here. I have sent for her that she may tell you how She-She-Note came to the lodge of Eagle Feather, where White Fawn and the white girl now sleep. Let White Fawn speak."

The young girl told her story in a straightforward way. When she came to the part about the mad wolf, a warrior asked her for more information. She said that she did not see the beast come nor did she see it go. After finishing her story, she departed, and La-Ki-Ma-Ha came forward and told what he had seen and done. Being asked about the wolf, he said he did not at first see the animal. He had sprung at She-She-Note, who had just slashed an opening in the lodge. Then he saw the wolf as it seized the villain and threw him down. He, La-Ki-Ma-Ha, then struck the assailant of his sister, and She-She-Note had not since raised his head. The wolf vanished before his eyes, and he had not seen where it had gone. Finished with his story, La-Ki-Ma-Ha stepped back among the warriors.

Eagle Feather followed, saying, "White Fawn came to Eagle Feather where he slept. He woke and went quickly to where La-Ki-Ma-Ha stood near the fallen She-She-Note—just as an arrow came swiftly by the head of Eagle Feather. This is the arrow. It passed through the lodge, and here it is. Let No-Tok-Ho tell Eagle Feather if it is not from the quiver of Noh-Noh-Co." As he spoke, Eagle Feather handed the arrow to the chief. No-Tok-Ho took it with seeming surprise but made no move toward a comparison. Eagle Feather waited. When he saw that the chief made no answer and did not compare it with the arrows in the quiver of the fallen warrior, he said with emphasis, "Eagle Feather waits. Let the chief speak." No-Tok-Ho now stepped forward and took several arrows from the quiver indicated. After inspecting them, he replaced the arrows. Eagle Feather asked the chief, "Is No-Tok-Ho ready to speak?"

The latter answered, "No-Tok-Ho did not see the arrow fly from the bow of Noh-Noh-Co. He was not there when it was taken from his quiver."

Eagle Feather replied, "The chief need not tell Eagle Feather where the arrow came from nor whose bow sent it at the head of Eagle Feather. All the warriors here know who made the arrow and from whose bow it sped on its errand of death. Eagle Feather again asks No-Tok-Ho why he sent these men to the lodge of Eagle Feather and whose blood did he tell them to shed. Let No-Tok-Ho answer."

The chief, after a moment's hesitation, answered, "No-Tok-Ho loves Eagle Feather and his family. He did not send them to harm his friend. He did not know that they went to the lodge of Eagle Feather."

The old warrior replied, "Warriors, you have heard the words of No-Tok-Ho. He did not know that the two warriors who sleep in his lodge went out with their arms to the lodge of Eagle Feather when the watch of the moon was only half over. Warriors, let his words stay in your ears." Then turning to an old warrior, Eagle Feather said, "Take many young men and take these wounded warriors to your lodge. Bind up their wounds. When they can talk, send Eagle Feather word."

No-Tok-Ho here spoke up and said that he would take them to his lodge and take care of their wounds. Eagle Feather replied, saying, "The chief sleeps too sound. Someone might take the sick men away, and No-Tok-Ho might not hear them go. When they are well, they will tell Eagle Feather who sent them to murder him." Turning upon his heel, Eagle Feather left the lodge, and the gathering broke up.

The only occupants of the hospital lodge were the sick hunter, White Fawn, and Maria, who refused to leave the bedside of her friend for a moment. She mildly censured White Fawn for not waking her as soon as she had escaped the grasp of the treacherous invader, for the excitement that the patient had undergone had heightened his fever to an alarming degree. Star-eyes gave the patient her fever medicine at frequent intervals. The señorita was most tender in her attentions as the young hunter tossed feverishly on his couch of furs. She often heard her own name drop from the lips of the raving sufferer, and she wept almost constantly.

"Why does my sister weep?" asked the gentle White Fawn.

"Oh," said the distressed señorita, "I know he cannot live. See, his mind is wandering, and I am so helpless."

"Let my white sister fear not," said the Apache girl, "for she and the little chief shall return to the people of the Great White Father. White Fawn will see them no more, but their faces will always remain in her heart. She believes that the Great Spirit will guide her white sister and the little chief safely back to their friends. Let my sister dry her eyes. Hush, the little chief awakens."

At that moment, the sufferer opened his eyes and looked around. It was evident that he was now rational. It was the ninth day of his fever, and toward evening, it left him. The fever did not return. He grew stronger and was soon able to walk around the lodge. Star-eyes made the patient the most attractive and savory dishes. La-Ki-Ma-Ha brought fresh trout from the stream, and soon the young man had so far recovered that he joined White Fawn and Maria at bow practice. White Fawn was expert with the bow. She could bring down birds and small game, rarely missing, and Walter renewed his determination to improve his proficiency with the bow and arrow as a means of subsistence in traveling through hostile districts where it was unsafe to fire a gun. He was pleased, too, that the gentle Maria was taking this time to practice with the bow.

BOOK FIVE

Shortly after Walter's recovery from his tortures, the Apache village held its annual sports and games. The contests included "archery, casting of the tomahawk, throwing the knife, casting the lance . . . [and] footraces. . . ." When he was not watching the games, Walter exercised, "hardening himself for the coming travels."

During the games, Walter met To-Bo-Ca, known as Young Antelope, a "fine-looking young man" who —despite his youth—defeated a visiting Comanche chief in a contest of archery. At the end of the contests, Walter and Maria departed the Apache village, after bidding an "affectionate farewell" to Eagle Feather, Star-eyes, and White Fawn. They were joined by the Apache boy Antonio, and Young Antelope and two other young warriors guided them for a few days. Lion—"gaunt and thin"—soon reappeared, and the "meeting was affectionate indeed."

Soon after Young Antelope and his companions left them, they entered a "terrible, lone, silent desert" and spent many "cheerless" days traveling mostly after dark from waterhole to waterhole. Walter managed to keep them alive, finding water, quail, and wild honey in the wasteland, but the señorita, in particular, suffered "terribly from thirst." From time to time, she lapsed into a "deadly fear and a belief that death was near at hand." They were threatened by hostile Mojave warriors, rattlesnakes, "oppressive" heat, and a violent storm.

Finally, they reached the edge of the desert and found plenty of water, grass, and game, including a pair of wild turkeys which Walter quickly dispatched with his recently improved archery skills. And scarcely a day later, they learned that the camp of their friends was nearby.

✳

The señorita requested that the party travel fast for, said she, "I will be tired no more until I see my father and sister and friends." It was close to midnight when they approached the camp of the white travelers. The young hunter went forward and made himself known to his friends. Approaching as near as he thought safe in the darkness, he took out his whistle and gave the usual signal announcing his approach. Almost instantly, the answer came, and presently the voice of Old Tex told him to come on. Walter went forward slowly, giving his companions time to come up—and they all entered the encampment together. It would be impossible to describe the joy with which their coming was hailed. The young señorita was instantly reunited with her father and little sister. The old priest and Mr. Collins repaired to the Castillo lodge, and the old father offered up a fervent and heartfelt prayer. All noted the worn-out condition of the señorita and urged her to go to bed, which advice she readily acted upon. Before leaving the lodge, she begged the good father to pray for their noble and generous friend, the young capitan, saying, "He has been so good, noble, and brave, and has suffered so much for us."

In the course of ten days, the travelers found themselves deep into Mexican territory and finally reached the villa of Señor Castillo. Here Walter got the rest he so much needed after the hardships he had so lately undergone. Maria took great pains to entertain him, and he spent a good part of each day in her company. She continued to give him daily practice speaking the Spanish language; he was an apt scholar, especially since no other language was spoken at the good señor's home. She even showed him the steps of the most popular and charming Spanish dances and coaxed him to practice with her while she hummed the enchanting tunes.

A regiment of Mexican cavalry went into camp about this time, a short distance from Señor Castillo's villa, and many of the officers visited the good señor to pay their respects. A young lieutenant named Juan de Rodrigues was among them. He had several years before brought a letter of introduction to the Castillos from a distant relative, and, typically, the Castillos had welcomed him as a cousin in their household. They urged him to make his presence known whenever his regiment was in the neighborhood, and he grew to enjoy the intimate warmth of "belonging" to this distinguished family. And they were proud that he had made a brilliant record as a soldier in the Indian wars and so had been promoted to first lieutenant and was now in command of a company. The family adopted him wholeheartedly.

The troops soon heard of Maria's captivity and her marvelous escape due to the courage of her young American protector. The officers were wild to make his acquaintance. Walter, in the meantime, had just returned from a prospecting expedition. He was welcomed by Señor Castillo and was soon ushered into the presence of the ladies—whom Lieutenant Rodrigues was also visiting. Walter was most warmly greeted by the young señorita and her mother. The little sister ran to him and threw her arms around his neck and kissed him as she would a brother. "Capitan," said Maria, "my dear madre has been much worried about you. You have been gone so long." The youth greeted the sick woman warmly, kissing her hand.

"And now, Lieutenant, let me present my very dear and kind friend, el Capitan, to whom we all owe our everlasting gratitude for saving the life of our sweet little sister, whom he snatched from the cruel Indians and the very jaws of death. Come here, darling," said the mother, and she embraced the little one while tears ran down her white cheeks.

The lieutenant offered Walter his hand, saying, "Sir, I am most pleased to meet you and to thank you on behalf of my good friends here."

The young scout said, "I assure you, sir, that I feel that the very small service I have been fortunate enough to render is quite outweighed by the pleasure it has given me to serve the señor and señora and their children."

"Lieutenant," said Señora Castillo, "you must be very kind to our young friend. You see how great our debt is to him."

"I will introduce you to my friends," said the lieutenant. "I invite you, sir, to our camp, and I will present you to our general."

"I shall be very pleased to visit you," replied the young scout. Turning to the señora, he said, "Madam, I wish you a pleasant evening." Bowing low to the señorita, he prepared to go.

"Capitan," said Maria, coming up to him, "you must not go. You must stay with us tonight and all the time."

"Yes," urged the señora, "you must not leave us."

But the young man could not be induced to change his mind. Some of his companions were about to return to Santa Fe with a caravan that started at sunrise, and he had promised to be with them for supper. "But," he said, "I will come to you tomorrow." With a hearty handshake, he departed.

"What do you think of our new friend?" Maria asked the lieutenant. "Is he not a noble-looking young man?"

"I must say," answered the young officer, "that he looks very common to me. Poorly clad, awkward, and I think, ill bred also."

"How can you be so ungenerous?" said Señora Castillo with great dignity. "A more noble youth I am sure I have never known."

"He is generous, brave, and so kind," said Maria with some show of feeling. "I am surprised at you, Juan, to be so unkind. I admire the young capitan more than anyone I ever met. He is well bred, he is brave, he is generous, and he is handsome. If all Americans are like the capitan, they are a noble race."

"Yes," said the lieutenant, "a race of robbers and cowards."

"Well," said Maria, "you may speak of Americans as a race as you see fit, but of the capitan, you shall not speak insultingly in my presence, nor in the presence of my mother and sister. I bid you good day, sir," and she left the room.

"Juan, why do you speak so in our presence?" asked the señora. "You know our obligation to this young stranger. He is entitled to our protection and our respect, and he shall have our warmest esteem while he sojourns here."

"Pardon me, Señora, I was hasty,"

"Hasty, indeed. Why is it necessary for you to be hasty? We owe him much more than we owe you. Your action is outrageous."

"Señora, I again ask your pardon, and I also ask you to send for Maria."

"No, I will not," said the señora coldly. "Her rebuke was just. You must make your own peace with her, and at another time."

With much chagrin, the lieutenant took himself away and was not seen at the villa for several days. Neither Maria nor her mother could account for the lieutenant's attitude toward the young American.

*

When Walter went to the tent of Old Tex, Tex greeted him warmly and suggested some exercise. The veteran unrolled from a ragged blanket two rusty swords. "I have always kept these old toadstickers. Good exercise. Take your choice, sir, and get out here and defend yourself."

The two men faced each other and, for an hour, engaged in a fencing match. Old Tex seemed to be a master of rare skill. As they finished, Tex said, "Boy, you have the makings of a swordsman. The strength of that arm of yours astonishes me. Tomorrow, I want to show you the most important of all guards, as well as the best offensive tactics. It is mighty good to know these things, boy, and never forget: The man who lifts his feet too far off the ground is sure to be buried in it. You could hold your own with any ordinary fencer now, and I'll soon put some new tricks in your bag. If you're like me, you'll enjoy the exercise and the excitement."

"You have probably fought lots of duels," said Walter.

"Ah, yes, boy—most often with pistols. But these swords here have tasted blood." Tex paused, wrapped in thought. Suddenly he shook his head and looked at Walter. "And therein lies the secret of my life—how I became an outcast and desperado." His voice trailed off.

"Don't say that, Mr. Tex. You may have appeared so to me at first, but your kind heart has won me as a friend."

"Never mind, boy. I'm feeling a trifle sad tonight. It is a presentiment of evil. I've felt it before. When I was young, a terrible evil befell me and drove me from my home. You see, I was born in the state of Tennessee. My name was Allen Gary. My father was a planter of the old school. My mother was a Creole of good family, and I had a brother. When we came of age, my father gave each of us a part of the plantation. I built a house on my land and adorned it with such luxuries as I could afford. We were prosperous. Crops were good, prices high. I asked a fair and beloved sweetheart to marry me, and she accepted. Now, there was another pursuing my bride-to-be. She was not interested in his advances, but she was a southern lady and treated all with the courtesy due gentlemen in good standing. Thus encouraged, no doubt, he was persistent in his attentions. He had to know, of course, that we had made our plans and had our parents' blessing—yet he returned again and again to press his suit.

"Our wedding was but two weeks off when, one afternoon, I visited her at her father's house. To return home, I had to ride five miles through a pine forest. In the middle of the wood, I met my rival. He blocked the way. 'You have stolen Jenny from me,' he shouted like he was out of his mind. 'One or the other of us must die.'

"I was young then, only twenty-four, and yet I was coolheaded. I tried to pacify him, for I knew well what the consequences of a conflict could be. Although I had been taught to handle a sword and pistols, I knew Jenny would disapprove of a duel. I was well aware, too, that such a thing would break my mother's heart. She detested dueling and had many times lectured my brother and myself on the subject. Finally, I said, 'I bear you no ill will, man. I do not want to fight you. We are neighbors. Our mothers are like sisters. Think of the consequences. Come now, why can't we let Jenny make the choice?'

"He laughed a wild, reckless laugh. 'You can't put me off that way.'

"I saw that the man was desperate. I said, 'Well, if you must fight, let us fight like gentlemen and let the code of Tennessee shield the victor from the charge of murder. I accept your challenge. I refer you to Silas Moses. He will be my second.'

"'No, no, that will not do,' he cried. 'Now is the time. This is the place. You fight me here and now.'

"But I said, 'I am not armed. I have no weapons. You have no right to set upon a man in this manner.'

"'Oh,' he said, 'I have foreseen all this. I have pistols, swords, and Bowie knives for both. Take your choice,' and sure enough, he produced a regular arsenal.

"My southern blood began to boil, but I felt that if I fought Jenny would be lost to me forever.

"'Choose. Choose. Don't be a coward which I believe you are,' he shouted.

"It seemed to me that I could resist no longer. We both dismounted and faced each other. I took one of the pistols. He said, 'There is but one shot here. This is to the death, remember. Better take a Bowie knife, and you will have something left to defend yourself with.' I took a knife.

"He said, 'I want no advantage. Step away ten paces. I will count three. At the last word, fire.'

"'Count,' I said.

"He counted, 'One. Two. Three.' I was still dazed and did not fire. I felt a sharp pain in my left shoulder and knew I was hit.

"He drew his knife and shouted, 'Come on now—for the finish.'

"We met and fought. He was the larger and stronger, but I was the quicker. How long we fought I know not. He cut me beyond recognition, but I killed him. I was weak, but I rode to my father's plantation. I went to the negro quarter and sent for my father. They bound up my wounds. I told him all.

"He said, 'My son, I am sorry for you. You will be held for murder. Your friends will believe you as I do, but oh, my son, the law will demand proof. This you cannot furnish. I fear, my boy, you must leave home forever.' My father sent for the family doctor. My wounds were cared for, but I was terribly disfigured.

"At this time, Texas was a new country. When I had recovered enough, I went there and began life anew. I got into some trouble, and a kind friend gave me a letter to General Taylor and I served through the Mexican War. I drank, got into more trouble, fought duels—yes, sometimes with swords. I became an outlaw, an outcast, a desperado." The old man had risen to his feet. "There," he said, "you know all. You'd be best off forgetting you ever knew me."

Walter threw his arms around the hardened man. "Mr. Gary, I cannot ever forget you."

"Silence, son. Don't ever call me by that name. I am forever Old Tex."

"Mr. Tex," said Walter, "I already have had so many evidences of your goodness of heart that you have my full confidence. We will be forever friends, if you wish."

✴

When the good señor learned that Tex's companions had drifted off, going their separate ways, he suggested that Tex discontinue his camp and take possession of the little house half a mile from the villa. Tex accepted this kind offer, confessing that he was lonesome with so much time on his hands. Now so available was he that Walter could duck in several times a day for sword practice with the now cleaned and polished swords.

Tex prided himself on being as perfect as a man could get in the art and science of fencing and use of the sword. Walter was an avid student, fascinated by the whole progression of the footwork, positions, attack, and defense.

One day, there arrived at the Castillo villa a young Mexican whose cheerful posture seemed to infect the whole family. Maria introduced Walter to the newcomer, saying, "I want you to know my own, good, dear cousin, Don Roberto Castillo, my uncle's only son." Maria laid her hand lightly on her cousin's arm and, placing her other hand on Walter's arm, she said, "Cousin, this is the brave, noble American who suffered so much for our family and to whom we all owe our lives."

The young Mexican grasped Walter's hand and said, "Capitan, your fame has gone before you. I meet you with the greatest pleasure, and I pledge you my everlasting friendship for the service you have rendered our family. If you ever need the arm of a friend, mine will be yours."

"Capitan, do not mind Roberto," cautioned the señorita. "He is my best friend in all Mexico. He is an officer of the Mexican government now on leave for six months. He will live with us and is a privileged character, as are you also."

✳

Two weeks later, Tex decided to accept a position with Señor Castillo, superintending a large hacienda property some distance from the villa. He was to leave as soon as he was able to gather needed equipment and supplies. In the meantime, whenever there was time, he would ride with Roberto and Walter hunting doves or deer or on expeditions of exploration into the mountains. In the evenings, the three would take their turns with the swords.

One evening, after an especially laborious practice, Tex told Walter, "Son, you are an apt scholar. You have a good eye, your calculation is good, your quickness and coolness will save you if you ever are unfortunate enough to have a sword encounter."

Walter replied, "Yes, but Mr. Tex, the sword is the last weapon I would choose for self defense."

"Well," said Tex, "one never knows when he may be called upon to defend himself or others in a wild country like this."

When Tex moved to his new home, he left the swords for Walter and Roberto with the admonition to keep in practice.

The young men were so busy with their various activities that they seldom saw much of their military friends. Lieutenant Rodrigues, however, continued to be attentive to Maria. He had, to all appearances, succeeded in reinstating himself into the good graces of the señora and the señorita. When the young men met, they were passably cordial—and yet a close observer could have detected the lack of warmth between them.

One evening, however, the three—Walter, Roberto, and Lieutenant Rodrigues—met at the dinner table of the good Señor Castillo. During the meal, the lieutenant made rude remarks concerning Americans. Roberto tried to change the thread of the conversation, but failed. Finally, the good señor, with dignity and force, informed the young lieutenant that the subject was a delicate one, and the old gentleman abruptly introduced other subjects. The other two young men entered into the discussion with interest and zest, and the meal ended without further controversy. After brandy and cigars, the men retired to the drawing room where the ladies were already waiting. Maria was unusually lively and cordial. She sang ballads and played on the harp, entertaining all. The lieutenant responded to both the departing young men with the barest possible courtesy.

When they had retired to their lodgings, Roberto said, "Did you ever see such meanness? I understand that the regiment will remain in this neighborhood some two months yet. Juan Rodrigues, strange to say, is reported to be very popular among the young officers. He is rich, you know, and his family is most indulgent, setting no bounds on his expenditures. Thus he is able to shower favors upon his friends which, I presume, is the secret of his popularity. Some months ago, he engaged in a duel with a foreign attaché who, he fancied, was calling on Maria. Half the regiment clamored to take it off his hands, but he likes that sort of thing. And now I hear he is a hero largely on that account."

As the days and weeks went by, Walter and Roberto were constant companions. They undertook excursions far and near, often with Tex. Sometimes they took turns engaging in sword play with the master. One evening, Walter—thinking it might be best all around to leave Maria to her choices, and hoping he'd not regret it—announced that he was going to visit Tex at Señor Castillo's hacienda about one hundred miles distant. The ladies at once raised a most decided protest and were heartily joined by Roberto.

"My son," urged the señora, "we insist so strongly because we are going to host a great company and ball. You see, our neighbors are far apart and we cannot, without much preparation, get them together. We expect relatives and friends from long distances—and more than half our pleasure would be destroyed if you would leave us, because we intend this function to be largely in your honor. Also, the regiment has now been here a long time and we must do something for their entertainment since we have many old friends among the officers. Now, Capitan, you will not disappoint us, will you?"

The young man replied, "I will remain, and I beg of you to call on me if I can be of any assistance to you."

While the preparations for the grand occasion were underway, Walter and Maria saw much of each other. They often met in the grove beyond the gardens under the branches of an old laurel tree. And it was there that the young American finally told the dark-eyed beauty of his love and that she promised to be his wife.

"Capitan," asked the girl, "why did you never tell me of your love when we were alone so many long days on that awful desert and while we were prisoners? If you had told me then, my captivity would not have been half so dreary and the future not nearly so hopeless. I sometimes thought you harsh and cold. It was only when great dangers threatened and I was on the brink of despair that you were gentle, kind, and tender in your attentions. When I was cheerful, you turned iceberg again. Capitan, you nearly drove me mad. I insist that you tell me why this was so."

"Señorita," answered the young man, "you were a young girl. Circumstances placed you in a most unfortunate position. What would you have thought of your protector if he had taken advantage of your helpless and friendless condition to press his suit? Truly, I loved you all the time, but I considered that it would be dishonorable to make advances under such circumstances. Am I not right?"

"Madre and Cousin Roberto and Father say you are right," answered Maria.

"Do they know our secret?" asked Walter in a surprised tone.

"Yes, they know—that is, Father and Roberto know, but not Madre, since she does not think I should marry any but a Mexican."

At this point, the lovers were interrupted by Lieutenant Rodrigues. Maria asked Walter to accompany her back to the villa, which he did and immediately took his leave in search of Tex, who had just returned from Señor Castillo's distant hacienda. Notwithstanding the busy days, Walter and Tex found time to indulge in their favorite pastime—bouts of fencing. Tex had taught his young pupil everything he knew of the art, and yet he insisted that they practice over and over the art of disarmament. This movement required great strength and quickness as well as the keenest eyesight in order to decide upon the exact instant to make the attack. Tex was a powerful adversary, but it required all his strength and skill to foil the young man. Roberto, who could pretty well hold his own with a sword in his hand, benefited from the lessons also.

The day of the grand ball finally arrived with guests from distant parts gathering at the villa. All was bustle and excitement. Friends who had not met for years found themselves guests together under the hospitable roof. The fame of the young American had spread far and wide, and all relations and immediate friends of the Castillo family were eager to make his acquaintance.

A sister of the good señor, with her daughter, had traveled more than one hundred miles to take part in the festivities. Maria presented these relatives to Walter. "This is my dear aunt, Señora de Almond, and my cousin Christina Almond." The ladies were warmly cordial and very generous in their expressions. The aunt was a beautiful woman, about forty-five, with charming manners. The daughter was a lovely girl of eighteen, almost the exact age of her cousin Maria. When Maria proposed a walk in the grove, the elder lady excused herself and the two young girls left the house.

"This," said Maria as they reached the rude bench under the great laurel tree, "is my favorite retreat."

"Why," replied her sweet cousin, "it looks to me like a real lovers' retreat." She continued, "Dear, I think your American is charming. He is very handsome. Is he a nice dancer?"

"Oh, yes. Roberto and I have shown him the steps of our classic Spanish dances. He can do almost everything nicely."

The two young señoritas, exquisitely groomed, were everywhere present, visions of loveliness, ministering to the wants of all. The ball started promptly, immediately after twilight according to the custom of the country, and it was the crowning feature of the gathering. The crowded ballroom was a sparkling collage of gaily dressed officers, ladies in rustling silks, Spanish gallants, and distinguished gentlemen from neighboring villas. The young American found himself quite the lion of the hour. His modest manners and obliging assistance to the señorita and her cousins had further endeared him to them all.

When it was determined that the señora was unable to attend the party and had retired to her apartment quarters, Maria reminded Walter, "You are my father's honored guest, and as a member of our household, you must open the march and lead the first dance with me."

Walter answered soberly, "I will esteem it a very great pleasure."

Maria was proud of the way he looked in his new, well-tailored suit. She stood for a moment admiring him and then asked, "Why did you not ask me first?"

The young man finally stammered, "I thought one of the fine officers would claim the honor. You know, Señorita, I do not yet know all of your customs."

She laughed, peering over her fan at him, eyes dancing, "I will forgive you this time, Capitan."

As the music started, the señorita led the march with the young American on one side of the ballroom, while the good Señor Castillo, with his sister, Señora de Almond, led the march on the opposite side. Following came the officers and their ladies. But Lieutenant Rodrigues did not fall into line. Señorita Almond, seeing this, picked him up and made herself very agreeable indeed.

When the most exquisite of the Spanish dances were finished and the ladies were seated, Walter was most gracious in his attendance, especially on the elder ladies. And Señor Castillo took special pains to introduce him to the gentlemen. He was pressed on all sides to tell something of his adventures with the fair señorita. This he did only when it could not be avoided, as he was so naturally modest.

The señorita herself was much occupied in the double duties as hostess on behalf of both her mother and herself. And she became more and more disturbed that Lieutenant Rodrigues seemed so morose. He quarreled with the servants and with Christina Almond, and he became so abrupt that he made others ill at ease here and there throughout the hall.

Just after refreshments were served, while the señorita was engaged elsewhere and Walter was surrounded by guests eagerly urging him to explain the customs of his own country, Lieutenant Rodrigues forced his way into the circle and, with his folded gauntlet gloves, struck the young American full in the face, accosting him in Spanish as a spy and instantly withdrawing.

Walter was stunned and for a moment speechless. Christina gave a little scream and called after the assailant, "Oh, Señor Lieutenant, how could you be so rude at such a time?"

The young ladies huddled together and the gentlemen fell back, all look-ing at the young man expectantly. Walter recovered himself almost imme-diately and continued his recital calmly until he had finished.

As soon as she could do so, Señorita Almond withdrew to inform her cousin of the assault. Maria was with her father. Both seemed horror stricken at Christina's account, and Señor Castillo immediately departed in search of the lieutenant. At this moment, Roberto joined them, and seizing his arm, the señorita said, "Dear cousin, listen." And Christina again recited the circumstances of the insult. When she had finished, Maria asked quickly, "Cousin, dear, what did el Capitan do?"

"He did nothing," said Christina. "I thought that his head inclined slightly as a half bow, his face flushed a little, and a white dimple came in his cheek, but he then began speaking as though nothing had happened. Then I left to find you."

"Let us go and find him," said Roberto. The young capitan was nowhere in sight. One of the ladies said she had seen him go out the south door. They searched carefully but failed to find him.

As soon as he could excuse himself, Walter had left to find a servant, whom he sent to find Antonio, the Apache boy. When the boy appeared, Walter handed him a small scrap of paper upon which was written: "Tex, my friend, come quick! Trouble!" He said to the boy, "Take my gray horse and ride fast. Bring Tex."

The boy answered, "Me go fast. No sleep."

Walter then reentered the ballroom by another door. As he passed in, he met Señorita Almond and smilingly asked her for the pleasure of the next dance. The young American chatted pleasantly to his partner, hardly know-ing what he was saying, but never once alluding to the occurrence half an hour earlier. When the dance ended, Walter paid his young partner a high compliment as a dancer, and they joined Maria and Roberto.

Walter gave them no opportunity to bring up any mention of the un-pleasant affair, and so ardently did all four enter into the enjoyment and entertainment of the evening that the assault seemed forgotten, and the dance continued until the light of dawn.

Walter then took his leave of the ladies and repaired to his own quarters. He did not again see Señor Castillo or Roberto. Among the young bloods, there was much talk as to what course this young American should pursue after so vicious an insult, especially in the presence of ladies. Some set him down as afraid to meet the lieutenant, who was known to be the best swordsman in the regiment. Walter must challenge, and the challenged would, of course, have his choice of weapons. Rodrigues would certainly choose swords.

When Roberto was questioned, he said he knew nothing about the matter and had not been consulted. He said he had not seen the insult—had only heard about it later—and had not even exchanged a word with his friend since Walter had left after the party. "But," said Roberto, "we have been led to believe his courage is of the highest order. In his own time, he will act. I do not know why there is delay."

The lieutenant, in the meantime, was loud-mouthed in his denunciation of all Americans, and this one in particular. He especially denounced Walter in the presence of Roberto, whom he knew was the young American's friend. Roberto had expected to be called to act as Walter's second, and he ground his teeth to think that such an insult had been allowed to rest unpunished for so long. "To think," said he, "that it is now the middle of the second day since the affair occurred."

Meanwhile Walter had estimated the time it should take Tex to come the distance and went to meet him. Finally, he saw Tex approaching. They embraced with relief and even joy and rode in together. As they neared the villa, they separated. Tex went to the barns and Walter to his room. When they reappeared, Tex was leading a fresh horse.

Roberto and Maria came from the villa and hurried forward to intercept Walter. They heard him tell Tex, "I am sorry to insist upon your going to the regiment tonight, but I cannot wait longer. Here is the document."

"Never mind, my boy," said Tex. "I will be back in an hour or two and will come to you."

The young American's words, Roberto saw at a glance, brought sorrow to the señorita. The girl had readily divined the full meaning of the appearance of Old Tex, as well as the errand upon which he had been dispatched. She was pale as death, and her hand on Roberto's arm trembled.

When Walter excused himself, saying he had letters to write and business to attend to, Maria said to Roberto, "Cousin, you know what this means. They will fight. Will Lieutenant Rodrigues kill him?"

"Oh, that I cannot say."

"Rodrigues is said to be the best swordsman in the regiment. Is that not so? Yes, I have heard him called invincible. Now, cousin, answer me. Will Rodrigues kill him?"

"No," replied Roberto, "I don't believe you will lose him."

At this moment, Christina came from the villa. "Are they going to fight?" she asked. "I thought by the way the officers talked last night there would be no fight. Lieutenant Rodrigues is calling him a coward and boasting all the time."

The ladies now left for the house, and Roberto went to find Señor Castillo to tell him what had occurred. "Well," said the señor, "of course, he must fight Lieutenant Rodrigues or leave here at once. I have wondered at the delay. I fear it will be his last fight. Juan Rodrigues is known as a great fighter, but has not the manly qualities that would prompt him to waive the choice of weapons. Has the young man consulted you, Roberto?"

"No, uncle, and I have been surprised and hurt that he has not done so. On the contrary, he has avoided me and given me no chance to refer to the unpleasant subject. There is much talk of the delay of a challenge. Indeed, I could find no excuse for it. Yet he must have one, of course."

"If they fight, and of course they will," said Señor Castillo, "you must go and see to fair play, Roberto. You know our young men sometimes show scant courtesy to strangers, and we are so deeply indebted to this young man that I feel almost impelled to go myself and witness the encounter and even volunteer to stand by him—notwithstanding it would be such an unnatural thing for me to do."

"Well," replied Roberto, "I must go. If he would only ask me, it would be easy, but I do not believe he will, so I will ride over and intrude myself upon him." After further talk, Roberto took his leave, but before going, he said thoughtfully, "As a member of your household, uncle, I might go to him and say that you sent me and ask to be of service in some way, saying that you regret that he has been placed in such an unpleasant position while under your roof as your honored guest."

Roberto took himself to the room of the young American and knocked. Walter welcomed him with a smile. Old Tex was present. Roberto came immediately to the business that brought him. "I come to you, Capitan, as a member of Señor Castillo's household and beg as a favor that you will let me serve you in any way you may name. I am at your service."

Walter replied, "My friend, I am deeply sensible of your kindness and regret that my presence at the home of the kind Señor Castillo has cast a gloom over his household. I thank you for your solicitude. I know something of your customs and therefore understand that you are anxious for my reputation as a gentleman as well as my mental and bodily comfort. I shall be very frank with you and ask you to make my peace with your family. When this unpleasant affair occurred, I first dispatched a messenger to Mr. Tex here. I did not allow Mr. Tex to rest until he had delivered my message to Lieutenant Rodrigues. Tex has arranged a meeting that takes place near the spring in the fir grove on Black Mountain at sunrise tomorrow. Swords are the weapons. I deeply regret that it was necessary to delay so long. Mr. Tex will be my second on this unfortunate occasion. I cannot, for reasons you doubtless understand, ask you to join us."

Roberto rose, saying, "My friend, from my heart and soul I wish you success. Count on me under any and all circumstances. May God shield you." Grasping the hand of the young American, he pressed it with great warmth and hurried out.

Tex then spoke, "Come, boy, we must practice."

"No," said Walter, "you must sleep. It is now three-thirty. You shall sleep three hours, and then I will wake you. I will write until then. When you get up, we will practice for one hour and sleep again."

At six-thirty, Walter laid his hand on Tex, who woke instantly. "All right, my boy," the old man said cheerfully, "I feel fine now. My sleep has refreshed me wonderfully."

Tex soon produced the swords, and the two stripped to the waist. The two circled around, and a perfect stream of sparks flew from their weapons. Tex said, "Boy, the lieutenant is a giant and may disarm you. It will be best to take great care. I don't want to unnerve you. I believe you can wear him out notwithstanding his great bulk. Now to bed, for we rise an hour and a half before the sun."

"Yes, Mr. Tex," said the young man, "go to bed. You are tired. I am going for a walk. I shall be gone for an hour and will not disturb you when I come in. Good night, sir," and the lad passed out into the twilight.

At first light, two horsemen directed their course toward the canyon to the east of Black Mountain. They rode in silence. The elder of the two men rode in advance. They spoke not a word until they reached a spring of cold, clear water at the edge of a dark fir forest. The spring burst in great volume from under a high limestone cliff and formed a beautiful stream some eight or ten yards wide. The valley was twenty or thirty acres in extent.

As the men reached the stream, they rode into it and their horses drank freely of the clear, pure water. "Well, boy," said the elder, "we are the first here. If we were a little slow in getting at this business, we are at least the most prompt at the closing scene."

"I am glad we are here first," replied Walter.

"Shall we cross blades?" inquired Tex.

"No," said the young man. "I do not care to cross blades with so good a friend on this spot, the soil of which may drink the lifeblood of one of the principals in the coming combat—and perhaps both. If we ever practice at fencing again, it must be on peaceful ground. Mr. Tex, I have a request to make of you. In my hurry this morning, I forgot to give you a package addressed to yourself. In the package you will find letters and full instructions as to what to do with them should I not leave this field."

"You may rest easy, boy," said Tex. "I will travel to the ends of the earth to do you a service. But what's the use of talking? You will come out all right. No pupil of mine can lose."

Presently they heard the tread of horses, and the Mexican party came into view. Roberto was among the first to dismount. He advanced and shook hands cordially. The lieutenant and his party took possession of the opposite side of the grove. Presently an officer in civilian dress walked over and met Tex, saying, "Well, Señor, we are here, ready for business."

"All right," said Tex. "I am at your service."

The two walked down, and after looking over the ground, the Mexican said, "Well, we select this position." The position he had chosen placed the lieutenant with his back to the east, with his opponent facing the rising sun.

"You can have that position if you win it," said Tex, "not otherwise."

To which the other replied, "We are the challenged and claim that right."

"Señor," said Tex, "you have exercised every choice you are entitled to under the rules of the code. You selected weapons, time, and place. You can choose nothing more, and really I am amazed that you make such a demand. We are ready to meet your man, but will surrender no right that is ours."

By this time, several other Mexicans had joined them. Tex stood his ground and finally an officer spoke up, rebuking the lieutenant's second, sustaining the contention of Tex. Tex then produced a Mexican dollar and handed it to the officer, saying, "Capitan, will you throw the coin for choice of positions?" The coin flew into the air, and the Mexican chose heads. The coin fell heads up, giving the lieutenant choice of positions. His second promptly chose the east, giving Lieutenant Rodrigues the advantage.

When all was ready, the lieutenant came slowly forward. Tex handed Walter his sword. The young American dropped the point on a piece of wood on the ground and stood at rest. The lieutenant wore around his waist a small Mexican flag, and Tex noticed that Walter wore a tiny rosette of red, white, and blue ribbon pinned to his breast just over the heart. When the two men faced each other, the difference in their sizes was apparent to all.

All now were impatient to see the combat begin. Walter seemed calm and composed, and this attitude in the face of his seemingly invincible opponent proved conclusively that his courage was of the highest order.

The principals were ordered to be on guard. As their weapons met, a metallic sound rang out on the morning air with a musical ring. As the eyes of the opponents met, a dark scowl overspread the Mexican's visage. The calm, confident air of his opponent seemed to anger him. The lieutenant, after a few preliminary feints, made a savage thrust at his wary enemy. After several ineffectual thrusts, he became more violent and threw himself upon the smaller and lighter opponent with all his weight and strength. The smaller man was alert, and the lieutenant was not able to force Walter back an inch, and in fact, he lost ground which he was not able to regain. It was noticed that the sword of the American had drawn blood from the lieutenant's neck.

Foiled and forced back, the Mexican fumed and allowed his temper to get the upper hand. He called his opponent foul names and cried, "Come on and fight."

His second spoke to him in Spanish, "Keep cool. Take it easy and your time will come. You are settling your dispute. You have no right to resort to abuse. Your opponent stands upon the same spot where he began the contest." While this rebuke was administered in a friendly tone, it had the effect of cooling down the Mexican giant.

Still, he could not seem to ruffle the young American. Walter met and parried every thrust and seemed to divine in advance every move of his antagonist. Having tried every device known to the art without avail, the lieutenant adopted a series of sudden lunges. These were met with skillful parries by the youthful defender. All at once, the Mexican jumped aside and, with a fearful yell, made a terrible lunge at his opponent. This was said to be a trick resorted to by Oriental fencers when all other tactics failed. Walter parried the mighty thrust, and with lightning quickness, he drove his sword straight to the breast of the Mexican giant. Tex, who was watching closely, thought the lieutenant was wounded. The Mexican fell back, and Tex noticed a strange, puzzled look on Walter's face. Was he deceived, had the Mexican's blade been quicker than the eye? Could the boy be hurt?

The old fighter held his peace, but he noticed that his charge now assumed a different attitude. His face grew pale, and the white dimple on his cheek warned Tex that something indeed had happened to excite and madden him. Walter seemed to gather himself up and throw himself into the fight with renewed force. His eye fairly blazed, and his every motion was like lightning. He ignored every opening to the lieutenant's body and fought fiercely for his head and neck.

Tex noticed that the Mexican also grew pale and excited. It took all his skill to parry the fierce assaults of his savage opponent. Suddenly Walter sheathed the point of his sword in the neck of the lieutenant. It was a glancing thrust, however, and only served to make the Mexican attack more recklessly.

Tex was now satisfied that his charge was at least safe from serious harm. The younger man was forcing the fighting, and his thrusts came fast, savage, and forceful, taxing the lieutenant to the utmost to save his face and head. As the combatants surged back and forth, the young American made a dash at the Mexican's throat. The latter fell back, stepped on a rolling stone, staggered, fell to his knees, and was at the mercy of his opponent. Walter dropped the point of his weapon, stepped back to his place, stood on guard, and waited. A murmur of admiration came from the Mexican witnesses.

Tex shook his head in disapproval. The giant lieutenant neither acknowledged nor in any way recognized the courtesy, but returned the assault with yet more vehemence. The swords clicked in rapid succession as the men fought with a fierceness seldom witnessed. At the end of a long siege, the sword of the younger man split the nose of the Mexican, who was now bleeding from three wounds and covered with blood. Wild with fury and uttering imprecations of the vilest sort, the lieutenant tried to beat down the alert guard of the young American. All at once, the giant bounded like a tiger and aimed a terrible blow at his opponent, but the sword of the smaller man parried the thrust, and he again sheathed his sword in the Mexican's neck. This also was a glancing blow, skin deep.

The Mexican shook his head and, with a curse and a sneer, cried out, "Only a second! I will have the American pig in a second." Again, the fighting grew fierce. The sun was now up and shone brightly in Walter's face, but nothing seemed to daunt his piercing eyes, which were riveted on his big antagonist. Walter now drove the Mexican far back from his original position. The Mexican had all he could do to protect his head, which the young fighter seemed determined to disfigure. Walter had not yet received a scratch, though the lieutenant's weapon had twice passed through the folds of his shirt.

So furious had the combat become that it did not seem possible that either could hold out longer. Suddenly Walter stepped on a rolling stone, staggered, and for a second, lost his poise. With a savage yell, the lieutenant lunged forward and, with villainous thrust, drove his sword seemingly through the side of his antagonist, whose effort to parry did not appear to have been entirely successful. "I have his blood," shouted the Mexican as he thrust again, but his youthful opponent had regained his poise. He met the onset with a lightning stroke that opened the Mexican's throat and followed that with a thrust that drove the point of his weapon with terrible force through the lieutenant's neck. The Mexican's weapon fell from his grasp. He staggered and plunged forward on his face and expired almost instantly.

The youthful fighter dropped the point of his weapon on the ground and leaned heavily upon it, panting, perspiration streaming from his face. Tex rushed to him. "Son," asked the old man, "are you hurt?"

"Only scratched," Walter said between gasping breaths.

"My boy," asked Tex, "why did you ignore so many body openings and fight so desperately for the head?"

"Because he wears a coat of mail that my weapon could not penetrate."

Tex stepped to the side of the fallen man and said, "Gentlemen, I request that you remove the shirt from this man. I charge that this man wears body protection."

The attending doctor instantly ripped open the dead man's shirt and revealed the presence of a steel chain covering that served as a perfect body shield. Beneath it, the lieutenant's skin was broken in two places where the point of the young American's sword had found the Mexican's breast. At this discovery, the Mexicans fell back from the body with disgust stamped on their faces. Tex took hold of his young principal and said, "Come on, my brave boy. You must cover your body. Let us go."

The Mexican's second called Tex to one side and expressed with chagrin his deep regret that he had unwittingly seconded a man who would stoop to shield himself on the field of honor by the use of so unworthy a device. With but one exception, every witness expressed horror and disgust. The exception was a young lieutenant in the same company. He raved and declared it to be his purpose to challenge the young visitor, but Roberto stepped forward, saying, "You may fight him, but it will be after you have disposed of me."

Walter left the field with Tex, after taking leave of Roberto. As soon as Roberto reached the villa, he reported the results of the encounter to Señor Castillo, who listened with heartsick attention. "Our poor Rodrigues. He certainly took leave of his senses," mused the old man. "Did the boy fight well?"

"Uncle," answered Roberto, "I have seen some of this kind of work. I have seldom seen a man exhibit such unflinching courage and such masterly control of himself."

When told of the final discovery that the lieutenant wore a jacket of mail, Señor Castillo held up his hands in horror, saying, "And we welcomed him as a son into our home!"

"No!" thundered Roberto. "At least he did not bear our name."

"Right, my son, he did not," answered the old man. "You are right, my son." The good señor went on to say, "I am convinced from what you tell me that Walter cannot remain here with us."

"That is true," answered Roberto. "He would have to fight the whole regiment. He must go at once. He is in great danger of assassination. These young bloods have no heart, no appreciation of a noble, generous foe. I will go to him."

As Roberto departed, he was accosted by the señorita and her cousin Christina. "Dear cousin," Maria cried urgently, her face white as marble "tell me of the duel. Does the capitan live?"

"Yes, sweet cousin," answered Roberto, "the capitan lives. He is unhurt." And he then gave them a history of the fight, touching upon the scenes of the duel as delicately as possible.

With this, Roberto bowed and passed on to the quarters of the young American, whom he found at his table busily writing. Roberto hastened to compliment his friend on the dignity he had displayed throughout the affair. "You will be at lunch?" asked Roberto, rising.

"I have thought," replied Walter, "that it might be embarrassing to meet the ladies after what has happened."

"I think not," answered Roberto. "I think Aunt and Uncle will be disappointed and further distressed if you should fail to meet them in the regular way at meal time."

Roberto had scarcely left the room when a knock came at the door, and the old priest entered. He was very cheerful and at once broached the subject of the morning's duel. He spoke no unkind word, nor did he lead Walter to believe that he had any criticism to make concerning the young scout's actions. Before leaving, he asked permission to pray, which he did most fervently, alluding to Rodrigues as the aggressor who had abused every rule of propriety and honor. On leaving, he said, "My son, I will see you at lunch."

Shortly after the father left, Señor Castillo himself called, saying, "It is my extreme happiness and pleasure that you, my son, came out of that affair this morning unscathed and unwounded. I shall see Rodrigues's foster father tomorrow and shall attend the funeral and explain to him that, owing to the outrageous behavior of the lieutenant, had he lived he could never again have entered my house. I wish to say to you, my son, that every possible assistance I can render you shall be forthcoming. While I deplore what has happened, I exonerate you from any blame and say to you freely and frankly that you could not have been expected to do otherwise. Now, my son, I will expect you at lunch."

In the villa, Señora Castillo called the young American to her couch and begged him to sit with her. While she did not discuss the hostile meeting, she was gracious, kind, and affectionate. Señora Almond was reserved and somewhat cool, but all the rest of the ladies, including Christina, were cheerful, treating Walter with the utmost cordiality. The old priest made an eloquent prayer, asking for divine protection for his worthy son, the brave young American, and the repose of the soul of the departed officer.

Shortly after lunch, Roberto and Walter left the villa on their horses, taking a course across the valley. They returned toward evening by another road. About two miles from the villa, while they were crossing a small stream through some brush, an unseen enemy fired upon the young scout, who was riding in advance. One ball passed through his coat, barely touching the skin, the other through his hat. Like a flash, he wheeled his horse and charged in the direction from which the shots had come. So quick was his action that the assassin—to escape recognition—plunged into the stream and entered the brush on the opposite side. Roberto, quickly realizing the danger from the would-be assassins, seized Walter's reins and led his horse away from view.

"Saw you the villains?" asked Walter.

"No," was Roberto's answer, "I was a little late."

"They wore the uniform," said Walter, and he did not again allude to the occurrence.

When they arrived back at the villa, the señor called the young men into his office and told them that he had information that the younger officers had formed a conspiracy to bring a quarrel and ultimately the death of the young American. Roberto then related their recent experience.

After a long silence, the old señor said, "My son, assassins cannot be foiled for long. I fear, my boy, that you must leave us."

"Yes," said Roberto. "As much as we regret to lose you, we cannot see you murdered."

"I will at once station trusty men to guard these grounds," said Señor Castillo.

Roberto sought old Tex and consulted him on the subject. The old American became excited at once and insisted that they immediately depart, but Señor Castillo advised otherwise, saying, "We must avoid pursuit. Therefore you must not start until midnight or later. We can thus mislead watchers."

Roberto took charge of all the arrangements. He decided to give out the report that the two young men had gone into the interior for a few days. Walter bid an affectionate adieu to the members of the Castillo family early in the evening. Roberto wanted to accompany his friend, but Señor Castillo decided it would be better for him to remain at the villa in seclusion. Walter was quite unconscious of the real seriousness of the situation, but he was anxious to spare his friends any further concern. He placed himself in their hands and was ready at a moment's notice for a hasty departure.

Late that night the señorita met the young scout under the laurel tree. Here, he again told her of his love and offered to take her with him. "I could do so easily," he said. "I have horses ready, and I will try to convey you quickly to a place of safety."

But Maria replied, "No, Capitan, I love you and can never love another— and yet, as you know, my madre is in poor health, my father is old and not very well, and I could only leave them by running away. Neither would consent to my going now under the circumstances. If you love me, dear, brave, generous Capitan, do not take me now. I am yours when you claim me.

"Capitan, I fear for your safety. They will kill you. The thoughtless, reckless young officers will hunt you to the death. Do not smile like that, Capitan. I have seen that smile before. I saw it when Death surrounded you when we were set upon by Tee-Clee and his warriors. I saw it when you were bound to that awful tree. I saw it at the fearful moment of our capture. Capitan, don't smile. My heart stands still. Please don't smile. I must not lose you.

"You must go. Father says it is the only course. Do you see the seven stars that revolve around the bright beacon of the North? Do you see the two stars that stand in line with yonder statue and this grand old tree, our "betrothal tree," as you call it? They will soon pass this spot, Capitan. Three years from tonight, meet me here at this hour, at the very moment when their shadows touch this place. I will be here, Capitan. If you do not come, my heart will be buried here. I will follow wherever you shall lead. And, I hope, with the blessing of Father and Madre and the good priest. You do not speak, Capitan. Tell me, 'yes,' or my heart will burst."

"Señorita," answered the young man slowly, "I will come. I will be here at the hour, at the moment the two stars' shadows touch this place." Taking the hand of the beautiful girl, he pressed it to his heart and his lips.

Hearing footsteps, Walter rose quickly. The intruder was the old priest, who grasped the youth's hand. "My son," he said, "I rejoice that you are here and safe, but you must fly. You, too, must go, my child," he told Maria. "Speed to the house quickly." He told Walter to wait under the old laurel tree until he sent him a trusty guide to direct him to safety.

Still holding the hand of the young girl, Walter now folded her to his breast in one long, ardent embrace. Once again kissing her hand, he turned to go. She whispered, "Will you remember, Capitan?"

"I will be here when the shadows touch this place. Until then, farewell."

"Farewell, dear Capitan."

The priest turned with the young señorita. Walter had waited scarcely five minutes when he felt a light touch on his shoulder. The young Apache, Antonio, stood at his side. "Come quick," said the boy, and they strode rapidly from the spot, walking five minutes to a thick clump of trees where they found Señor Castillo and Roberto. The señor grasped the young scout by the hand, saying in a tremulous voice, "My son, I regret that we must so soon part. I feel the deepest humiliation that we are powerless to protect you. Come to me later, my son, when the present unpleasant conditions exist no longer."

"Sir," replied the young man, "my concern is for you and the friends I am leaving behind. I shall never to cease to regret that I have been the cause of worry to you and yours."

"Say not so, my son. You have been the source of the greatest happiness to us all. It is our own people that we have to thank for your untimely departure. But I must not detain you. Time is precious."

"Is it," asked Walter, "so urgent that I depart?"

"Yes, my son, trust us. It is."

Roberto embraced his friend and then laid his hand on Antonio's shoulder, saying, "Stay with our friend here as long as he needs you. Farewell."

Traveling rapidly forward for a half an hour, Walter and Antonio came upon the young scout's horses already loaded with provisions and gear for the journey. Mounting his gray, Walter urged Antonio to mount the other horse. The boy refused and pushed on rapidly. As Walter set off, the gaunt form of Lion rose from the grass and followed at a slow pace. Antonio led them through a deep, narrow gorge. Walter caught up with him as he stood making signs to a solitary horseman. It was Tex.

"Now, boy," said the old veteran, "we must get out of this place. Come on."

The Indian boy passed on up the gulch, but soon reappeared mounted on a mustang that had been waiting with Tex. The party now took a south-westerly course across the hills, apparently barren except for cactus and comfortless with much sand. After riding rapidly forward for many hours, they halted as light was promising to appear in the east. Entering a thick grove of pines, they prepared to bed down—and were soon wrapped in sleep for a few hours. Shortly after sunrise, a heavy wind set in from the east and blew a hurricane for nearly two hours. When the Apache boy came in from caring for the horses, he said, "No trail. Now wind fill tracks with sand."

It began to rain, and they did not move that day. They constructed a brush lodge, covering it with boughs of the fir tree, and huddled there for two days while the storm raged. In discussing their future course, Tex and Antonio confirmed that a conspiracy had existed among the young officers of the regiment to waylay and kill the young American, and that scouts and prowlers had been seen around the villa the night of their departure. So serious was the situation that both the good señor and Roberto believed that Walter would be hunted even to Santa Fe. Therefore Tex proposed to avoid the regular trail to Santa Fe.

On the morning of the third day, the little party made a start and traveled forward until far into the night, estimating that they had covered eighty miles. For three days thereafter, they made good progress, covering nearly sixty miles per day. Then Tex became indisposed with severe stomach pains, and they rested for two days. On the evening of the second day, Tex said that he was all right and proposed that they start the next morning.

About midnight, a storm rose suddenly, accompanied with the most violent visitation of thunder and lightning. The party's horses stampeded, and in the morning, not a horse could be found. The storm had obliterated every trace of the trail. Antonio started early, but after searching all day, he returned without having seen a sign of the missing animals. The boy and the young hunter searched the country late and early for seven days without success, until they finally overtook the animals along a small stream.

They pushed on and soon came upon a large caravan of travelers. The party included several Americans and quite a large number of Mexicans. The caravan included three women. Walter soon learned that this party had been traveling carelessly, paying little attention to properly guarding their horses. The evening before, Indians had cut out a portion of their horses and driven them off. The party had then sent out a small pursuing party, which pushed on after the savages in hopes of recovering the stock. Tex, who had been ailing for several days, proposed to rest, and Walter agreed. They accordingly went into camp, much to the satisfaction of the larger party, many of whom were thoroughly cowed and felt that the larger the party the greater would be the safety of all.

That evening, the travelers discussed the possibilities of a new raid and the probable fate of the party that had gone in pursuit of the stolen animals. Tex and Walter were of one opinion as to the situation. "Mr. Tex," said Walter, "I think I will pick up the trail in the morning and scout the country carefully and be of some service to these people, who seem from what I can learn to be mostly inexperienced in such work."

The Indian boy, who had spoken no word, said that there was an Indian woman in the camp. He said that the woman had told him that two Mexicans had joined the party two days before and had asked about two Americans, an old man and a young man who rode a big gray horse. Antonio said that he had seen one of these Mexicans, adding, "Me watch close." Tex was very concerned and considerably excited. Walter, however, was apparently unconcerned. He just took his blankets and went to sleep near the horses.

After Walter had gone, Tex took the boy and made the rounds of the camp, hoping to get his eyes on the two Mexicans who were evidently on their trail. On the extreme edge of the camp, they came to a campfire over which an ugly-looking Mexican was roasting meat. The man paid no attention to them, but the boy gave Tex a sign that this was one of the men. Tex examined the visage of this man as best he could in the uncertain light, and after they returned to their tent, he told the boy that he must see the other Mexican in the morning. "We must watch them very close," he said.

"Yes," said the boy, "me watch."

Long before daylight, Walter saddled his gray and left camp. Back at camp, about midday, the two Mexicans came along and tried to engage Antonio in conversation. Failing that, they went out to the horses. Presently they came back and asked where the gray horse was. "Gone," said the boy.

They asked then for the young man.

"Gone," said the boy.

"Where?" was their next question.

The boy was silent. The men urged, but the boy would not talk. Presently, the bigger Mexican came near the boy with his hand on his revolver and asked in a savage tone, "Where has that young man gone with the big gray horse?"

The boy was slow to answer.

The Mexican drew his revolver and repeated the question.

The boy, with apparent reluctance, said, "Santa Fe."

The fellow replaced his revolver, and the two left in the direction of their own camp. When Tex returned, the boy related to him the episode. The old man seized his weapons and was about to follow the Mexicans. Antonio said, "No, don't go. Maybe Mexicans go Santa Fe, too. Wait."

Tex said, "Good, my boy, I guess that is best. We will see what they do."

An hour later the Mexicans mounted their horses and rode away toward the Santa Fe trail. Tex told Antonio to saddle his horse and follow them, which he did. Upon his return, he reported that the men—the last he saw of them, twelve miles up the trail—were traveling fast toward Santa Fe. Tex had a good laugh and told the boy he had done a smart thing.

The day passed, and Walter did not return. Neither did the pursuing party return, nor was any word of them received. Meanwhile, Walter had followed the stream until daylight. He then took the high ground north, his object being to watch the whole country and avoid being seen. Having gained a high eminence bordering a small stream, he kept carefully under cover of a heavy pine forest. Having gained a point for observation, he halted. He saw that the trail seemed to pass through a closed canyon at the head of the stream. Suddenly a breeze sprang up and the wind blew freshly from the direction of the canyon. Lion rose and sniffed the air. Walter at once concluded that either game or Indians were lurking in the vicinity. He could see nothing unusual. Yet Lion continued to exhibit uneasiness. Walter tightened his saddle girth and was about to mount when he noticed that his horse seemed also to scent danger. Leaning over the gray's neck, he again directed his attention in the direction indicated by both dog and horse. Finally, at the summit of the hill, just above and about in the center of the closed canyon, he saw plainly a solitary horseman standing under a clump of large, scrubby pines.

His first care was to lead the gray behind a thick clump of pines. He then surveyed the immediate surroundings. The horseman's attention seemed to be directed toward the west. Watching closely, Walter saw the horseman ride over toward the canyon and down the eastern slope. Then he executed a series of signals with his arms. Presently Walter saw other men appearing at the mouth of the canyon. They were not mounted. Walter now made up his mind that these were savages lying in wait for the pursuing party of white men who were doubtless returning from their fruitless effort to recover their stolen horses.

Walter decided that he must get to the opposite slope of the mountain if he was to render the white men any assistance. Mounting the gray, he presently came to a new trail where many animals had passed recently, all going west. After a careful examination, he concluded that this was the trail over which the stolen horses had been taken—and it was also the route which the pursuers had followed, as some shod horses were among the last to have passed over the trail. Leaving his horse to graze, he walked up the mountainside to a prominence from which he could see the trail for a long distance westward. He sat under a small pine tree for twenty minutes, watching. Presently a number of horsemen rode out into plain view about half a mile distant. He could see that they were white men, seven in number.

He now slipped quietly from the mountain. He did not wish to be taken for an Indian, and so he remained in the bushes along the stream. As the men approached, he could hear them talking and he had no difficulty in determining that they were all novices in woodcraft. They traveled in single file, well scattered, making no pretense to guard against surprise. As they crossed the stream and the first horseman emerged from the bushes, Walter stepped out, speaking to the leader, who proved to be a Mexican. The others followed and were much surprised to see a white man in this lonely place. Walter quickly explained how he came to be there. He also explained that their way was barred at the little canyon and that the only safe way back was the trail he had just passed over. They all readily consented to follow his lead. From an Englishman with the party, he learned that they had never overtaken the lost horses, that they had fallen into an ambush and four of their number had been killed, and that they had been unable to recover the bodies. They were all badly wrought up and terribly frightened and did not want any more Indian or horse hunting. Their horses were pretty well jaded and rapid progress could not be made. Three of the men who had been killed were Mexicans and one American. The skirmish had only taken a few minutes. They claimed they had killed several Indians.

They were much discouraged at hearing of the new danger; they had supposed that the enemy were all behind them. Walter took charge of the party
and conducted them into their camp about midnight.

Having abandoned all hope of recovering their lost stock, the caravan
moved on the next day. They traveled about twelve miles and camped on a
small stream where there was abundant grass. Walter advised throwing out
a strong guard along the stream and a deep ravine lined with heavy chaparral. There being no fresh meat in camp, he and Antonio went out with a
pack horse as soon as they arrived. Shortly after he left, a party of Americans joined the caravan. Among these was the old priest from the Castillo
villa who had grown restless and wished to visit his former charges near
Santa Fe. He was traveling with one man, a Mexican, and they had been
overtaken by the Americans. When they came upon the larger caravan and
heard of the trouble with Indians, the newcomers decided to join them for
added protection. When Tex saw the good old priest, he took him and his
companion into his camp, to the delight of the old father.

About 4 o'clock in the afternoon, the horse herd became scattered. Some
of the guards had come into camp, and the party's horses and mules had
strayed well out into the foothills, and there were scarcely any horses in
camp for use. Tex saddled his horse, as did four or five others, and they
rounded up the strays. After urging the travelers to look after their animals
and bring them in closer, Tex returned to camp just as two parties of Indians, one from the ravine on the north, the other from the timber bordering
the stream on the south, rode rapidly through the herd.

Giving the alarm, Tex rode swiftly forward and was soon joined by four
others. They succeeded in saving part of the herd, but in the mix-up Tex
received a painful wound in his left leg, near the thigh. It bled profusely,
and he barely reached camp before fainting. The priest took charge of the
wounded man and did all in his power for him. The caravan had lost most
of its stock, but the Americans quickly gathered a pursuing party of men
who still had mounts. They overtook the savages in the foothills, where a
fight followed. Night came on, and only a few of the pursuers got back to
camp that night.

Shortly after nightfall, Walter returned with his horses loaded with fresh
meat. He was alarmed at the condition in which he found his old friend
Tex and at the general distress of the entire camp. The loss of so much stock

was a very disturbing development, as was the uncertainty of the fate of the pursuers, several of whom were yet absent. The night was dark and cloudy, and nothing could be done beyond guarding the stock that had been saved.

Early in the morning, taking with him such men as had mounts and arms, five in all, Walter set out on the trail of the pursuing party, following the high ground. About midmorning, he met ten of the absentees returning empty-handed. They reported camping some miles farther west. Among them were two slightly wounded. After traveling some distance, the returning pursuers had discovered some lost horses, and five of their number had turned off in hopes of being able to drive them into camp. Walter proposed that the whole party go that way. "Those loose horses," he said, "may have been a decoy to draw your companions into an ambush." The men, however, would not hear of this plan, saying that they were going back to camp as quickly as possible. Two of Walter's companions joined the party returning to camp. With the other three, the young scout pushed on. They soon found the horses, but saw nothing of the men. As they turned the horses toward camp, several Indians made their appearance and tried to cut them off. Walter finally succeeded in rounding up the horses, avoiding a skirmish. Sending his companions on with the stock, he lingered behind and covered the retreat. The Indians pursued Walter almost into camp. They were well mounted. His guess had been right. They had laid a trap in hopes, doubtless, of securing some scalps.

Noticing the Indians turn suddenly and dash up the creek, he wondered what had attracted them so suddenly. He had supposed that the returning party had already reached camp. Hearing shots, he with two of his companions dashed after the savages and soon discovered his friends at bay. The savages were making a most determined attack. He at once charged them from the rear, united his forces with the besieged, and was making good headway toward camp when the Indians were reinforced from the west. Walter finally got his men into the timber and they gradually fell back until they reached camp. Walter was the last to enter camp, having done most effective work in checking the onslaught of the savages—who soon learned to their sorrow that it was not safe to come within range of his deadly rifle.

The young scout rode up to his own tent and asked how Tex was getting along. The priest told him that the wound was much swollen and was giving

Tex trouble. Walter was about to remove his saddle when a young man came to the tent and spoke to him, saying, "Sir, I wish to thank you for saving our party. We had no leader, sir, and we were surrounded. There could have been but one outcome, a massacre. I confess I lost my head completely, but as soon as you gave your orders, every man obeyed and all got in safely, although several were wounded. Hudson and I were together, but we got separated down in the timber and I think he must have gotten in with the others."

At this moment, another American stepped up and said, "We have four men missing. One of the Mexicans states that he saw four cut off and they climbed yonder hill. Of our party, Graves, Hudson, and Goddard are missing. I do not know the fourth man."

The first arrival now introduced himself as Charles Overton of St. Louis, and his friend as Alfred Stover of San Antonio. Walter greeted them warmly and asked, "You spoke of a Mr. Hudson. Who is this man?"

"He is a very dear friend of mine from Missouri boyhood days," said Overton. "His father, Colonel Hudson, is one of the most prominent men in St. Louis."

"I have letters for Hudson," answered Walter, "and would very much like to meet him."

At this moment, several men came up and stated that the missing men could be seen from the upper end of camp and that they were in plain view on the side of the steep hill some half a mile distant. Walter, after a moment's examination of the hill, remarked, "Those men are in a very dangerous situation. I am sure that they are entirely surrounded. They must be relieved at once, gentlemen. Saddle your horses quickly, and I will join you at the upper end of the camp."

Tex had moved from the tent into the sunlight, where he said he was more comfortable in the open air. He now addressed Walter, "I am afraid you will get into serious trouble. I don't believe those men will stay with you. They are a pack of cowards."

"I can't help that," answered Walter. "I must do what I can to aid those men. I promised Hudson's father and sister that if ever I could aid him, I would." Stepping to the side of the wounded man, the young scout kneeled and took Tex's hand. "My dear, kind friend," he said, "do not be discouraged. Your wound will soon heal."

"My wound," replied the veteran, "does not concern me. I fear for your safety. This place is alive with redskins. So far, yours has been a charmed life. Somehow I feel this cannot last. Be careful, son. Be careful for my sake."

"I will try to be," answered Walter. Before mounting, he called Antonio and the old priest to his side, saying, "Those Hudson letters are in a pocket of my saddlebags. Should anything happen to me, promise that you will not desert Mr. Tex."

Each gave the desired promise, and Walter galloped to the upper camp. Shortly, nine horsemen rode toward the hill. As they approached, Indians appeared on both ends of the hill and rode slowly toward the relief party. Walter took Overton with him at the center of the line. He sent instructions to the men: "If the enemy makes a dash, dismount and kneel down, but hold your fire for close quarters. Those warriors will not charge a loaded rifle. Let the end lines hold back a little, as I wish to get as close to the hill as I can to give your friends a chance to get inside our lines. Then we can fall back and protect them."

The relief party was in full view of the camp. Tex called the old priest to his side, saying, "Father, will you bring me that old army field glass. You will find it in my saddlebags." The priest brought the glass, and Tex settled himself to watch the maneuvers in progress near the base of the hill.

"I see the four men on the hill huddled together," he remarked. "The boy is motioning to them. Father, that boy is a general. If his men will stand, he will save those men. The reds are approaching the flanks slowly. The boy seems to be calling to the men. They start down the hill. There are two reds in the edge of the timber between the boy and the men. The boy makes a sudden charge. The reds scatter. The men are rushing down the hill. They are close to the boy. The boy drives them before him like sheep. They seem dazed. Now they run for their lives toward camp. Seven Indians charge him from the north end of the hill. They are trying to cut off the men the boy has just relieved. The boy keeps between the fugitives and the Indians. One big fellow rides a black horse. He has a war bonnet that floats behind in the wind.

"My God! The boy rides forward to meet the whole seven. He does not lose sight of the men he is protecting. They seem to have forgotten that they have guns themselves. That fellow on the black horse is the chief, sure. The boy swings around on the right end of the line of the reds and cuts them off from their prey. The fugitives will reach camp if they don't let up.

"My God! A dozen reds are charging from the south end of the hill. Our men are all on the run. They have stampeded. The boy is alone. The chief and his six warriors charge the boy. Why doesn't he fall back? There is no horse the match of his gray in that crowd. He whirls and charges straight for the chief. The big red is shooting arrows at him. He is down!"

"Who is down?" shrieked the priest.

"The chief! The others fall back. The boy swings to the left and is meeting the reds from the south end. He stops them. Two more are down. What cowards our men are! They are rushing for camp and leaving the boy to himself. More reds are coming from the south and from over the hill. They are between the boy and camp. He is falling back slowly to the north. He seems to be resting his horse. The reds don't approach too close. He is loading his gun. He's now going into that thick chaparral in the draw to the north. He can never get to camp alive. The reds are closing up. At this moment, they could capture this camp and not lose a man. Our half-armed men are cowed and won't fight. Ah, I now see the boy's plan. I read it like a book. He has sacrificed himself to save these men!"

At this moment, several men—including Hudson, Overton, and Stover, with several Mexicans—came running up, out of breath. Tex called to them, "Men, go to the assistance of that brave boy. Don't you see he is alone?"

Overton came forward and said, "Sir, can you not see that it would only be throwing our lives away? There are over thirty Indians in that party."

"What is thirty Injuns," roared Tex, "against six or eight brave men, armed with rifles? Out, I say, go to the rescue."

Stover came up, leading a horse. "I will go," said he, "with any five men," but none moved. Tex begged, and the priest prayed, willing them to go quickly to the rescue.

"Oh," Tex moaned, lifting the glass to his eye. "It is too late. They are closing in on him. He will not have it so. He charges. They fall back. That deadly rifle brings terror to their coward hearts. He tries to break through them. They close up and stand their ground. He whirls and breaks for the chaparral. Such horsemanship I never before witnessed, I who have served in two bloody wars. They charge him from all sides. My God, how the arrows fly! The gray staggers. No, he recovers. Oh, what a spirited, noble creature. The horse is down! The boy rises, and the savages scatter and enlarge their

circle. He kneels at the gray's head. He rises and leaves the horse. They narrow the circle. Now he moves toward the chaparral. He is wounded! He
falls! No, he is up again. He sways, staggers, falls. They rush upon him. He
rises, fires both barrels. They scatter. Two fall from their horses. He stops to
reload. They rush. He draws his pistol. Every shot tells. They fall back. He
finishes reloading. What courage! Boy, I would give life, soul, to be by your
side! My God! He is gone. He has disappeared!"

The old Texan fumed, cursed, and groaned, addressing those around
him, "Oh, you cowards. Go bring his body here. He is no more. But no, can
such courage fail to triumph? Yes, I know he lives. Why was I stricken down,
I, a worthless, worn-out hulk? Why was I denied the boon of laying down
my wasted life for that gallant lad?"

Tex lapsed into a raving, delirious sleep from which he awakened with a
high fever. The next morning, when it was proposed to break camp, Tex
sent for the Americans and begged them to go and investigate. When they
refused, he said, "And you, whose lives he saved, propose to leave this spot
without discovering that boy's fate!" Tex raved on, exclaiming vehemently,
"May the gods curse you!" His fever took over, and he was out of his mind
again. The old priest and Antonio fixed up a travois, and they followed the
caravan as far as the little town of Valencia, where the old priest decided to
stop with the sick man and await his recovery.

*

After covering the retreat of the Americans, Walter had found himself
quite alone as his companions fell back before the rapidly approaching
savages. Before leaving them, he addressed his men. "These Indians," he
said, "are armed, for the most part, with bows and arrows. These have only
a short range. You have nothing to fear, for you have rifles of much longer
range. These people will not charge you as long as you stand your ground
and face them with your guns. Keep a clear head and boldly face the enemy.
Then you will come out all right, and we will save our friends without loss
of life."

Finding that the fugitives could not reach safety unless their retreat was
covered, he was forced to put his horse to the severest test, first threatening
one advancing column of savages and then another. At last, he found himself

hopelessly cut off from camp. He decided to make for the chaparral where he could get protection. The enemy saw through his scheme and decided to kill his horse. Finally, a well-directed arrow pierced the gray's flank. Walter reached down and pulled out the shaft. Still the animal did not lose heart. But shortly he was pierced by other arrows. The noble creature struggled to the very last. In fact, when he fell, he scarcely moved a muscle. Walter raised the creature's head, and he thought the gray responded to his last caress.

The enemy now tried to run him down, but he made this too expensive an undertaking. Still, shortly after he left his horse, he received a painful wound from an arrow. At last, after a desperate struggle, he reached the edge of the chaparral. A warrior rushed upon him. With his last shot, he mortally wounded this savage. Entering the thicket, he reloaded his rifle, crept to the edge of the bushes, and fired two more shots with deadly effect.

The enemy now drew off, removing their dead, evidently satisfied that their enemy was too dangerous to attempt to dislodge from his now-sheltered position. Falling back again out of sight, he reloaded his rifle, and then he withdrew the broken shaft that had penetrated his thigh. This was the last act of which he had any realization.

When Walter next came to his senses, Lion was licking his face, but his limbs were stiff and cold. His lips and throat were dry and parched. He was unable to rise. It was very dark, and there was a deathlike stillness everywhere. He couldn't locate where he was. Was he dreaming?

Now he knelt at his mother's knee, saying his prayer, "Now I lay me down to sleep; I pray the Lord my soul to keep." Now, he found himself in the little log schoolhouse in far-off Michigan. Now, he was raking hay in his aunt's meadow. Now it was noontime, and he was at the well of his aunt's farm. He could hear the old well sweep squeak and groan as the oaken bucket rose from the watery depths. The bucket poised upon the well curb. It tilted forward. He drank from the old bucket such delicious draughts as cannot elsewhere be found. He could feel the cold water running down his face and neck with sensations of delight experienced only by the farm boy at night when the work of the day is done. He lived over again his trials in the West. He ran over again the great race at Council Grove, felt the race must be lost because his limbs were stiff and cold. He again experienced the fine moment when he became the proud owner of that magnificent horse. By a campfire, he listened to Jim Bridger telling stories.

Gradually he fell again into forgetfulness, only to be quickly aroused by the thundering tones of Eagle Feather closing his great speech at the Apache village. He passed again through the privations of the desert. Consciousness faded again while he struggled, wielding his sword, on the field in Mexico against Lieutenant Rodrigues.

Acutely conscious of a burning thirst, he hears the ripple of running water. It sounds so sweet. He struggles to reach the little creek, so near and yet so very far. He drags his stiffened limbs through the tangle of brush and faints again. Then he hears the voice of a wren on a bush overhead. The robin's merry voice is in his ear. A lark's rich, melodious tone awakens his slumbering faculties, and daylight begins to brighten and color the surrounding peaks. What sound is that which comes from yonder thicket of chaparral, where the willow sways and bends, where the stately evergreen grows, where the somber alder extends its softening touch? Entwining here and there, the chaste white clematis spreads its tender shoots high and wide, and the lovely señorita fades in and out of the dark retreat. The wild rose rises in full flower, the white syringa, the fragrant mock orange perfumes the air. The señorita's soft, cool hands stroke his throbbing brow. That sound again, that wondrous tone.

From an untrained throat comes those heavenly notes: the sound of the matchless thrush. There it is again. Lion raises his sleepy head and cocks his ear to one side as if determined that no note shall escape him. Walter muses, "When the life spark has ebbed out of this poor human frame, drop by drop the life blood flows out on these bare sands. Could I but drag this helpless form to yonder bower, death would come calmer, sweeter, easier at the last."

❋

As the sun shed its first rays on the mountain tops, two men on foot emerged from the edge of the timber skirting the battlefield of yesterday. They looked out over the plain, a small donkey following them. One spoke, "Peter, over there is a dead animal. Let's step down and look at it."

"Judging from the disarray," said Peter, "I'd say it was a battle royal."

Approaching the carcass, the two men looked it over. "Full of arrows. The work of savages," remarked one.

"Belonged to a white man. That's sure," said the other.

From their rough, unkempt appearances, it was apparent these men had been in the wilds for some time. And it turns out that they were no other than Mr. Grey and Peter Stanford, recently of California Gulch, Colorado. Walking around the body of the horse, Grey stood looking at its sloping head. "Peter," he called excitedly.

"What is it?" responded Peter quickly. "Do you see Indians?"

"No," answered the other more calmly. "I recognize this horse. It's the thoroughbred that belonged to that boy we knew at California Gulch."

"Walter Cooper?" Peter asked.

Grey quietly answered, "Look him over, Peter, and see if you do not recognize him."

"If this is the same horse, he will be branded on the hoof of one of his feet. Don't remember which one. I wanted the boy to brand the horse. He said he didn't want to be so cruel to such a sensitive animal, so he compromised by cutting the letters into the hoof."

"Here is the brand," answered Grey, and sure enough, there it was, WC on the left front foot on the inside. "The boy has been here, that's certain, for he never would have parted with that horse."

"Could have been stolen from him," suggested Peter, who was still looking over the ground. "The earth is all cut up with pony tracks. Come here, Grey," he called. "Someone has been killed," and he pointed out a big patch of blood on the ground. He picked up a knife from the grass. The two men began a careful search in all directions. Presently Peter spoke up, saying, "Grey, we're pretty careless. We're in plain sight on this open plain." They drifted down toward the chaparral.

"Hold there, Grey!" called Peter excitedly. "There is a mountain lion." A great, gaunt hound raised up from the grass. "Don't shoot. It is a dog."

Grey now advanced toward the great creature, speaking softly and making friendly gestures. "Come here, Peter," he called. "Here is his master, dead." The dog made no objection when the friends knelt over the prostrate form.

"My God," said Peter. "It is our boy." He felt for a pulse. "He still lives!" he cried out. "His heart beats faintly. Let's fix up a camp in that thicket. Look how he dragged himself through the bushes, hunting for water. Here's the boy's gun and revolver. And here is where he made his last stand."

Grey brought the donkey forward and took charge of the wounded man while Peter prepared the camp. They kindled a small fire, heated water, and washed and dressed the boy's wounds as best they could.

"None of these wounds are fatal," said Grey, "but he has lost all of his blood. It will take a long time for him to build up so he will have strength enough to travel. Peter, could you find a grouse? We might make him some broth and give him a little strength."

"Yes, I'll take his gun. I see one barrel is empty. I will use just a little powder and make as little noise as possible. This country must be alive with Injuns."

At the end of half an hour, Peter returned with three nice grouse. They dressed them, and Grey proceeded to make the broth.

"Does this fire show up from a distance?" asked the cautious Grey.

"Very little," answered Peter. "The smoke is scattered in the trees."

It was a very comfortable camp. They found a little grassy bank close at hand where the timid donkey could feed, and they fed the great hound, who rested contentedly now that his young master had found friends.

After a careful scout, Peter returned and suggested that a new camp be found. "This one," he said, "will be untenable in another day. I found two more dead horses just back of the point there. That boy must have played havoc with those reds. The ground is all cut up where they circled around him."

After a hasty breakfast, Peter set out to find a favorable location for a safe camp where they could stay for a few days. He soon returned and said that there was no place suitable down the draw, as there was no chaparral of sufficient density to form a safe cover. About noon, he returned again and reported that he had found a fine place two miles up the draw, with a spring close at hand, large fir trees, and thick chaparral. He proposed that they move as soon as the shades of evening made it possible to do so unobserved. They constructed a hand barrow by taking two poles, eight feet long, and weaving willows across them, forming a foundation for a bed. Upon this, they laid blankets to support the wounded man. The two strong men then bore their charge to the new camp.

For many days, the patient, silent Grey watched at the bedside of the wounded scout, while the boy's life fluttered precariously. Peter would leave camp at dark and travel far back into the mountains, hunting deer in the early morning and jerking the meat during the day. He would then return at night. In this manner, he kept the camp well supplied with food and accumulated a quantity for the journey after their charge had recovered sufficiently to travel.

On Peter's return to camp early one morning, Grey told him that there had been a change for the better in their patient. "Yesterday morning," he said, "very early, I noticed that he was awake. He was listening to the song birds. One in particular held his attention, that thrush that we've heard so much here of late. I think he called me Mr. Tex. Of course the light was uncertain. He has not spoken since, but perhaps the worst has passed."

Day by day, the patient took a little more nourishment, and yet he did not again speak. About a week later, Grey met Peter on the outskirts of the encampment and reported, "The boy is better, yet he does not talk of passing events. I listened to him last night for a long time. His mind was wandering from one thing to another. He seemed to be present at an Indian council. He talked of making a speech. Then he was traveling in the desert. He was in search of water for someone he called 'Señorita.' Once he gave a shrill whistle that startled me. He talks about a Mr. Tex, a Señor Castillo, a Maria. This morning, about 3 o'clock, he was awake when that song bird began his song. He seemed greatly interested and talked of the bird, of the beauty and sweetness of its song. At the sound of the boy's voice, the dog rose and stood over him. He put out his wasted hand, and the great dog licked it with real affection. I thought he recognized the dog. He soon dropped off to sleep and slept peacefully and soundly. When he awoke, he was rational, though still very weak. He did seem cheerful and talked considerable."

Walter finally told Grey that he felt able to move. They found that his right leg was stiff and bent at an angle that made it impossible for him to walk. They now decided to discard all articles that could be spared and make the sick boy a bed on the back of the donkey. The weight was not excessive as the usually compact body of the young scout was much shrunken and wasted. His fever had passed away entirely, and he was able to take ample nourishment. They finally made a start, and for several days, they made short marches with frequent rests. The boy continued to thrive and gradually gained strength.

The country seemed to be completely overrun with prowling bands of savages, making it necessary to travel almost entirely at night and lie in hiding during the day. After ten days of tedious labor through the mountainous country, they came to a raging mountain torrent and camped on its bank. At the first signs of coming day, Peter made a careful scout for a safe ford. He found a place about a mile above camp where he thought a crossing might be made.

On reaching the spot, they found the outlook extremely perilous, as the bed of the stream was rocky and the current very swift. All hands agreed that it was necessary to make the effort since they had again encountered fresh Indian signs. Peter reasoned, "It is unsafe to remain here. I don't believe the red devils will follow us across this stream."

He proposed to carry the wounded boy on his back, but the latter said, "No," decidedly. "I will my take my chances on the back of the donkey. If he fails, I will do my best to get out on one side or the other."

Before it was fairly light, they started, leading the donkey well upstream. While crossing, the donkey made good progress to a point near the middle of the stream. Here he drifted down onto a bar which proved to be the upper end of an immense shelving rock. When the water commenced to deepen, the small animal could not resist its force and was swept over the rock's edge into a seething whirlpool. The wounded boy became separated from the donkey and, after a hard struggle, was swept to the same shore from which he had started. He was fortunate enough to come in contact with some willows, by the aid of which he helped himself to a safe landing.

After a short rest, he made his way up the stream and plunged in. With the help of a stout stick, he reached the opposite shore, very much exhausted. He noticed that both Peter and Grey seemed much excited, and he thought that, perhaps, they had made up their minds that this shore was more dangerous than the one they had just left and they were trying to stop him. After recovering sufficiently from his exertions, he asked what was the matter.

"Why, man," shouted Peter, "your leg! Your leg is straight again!"

"That's so," answered the young man, rising to his feet and walking around. "That's so, it is all right again."

After a careful search, they found the poor donkey a quarter of a mile below in a big drift, nearly exhausted. After rescuing the animal, they found a secure camp and rested for the remainder of the day. About the middle of the day, some dozen savages examined the shore opposite, but made no effort to cross.

As soon as it was dark, the friends were on the move again, and in good time, they reached Taos. Here, they made careful inquiry for the caravan with which Tex had been traveling, but no news could be had of it. They finally decided to pass on to Denver and then split up.

Walter called at once upon Mr. Carson, who received him with great kindness, and both he and his friends became guests of the great scout.

After resting a few days, they made a start for Denver, riding horses furnished by Kit Carson. They reached their destination in due time. Upon calling on Captain Scudder, Walter found that John J. Pierce, the honest Texan who had taken his claim at California Gulch, had—true to his promise—paid the five hundred and fifty dollars yet due on the claim.

CODA

The manuscript of A Most Desperate Situation *ends abruptly with Walter Cooper's return to Denver, where he discovers that John Pierce has paid him for the rights to his claim at California Gulch. Luckily, Walter left among his papers a much briefer, first-person narrative that recounts his adventures as he came into the Montana gold fields in the autumn of 1863. This short text, unlike* A Most Desperate Situation, *has the feel of a straightforward memoir and lacks some of the drama—and melodrama—of the more fictional longer work. While Walter is still the hero of most conflicts, he also faces setbacks and disappointments. And because of the first-person narration, there is less commentary from others about the young prospector's many exemplary qualities. Still, in his own telling, Walter Cooper, "the young scout," remains an appealing protagonist and, as always, a master storyteller.*

During the latter part of 1863, including the summer, I made my headquarters at Colorado City, Colorado Territory. The town was located on the Fountain Qui Bulla River, a tributary of the Arkansas River. I had located a farm on a quarter section of land on the river bottom about seven miles above Colorado City.

The latter part of the summer, we began to hear reports of the rich gold discoveries at Alder Gulch, Bannack, and other points in what was then known as Idaho Territory. I had a good saddle horse and wanted to go to Denver to look after some small matters. While at Denver, I met a man by the name of Jack Olinger. He was in touch with some young men who had just arrived in Denver from Alder Gulch. They were on their way home, which was at Leavenworth, Kansas. They had plenty of gold dust from Alder, and they intended to return to their claims in the early spring. They gave Olinger letters to friends at Alder. Jack was wild to start at once and wanted me to join him in making up an outfit for the trip. I really wanted to go back to my claim on the Fountain.

While we were discussing the proposed journey, I met a man by the name of MacGilvra. He was two or three years older than I and was a tinner by trade. He was working for a hardware store at his trade. He did not have the gold fever and rather wanted to settle down on a ranch. After a few days, I decided to join Olinger, fit up a good team, and go to Alder Gulch. In the meantime, MacGilvra wanted to go over and see my ranch. We went over, and I gave him permission to take the ranch and work it and keep all he could make.

I joined Olinger, and we started for Alder Gulch on September 1, 1863. We had fitted out a good team of horses of about 1,200 pounds weight each, a new harness and wagon, and a No. 1 outfit all around, with sufficient corn to last the team for the trip. We each had some spare money that we wanted to invest in goods that we could sell when we arrived in Alder, as reports said that all staples brought high prices. I bought six hundred pounds of bacon, and Jack bought ten gallons of whiskey. He was told that it would bring fabulous prices. We had a good outfit and made a comfortable trip, making good time after our team got used to the harness and thoroughly acquainted with each other.

On reaching the site of future Fort Phil Kearny, we were overtaken by a fearful storm. The wind blew terribly, and the snow accumulated quickly. We were advised to push on and cross the range onto Bitter Creek, which our informant told us would be quiet with no wind and likely less snow. As I left, our informant called to me, saying that there was a large party of heavily loaded emigrants' wagons with poor teams that had started to cross the divide some two hours ahead of us. He said, "They can never make it over the hill onto Bitter Creek, and I fear they may perish." The last words of his report I heard indifferently, owing to the high wind.

We pushed on rapidly. It was then about 2 P.M. The wind increased constantly and seemed to grow stronger each moment. We kept to the road with some difficulty. By the time we reached the summit of the pass, then called "Bridger Pass," we could scarcely see our horses' heads. At the highest point, during a lull in the wind, I saw a team to the right of the road, standing still. On examination, I found the occupants barely protected with the single thickness of their clothes—clothing wholly unfit for the inclement weather.

I finally found the road and, with the utmost exaction, started the teams and got the wagons moving, rousing the men to fair exertion. One man threatened to shoot me for, he said, interfering. We finally started down a grade. Our own wagon tipped over. Jack and I fell out, but we finally got down to Bitter Creek just as night set in. There was no wood, but plenty of sagebrush. We grouped the wagons in a circle within which we kindled a great sagebrush fire and kept it burning all night. One of the teams was owned by a brute of a man. He insisted on having his team planted in the center of the circle, and we finally had to knock him down and banish him to the extreme end of the circle, as we wanted to save the women and children from unnecessary exposure and discomfort, not knowing how long they would need extra protection from the storm. During the latter part of the night, the weather moderated very much, and shortly after daylight, we found we could dispense with the fire. The fire had been a godsend to the needy since it gave out great heat, though we had had to expend much exertion to keep it alight as the brush burned up very quickly.

Jack was up early, made breakfast, and had gotten into our wagon and was gathering up his lines for a start. I was about to get into the saddle when a woman got down from her covered wagon, walked out near us, and said, "Gentlemen, I cannot permit you to drive away from this place without expressing my heartfelt feelings. You young men, who are strangers, have done a most Christian act. You have rescued more than twenty people from certain death. You found us entirely exhausted; our stock powerless to move these over-burdened wagons from those nameless hills and frozen heights, our men exhausted, beating the workout mules and searching for the lost and covered roads, doing which they expended all their strength and had surrendered to the inevitable; and ourselves exhausted, walking and protecting our little ones from the cold, our last act having been to bind our small children between our featherbeds, by which means the loving mothers hoped to protect the helpless who could not help themselves. You have saved us from the horrors of a death upon yonder pitiless mountain and brought us to this haven of rest and comfort. Can we hope that you will permit us to petition our Heavenly Father to protect you on your dangerous journey?"

The prayer which followed was couched in the most beautiful and touching language, mingled with warm, grateful tears. All the women and children and part of the men joined the eloquent suppliant. This exhibition of grateful appreciation warmed our own hearts greatly, and Jack—usually stubborn and sour—was much affected. He got off his wagon and said, "Walt, suppose we give them a couple sacks of corn to help them to the Mormon settlements?" I at once agreed. Soon we bade them good-bye and proceeded on our journey.

We constantly met travelers and returned miners and gold hunters, and scarcely a night passed that we did not camp with outgoing people who told us of the dangers of the road from frequent robberies. Even murders were reported to have been committed. The outlaws were reported to be constantly preying upon both the outgoing travelers and the incoming people, indeed upon all who were possessed of sufficient wealth to offer suitable inducements to warrant the reckless element taking chances to enrich themselves.

After crossing Bear River, we met many travelers on their way to Denver, Salt Lake, and the states. Among them were men who had mined at and about Bannack, Alder Gulch, and other districts. They all knew more or less concerning robberies having been committed by so-called "road agents," as well as of murders perpetrated by the same band of outlaws. The fact was that the very rich mines at and in the vicinity of Bannack, Alder, and Summit had attracted the desperadoes from all the mining districts.

Such was the condition of society at the time of our arrival at Virginia City. We looked around for a few days and went all over the claims from Nevada City to the summit. After talking with the miners extensively, I made up my mind that Alder was the greatest mining camp, at least the greatest that I had ever seen or heard of. Every bank, store, saloon, and place of business had gold pans full and part full of gold. There were no claims for sale, and nothing doing but work. We sold our bacon at $2.10 per pound in gold. Jack could not get a bid on his whiskey for any more than he paid for it in Denver—so he said he would keep it. A ten-dollar greenback was only worth four dollars, or forty cents on the dollar, four dollars in gold for a ten-dollar bill.

I got a job from a son of Captain Scudder of Denver, with whom I was somewhat acquainted, at ten dollars per day. I worked in the mines and was put in the tailrace to shovel the tailings. There were four men below shoveling into the sluice boxes. At the end of the day, young Scudder came around and looked me over. He remarked the condition of my hands and asked if they were sore.

I said, "Oh, not much."

"Will you be here in the morning?"

I said, "Yes, sir. I will be here on time."

I went up to a restaurant for supper. When I went to pay for supper, the man was pretty busy and said, "Will you be here for breakfast?"

I said, "Yes," and he told me to pay the next morning. In the morning, I took out a ten-dollar bill and offered it to him.

He turned it over and asked, "Haven't you got any gold?"

I said, "No."

He said, "All right. I don't want that stuff. When you get some gold, you can pay me."

I stayed with the tailrace through the week, and Saturday night, I was paid seventy dollars for my seven-days work. As I was paid, I remarked that I knew Captain Scudder of Denver. Young Scudder said, "I am his son." He took me to his mess, which was less expensive and more pleasant than the restaurant.

I stayed with Scudder until May 15, 1864. I had accumulated quite a sum of money in nearly four months without the loss of a day. I then purchased a half interest in an ox train of seven teams, with large Murphy wagons and six yoke of oxen to the team, and I started for Fort Benton, head of navigation on the Missouri River. On reaching the fort, we found that due to low water, no boats had arrived. Old residents predicted that few, if any, would reach Benton. There were hundreds of teams at and around Benton waiting for freight. Only one or two of the teams had horses, and since I had a good saddle horse and pack mule, I was kept pretty busy keeping track of rumors of boats.

I made a trip to Cow Island and met the steamer, *Yellowstone.* The boat was tied up opposite the mouth of Cow Creek, stranded because of low water. The afternoon that I reached Cow Island, a cloudburst some distance up the Missouri caused a very sudden rise in the river. When the flood struck the *Yellowstone,* half her crew was on land and out of reach. By the use of oil, bacon, and other quick-burning materials, the rest of the crew made enough steam to control the boat in midstream. When I talked with the crew, I found that her freight was all under contract. Thus our trip was fruitless. We returned to Benton to find that our train had moved down to Milk River for grass for our cattle.

A rumor soon reached us that a boat had reached the mouth of Milk River, and we thought that there might be a chance to get loading for our teams. I at once proceeded to the mouth of the Milk, not only to secure loading, but our people were out of coffee, meat, and sugar, with but little flour on hand. The country was alive with Indians, and I could only travel at night. I got away alone and went into cover as soon as it was light and lay concealed until nightfall.

I started out knowing that I must cross Milk River at once. I took some chances by going down a steep gulch and reaching the Milk as it was growing dusk. As I led my horses through the bushes, I saw a number of Indians. They had evidently seen me first. They were, it seemed, under excitement, and one among them—I thought a man—motioned to me to get to the river neck, which was much swollen. I sprang into the saddle, seized the reins of my pack horse, and rushed for the river. We were caught by the current and swept down. This movement certainly surprised the Indians, for we were a full hundred feet below them and well out into the current when they reached the bank. Several arrows struck the water behind me, and I had, by this time, gotten my horses in the right shape to take some advantage of the strong current. The stream was about three hundred feet wide and very swift where we crossed. As I entered the brush, I imagined that I got a friendly sign from one Indian.

Long, long years thereafter, I was at the Crow Agency endeavoring to secure the ratification of a treaty that Congress had granted to the Rocky Fork and Cook City Rail Company. President Cleveland had stipulated that the treaty must be approved by a majority of the Indians. After a majority of the Indians had touched the pen in approval, their interpreter, Pierce Shome, came over to where I was standing. He said, "Did anybody save your life on the Milk River in 1864?"

I took in his measure and profile at a glance and promptly replied, "Yes, and it was you, you old Indian, a Blackfoot then, now a Crow."

Shome laughed in his quiet way. "Very close. Pretty close that night. You made quick escape by jumping then. I no see you since that time. You live Bozeman?"

"Yes," I said. "You come see me at my home, and I will take care of you for a long time." I then said that I had a fine horse worth two hundred dollars for him.

He promptly replied, "I don't want horse. If you will send me a match-box, I won't forget." There were at that time many French half-breeds in the mountains. They were all great, big-hearted men, honest and true. This man was one of the greatest of that noble bunch. Before leaving the agency, I had a long talk with him. He said that he was with that party of Blackfeet. They were watching the crossing. He said that they had discovered me when I entered the steep gulch. They knew that I was aiming to cross the river at that point, and they meant to take me in. They were close to the trail where it entered the river, but they had no idea that I would jump into the river where the bank was so high. He said that if I had tried to get to the ford they would certainly have gotten me. He was much pleased that I saw his signs of danger and acted so quickly. He said that those Blackfeet had all had black hearts and wanted to kill.

Those many years earlier, after evading the Blackfeet, I pushed on, taking a chance on the trail over the prairie to the mouth of the Milk River. On my arrival, I found Jerry Mason with a large train of wagons, plus several independent outfits, among whom were Al Nichols and several others of the Gallatin Valley. I entered the train but found no one. It was just daylight. I heard quite a noise some distance east, where I imagined that the Milk River joined the Missouri. While I hunted around among the wagons, I awakened a man who said he was the night herder. I finally climbed up on the hind wheel of a great Murphy wagon, from which I saw the smokestack of a large steamboat half a mile or more distant.

I turned my eyes down the river along a high bluff and saw a great dust rising from the edge of the bluff. At first, the wind prevented me from learning what caused the dust, which was several miles below and bordering an immense river bottom. Finally I decided that the dust was caused by horsemen, who gradually grew more distinct to the east of the wagons. There a large slough came in, bending toward the bluff. It turned just below the train and ran down parallel with the bluff, some hundred yards from it. When I first saw them, the horsemen seemed to be riding rapidly along the face of the bluff, which was of considerable height. I saw that they were Indians, almost all or partly naked. I could make out their number as eighty or one hundred, moving forward rapidly. When they were some three hundred yards below me, they divided, with one group turning suddenly to the left and plunging into the slough. Another group of thirty-two horsemen swept on and rode past the train of wagons. The party that had forded the slough rode up to the train's great herd of cattle, horses, and mules and at once began cutting out the horses and mules. Some of them launched their arrows into the cattle as they passed.

I finally saw a white man riding a large mule come down the opposite side of the slough. I at once concluded that he had been with the stock as a herder. The Indians were all around him. He urged his mule forward at its utmost speed. Coming to a slight bend in the slough, he tried to force the mule into the slough, but the mule stopped and would not enter. As the bank was somewhat high, after two or three trials, the man jumped off and plunged into the slough and swam across. The Indians, five of whom were some sixty or seventy feet behind him, jumped their horses into the water and followed him. He reached the bank just in advance of the Indian riders, who began shooting arrows at the man as he did his best to escape.

About this time, I deserted my elevated position on the Murphy wagon and ran over to where the night herder stood. I told him what was happening, saying, "Take that gun on the side of the wagon, and come with me to help that man the Indians are chasing."

He answered that there was no hammer to that gun.

"Well," said I, "get the gun and come on. It is as good as mine that I have soaked in the river."

Acting on my suggestion, he seized the old Kentucky rifle and followed. We ran as fast as we could to meet the man who was running slowly toward the train. I called to him to hurry. The five Indians were about forty yards behind him, and they were launching a stream of arrows at the poor fellow. The Indians halted as we approached the river and brought our rifles into firing position. They turned and rode back toward the slough and the herd. Most of the cattle had dropped out, and the Indian riders were pushing the horse herd forward to the crossing of the slough. The Indian horsemen rushed their plunder as fast as possible, evidently believing it necessary to get their captured property as far beyond the reach of their late owners as possible.

As his pursuers turned back, the white man fell on his face. There were two arrows sticking in him, one in the shoulder; the other had entered from behind and protruded from his breast about four inches. I took hold of the arrow point and pulled it out. Much frothy blood followed the extraction of the arrow, which the night herder said came from the lungs. We carried the man to the train about one hundred yards away. As we reached the wagons, the men from the boat began to arrive and continued to come until there were upwards of forty, some of whom I had met before. Jerry Mason, the owner of the train, was among them. I explained what I had seen of the Indians and their movements.

From my viewpoint on the old Murphy wagon, I had had a splendid opportunity to see and mark minutely the thirty-two Indians as they passed not more than sixty feet from where I stood. It was the most magnificent and remarkable native military exhibit that could be produced. Stripped of every superfluous article, the warriors represented a type of cavalry, from a primitive standpoint, that was certainly perfect. They were naked, save for their well-kept hair falling in two heavy braids down their backs. Some had one or two feathers in their hair. Most had a band of skin about the neck, to which was attached some ornament from fowl or animal. I did not see any ornament attached to ears. Some had bands of skin, hair out, on their arms. All had a belt about the waist and carried a knife thereon. All carried a bow with a bunch of arrows grasped in the left hand. A part of them carried a lance, long and slim, with which they wounded many cattle. All rode bare-backed. I saw no saddle or other contrivance to take its place. All had a rawhide strap attached to the lower jaw of the horse, some twenty feet in length, and yet the animal was guided by the body of the rider. All had lariats. The animals were, it seemed to me, perfectly trained, responding to the wills of their riders instantly. All animals were sleek and fat. Being thoroughly familiar with the mounts of many tribes, including Mexicans, I never saw a finer mounted body of men. The train was powerless to make any move whatever, as they had no horses or other means with which to attempt to recover the lost animals. About twenty head of cattle had been killed outright, and many others wounded, some sorely.

The wounded man was one of the herders employed by Jerry Mason for his large train. Mason, having come down under contract, took the entire cargo of the boat that unloaded at the mouth of the Milk River, and yet he did not have a full load for his teams. I was able to get the few supplies that

I could take on my packhorse, which included a small quantity of beef taken from one of the fat animals that the Indians had killed. I started back at midnight for our camp on the Milk, which was about seventy miles above the mouth.

I pushed on as fast as I could, encumbered with a pack animal heavily loaded. I concluded that I had traveled about twenty-five miles. I hurried over a divide into a considerable gulch, where I cached my horse for the day. I went to sleep in an elevated place at the end of the gulch, where I imagined I would not be discovered. When I awakened just past noon, feeling much refreshed, I turned my eyes to the north and saw a bunch of people whom I took for Indians. When I put the glass on them, I found there was quite a party of them. Their attention seemed to be focused on other objects, and when I put my glass in the direction their attention seemed to be directed, I concluded that I was safe, as they evidently had not discovered me. I lay quietly in my snug retreat until dusk, when I saddled my horse and pulled out.

About midnight my packhorse wanted to rest. I had no way of judging just where I was. The country was quite overcast with clouds, and I could see only a short distance. I finally saddled up again and pushed on. I traveled as fast as I could force the packhorse along. Finally, I made up my mind—from the way the saddle horse acted—that we were being followed. He kept constantly turning back, and I began to feel that it was dangerous to travel farther until I could get more light. In the course of half an hour, I came to the conclusion that I was being followed by some animal that likely was attracted by the meat. Therefore I went on. It grew a little lighter. I came to fear that I might pass our camp. Finally I saw what I believed to be either our camp or some other camp, most likely freighters like ourselves. I made for it, but it was farther away than I expected. Day now began to break, and I soon discovered that my pursuer was a half-grown bear attracted by the meat I had on the pack. The camp I found to be our own. My fellow freighters were overjoyed to see me, as I was to see them.

Being almost worn out, I crawled into a wagon and slept most of the day. The next morning, we turned our heads toward Fort Benton again. We struck the Missouri near the mouth of the Marias, where we camped all night. On reaching Fort Benton, we made up our minds that no more boats would come up close enough for us to reach them during the freighting season. Quite a number of the teams with whom we had been neighboring and traveling wanted to start back at once. The only trouble was that so much stock had been maintained along the wagon road back to the mines that our stock would reach the mountains in poor condition. So far as our case was concerned, we wanted our cattle fit for beef, as we had to sell some of it in order to pay our help.

We needed a road where there was good grass. The next day, I met a man by the name of Jo Cabelle, who was an Italian who had been in and about that country for twenty-five years. He told me he knew the country well and that we could cross the river at Benton. He felt sure that we could find a road through the country as far as the Gallatin River. He had not been all the way but had hunted for more than thirty miles and said he believed we could find a road for empty wagons all the way.

Five or six men started out in the morning to find a ford. At night, they reported that the river could not be forded. In the morning, several of us sat on our horses, discussing the matter of fording. I rode my horse down to the river and up and down for a half mile. I was with a Mr. Miller. I said to him, "In my opinion, the best ford in miles is right here in front of the old fort." I rode down to the river and into the water. It was pretty swift. I finally started across and succeeded. There were only thirty feet of the crossing where my horse did not touch bottom. I came back in the same place that night. We decided to cross the teams in the morning.

When all was ready, our seven Murphy wagons took the lead, as did the larger cattle. In all, there were sixty wagons and twenty-five men. We camped on the other side of the river and proceeded to get our supplies over, ready for a start on the new road to the mines. Many predicted that we would fail and have to turn back. Jo Cabelle went with the train for two days and then returned to Benton. We had no serious trouble. We found most excellent feed for our cattle.

We were short of horses, having only one besides my saddle horse, Billy. We were very short of provisions because all of our surplus supplies had been loaded into Ruffner and Miller's sutler wagon, which had capsized in the river. Our supplies were lost, and as about all our money had been exhausted in their purchase, we had to depend largely on my ability to supply wild meat sufficient for the crowd. The trip consumed nearly a month, as we were trying to fatten our cattle by making short drives. This plan proved a success. I was in the saddle every day, made necessary by the demand for fresh meat. We had a colt and a very gentle team of oxen that made short side trips to bring the heavy game to the train. We killed many elk, which were the best of food. While out one day some miles to the east to the train, passing through a dense patch of tall sagebrush, I came onto the complete equipment of a large Indian village, which had been cached by a large number of Indians who, doubtless, had been forced to retreat at a rapid pace to escape a much larger belligerent force. The cache was in perfect condition and had not been disturbed. The indications were that the deposit had lain for a considerable length of time in hiding.

Another afternoon, while on a hunt in plain view of the train, I saw a very large bear in my path. I had left my horse on a ridge higher up the hill. The bear rolled over two or three times and, finally getting to its feet, came directly toward me. I had a muzzle-loading gun only partially loaded, the ball having stuck in its barrel. Behind me, there was a perpendicular ledge of rocks. I looked about to see where I could get up on the ledge, which was some twenty feet high. The bear was coming toward me at a pretty fast gait. I did not think he had seen me. I noticed a crevice in the wall of rocks and just had time to step in. The bear passed me and went up on the ledge about one hundred feet below where I stood—which was in sight of the train. Several of the boys started up to where I was. I finally got the ball down and fired at the bear. I thought I had hit him, and with several of the men, I passed up to the top of the ledge, discovering that the wounded bear had gone into a dense aspen thicket about one hundred feet from the ledge.

We had two dogs with us, and all the men were anxious to send them in after the bear. My shot had struck the bear a little too far back, and he must have been very sick. I advised them not to send the dogs in, as they were unused to such game and the brush was very thick, with little room to maneuver. By this time, more men had arrived and most of them were keen to have the dogs go in. The owner of one of the dogs, Greene, said, "I will chance my dog."

"Well," said I, "there is my bear. I will not be responsible for any damage he may do to the dogs, for it will be done in self-defense."

In went the dogs with many yelps. My bear was silent. About three minutes later, there was something doing in the brush. Out came one dog with a bunch of skin hanging from his rear end. He was giving two yelps to each

jump. When he came to the ledge, he did not see it and he went over, landing on his back at the bottom. Just then, several more men came up from
the train. One of them had a No. 8 shotgun, which he said was loaded with
thirty-six buckshot in each barrel. In the meantime, the bear, which had
followed the dogs out, went back to cover.

Greene said his dog would go back in, and the man with the big shotgun
spoke up, saying, "I would like a chance at that bear. I will guarantee to fix
him."

I remarked, "Gentlemen, as I told you a while ago, the bear is mine. I
expect to get him but am in no hurry about it. I have been pretty close to
him once and don't care to be as close again. If you gentlemen have any
curiosity about seeing him, he is in there and will, I think, if persuaded,
come out for inspection."

The shotgun man, addressing Greene, said, "Let your dog go in. If the
bear comes out, I will give him both barrels and I guess he will stop."

Greene then suggested that the dogs be encouraged to go in and rout out
the bear. Greene led his dog in about thirty feet. Another fellow went in
with him. They left the dog and came out and had just reached the edge of
the brush when the dog reached the bear. To judge by the sound, the dog
must have given the bear a start, for he gave a roar that raised our hair. The
dog was evidently nervy and must have started out backwards and slowly.
He came out on the run, with the bear right at his tail. The pace was so fast
that the shotgun man was taken by surprise, and the dog and the bear were
right on top of him. He was in their very path. He turned and ran at the top
of his speed. The bear's paw was really on his heels. He had no time to act
or think. He was blind as to his trail. He went over the ledge, gun and all.
The gun was smashed, and the man nearly dead. Though badly used up,
the bear turned and very leisurely went back into the thicket. By the time
the excitement was over, it was dark and all hands went back to the train.
On examination the next morning, the bear was found to be dead. His first
rifle wound—while a little slow-acting—had proved fatal.

The train rolled down into the Missouri Valley near where Confederate
Creek enters the river in the present county of Broadwater. We then passed
over the hills and reached the West Gallatin River near its entrance into the
Missouri, from which we passed up the Madison River and crossed it. Thereafter, we followed the regular pioneer route to Virginia City, reaching there

about August 10, 1864. Our mixed train disbanded, and I then disposed of what was left of my interest in the train and went back to work in the mines.

The last of October, I purchased some cattle and a wagon and returned to the Missouri River. I expected to meet Jack Olinger. I was traveling alone at rather a slow gait, and at a point near the Jefferson River, I was overtaken by a fine-looking man somewhat older than myself. I was riding a saddle horse and had another hitched behind the wagon. I had four yoke of oxen on the wagon. As this man overtook me, I asked him if he would be willing to drive the team, and he agreed. We soon reached the Jefferson, where we camped for the night. He pitched in and got supper while I looked after the stock. In the morning, he got breakfast while I got up the cattle. At breakfast, I asked him his name. He answered that it was Yank. He had no baggage whatever except a change of underclothes. We traveled together to a little below the summit of the belt range at the end of Boulder Valley. I had found this man to be a decent sort, a good cook, willing to do cheerfully all the work about the camp, including washing the clothes for us both.

I asked him if he had any plans for the future, and he replied that he had none. I said, "Well, do you want to stay with me?"

He said, "Yes. I have no money, not a cent."

"Well," I said, "I have no plan at present. I started out with the idea of putting in the winter hunting."

He said he had no gun, was no hunter, but could pack in the game.

"Well," said I, "this is a very good camp, and we need meat. If you fix up camp, I will go hunting."

We had a tent, which he proceeded to put up, and I shouldered my rifle and started out. Directly I saw plenty of signs of elk. About noon, I struck a band of about a dozen and killed three, one large cow, one two-year-old bull, and a yearling calf, all fat and fine. We packed in the meat before dark, and in the morning, we started on toward the Boulder. At or near the crossing, we came to a partially built house where the Diamond R had a train. We gave them an elk and stayed all night. They had a yearling bear that was sucking his paw and evidently wanted to go to sleep, as it was about the time of year that bruins hunt a warm place in some nook or corner of the mountains and hole up for about five or six months or until fair weather in the spring. Just below the road about a mile, there was a hot spring with a strong flow of hot water, and we took a nice, warm bath.

The Diamond R train was in the charge of a wagon master who was a fine fellow and from whom we got some bacon in exchange for some maple syrup, of which we had a surplus. We drove on down to the road leading to the three forks of the Missouri River, where we camped for a couple of days and prospected for gold. Small prospects could be found almost any place on the banks of the creek called Prickley Pear, which flowed to the east, joining the Missouri lower down. We went on in the direction of Three Forks. On reaching the Missouri at a point just above where Confederate Gulch Creek entered the Missouri, we crossed the river, camping near the Lewis and Clark Trail at Round Grove, a short distance from the river.

In the morning, I rode toward the high hills up the stream that passed through Round Grove to the east. At the mouth of the canyon at the base of a tall, timbered butte, I selected a location for a winter camp. We moved up and made our camp under a number of tall, sheltering fir trees where there was plenty of dry aspen wood of all sizes. Entirely out of the wind, we selected a camp in the open. We covered our shelter entirely with fir boughs, the rear being at the base of a large fir tree and the front entirely open at the fire, which burned all winter. We had a good tent, but we never put it up as we were perfectly comfortable in all kinds of weather during the entire winter. The first morning in camp, I went out to hunt and killed two deer and half a dozen fat young grouse, which furnished a meal fit for the gods. We were very comfortable indeed.

After a day or two, I got limbered up and used to walking over the hills so that I was practically tireless. I was out every day and never failed to get at least one deer. At one time, we had fifty fat deer hanging at our camp. As I did not wish to kill them in a wasteful way, I was thinking of a stop in hunting. Yank reminded me that Christmas was but two days off, and, said he, "I have never seen a Christmas without a good dinner on that day."

"Now, Yank," I said, "name anything that I can get in these hills to help out the dinner and you shall have it."

After a moment's thought, he said, "We have not had any of those nice grouse for a month."

"Well," I replied, "I will get all you want tomorrow."

"I don't know of anything better," he answered, "than roast venison and chicken potpie. I believe," he added, "that we might have some company. I saw a fellow the other day when I was looking for the cattle. He asked me if

I knew where he could get some meat for his camp. I told him we had plenty. He said he would be over, and I believe he will be over, with a few friends, Christmas or before."

I went out the next day and got ten grouse, as fine and fat as I had ever seen. The next day I hunted up a fishhook and got a dozen trout that would weigh better than a pound each—and some at least two pounds.

Christmas day came. A heavy snow fell the night before, and it was cold and cheerless. And yet Yank was up, and his voice was cheerful. As I stepped before the fire, he said, "Walter, I am happy. I know what is being done at home. They are going to have a Christmas dinner, and we will have one, too. I am afraid our expected guests won't come, but come or not, the dinner will be ready at 2 o'clock."

"Well, Yank," I asked, "what can I do to help it along?"

He said, "Nothing, except give me full swing about the fire and camp."

So I watched his antics. We had a very large cast iron or Dutch oven with a tight lid on top. He took the shovel at the proper hour to the creek and soon returned with several pieces of green willow sticks. These he set up by the fire and thawed the frost out of the wood. At his leisure, he peeled these pieces of wood and laid the bark in a clean place near at hand. Then he scraped the ashes from a section of the fire and dug a good-sized hole, removing the loose earth. He filled the hole with live hot coals, covering the place with hot ashes. At the proper time, he cleaned out the hot coals and then took the clean white willow bark and covered the bottom, sides, and ends of the hole with the bark, rough side down. In this bed, he placed the blue grouse, whole, nicely dressed. At the other end, he placed his trout. These he carefully covered with the clean bark, well pressed down. Then he neatly covered the grouse and trout with live coals, six or eight inches deep. It was now close to noon.

Yank then made his bread in the Dutch oven. I noticed that his eyes constantly roamed over the hills. It was now between 2 and 3 o'clock. Yet, Yank waited. We were both half starved. And yet, he waited.

After a while, he quit looking toward the hills and said, "Well, Walt, I don't want to starve you any longer. I don't want any dinner myself. I believe those men are lost. I have a mind to start to meet them." He got his old everyday coat and fixed the fire with some heavy logs nearly twelve feet long, for we thought it best to have a long fire so all could get its full benefit.

He had walked out a few steps when he gave a regular Indian whoop and hollered that they were coming. Presently, four tired men reached our camp.

"Where is Jeff?" asked Yank.

"He went over to help the old man. He is on the way."

Soon the two men hove into sight, traveling very slowly. They soon reached our fire. The old gentleman was fairly staggering. They all pulled off their frozen shoes before the great warm fire. The old gentleman toppled down on a robe. I crawled into the wagon, and out came a gallon keg of good old whiskey. I poured out a tin cup full of the beverage, saying, "Boys, this is Christmas. This keg has never been opened or sampled until now. Just let our old friend over there take a good drink of this. It will rest him up and help all of you."

I could see Yank's eyes fairly sparkle, for he knew what the old man really needed. All except Yank took a good drink from the cup. The old man soon brightened up, and all were ready for Yank's dinner. Each was served with a whole grouse uncut, a good big trout, hot bread and butter, coffee, and old maple syrup. All, including ourselves, had fasted since early morning, and we soon disposed of this most hearty meal. Every one of our guests declared that he had never sat down to a finer dinner.

Five of our guests belonged to one party of miners called the Harwood Company that had come down from the mines to pass the winter and expected to soon return to their claims located on a small tributary near the summit of Alder Gulch. The old man was with a small party from Iowa which had only arrived at Alder a few weeks previous to their coming down to the river for a hunt. They had had no success hunting. I told the old man that he could have a half-dozen deer by returning their skins to our camp before we left our present location. He said he would like to have the meat and would soon come down to take it away.

It was snowing quite lively, and our guests began to talk about starting back to their camp. I proposed that they stay all night, saying that I thought we could arrange sleeping accommodations by keeping the fire burning. This Yank heartily seconded. The old gentleman said he could not make it back that night. All accepted our invitation, and Yank made special arrangements about the fire.

*

While out hunting one day, I passed through some pretty thick timber. The snow was quite deep and there were many fresh tracks in the fresh snow. When I passed under a large, leaning pine, a piece of bark dropped directly in front of me. I looked up and saw in the crotch of the tree the head of a very savage-looking creature with large blazing eyes. I instantly covered the head and fired. There followed a most unearthly scream. I was covered with bark and dirt as the animal scratched violently at the tree, and a moment later, he fell headlong into the snow a few feet ahead of me. At this moment, another screech came from directly in front of where I stood, and I saw another similar animal going rapidly up a tree. It went too fast to get a shot at it in the swaying limbs. It sprang to another tree on my left, and while it was adjusting itself, I gave it my second barrel. Down it tumbled. The creature directly in front of me was dead. The other still struggled, but by the time I reached it, it too was dead. The first animal I shot was a monster mountain lion, and its weight I judged to be upwards of 250 pounds. The smaller was a female and would weigh about 150 pounds. Both had fine skins. Of course, they were valuable only as rugs or for ornament. I went directly to camp and got Yank and the mare, and he took the two lions in on one load on our sled.

Another day, I shot a marten, and while I was examining the fur, I noticed the size of its head. We had no traps for these small creatures and to make a deadfall required considerable labor. I began to study out some better plan that required less labor than was expended by the trappers of that day. That evening, Yank was at work on a proposed light sled for use in bringing in game. He had a two-inch auger that was too large for his purpose, and he threw it aside. I took the auger and bored straight into a tree. I thought the bait might be put into the back end of the hole if some way could be devised to capture the little creatures. I thought of many plans but could not decide upon a practical method. While in my bed, I finally studied out a plan that I decided to try. Taking the auger, I bored into the tree, took a ten-penny nail nicely sharpened, and drove it in standing upwards, leaving sufficient room for the animal to force its head into the hole. My thought was that, when the marten seized the bait and withdrew its head, it would be caught on the sharp nail and killed. On the third trial, I refined the plan by boring the hole somewhat downward, leaving the outside or edge of the hole higher than the back part of the hole and then driving the sharpened nail in with an upward slant. This plan succeeded, except that the two-inch hole was just a little too small for the heads of some marten to enter. I did catch some of the little animals with this method.

✱

During January, the white-tailed deer drifted into the valleys bordering the river. During February, a great thaw set in and the snow disappeared. These valleys were free from timber or brush, and the hunting then was practically at an end. The blacktail deer remained in the rough mountains. While hunting these animals one day, I had quite an exciting time. I had killed one deer on a bound and shot another. I thought I had killed the second deer, too. After I loaded my gun, I passed along to where I thought the second animal had fallen. I was on a steep sided hill, believing that I was near the spot where the deer lay. Suddenly I saw it some thirty feet above where I stood. As I saw it, it rose to its feet and, like a flash, dashed down the hill directly at me. Just in front of me stood a fir sapling some three inches in diameter. This I seized with my left hand. The animal in its downward charge struck the sapling, with one horn on each side of the tree. The force of the stroke bent the tree considerably downward. The animal fell and went some twenty or thirty feet below the tree. It gathered and charged back. I lost my gun in an effort to keep my feet. It continued the battle and displayed such activity that I could not get possession of my gun. I only saved myself from being gored to death by keeping possession of the sapling and, at the same time, keeping my feet on that steep, slippery hillside.

After many fruitless charges, the creature stopped to rest some distance below me. After I rested a bit, I started down to recover my gun. The animal was on its feet in a flash and bounded forward at the attack. I then got a lesson on the tremendous agility of the blacktail buck when in his native element. He kept me for a full hour at that sapling and almost wore me out with his savage and tireless thrusts. He finally went a little farther down the hill, but was still watchful to prevent any act of mine. I sat down in the snow and, inch by inch, slid down to where I supposed my gun lay. Twice I had to climb back. Finally I got hold of my gun, and I shot the creature in the head and thus secured my liberty.

Having secured his liberty, overcome innumerable obstacles, and passed from boyhood into manhood, Walter Cooper now settled down in the country where he would spend the rest of his days. For more about his career as a Montana entrepreneur and public figure, see Larry Peterson's Afterword, which follows.

AFTERWORD

Walter Cooper's adventures and achievements had only begun. He arrived in Virginia City in February 1864, and over the next four decades led a most distinguished life as a professional and as a public servant. Cooper left his mark on the town of Bozeman and made numerous and significant contributions to the entire state of Montana.

After four years of mining for gold with little success, Cooper headed to Bozeman, where he would live the rest of his life. In 1870, he married Mariam D. Skeels of Boulder Valley, Montana. At the time of their marriage, Walter had been engaged for several years in the gunsmith business in Bozeman. He later characterized his gunsmith business as "the first house of this kind started in the State or rather Territory of Montana for handling and manufacturing guns, ammunition, and fishing tackle. At that period most of the ammunition used for large game was loaded in empty cases either by the hunter or the dealer who assembled the ammunition for the hunter or user."[1] Because of his expertise in this area, Cooper seized the opportunity in 1870 to refurbish a little 4.62 single-bore cannon left behind when a group of gold prospectors from the Bighorn River area of Wyoming disbanded in Bozeman. The cannon became famous throughout the Gallatin Valley.

At the time, Bozeman was second only to Fort Benton in importance in the Montana Territory as a shipping point for hides and robes. By 1871, Walter was advertising that he was the "agent for Sharps Sporting Rifles."[2] But he was not content to just sell Sharps and started making improvements on them. Some of his improvements led to U. S. patents. His innovations included a rebounding hammer and a large, buckhorn rear sight of Cooper's own manufacture that fit a standard Sharps dovetail. With increased competition from other Sharps salesmen in the 1870s, Cooper's business ran into financial difficulty. He fell behind on payments to the factory and by 1875, Sharps was threatening legal action for nonpayment.

Walter turned to other business interests but left an important legacy for gun collectors. Sharps rifles inscribed with Cooper's mark are highly collectible today.[3]

Cooper always had many irons in the fire. In 1873, he joined others to form the Yellowstone Transportation Company with the intention of finding a route for a wagon road to connect with boats on the Yellowstone River to carry goods to Bismarck, in the Dakotas.[4] When this venture failed, he still had his lucrative fur trade business, among others, to fall back on. Over the years, he organized a company to supply water to Bozeman (Bozeman Water Works Company), developed the large coal fields of Rocky Fork, headed one of the largest flour mills in the state (Bozeman Milling Company), and continued prospecting for gold (Bozeman Gold and Silver Mining Company).

Business was going well enough for Walter to take what he called "his wedding trip" in 1876 to the Centennial Exposition in Philadelphia. On display there was a large collection of his minerals and Indian paraphernalia. His collection was later donated to Syracuse University and is known today as the "Cooper Collection."[5]

While gold prospecting had been a bust for many, enough gold was being mined to convince the Northern Pacific to run its rail line through Bozeman. March 1883 was an important month in the history of Bozeman. Many citizens, including Cooper, who had been recently elected the first president of the Board of Trade, joined in celebrating train service to Bozeman. Within days the town incorporated.

At the state level, Cooper was elected delegate-at-large to the Montana Constitutional Convention in 1884 and was made chairman of the Committee on Privileges and Elections. He was again elected to the convention in 1889, the year Montana was admitted to the Union. This time, he chaired the Committee on Appointment and Representation, giving each county one senator, and spearheaded the ratification effort. This success led to his selection as a delegate to the National Democratic Convention held in Chicago in 1892. Walter and Mariam visited the World's Columbian Exposition that year and again in 1893, where Mariam was one of the Lady Managers of the Exposition.[6]

That same year, Governor John E. Richards signed a bill to establish a land grant college in the Gallatin Valley. Five Bozeman area men, including

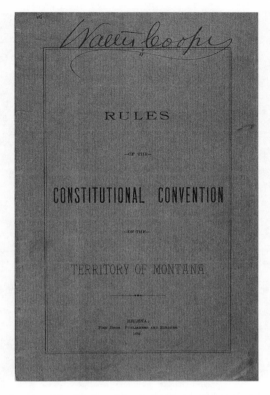

*Cooper's copy of the "Rules of the Constitutional Convention of the
Territory of Montana," Helena, 1884.*

Walter Cooper, were chosen to select a site. They selected a 160-acre parcel next to Eighth Avenue. One hundred and thirty-nine students were enrolled by 1896 at the Montana State College of Agriculture and Mechanic Arts. Cooper's name stands forever on the cornerstone of Montana Hall at what is today known as Montana State University.[7]

Charlie Russell, a contemporary of Cooper, cared little for politics, but there was one group that they both supported enthusiastically. The Society of Montana Pioneers, an organization founded in Helena in 1884, was especially appealing to Russell since the society sponsored annual conventions in various Montana communities to promote interest in local history. Membership was open to all persons who were residents of the Montana Territory before December 31, 1868, with dues set at $2 a year.

Invitation and admission passes to the World's Columbian Exposition in Chicago, October 1892. Mariam Cooper's photo appears on her passes to the exposition.

Walter Cooper, the first president of the Pioneer's Society of Gallatin County, served two terms as president of the Society of Montana Pioneers from 1892 to 1894, and Charlie Russell illustrated the society's convention brochures for decades.[8]

Cooper remained politically involved after the turn of the century. He observed the proceedings of the 1900 U.S. Senate from the reserved gallery as a guest of famed Montana senator and personal friend, W. A. Clark. A year later, Governor Toole appointed Cooper as commissioner to represent the state of Montana at the South Carolina Inter-State and West Indian Exposition in Charleston. In 1902, Walter served as chairman of the state's Democratic committee at the state convention hosted in Bozeman.[9] Two years later Walter, with his wife Mariam and daughter (also named Mariam), traveled to St. Louis for the Louisiana Purchase Exposition, where they represented Montana at various functions.

With the demand for rail service throughout the region on the rise, Cooper formed the Walter Cooper Company in 1901 to provide rail ties to the Northern Pacific, Burlington, and other railroads. Along with Helena investors, Cooper bought land along the Taylor Fork from the Northern Pacific Railroad, set up three tie-cutting camps, and started logging. Historian Michael Malone stated, "It was a colorful, boisterous operation, but it didn't last long."[10] With the Great Panic of 1907, a downturn in the national economy destroyed many businesses, including Cooper's.

With the loss of income from the railroad tie business, Walter's worries mounted. He still participated in many reunion-type gatherings of organizations, but extensive and expensive travel was restricted. A bright spot in his increasingly troubled life occurred in 1909 when his daughter Mariam was named Queen of the Bozeman Annual Sweet Pea Carnival.

Montana Hall, completed 1889, on the campus of Montana State College of Agriculture and Mechanic Arts. Photo appeared in Souvenir of Bozeman and the Gallatin Valley, Montana, 1905; *photo by Evan Davis of Bozeman; published by Albertype Co., Brooklyn, New York.*

Front page of Butte Miner, *September 21, 1902, announces Walter Cooper as the chairman of the Democratic State Convention in Bozeman.*

The Anaconda Standard reported:

> At 8 o'clock on Wednesday evening Miss Marion [sic] Cooper will be crowned queen of the carnival at the large stand built in front of the courthouse. An elaborate program has been arranged for this part of the carnival. Miss Cooper is one of the best-known young women in Bozeman. She was born and reared in this city. She is the only child of Walter Cooper, the Gallatin county pioneer, who is perhaps better known throughout Montana than any other of the old-timers. Her selection as queen has met with universal approval. George D. Pease will have charge of the coronation ceremonies. He will deliver the address and place the crown upon Miss Cooper's head. She will respond. The regular pages, maids, attendants and general retinue of the queen will all be dressed in the handsomest costumes available.[11]

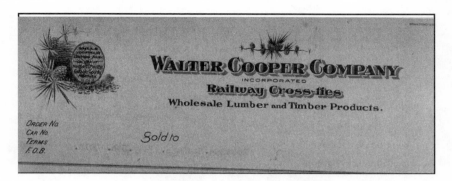

Walter Cooper Company letterhead.

The Coopers' Hellroaring Creek cabin, located twenty-seven miles into the Gallatin Canyon, afforded Walter quality time in the summer with family and friends. Fishing, swimming, games, and wonderful conversation helped him to forget his mounting financial problems.

By 1911 Walter was sixty-eight years old and should have been enjoying and reflecting on a productive and rewarding life. Unfortunately, his substantial landholdings in Bozeman that had been secured by loans were draining his finances. His longtime friend from Butte, Senator W. A. Clark, apparently had loaned him a large sum of money to purchase fifty-six lots in Bozeman years earlier. Walter subsequently had taken out a loan with the Commercial National Bank of Bozeman, using the property as collateral. After not receiving payment on the loans from Cooper, the bank sued him and Clark in 1913. After a lengthy legal battle, W. A. Clark reluctantly sued Cooper in 1915 and foreclosed on a mortgage in excess of $52,000 owed by Cooper. Cooper's extensive landholdings in Bozeman were gone.[12]

One could surmise that the manuscript Cooper had been working on after the turn of the century changed from a labor of love to a possible source of income for his ailing financial situation. In 1913 he turned to Charlie Russell, who by then was the most famous Western illustrator in the country, to illustrate this story. Most likely he reasoned that a book accompanied by Russell illustrations would sell quite well and would be a much-needed extra source of income. However, with mounting debts, by 1915 there probably wasn't enough money available for Cooper to even think of publishing his work.

Cooper's railroad tie camp near Bozeman.

Although there was still some income from the lumber business, the Coopers' asked their daughter and her husband, Eugene F. Bunker, to move in with them to make ends meet. Two granddaughters soon arrived, Virginia and Mariam. Bunker was elected county attorney and supplemented his modest income by moonlighting as temporary football coach at the state college.[13]

Even approaching eighty, Walter remained physically active until a fall from a flume restricted his activity. By 1920 W. A. Clark and Walter had apparently patched up any hard feelings over the earlier lawsuits, since Walter took an active role at the meeting in Helena of the Society of Montana Pioneers to honor Clark. The fiftieth wedding anniversary of Mr. and Mrs. Walter Cooper took place on April 19, 1920, at the family home of Mrs. Cooper, in Boulder Valley, Montana. There were still trips to the family cabin, and in 1921 the family traveled to take part in the forty-fifth anniversary of the Custer battle in Hardin. Frank B. Linderman of Somers, Montana, and Charlie Russell were honorary vice-presidents of the anniversary event.[14]

The end for this great Montana pioneer came on April 24, 1924. Reported cause of death was "a general breakdown" at almost eighty-one years of age. Cooper was survived by his wife and daughter, two granddaughters,

Walter Cooper (top left), Mariam Cooper (just right of Walter),
daughter Mariam (bottom left), and family friends at the
Cooper's Hellroaring Creek cabin near Bozeman.

and three brothers: George Cooper and David Cooper of Syracuse, New York, and Ransom Cooper of Great Falls. Services were held the next day at the Presbyterian church in Bozeman.[15] Telegrams from all over Montana and the nation poured in. W. A. Clark's said "Dear Mrs. Cooper. It is with great regret that I have been advised of the death of your husband and my lifelong friend honorable Walter Cooper. Please accept my deepest sympathy for yourself and daughter on this sad occasion."[16]

His partner on his book project, Charlie Russell, also had taken a fall in the early 1920s, and, along with congestive heart failure and a goiter, he experienced declining health until his death in October 1926 at age sixty-two. Within two years, Montana had lost two of its greatest citizens. Both came from the East to a land full of adventure and "most dangerous situations," both made huge contributions to Montana, and both left legacies larger than life.

[1] Walter Cooper, undated manuscript (Montana State University, Bozeman, Special Collections).

[2] *The Avant Courier*, Bozeman, Montana, December, 1871.

[3] Ralph A. Heinz, "Montana Sharps: The Story of Walter Cooper," *Man at Arms*, 3:6 (November/December ,1981): 25–37.

[4] Ref. 2, 133.

[5] *The Bozeman Daily Chronicle*, Bozeman, Montana, April 29, 1924.

[6] Ibid. & numerous pieces of correspondence and surviving Exposition memorabilia, now are in the author's possession.

[7] Ref. 2, 171.

[8] Larry Len Peterson, *Charles M. Russell, Legacy: Printed and Published Works of Montana's Cowboy Artist* (Helena: TwoDot Books, An Imprint of Falcon Publishing in Cooperation with the C. M. Russell Museum, Great Falls, Montana, 1999): 127.

[9] *Butte Miner*, Butte, Montana, September 21, 1902.

[10] Michael P. Malone, "The Gallatin Canyon and the Tides of History," *Montana, The Magazine of Western History*, 22 (Summer, 1973): 7.

[11] *The Anaconda Standard*, Anaconda, Montana, September 12, 1909.

[12] Court papers, graciously supplied by Ellie Arguimbau, archivist, Montana Historical Society in December, 1998.

[13] Personal notes of Walter's granddaughter, Virginia, now in the author's possession.

[14] Ibid.

[15] *Bozeman Daily Chronicle*, Bozeman, Montana, April 29, 1924.

[16] Western Union telegram, dated April 30, 1924, now in the author's possession.

Larry Len Peterson, author of *Charles M. Russell Legacy: Printed and Published Works of Montana's Cowboy Artist,* has written numerous articles on the art of Charles M. Russell. He has served as a juror for the C.M. Russell Museum Art Auction and as chairman for its National Advisory Board. Peterson has given lectures to Russell followers everywhere, including recent events at the C.M. Russell Symposium in Coeur d'Alene, Idaho, and Glacier National Park. A native of Plentywood, Montana, Peterson is a graduate of the University of Oregon and Oregon Health Sciences University.

A native Montanan, editor **Rick Newby** is the author of two collections of poems, *A Radiant Map of the World* and *Old Friends Walking in the Mountains.* He is the editor of *On Flatwillow Creek: The Story of Montana's N-Bar Ranch* by Linda Grosskopf, and co-editor of *Writing Montana: Literature under the Big Sky* and *An Ornery Bunch: Tales and Anecdotes Collected by the WPA Montana Writers' Project, 1935-1942.* His articles and reviews on contemporary artists of the West have appeared in *American Craft; American Ceramics; Ceramics: Art & Perception;* and *Sculpture.*

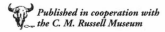

Charles M. Russell

TWODOT®

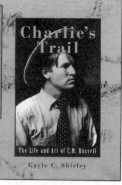

Charles M. Russell, Legacy
By Larry Len Peterson
Co-published with the
C. M. Russell Museum.

$95.00 cloth binding
456 pp

**The C. M. Russell
Postcard Book**
Co-published with the
C. M. Russell Museum.

$8.95 sc
22 color postcards

Charlie's Trail
The Life and Art
of C. M. Russell
By Gayle C. Shirley
Co-published with the
C. M. Russell Museum.

$10.95 sc
72 pp

MONTANA
HISTORICAL
SOCIETY
PRESS

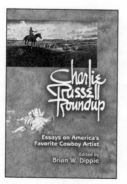

**Charlie Russell
Roundup**
Essays on America's
Favorite Cowboy Artist
*Edited and with an
introduction by
Brian W. Dippie*

$39.95 hc $19.95 sc
356 pp

**Charlie Russell
Journal**

$12.95 hc
128 pp

*To order, check with your local bookseller or call Falcon at **1-800-582-2665**.
Ask for a FREE catalog featuring a complete list of titles on
nature, outdoor recreation, travel, and the West.*

www.falcon.com

FALCON®